# Nation of Nations

# Nation of Nations

## A CONCISE NARRATIVE OF THE AMERICAN REPUBLIC

### FOURTH EDITION

James West Davidson

William E. Gienapp
Harvard University

Christine Leigh Heyrman
University of Delaware

Mark H. Lytle
Bard College

Michael B. Stoff
University of Texas, Austin

Boston   Burr Ridge, IL   Dubuque, IA   Madison, WI   New York
San Francisco   St. Louis   Bangkok   Bogotá   Caracas   Kuala Lumpur
Lisbon   London   Madrid   Mexico City   Milan   Montreal   New Delhi
Santiago   Seoul   Singapore   Sydney   Taipei   Toronto

**The McGraw·Hill** Companies

## Mc Graw Hill **Higher Education**

Published by McGraw-Hill, an imprint of The McGraw-Hill Companies, Inc., 1221 Avenue of the Americas, New York, NY 10020. Copyright © 2006. All rights reserved. No part of this publication may be reproduced or distributed in any form or by any means, or stored in a database or retrieval system, without the prior written consent of The McGraw-Hill Companies, Inc., including, but not limited to, in any network or other electronic storage or transmission, or broadcast for distance learning.

This book is printed on acid-free paper.

1 2 3 4 5 6 7 8 9 0 DOC/DOC 0 9 8 7 6 5

ISBN 0-07-297087-1

Editor in Chief: *Emily Barrosse*
Publisher: *Lyn Uhl*
Sponsoring Editor: *Steven Drummond*
Marketing Manager: *Katherine Bates*
Director of Development: *Lisa Pinto*
Developmental Editor: *Kristen Mellitt*
Managing Editor: *Melissa Williams*
Project Manager: *Holly Paulsen*
Manuscript Editor: *Jan McDearmon*
Art Director: *Jeanne Schreiber*
Design Manager: *Gino Cieslik*
Text and Cover Designer: *Gino Cieslik*
Art Editor: *Emma Ghiselli*
Photo Research Coordinator: *Nora Agbayani*
Photo Research: *Deborah Bull and Deborah Anderson, Photo Search, Inc.*
Print Supplements Producer: *Louis Swaim*
Production Supervisor: *Randy Hurst*
Media: *Kathleen Boylan*
Composition: *10.5/13 Janson Text by The GTS Companies, York, PA Campus.*
Printing: *PMS 202, 45# Pub Matte Plus, R. R. Donnelley & Sons/Crawfordsville, IN*

Cover: *(left to right)* © Gianni Dagli Orti/Corbis; © The Corcoran Gallery of Art/Corbis; National Archive; © Corbis; Buzz Orr; Library of Congress; Prints & Photographs Division; *(background/dome)* © Peter Gridley/Getty Images.

Credits: The credits section for this book begins on page C-1 and is considered an extension of the copyright page.

Library of Congress Cataloging-in-Publication data has been applied for.

www.mhhe.com

# William E. Gienapp

## 1944–2003

Inevitably, the contingencies of history bring grief as well as joy. We are saddened to report the passing of our dear friend and co-author, William E. Gienapp. It would be hard to imagine a colleague with greater dedication to his work, nor one who cared more about conveying both the excitement and the rigor of history to those who were not professional historians—as has been attested by so many of his students at the University of Wyoming and at Harvard. Bill had a quiet manner, which sometimes hid (though not for long) his puckish sense of humor and an unstinting generosity. When news of his death was reported, the *Harvard Crimson*, a student newspaper known more for its skepticism than its sentimentality, led with the front-page headline: "Beloved History Professor Gienapp Dies." Bill went the extra mile, whether in searching out primary sources enabling us to assemble a map on the environmental effects of the Lowell Mills, combing innumerable manuscript troves in the preparation of his masterful *Origins of the Republican Party*, or collecting vintage baseball caps from the nineteenth and twentieth centuries to wear (in proper chronological sequence, no less) to his popular course on the social history of baseball. When an illness no one could have predicted struck him down, the profession lost one of its shining examples. His fellow authors miss him dearly.

CHAPTER TWELVE
The Fires of Perfection (1820–1850)   313

## CHAPTER THIRTEEN
# The Old South (1820–1860)   340

CHAPTER FOURTEEN

# Western Expansion and the Rise of the Slavery Issue (1820–1850)   370

## CHAPTER SEVENTEEN
## Reconstructing the Union (1865–1877)    459

# PART FOUR
## GLOBAL ESSAY: THE UNITED STATES IN AN INDUSTRIAL AGE   485

## CHAPTER EIGHTEEN
# The New South and the Trans-Mississippi West (1870–1896)   487

CHAPTER NINETEEN
# The New Industrial Order (1870–1900)   519

## CHAPTER TWENTY
## The Rise of an Urban Order (1870–1900)  550

## CHAPTER TWENTY-ONE
## The Political System under Strain (1877–1900) 578

## CHAPTER TWENTY-TWO
## The Progressive Era (1890–1920) 615

### CHAPTER TWENTY-THREE
## The United States and the Old World Order (1901–1920) 648

## PART FIVE
### GLOBAL ESSAY: THE PERILS OF DEMOCRACY 679

### CHAPTER TWENTY-FOUR
## The New Era (1920–1929) 681

CHAPTER TWENTY-FIVE
# The Great Depression and the
# New Deal (1929–1939)   715

## CHAPTER TWENTY-SIX
## America's Rise to Globalism (1927–1945)   756

# PART SIX
## GLOBAL ESSAY: THE UNITED STATES IN A NUCLEAR AGE 796

## CHAPTER TWENTY-SEVEN
## Cold War America (1945–1954) 798

## CHAPTER TWENTY-EIGHT
## The Suburban Era (1945–1963) 826

### CHAPTER TWENTY-NINE
## Civil Rights and the Crisis of Liberalism (1947–1969)   857

CHAPTER THIRTY
# The Vietnam Era (1963–1975)   886

# CHAPTER THIRTY-THREE
# Nation of Nations in a Global Community (1980–2004)   966

# List of Maps and Charts

# Interactive Map Portfolio

An interactive version of each of the maps in this section can be found
on the Primary Source Investigator CD-ROM and in the book's Online
Learning Center at www.mhhe.com/davidsonconcise4

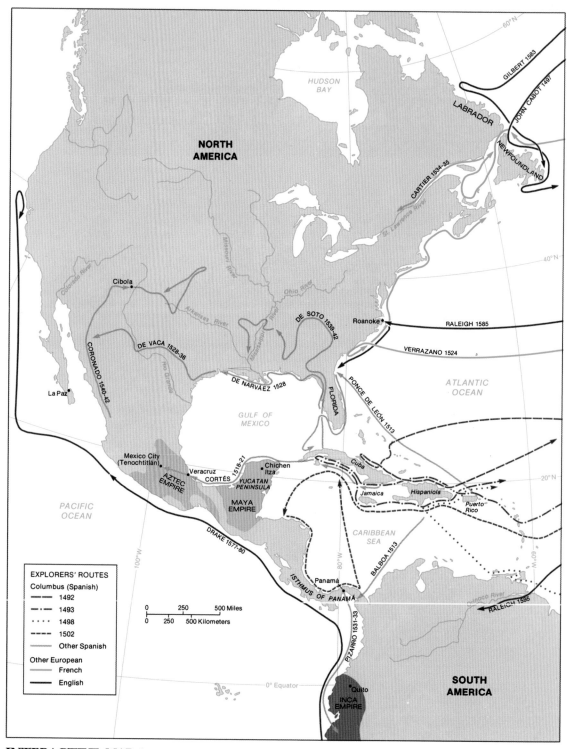

**INTERACTIVE MAP 1** PRINCIPAL ROUTES OF EUROPEAN EXPLORATION

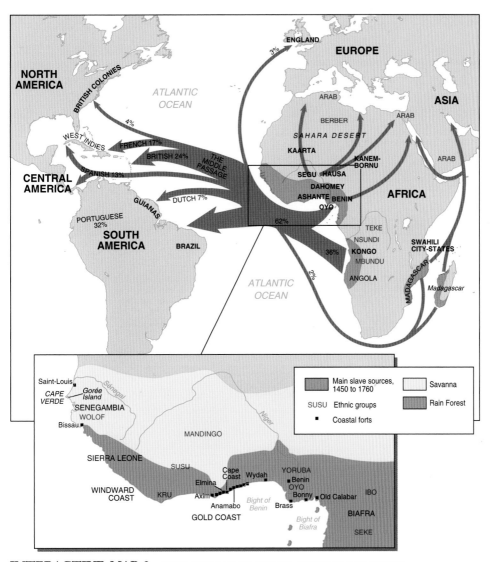

**INTERACTIVE MAP 2** THE AFRICAN TRANSATLANTIC SLAVE TRADE,
1450–1760 Toward the end of the seventeenth century, Chesapeake and Carolina
planters began importing increasing numbers of slaves. In Africa, the center of that
trade lay along a mountainous region known as the Gold Coast, where over a hundred
European trading posts and forts funneled the trade. Unlike most of the rest of West
Africa's shoreline, the Gold Coast had very little dense rain forest. Despite the heavy
trade, only about 4 percent of the total transatlantic slave trade went to North America.

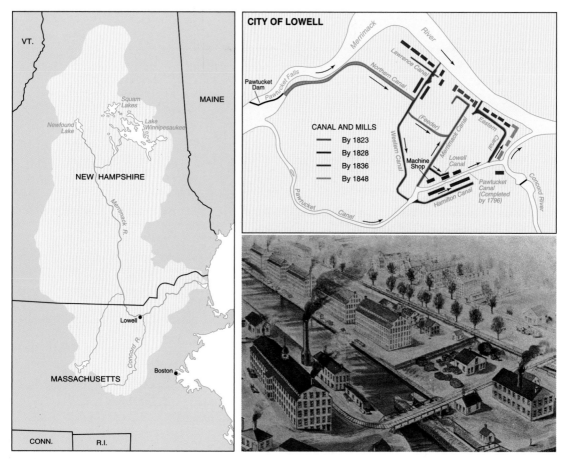

**INTERACTIVE MAP 3** DEVELOPMENT OF THE LOWELL MILLS   As more mills were built at Lowell, the demand increased for water to power them. By 1859 the mills drew water from lakes 80 to 100 miles upstream, including Winnipesaukee, Squam, and Newfound. The map at left shows the watersheds affected. In the city of Lowell (right), a system of canals was enlarged over several decades. In the painting (done in 1845), the machine shop can be seen at left, with a row of mills alongside a canal. Rail links tied Lowell and Boston together.

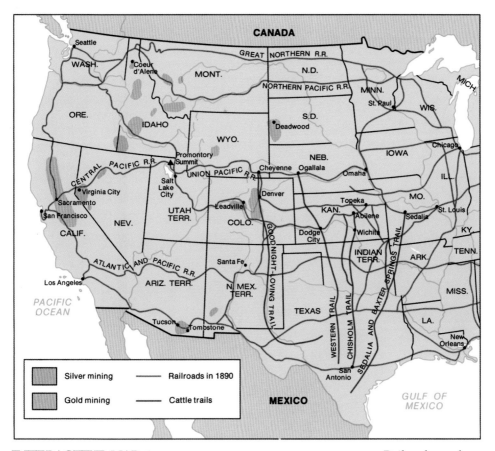

**INTERACTIVE MAP 4** THE MINING AND CATTLE FRONTIERS Railroads, cattle trails, and gold mines usually preceded the arrival of enough settlers to establish a town. Cattle trails ended at rail lines, where cattle could be shipped to city markets. By transecting the plains, railroads disrupted the migratory patterns of the buffalo, undermining Indian cultures and opening the land to grazing and farming.

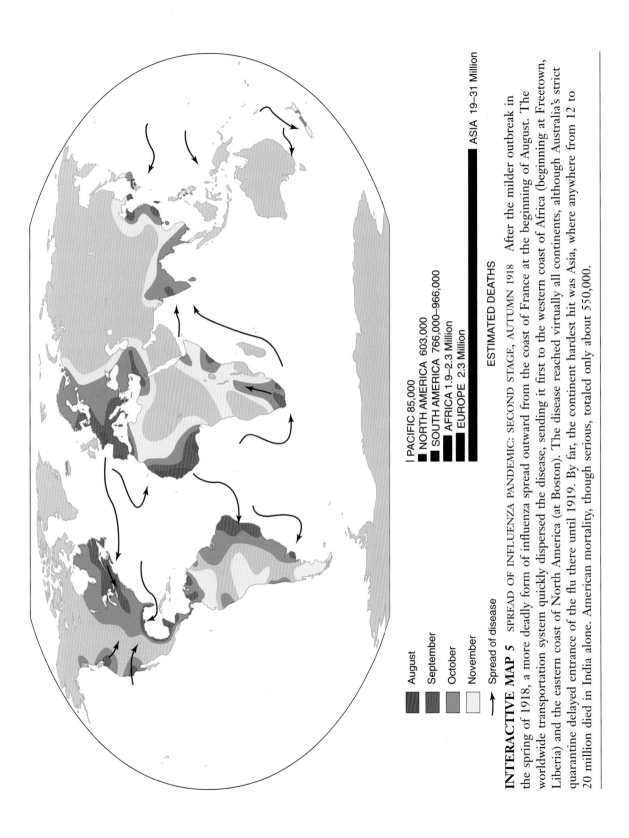

August

September

October

November

→ Spread of disease

| PACIFIC 85,000
■ NORTH AMERICA 603,000
■ SOUTH AMERICA 766,000–966,000
■ AFRICA 1.9–2.3 Million
■ EUROPE 2.3 Million

ASIA 19–31 Million

ESTIMATED DEATHS

**INTERACTIVE MAP 5** SPREAD OF INFLUENZA PANDEMIC: SECOND STAGE, AUTUMN 1918    After the milder outbreak in the spring of 1918, a more deadly form of influenza spread outward from the coast of France at the beginning of August. The worldwide transportation system quickly dispersed the disease, sending it first to the western coast of Africa (beginning at Freetown, Liberia) and the eastern coast of North America (at Boston). The disease reached virtually all continents, although Australia's strict quarantine delayed entrance of the flu there until 1919. By far, the continent hardest hit was Asia, where anywhere from 12 to 20 million died in India alone. American mortality, though serious, totaled only about 550,000.

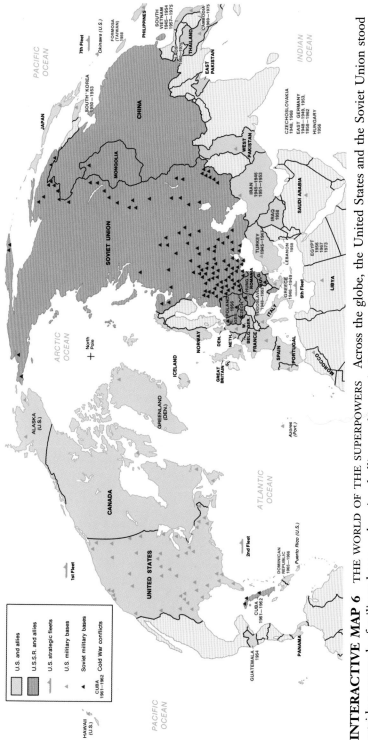

**INTERACTIVE MAP 6** THE WORLD OF THE SUPERPOWERS Across the globe, the United States and the Soviet Union stood astride a network of military bases and regional alliances that marked the extent of their powers. Around these strategic perimeters, centers of conflict continued to emerge.

# PART ONE

# The Creation of a New America

It is now half a millennium—a full 500 years—since the civilizations of Europe and Africa first made sustained contact with those of North America. The transformations arising out of that event have been astonishing. To gain a rough sense of the scale involved, in both time and space, it is worth standing for a moment not at the beginning of our story but somewhere nearer its midpoint: with Meriwether Lewis and William Clark in August 1805, atop the continental divide on their traverse of North America. The two men, on orders from President Thomas Jefferson, had been sent on the first U.S. mission to report on the lands west of the Mississippi. From Lewis and Clark's vantage point, high in the Rocky Mountains, what can we see?

At first glance we see pretty much what we expect to see: a vast, seemingly endless land stretching from sea to sea. But living as we do in the late twentieth century, we tend to take for granted that the domain spread before us is united as a continental republic under a single national government. Only hindsight makes this proposition seem natural. In 1800 the sheer size of the land made the notion of political unity difficult to grasp, for the United States itself remained a group of colonies only recently unified. Even Jefferson, who possessed the vision to send Lewis and Clark on their mission, had long been in the habit of referring to Virginia as "my country." And the lands west of the Mississippi were still controlled primarily by scores of independent Indian nations.

Just how diverse the landscape was can be seen by the methods Lewis and Clark used to communicate. With no common language spanning the territory,

2

# Nation of Nations

speech making became a series of translations that reflected the route over which the party had traveled. In present-day Idaho, Clark addressed the Tushepaw tribe in English. His speech was translated into French by a trapper in the party; then a second trapper translated into Minataree, a language that his Indian wife, Sacajawea, understood. Sacajawea, the only female member of the party, had grown up farther west with the Shoshone, so she in turn translated the Minataree into Shoshone, which a boy from the Tushepaw nation understood. He translated the Shoshone into his own people's tongue.

If the Louisiana Territory seemed a patchwork of governments and cultures, the young "United States" appeared nearly as heterogeneous. Dutch-speaking patroons could be found along New York's Hudson River, Welsh and German farmers along Pennsylvania's Lancaster Pike, Swedes in Delaware, Gaelic-speaking Scots scattered up and down the Appalachian backcountry, African Americans speaking the Gullah dialect along the Carolina coast. In 1800 many of these settlers knew more about their homelands in Europe or Africa than they did about other regions of North America.

Thus our first task in studying the American past becomes one of translation. We must view events not with the jaded eyes of the early twentieth century but with the fresh eyes of an earlier era. Then the foregone conclusions vanish. How does the American nation manage to unite millions of square miles of territory into one governable republic? How do New York and San Francisco (a city not even in existence in Lewis and Clark's day) come to be linked in a complex economy as well as in a single political system? Such questions take on even more significance when we recall that Europe—roughly the same size as the United States—is today still divided into over four dozen independent nations speaking some 33 languages, not to mention another 100 or so spoken within the former Soviet Union. A united Europe is emerging only slowly and indeed seems at least as far away after the momentous breakup of the Soviet empire.

How, then, did this American republic—this "teeming nation of nations," to use Walt Whitman's phrase—come to be? In barest outline, that is the question that drives our narrative across half a millennium.

The question becomes even more challenging if we move toward the beginning of our story. In 1450, about the time Christopher Columbus was born, only the first stirrings of European expansion to the west had begun. To be sure, Scandinavian seafarers led by Leif Ericsson had reached the northern reaches of the Americas, planting a settlement in Newfoundland in 1001 C.E. But news of Vinland, as Leif called his colony, never reached Europe, and the site was soon abandoned and forgotten. In Columbus's day localism still held sway. Italy was divided into five major states and an equal number of smaller territories. The Germanic peoples were united loosely in the Holy Roman Empire, which (as historians have long delighted in pointing out) was neither holy, Roman, nor an empire. French kings ruled over only about half of what is now France. Spain was divided into several kingdoms, with some areas held by Christians and others by Islamic

Moors, whose forebears came from Africa. England, a contentious little nation, was beginning a series of bitter civil conflicts among the nobility, known eventually as the Wars of the Roses. The only country pushing beyond the boundaries of the known European world was Portugal, whose sailors were advancing down the coast of Africa in search of gold and slaves.

Localism was also evident in the patterns of European transportation and trade. For the most part, goods moving overland were carried by wheeled carts or pack animals over rutted paths. Rivers and canals provided another option, but lords repeatedly taxed boats that crossed their territories. On the Seine River, greedy tollkeepers lay in wait every six or seven miles. Travel across the Mediterranean Sea and along Europe's northern coastlines was possible, but storms and pirates made the going dangerous and slow. Under good conditions a ship might reach London from Venice in only 9 days; under bad it might take 50.

European peoples at this time had limited but continuous dealings with Africa, mostly along the Mediterranean Sea. There, North African culture had been shaped since the seventh century by the religion of Islam, whose influence spread as well into Spain. Below the Sahara desert the Bantu, an agricultural people, had migrated over the course of 2000 years from their West African homeland to establish societies throughout the continent. The tempo of these migrations increased as the Bantu learned to produce iron and—equally important—introduced bananas into their diet after the plants were imported to Africa from Asia around 300 to 500 C.E. As a result, the sub-Saharan African populations rose sharply from around 11 million at the beginning of the first millennium C.E. to over 22 million at the end of it.

Traditionally, Bantu agricultural societies governed themselves through family and kinship groups, clustered in villages of around a hundred people and linked with nearby villages in a district. But larger political states developed in response to the arrival of Muslim trading caravans penetrating the Sahara desert beginning around 800 C.E. The first was Ghana, a kingdom that flourished in the eleventh and twelfth centuries. It was followed in the thirteenth century by the even larger Mali empire. Mali's princes controlled almost all of the considerable trade in gold, ivory, and slaves, sending and receiving desert caravans that boasted as many as 25,000 camels. Yet Mali too was split by faction from within and military challenges from without. By the 1490s the Songhai empire had replaced Mali as the most important centralized kingdom in West Africa.

If Europe in 1450 was less unified and dynamic than we might have imagined, the civilizations of North and South America were more complex and populous than historians once thought. Earlier estimates suggested that when Europeans first arrived, about 10 million people were living in Central and South America, with another million living north of Mexico. More recently these figures have been raised tenfold, to perhaps as many as 100 million people in Central and South America and 5 to 10 million north of Mexico. In 1492, when Columbus landed on Hispaniola, that island alone may have held some 7 to 8 million people—a number roughly equal to the entire population of Spain. Tenochtitlán, capital of the Aztec empire, held an estimated 165,000 inhabitants, a population greater than those in the largest European cities of the day. Such dense urban populations were supported by sophisticated agricultural techniques, including canals, irrigation, and drainage systems.

North America was far from being as heavily populated, but neither was it sparsely settled. From one end of the continent to the other, native cultures actively shaped their environments, burning the forests and plains to promote the growth of vegetation as well as animal populations, which they harvested. As we shall see, Amerindian agricultural achievements were so remarkable that they eventually revolutionized eating habits across the rest of the globe.

In 1490 these three worlds—Europe, Africa, the Americas—remained largely separate from one another. Europe's fleeting encounter with North America had long been forgotten; the empires of interior Africa remained unvisited by Europeans. Yet currents of change would soon bring together these worlds in ways both vibrant and creative as well as violent and chaotic. What social and economic forces spurred so many Europeans—desperate and opportunistic, high-minded and idealistic—to turn west to the Americas in pursuit of their dreams? How did the civilizations of North and South America react to the European invaders? And not least, how did the mix of cultures from Africa, Europe, and North America create what was truly a new America, in which some of the most independent-minded individuals prospered in provinces that exhibited some of the harshest examples of human slavery? These are among the questions we seek to answer as our narrative unfolds.

# CHAPTER 1

All the world lay before them. Or so it seemed to mariners from England's seafaring coasts, pushing westward toward unknown lands in the far Atlantic. Since the time of King Arthur, the English living along the rugged southwestern coasts of Devon and Cornwall had followed the sea. From the wharves of England's West Country seaports like Bristol, ships headed west and north to Ireland, bringing back animal hides as well as timber for houses and barrels. Or they turned south, fetching wines from France and olive oil or figs and raisins from the Spanish and Portuguese coasts. In return, West Country ports offered woven woolen cloth and codfish, caught wherever the best prospects beckoned.

# Old World, New Worlds
## Prehistory–1600

**Preview**  *In the century after 1492, Europeans expanded boldly and often ruthlessly into the Americas, thanks to a combination of technological advances in sailing and firearms, the rise of new trading networks, and stronger, more centralized governments. Spain established a vast and profitable empire, but at fearful human cost. A diverse Mesoamerican population of some 20 million was reduced to only 2 million through warfare, European diseases, and exploitation.*

The search for cod had long drawn West Country sailors north and west, toward Iceland. In the 1480s and 1490s, however, a few English pushed even farther west. Old maps, after all, claimed that the bountiful *Hy-Brasil*—Gaelic for "Isle of the Blessed"—lay some-

*Cabot discovers Newfoundland* where west of Ireland. These western ventures returned with little to show for their daring until the coming of an Italian named Giovanni Caboto, called John Cabot by the English. Cabot, who hailed from Venice, obtained the blessing of King Henry VII to hunt for unknown lands. From the port of Bristol his lone ship set out in the spring of 1497.

This time the return voyage brought news of a "new-found" island where the trees were tall enough to make fine masts and the codfish were plentiful. After returning to Bristol, Cabot marched off to London to inform His Majesty, received 10 pounds as his reward, and with the proceeds dressed himself in dashing silks. Then Cabot returned triumphantly to Bristol to undertake a more ambitious search for a northwest passage to Asia. He set sail with five ships in 1498 and was never heard from again.

By the 1550s Cabot's island, now known as Newfoundland, attracted 400 vessels annually, fishermen not only from England but also from France, Portugal, and Spain. As early in the season as they dared, crews of 10 or 20 would catch the spring easterlies, watching as familiar roofs and primitive lighthouses burning smoky coal sank beneath the horizon. Weeks after setting sail the sailors sighted Newfoundland's fog-shrouded waters, which teemed with cod and flounder, salmon and herring. Throughout the summer men launched little boats from each harbor and fished offshore all day and into the night. With lines and nets, and baskets weighted with stones, they scooped fish from the sea and then dried and salted the catch on the beach. In odd hours, sailors traded with the native Indians, who shared their summer fishing grounds and the skins of fox and deer.

*The fishing season*

St. John's, Newfoundland, served as the hub of the North Atlantic fishery. Portuguese, English, and French vessels all dropped anchor there, and besides trading, there was much talking, for these seafarers knew as much as anyone about the world of wonders opening to Europeans. They were acquainted with names like Cristoforo Colombo, the Italian from Genoa whom Cabot might have known as a boy. They listened to Portuguese tales of sailing around Africa in pursuit of Asian spices and to stories of Indian empires to the south, rich in gold and silver.

Indeed, Newfoundland was one of the few places in the world where so many ordinary folk of different nations could gather and talk, crammed aboard dank ships moored in St. John's harbor, huddled before blazing fires on its beaches, or crowded into smoky makeshift taverns. When the ships sailed home in autumn, the tales went with them, repeated in the tiniest coastal villages by those pleased to have cheated death and the sea one more time. Eager to fish, talk, trade, and take profits, West Country mariners were almost giddy at the prospect of Europe's expanding horizons.

## THE MEETING OF EUROPE, AFRICA, AND AMERICA

Most seafarers who fished the waters of Newfoundland's Grand Banks remain unknown today. Yet it is well to begin with these ordinary fisherfolk, for the European discovery of the Americas cannot be looked upon simply as the voyages of a few bold explorers. Adventurers like Christopher Columbus or John Cabot were only the leading edge of a much larger expansion of European peoples and culture that began in the 1450s. That expansion arose out of a series of gradual but telling changes in European society—changes reflected in the lives of ordinary seafarers as much as in the careers of explorers decked out in flaming silks.

Some of these changes were technological, arising out of advances in the arts of navigating and shipbuilding and the use of gunpowder. Some were economic, involving the development of trade networks

*Changes in European society*

like those linking Bristol with ports in Iceland and Spain. Some were demographic, bringing about a rise in Europe's population after a devastating century of plague. Other changes were religious, adding a dimension of devout belief to the political rivalries that fueled discoveries in the Americas. Yet others were political, making it possible for kingdoms to centralize and extend their influence across the ocean. Portugal, Spain, France, and England—all possessing coasts along the Atlantic—led the way in exploration, spurred on by Italian "admirals" like Caboto and Colombo, Spanish *conquistadores* like Cortés and Pizarro, and English sea dogs like Humphrey Gilbert and Walter Raleigh. Ordinary folk rode these currents too. The great and the small alike were propelled by forces that were remolding the face of Europe.

## The Portuguese Wave

In 1450 all of the world known to western Europeans was Asia and Africa. Most sailors traveled only along the coast of western Europe, following the shores between Norway and the southern tip of Spain, seldom daring to lose sight of land. Beginning in the fifteenth century, bolder seafarers groped down the coast of western Africa, half expecting to be boiled alive in the Atlantic as they approached the equator. Europeans had traded with Asia through the Muslims of the eastern Mediterranean and across an overland route called the "Silk Road." But they had only vague notions about "the Indies"—China and Japan, the Spice Islands, and the lands lying between Thailand and India. What little they knew, they had learned mainly from Marco Polo, whose account of his travels in the East was not published until 1477, more than 150 years after his death.

But a revolution in European geography began in the middle decades of the fifteenth century, as widening networks of travel and trade connected Europeans to civilizations beyond western Europe. The Portuguese took the lead, encour-

*Revolution in geography*

aged by Prince Henry, known as the Navigator. The devout Henry, a member of Portugal's royal family, had heard tales of Prester John, a Catholic priest rumored to rule a Christian kingdom somewhere beyond the Muslim kingdoms of Africa and Asia. Henry dreamed of joining forces with Prester John and trapping the Muslims in a vise. To that end, he helped finance a series of expeditions down the coast of West Africa. He founded an informal school of navigation on the Portuguese coast, supplying shipmasters with information about wind and currents as well as with navigational charts.

Portuguese merchants, who may or may not have believed in Prester John, never doubted there was money to be made in Africa. They invested in Prince Henry's voyages in return for trading monopolies of ivory and slaves, grain and gold. A few may have hoped that the voyages down the coast of West Africa would lead to a direct sea route to the Orient. By discovering such a route, Portugal would be able to cut out the Muslim merchants who funneled all the Asian trade in silks, dyes, drugs, and perfumes through Mediterranean ports.

As Portugal's merchants established trading posts along the west coast of Africa, its mariners were discovering islands in the Atlantic: the Canaries, Madeira, and the Azores. Settlers planted sugarcane and imported slaves from Africa to work their fields. The Portuguese might have pressed even farther west but for the daring of Bartholomeu Dias. In 1488 Dias rounded the Cape of Good Hope on the southern tip of Africa, sailing far enough up that continent's eastern coast to claim discovery of a sea route to India. Ten years later Vasco da Gama reached India itself, and the Portuguese eventually reached Indochina and China. With the trade of Africa and Asia to occupy them, they showed less interest in exploring the Atlantic.

*The Portuguese focus on Africa and Asia*

By 1500, all of seafaring Europe sought the services of Portuguese pilots, prizing their superior maps and skills with the quadrant. That instrument made it possible to determine latitude fairly accurately, allowing ships to plot their position after months out of the sight of land. The Portuguese had also pioneered the caravel, a lighter, more maneuverable ship that could sail better against contrary winds and in rough seas.

As the Portuguese extended their influence along the Atlantic rim of West Africa, they were more likely to meet with native peoples who had had no earlier encounters with Europeans and, indeed, had no knowledge of the existence of other continents. On catching their first sight of a Portuguese expedition in 1455, the inhabitants of one village on the Senegal River marveled at the strangers' clothing and their white skin. As an Italian member of that expedition recounted, some Africans "rubbed me with their spittle to discover whether my whiteness was dye or flesh." Equally astonishing were the Portuguese ships and weapons, especially their deadly cannon and muskets. While some Africans concluded that these white newcomers must be either wizards or cannibals, to be shunned or killed, others eagerly enlisted Europeans as military allies and trading partners, hoping to gain both power and practical knowledge.

*Africans and Europeans meet*

The debate among West Africans about whether to resist or accommodate the new Europeans grew sharper as the interest of Portuguese traders in purchasing slaves increased. Before the end of the fifteenth century, most slaves in Europe were white, but among slaves of color, whether black or of mixed race (mulattoes), most were Muslims of North African ancestry and their numbers were concentrated in the Mediterranean. After the 1480s, however, darker-skinned, non-Muslim men and women from throughout West Africa began to appear in greater numbers among the ranks of slaves and servants, as well as among craftworkers and musicians everywhere in western Europe, even as far north as the Netherlands and England. Their presence was most pronounced in Portugal and Spain: by around 1550, people of African descent accounted for 10 percent of the population of Lisbon, Portugal's capital city.

Even so, this slave trade to the Atlantic islands and western Europe was small in scale compared with what was to come. The Atlantic slave trade did not take its full toll on Africa until Spain had made a much greater mark on the Americas.

## The Spanish and Columbus

From among the international community of seafarers and pilots, it was a sailor from Genoa, Cristoforo Colombo, who led the Spanish to the Americas. Columbus (the Latinized version of his name survives) had knocked about in a number of harbors, picking up valuable navigation skills by sailing Portugal's merchant ships to Madeira, West Africa, and the North Atlantic.

That experience instilled in Columbus the belief that the quickest route to the Indies lay west, across the Atlantic—and that his destiny was to prove it. Only 4500 miles, he reckoned, separated Europe from Japan. His wishful estimate raised eyebrows whenever Columbus asked European monarchs for the money to meet his destiny. Most educated Europeans agreed that the world was round, but they also believed that the Atlantic barrier between themselves and Asia was far wider than Columbus allowed. The kings of England, France, and Portugal dismissed him as a crackpot.

Almost a decade of rejection had grayed Columbus's red hair when Spain's monarchs, Ferdinand and Isabella, finally agreed to subsidize his expedition in 1492. For the past 20 years they had worked to drive the Muslims out of their last stronghold on the Iberian peninsula, the Moorish kingdom of Granada. In 1492 they completed this *reconquista*, or battle of reconquest, expelling many Jews as well. Yet the Portuguese, by breaking the Muslim stranglehold on trade with Asia, had taken the lead in competing against the Islamic powers. Ferdinand and Isabella were so desperate to even the score with Portugal that they agreed to take a risk on Columbus.

*The* reconquista

Columbus's first voyage across the Atlantic could only have confirmed his conviction that he was destiny's darling. His three ships, no bigger than fishing vessels that sailed to Newfoundland, plied their course over placid seas, south from Seville to the Canary Islands and then due west. On October 11, branches, leaves, and flowers floated by their hulls, signals that land lay near. Just after midnight, a sailor spied cliffs shining white in the moonlight. On the morning of October 12, the *Niña*, the *Pinta*, and the *Santa Maria* set anchor in a shallow sapphire bay, and their crews knelt on the white coral beach. Columbus christened the place San Salvador (Holy Savior). (Interactive Map 1 in the color insert shows the principal routes of European exploration.)

Like many men of destiny, Columbus did not recognize his true destination. At first he confused his actual location, the Bahamas, with an island off the coast of Japan. He coasted along Cuba and Hispaniola (Haiti), expecting at any moment to catch sight of gold-roofed Japanese temples or to happen upon a fleet of Chinese junks. He encountered instead a gentle, generous people who knew nothing of the Great Khan, but who showed him their islands. He dubbed the Arawak people "Indians"—inhabitants of the Indies.

*The four voyages of Columbus*

Columbus crossed the Atlantic three more times between 1493 and 1504. On his second voyage he established a permanent colony at Hispaniola and explored other Caribbean islands. On his third voyage he reached the continent of South America; and on his last sailing he made landfalls throughout Central America. Everywhere he looked for proof that these lands formed part of Asia.

Columbus died in 1506, rich in titles, treasure, and tales—everything but recognition. During the last decade of his life, most Spaniards no longer believed that Columbus had discovered the Indies or anyplace else of significance. Instead, another Italian stamped his own name on the New World. Amerigo Vespucci, a Florentine banker with a flair for self-promotion, cruised the coast of Brazil in 1501 and again in 1503. His sensational report misled a German mapmaker into crediting Vespucci with discovering the barrier between Europe and Asia, and so naming it "America."

## EARLY NORTH AMERICAN CULTURES

The Americas were a new world only to European latecomers. To the Asian peoples and their Native American descendants who had settled the continents tens of thousands of years earlier, Columbus's new world was their own old world. But the first nomadic hunters who crossed from Siberia over the Bering Strait to Alaska probably did not consider themselves discoverers or recognize what they had found—a truly new world wholly uninhabited by humans.

### The First Inhabitants

The first passage of people from Asia to America probably took place during a prehistoric glacial period—either before 35,000 B.C.E. or about 10,000 years later—when huge amounts of the world's water froze into sheets of ice. Sea levels dropped so drastically that the Bering Strait became a broad, grassy plain. Across that land bridge between the two continents both humans and animals escaped icebound Siberia for ice-free Alaska. Whenever the first migration took place, the movement of Asians to America continued, even after 8000 B.C.E., when world temperatures rose again and the water from melting glaciers flooded back into the ocean, submerging the Bering Strait. Over a span of 25,000 years settlement spread down the Alaskan coast, then deeper into the North American mainland, and finally throughout Central and South America.

Native Americans remained nomadic hunters and gatherers for thousands of years, as did many Europeans, Africans, and Asians of those millennia. But American cultures gradually diversified, especially after about 5500 B.C.E., when the peoples of central Mexico discovered how to cultivate food crops. As this "agricultural revolution" spread slowly northward, Native American societies were able to grow larger and develop distinctive forms of economic, social, and political organization. By the end of the fifteenth century, the inhabitants of North America, perhaps 5 to 10 million people, spoke as many as 1000 languages.

INDIANS OF NORTH AMERICA, CIRCA 1500

Although later Europeans, like Columbus, lumped these societies together by calling them Indian, any cultural unity had vanished long before 1492.

The simplest Indian societies were those that still relied on hunting and gathering, like the Eskimos of the Arctic and the Serrano, Cahuilla, Luiseño, and Diegueño of southern California, Arizona, and the Baja peninsula of Mexico. Stark deserts and frozen tundra defied cultivation and yielded food supplies that could sustain nomadic bands numbering no more than about 50 people. Families occasionally joined together for a collective hunt or wintered in common quarters, but for most of the year they scattered across the landscape, the women gathering plants and seeds, making baskets, and cooking meals while the men hunted for meat and hides. Political authority lay with either the male family head or the "headman" of a small band. "Shamans"—any tribesmen claiming spiritual powers—enlisted the supernatural to assist individuals.

## Societies of Increasing Complexity

In the densely forested belt that stretched from Newfoundland to the Bering Strait, resources more generous than those of the tundra to the north made for larger populations and more closely knit societies. Northeastern bands like the

paralleled Virginia's and Maryland's paths from violence, high mortality, and uncertainty toward relative stability.

### Paradise Lost

The English had traded and battled with the Spanish in the Caribbean since the 1560s. From those island bases English buccaneers conducted an illegal trade with Spanish settlements, sacked the coastal towns, and plundered silver ships bound for Seville. Weakened by decades of warfare, Spain could not hold the West Indies. The Dutch drove a wedge into Caribbean trade routes, and the French and the English began to colonize the islands.

In the 40 years after 1604, some 30,000 immigrants from the British Isles planted crude frontier outposts on St. Kitts, Barbados, Nevis, Montserrat, and Antigua. The settlers—some free, many others indentured servants, and almost all young men—devoted themselves to working as little as possible, drinking as much as possible, and returning to England as soon as possible. They cultivated for export a poor quality of tobacco, and profited little from it.

Then, nearly overnight, sugar cultivation transformed the Caribbean. In the 1640s Barbados planters learned from the Dutch how to process sugarcane. The Dutch also supplied African slaves to work the cane fields and marketed the sugar for high prices in the Netherlands. Sugar plantations *Caribbean sugar* and slave labor rapidly spread to other English and French islands as Europeans developed an insatiable sweet tooth for the once-scarce commodity. Caribbean sugar made more money for England than the total volume of commodities exported by all of the mainland American colonies.

Even though the Caribbean's great planters became the richest people in English America, they could not have confused the West Indies with paradise. Throughout the seventeenth century, disease took a fearful toll, and island populations grew only because of immigration. In the scramble for land, small farmers were pushed onto tiny plots that barely allowed them to survive.

The desperation of bound laborers posed another threat. After the conversion to sugar, black slaves gradually replaced white indentured servants in the cane fields. By 1700 black inhabitants outnumbered white residents *Slavery in the* by about four to one. Fear of servant mutinies and slave rebellions *Caribbean* frayed the nerves of island masters. They tried to contain the danger by imposing harsh slave codes and inflicting brutal punishments on white and black laborers alike. But planters lived under a constant state of siege. One visitor to Barbados observed that whites fortified their homes with parapets from which they could pour scalding water on attacking servants and slaves. During the first century of settlement, seven major slave uprisings shook the English islands.

As more people, both white and black, squeezed onto the islands, some settlers looked for a way out. With all of the land in use, the Caribbean no longer offered opportunity to freed servants or even planters' sons. It was then that the West Indies started to shape the history of the American South.

## The Founding of the Carolinas

The colonization of the Carolinas began with the schemes of Virginia's royal governor, William Berkeley, and Sir John Colleton, a supporter of Charles I who had been exiled to the Caribbean at the end of England's Civil War. Colleton saw that the Caribbean had a surplus of white settlers, and Berkeley knew that Virginians needed room to expand as well. Together the two men set their sights on the area south of Virginia. Along with a number of other aristocrats, they convinced Charles II to make them joint proprietors in 1663 of a place they called the Carolinas, in honor of the king.

A few hardy souls from Virginia had already squatted around Albemarle Sound in the northern part of the Carolina grant. The proprietors provided them

*North Carolina* with a governor and a representative assembly. About 40 years later, in 1701, they set off North Carolina as a separate colony. The desolate region quickly proved a disappointment. Lacking good harbors and navigable rivers, the colony had no convenient way of marketing its produce. North Carolina remained a poor colony, its sparse population engaged in general farming and the production of masts, pitch, tar, and turpentine.

The southern portion of the Carolina grant held far more promise, especially in the eyes of one of its proprietors, Sir Anthony Ashley Cooper, Earl

*South Carolina* of Shaftesbury. In 1669 he sponsored an expedition of a few hundred English and Barbadian immigrants, who planted the first permanent settlement in South Carolina. By 1680 the colonists had established the center of economic, social, and political life at the confluence of the Ashley and the Cooper rivers, naming the site Charles Town (later Charleston) after the king.

Most of the Carolina proprietors regarded their venture simply as land speculation. But Cooper, like others before him, hoped to create an ideal society

*The Fundamental Constitutions* in America. Cooper's utopia was one in which a few landed aristocrats and gentlemen would rule with the consent of many smaller propertyholders. With his personal secretary, John Locke, Cooper drew up an intricate scheme of government, the Fundamental Constitutions. The design provided Carolina with a proprietary governor and a hereditary nobility who, as a Council of Lords, would recommend all laws to a Parliament elected by lesser landowners.

The Fundamental Constitutions met the same fate as other lordly dreams for America. Instead of peacefully observing its provisions, Carolinians plunged into the kind of political wrangling that had plagued Maryland's proprietary rule. Assemblies resisted the sweeping powers granted to the proprietary governors. Ordinary settlers protested against paying quitrents claimed by the proprietors.

Political unrest in North Carolina triggered three rebellions between 1677 and 1711. In South Carolina opposition to the proprietors gathered strength more slowly but finally exploded with equal force.

## Early Instability

Immigrants from Barbados, the most numerous among the early settlers, came quickly to dominate South Carolina politics. Just as quickly, they objected to proprietary power. To offset the influence of the Barbadians, most of whom were Anglican, the proprietors encouraged the migration of French Huguenots and English Presbyterians and Baptists. The stream of newcomers only heightened tensions, splitting South Carolinians into two camps with competing political and religious loyalties.

Meanwhile, settlers spread out along the coastal plain. Searching for a profitable export, the first colonists raised grains and cattle, foodstuffs that they exported to the West Indies. South Carolinians also developed a large trade in deerskins with coastal tribes like the Yamasee and the Creeks and Catawbas of the interior. More numerous than the Indians of the *Indian slavery* Chesapeake and even more deeply divided, the Carolina tribes competed to become the favored clients of white traders. Southeastern Indian economies quickly became dependent on English guns, rum, and clothing. To repay their debts to white traders, Indians enslaved and sold to white buyers large numbers of men, women, and children taken in wars waged against rival tribes.

Provisions, deerskins, and Indian slaves proved less profitable for South Carolinians than rice, which became the colony's cash crop by the opening of the eighteenth century. Constant demand for rice in Europe made South Carolina the richest colony and South Carolina planters the richest people on the mainland of North America.

Unfortunately, South Carolina's swampy coast, so perfectly suited to growing rice, was less suited for human habitation. Weakened by chronic malaria, settlers died in epic numbers from yellow fever, smallpox, and respiratory infections. The white population grew slowly, through immigration rather than natural increase, and numbered a mere 10,000 by 1730.

Early South Carolinians had little in common but the harsh conditions of frontier existence. Most colonists lived on isolated plantations; early deaths fragmented families and neighborhoods. Immigration after 1700 only intensified the colony's ethnic and religious diversity, adding Swiss and German Lutherans, Scots-Irish Presbyterians, Welsh Baptists, and Spanish Jews. The colony's only courts were in Charleston; churches and clergy of any denomination were scarce. On those rare occasions when early Carolinians came together, they gathered at Charleston to escape the pestilent air of their plantations, to sue each other for debt and to haggle over prices, or to fight over religious differences and proprietary politics.

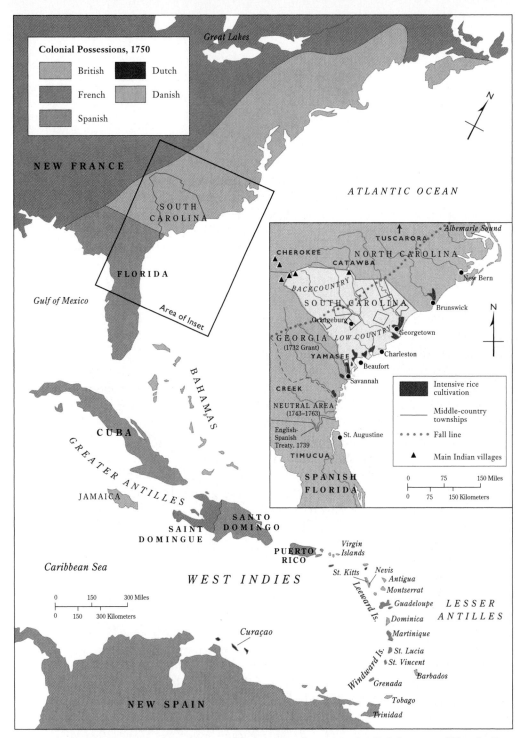

**Colonial Possessions, 1750**

- British
- French
- Spanish
- Dutch
- Danish

Great Lakes

NEW FRANCE

ATLANTIC OCEAN

SOUTH CAROLINA

FLORIDA

Area of Inset

Gulf of Mexico

*Albemarle Sound*

TUSCARORA

CHEROKEE    NORTH CAROLINA
            CATAWBA

New Bern

BACKCOUNTRY

SOUTH CAROLINA

Brunswick

Orangeburg

Georgetown

GEORGIA *LOW COUNTRY*
(1732 Grant)

YAMASEE

Charleston

Beaufort

Savannah

CREEK

NEUTRAL AREA
(1743–1763)

English-
Spanish
Treaty, 1739

TIMUCUA

St. Augustine

SPANISH
FLORIDA

Intensive rice
cultivation

Middle-country
townships

Fall line

▲ Main Indian villages

0    75    150 Miles

0    75    150 Kilometers

BAHAMAS

CUBA

GREATER ANTILLES

JAMAICA

SAINT
DOMINGUE

SANTO
DOMINGO

PUERTO
RICO

Virgin
Islands

St. Kitts

Nevis

Antigua

Montserrat

Guadeloupe

LESSER
ANTILLES

Dominica

Caribbean Sea

WEST INDIES

Leeward Is.

Martinique

0    150    300 Miles

0    150    300 Kilometers

Curaçao

St. Lucia

St. Vincent

Windward Is.

Barbados

Grenada

Tobago

NEW SPAIN

Trinidad

**THE CAROLINAS AND THE CARIBBEAN**   The map underscores the link between West Indian and Carolina settlements. Emigrants from Barbados dominated politics in early South Carolina, while Carolinians provided foodstuffs, grain, and cattle to the West Indies.

## White, Red, and Black: The Search for Order

By the opening decades of the eighteenth century, South Carolina seemed as strife-torn and unstable as the early Chesapeake colonies. In addition to internal tensions, external dangers threatened the very life of the Carolina settlements. The Spanish were rattling their sabers in Florida, the French filtering into the Gulf region, and pirates lurking along the North Carolina coast.

Most menacing were the Indians, and in 1715 they struck. The Yamasee of the coast allied themselves with the Creeks farther inland, launching a series of assaults that nearly pushed white Carolinians into the sea. All that saved the colony was an alliance with the Cherokee, another interior tribe that, in return for trading privileges, mounted a counterattack against their Indian rivals.

*Yamasee War*

As colonists reeled from the Yamasee War, opposition mounted against the proprietors, who had done nothing to protect their vulnerable colony. Military expenses had also forced Carolinians to fall into greater debt, to pay higher taxes, and to struggle with an inflated currency that month by month became worth less. Even Presbyterians, Baptists, and Huguenots, who had once defended the proprietors, shifted their sympathies because they disapproved of more recent attempts to establish the Church of England as South Carolina's official religion. During the 1720s, mass meetings and riots so disrupted government that it all but ground to a halt. Finally, in 1729, the Crown formally established royal government; by 1730 economic recovery had done much to ease the strife. Even more important in bringing greater political stability, the white colonists of South Carolina came to realize that they must unite if they were to counter the Spanish in Florida and the French and their Indian allies to the southwest.

*The end of proprietary rule*

The growing black population gave white Carolinians another reason to maintain a united front. During the first decades of settlement, frontier conditions and the scarcity of labor had forced masters to allow enslaved Africans greater freedom within bondage. White and black laborers shared chores on small farms. On stockraising plantations, called "cowpens," black cowboys ranged freely over the countryside. Black contributions to the defense of the colony also reinforced racial interdependence and muted white domination. Whenever the Spanish, the French, or the Indians threatened, black Carolinians were enlisted in the militia.

*Slavery in South Carolina*

White Carolinians depended on black labor even more after turning to rice as their cash crop. Indeed, the skills of West Africans in cultivating rice led to a greater demand for them. But whites harbored deepening fears of the workers whose labor built planter fortunes. As early as 1708 black men and women had become a majority in the colony, and by 1730 they outnumbered white settlers by two to one. Like Caribbean planters, white Carolinians put into effect strict slave codes that converted their colony into an armed camp and snuffed out the freedoms that black settlers had enjoyed earlier.

The ever-present threat of revolt on the part of the black majority gave all white South Carolinians an incentive to cooperate, whatever their religion, politics, or ethnic background. To be sure, the colony's high death rates and cultural differences persisted, while local government and churches remained weak. Yet against all these odds, white South Carolinians prospered and political peace prevailed after 1730. Any course except harmony would have exacted too high a price.

## The Founding of Georgia

After 1730 South Carolinians could also take comfort from the founding of a new colony on their southern border. South Carolinians liked Georgia a great deal more than the Virginians had liked Maryland, for the colony formed a defensive buffer between British North America and Spanish Florida.

Enhancing the military security of South Carolina was only one reason for the founding of Georgia. More important to General James Oglethorpe and other

*James Oglethorpe*

idealistic English gentlemen was the aim of aiding the "worthy poor" by providing them with land, employment, and a new start. They envisioned a colony of hardworking small farmers who would produce silk and wine, sparing England the need to import those commodities. That dream seemed within reach when George II made Oglethorpe and his friends the trustees of the new colony in 1732, granting them a charter for 21 years. At the end of that time Georgia would revert to royal control.

The trustees did not, as legend has it, empty England's debtors' prisons to populate Georgia. They freed few debtors but recruited from every country in Europe paupers who seemed willing to work hard—and who professed Protestantism. They paid their passage and provided each with 50 acres of land, tools, and a year's worth of supplies. The trustees encouraged settlers who could pay their own way to come by granting them larger tracts of land. Much to the trustees' dismay, that generous offer was taken up not only by many hoped-for Protestants but also by several hundred Ashkenazim (German Jews) and Sephardim (Spanish and Portuguese Jews), who established a thriving community in early Savannah.

The trustees were determined to ensure that Georgia became a small farmers' utopia. Rather than selling land, the trustees gave it away, but none of the

*Utopian designs*

colony's settlers could own more than 500 acres. The trustees also outlawed slavery and hard liquor, in order to cultivate habits of industry and sustain equality among whites. This design for a virtuous and egalitarian utopia was greeted with little enthusiasm by Georgians. They pressed for a free market in land and argued that the colony could never prosper until the trustees revoked their ban on slavery. Since the trustees had provided for no elective assembly, settlers could express their discontent only by moving to South Carolina— which many did during the early decades.

In the end, the trustees caved in to the opposition. They revoked their restrictions on land, slavery, and liquor a few years before the king assumed control of the colony in 1752. Under royal control, Georgia continued to develop an ethnically and religiously diverse society like that of South Carolina. In addition, its economy was similarly based on rice cultivation and the Indian trade.

Although South Carolina and the English West Indies were both more opulent and more embattled societies than were Virginia and Maryland, the plantation colonies stretching from the Chesapeake to the Caribbean had much in common. Everywhere planters depended on a single staple crop, which brought both wealth and political power to those commanding the most land and the most labor. Everywhere the biggest planters relied for their success on the very people whom they deeply feared: enslaved African Americans. Everywhere that fear was reflected in the development of repressive slave codes and the spread of racism throughout all classes of white society.

*Similarities among the plantation colonies*

## THE SPANISH BORDERLANDS

When the English founded Jamestown, Spanish settlement in the present-day United States consisted of one feeble fort in southeastern Florida and a single outpost in New Mexico. Hoping both to intimidate privateers who preyed on silver ships and to assert their sovereign claim to the Americas, Spain had established St. Augustine on the Florida coast in 1565. But for decades the place remained a squalid garrison town of a few hundred soldiers and settlers beleaguered by hurricanes, pirates, and Indians. Meanwhile, the Spanish planted a straggling settlement under azure skies and spectacular mesas near present-day Santa Fe in 1598. Their desire was to create colonies in the Southwest that would prove more richly profitable than even those in Central and South America.

*St. Augustine and Santa Fe*

Defending both outposts proved so great a drain on royal resources that the Spanish government considered abandoning its footholds in North America. Only the pleas of Catholic missionaries, who hoped to convert the native peoples, persuaded the Crown to sustain its support. But even by 1700, St. Augustine could boast only about 1500 souls, a motley assortment of Spaniards, black slaves, and Hispanicized Indians. New Mexico's colonial population amounted to fewer than 3000 Spanish ranchers, soldiers, and clergy, scattered among the haciendas (cattle and sheep ranches), presidios (military garrisons), and Catholic missions along the Rio Grande. There, the native Pueblo Indians numbered some 30,000.

Still, during these years the Catholic clergy remained active, creating mission communities designed to incorporate native tribes into colonial society. In New Mexico, Franciscan friars supervised Pueblo women (who traditionally built their people's adobe homes) in the construction of over 30 missions. By 1675 in Florida, perhaps 10,000 Indians were living in 35 Indian villages where the friars came to stay.

*Mission communities*

This Native American drawing on a canyon wall in present-day Arizona represents the progress of the Spanish into the Southwest. The prominence of horses underscores their novelty to the Indians, an initial advantage enjoyed by the invaders. "The most essential thing in new lands is horses," one of Coronado's men emphasized. "They instill greatest fear in the enemy and make the Indians respect the leaders of the army." Many Indian peoples soon put the horse to their own uses, however, and even outshone the Spanish in their riding skills.

Unlike the English, the Spanish projected a place in their colonies for the Indians. Homes, workshops, granaries, and stables clustered around the church. The missionaries taught Indians European agricultural techniques and crafts. At mission schools, adults as well as children learned to say prayers, sing Christian hymns, and speak Spanish. In 1675, when the Bishop of Cuba toured Florida's missions, he spoke enthusiastically of converts who embraced "with devotion the mysteries of our holy faith."

The Indians were selective, however, in the European "mysteries" they chose to adopt. Some natives regarded the friars' presence simply as a means of

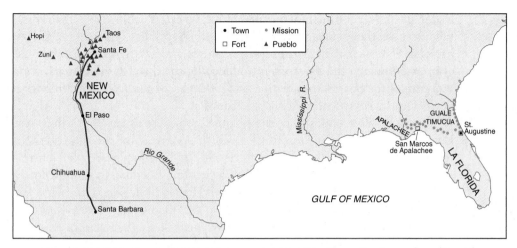

SPANISH MISSIONS IN NORTH AMERICA, CIRCA 1675   From St. Augustine, Spanish missionaries spread north into Guale Indian villages in present-day Georgia and westward among the Indians of Timucua, Apalachee, and Apalachicola. In New Mexico, missions radiated outward from the Rio Grande, as distant as Hopi Pueblo in the west.

protecting themselves against the harsher treatment of Spanish soldiers and ranchers. Other Indians used the Spanish presence to give them the upper hand in dealing with rival tribes, just as Powhatan had used white Virginians to further his own designs. And in their religious ceremonies, many natives simply placed Jesus, Mary, and Christian saints beside the other deities they honored.

Indian and Spanish cultures bumped up against each other in material ways as well. When the Spanish at St. Augustine found the climate unsuitable for growing wheat, olives, and grapes, they turned to Indian maize, beans, and squash. Indians adopted domesticated animals from Europe—horses, cattle, sheep, mules, and donkeys. Watermelons and peach trees, brought to the Atlantic coast by the Spanish, spread quickly along Indian trade routes, often ahead of Europeans themselves.

To their dismay, Indians discovered that, in the long run, becoming "civilized" usually meant learning to work for Spanish masters as docile servants. The labor was harsh enough to send many to an early death. European diseases, too, took a gruesome toll among mission Indians. As the population dropped sharply, the demand by Spanish colonists rose for increasingly scarce Indian labor.

As the abuses increased, so did the resentment. Indians regularly fled the mission settlements; others made life miserable for their "benefactors." One padre at Taos Pueblo was served corn tortillas laced with urine and mouse meat. On occasion discontent and anger ignited major insurrections. *Indian resistance*
The most successful was the Pueblo Revolt of 1680, which would drive the Spanish out of New Mexico for more than a decade. Popé, an Indian spiritual

leader in Taos, coordinated an uprising of several Pueblo tribes that vented the full force of their hatred of Spanish rule. They killed 400 people in outlying haciendas, burned their Spanish-style houses and churches to the ground, and even exterminated the livestock introduced by the Spanish. The attack wiped out one-fifth of the Spanish population of 2500 and sent survivors scurrying for refuge down Dead Man's Road to El Paso, Texas.

Despite native opposition, the Spanish persisted, especially as they saw their European rivals making headway in North America. By the end of the seventeenth century, English settlements in South Carolina were well entrenched, which prompted the Spanish in Florida to offer freedom to any escaped slaves willing to defend the colony and convert to Catholicism. The black fugitives established a fortified settlement north of St. Augustine, Gracia Real de Santa Teresa de Mose, which served as a barrier against English attacks and as a base for raiding Carolina's plantations. Meanwhile the French were building forts at Biloxi and Mobile near the mouth of the Mississippi River, signaling their designs on the Gulf of Mexico. As a counterweight the Spanish added a second military outpost in Florida at Pensacola and founded several missions in present-day Texas. After 1769, to secure their claims to the Pacific coast from England and Russia, Spanish soldiers and missionaries began colonizing California. Led by the Franciscan friar Junípero Serra, they established 20 communities along the Pacific coastal plain.

Empire . . . utopia . . . independence. For more than a century after the founding of Jamestown in 1607, those dreams inspired the inhabitants of the Chesapeake, the Carolinas and Georgia, the Caribbean, and the American Southwest. The regions served as staging grounds where kings and commoners, free and unfree, men and women, red, white, and black played out their hopes. Most met only disappointment, and many met disaster in the painful decades before the new colonies achieved a measure of stability.

The dream of an expanding empire faltered for the Spanish, who found no new El Dorado in the Southwest. The dream of empire failed, too, when James I and Charles I, England's early Stuart kings, found their power checked by Parliament. And the dream foundered fatally for Powhatan's successors, who were unable to resist both white diseases and land-hungry tobacco planters.

English lords had dreamed of establishing feudal utopias in America. But proprietors like the Calvert family in Maryland and Cooper in the Carolinas found themselves hounded by frontier planters and farmers who sought economic and political power. Georgia's trustees struggled in vain to nurture their dream of a utopia for the poor. The dream of a Spanish Catholic utopia brought by missionaries to the American Southwest dimmed with Indian resistance.

The dream of independence proved the most deceptive of all, especially for the inhabitants of England's colonies. Just a bare majority of the white servant immigrants to the Chesapeake survived to enjoy freedom. The rest were struck down by disease or worn down at the hands of tobacco barons eager for profit. Not only in the Chesapeake but also in the Caribbean and the Carolinas, real independence eluded the English planters. Poorer people were dependent on richer people for land and leadership; they deferred to them at church and on election days and depended on them to buy crops or to extend credit. Even the richest planters depended on the English and Scottish merchants who supplied them with credit and marketed their crops as well as on the English officials who made colonial policy.

And everywhere in the American South and Southwest, white people's lingering dreams were realized only through the labor of the least free members of colonial America. In the Southwest the Spanish made servants of the Indians. Along the southern Atlantic coast and in the Caribbean, English plantation owners (like the Spanish before them) turned for labor to the African slave trade. Only after slavery became firmly established as a social and legal institution did England's southern colonies begin to settle down and grow: during the late seventeenth century for the Chesapeake region and the early eighteenth for the Carolinas. That stubborn reality would haunt Americans of all colors who continued to dream of freedom and independence.

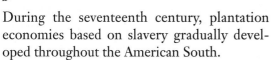

# chapter summary

During the seventeenth century, plantation economies based on slavery gradually developed throughout the American South.

- Native peoples everywhere in the American South resisted white settlement, but their populations were drastically reduced by warfare, disease, and enslavement.

- Thriving monocultures were established throughout the region—tobacco in the Chesapeake, rice in the Carolinas, and sugar in the Caribbean.

- African slavery emerged as the dominant labor system in all the southern colonies.

- Instability and conflict characterized the southern colonies for most of the first century of their existence.

- As the English colonies took shape, the Spanish extended their empire in Florida and New Mexico, establishing military garrisons, missions, and cattle ranches.

# interactive learning

The Primary Source Investigator CD-ROM offers the following materials related to this chapter:

- Interactive maps: **The Atlantic World, 1400–1850** (M2) and **Growth of the Colonies, 1610–1690** (M3)

- A collection of primary sources on the English colonization of North America, such as an engraving that illustrates the dress and customs of Native Americans living near Jamestown, a document about the peace resulting from the marriage of Pocahontas and John Rolfe, and the terrible collapse of that peace captured in a contemporary engraving of the Indian massacre of Jamestown settlers. Also included are several sources on the origins of slavery in America: a document that presents one of the earliest restrictive slave codes in the British colonies, images of Portuguese slave-trading forts on the coast of West Africa, and a sobering diagram of the human cargo holds of that era's slave-trading ships.

 For quizzes and a variety of interactive resources, visit the book's Online Learning Center at www.mhhe.com/davidsonconcise4.

refused to grant inland settlers equitable political representation or even basic legal institutions. In response to those injustices, two protest move- | *Regulation movements* ments emerged in the Carolina interior, each known as the Regulation.

Farmers in the South Carolina backcountry organized their Regulation in the 1760s, after that colony's assembly refused to set up courts in the backcountry. Westerners were desperate for protection from outlaws who stole livestock, kidnapped and raped women, and tortured and murdered men. In the absence of courts the Regulators acted as vigilantes, meting out their own brand of grisly frontier justice against these criminals. Regulator threats to march on Charleston itself finally panicked eastern political leaders into extending the court system, but bitter memories lingered among westerners.

Western North Carolinians organized their Regulation to protest not the absence of a legal system but the corruption of local government. Lawyers and merchants, backed by wealthy eastern planters, moved into the western parts of that colony and seized control of politics. Then they used local offices to exploit frontier settlers, charging exorbitant fees for legal services, imposing high taxes, and manipulating debt laws. Western farmers responded to these abuses with the Regulation: they seized county courts and finally squared off against an eastern militia led by the governor. Easterners crushed the Regulators at the Battle of Alamance in 1771 and left frontier North Carolinians with an enduring hostility to the seaboard.

Ethnic differences heightened sectional tensions between East and West. While people of English descent predominated along the Atlantic coast, Germans, Scots-Irish, and other white minorities were concentrated in the interior. Many | *Ethnic conflicts* English colonials regarded these new immigrants as culturally inferior. Charles Woodmason, an Anglican missionary in the Carolina backcountry, lamented the arrival of "5 or 6000 Ignorant, mean, worthless, beggarly Irish Presbyterians, the Scum of the Earth, the Refuse of Mankind," who "delighted in a low, lazy, sluttish, heathenish, hellish life."

German immigrants were generally credited with having steadier work habits as well as higher standards of sexual morality and personal hygiene. But like the clannish Scots-Irish, the Germans preferred to live, trade, and worship among themselves. By 1751 Franklin was warning that the Germans would retain their separate language and customs: the Pennsylvania English would be overrun by "the Palatine Boors."

## Boundary Disputes and Tenant Wars

The settlement of the frontier also triggered disputes between colonies over their boundaries. The most serious of these border wars pitted New York against farmers from New England who had settled in present-day Vermont: Ethan Allen and the Green Mountain Boys. In the 1760s New York, backed by the | *Green Mountain Boys* Crown, claimed land that Allen and his friends had already purchased from New Hampshire. When New York tried to extend its rule over Vermont, Allen led a successful guerrilla resistance, harassing Yorker settlers and officials, occupying Yorker courthouses, and setting up a competing judicial system in the Green Mountains.

The spread of settlement also set the stage for mass revolts by tenants in those areas where proprietors controlled vast amounts of land. In eastern New Jersey, proprietors insisted that squatters pay quitrents on land that had become increasingly valuable. When the squatters, many of them migrants from New England, refused to pay rents, buy the land, or move, the proprietors began evictions, touching off riots in the 1740s. Tenant unrest also raged in New York's Hudson River valley. In the 1680s the royal governor had granted several prominent merchant families large estates in that region. By the middle of the eighteenth century, there were about 30 manors around New York City and Albany, totaling some 2 million acres and worked by several thousand tenants. Newcomers from New England, however, demanded to own land and preached their ideas to Dutch and German tenants. Armed insurrection exploded in 1757 and again, more violently, in 1766. Tenants refused to pay rents, formed mobs, and stormed the homes of landlords.

### Eighteenth-Century Seaports

While most Americans on the move settled on the frontier, others swelled the populations of colonial cities. By present-day standards such cities were small, harboring from 8000 to 22,000 citizens by 1750. The scale of seaports remained intimate, too: all of New York City was clustered at the southern tip of Manhattan Island, and the length of Boston or Charleston could be walked in less than half an hour.

All major colonial cities were seaports, their waterfronts fringed with wharves and shipyards. A jumble of shops, taverns, and homes crowded their streets; the spires of churches studded their skylines. By the 1750s, the grandest and most populous was Philadelphia, which boasted straight, neatly paved streets, flagstone sidewalks, and three-story brick buildings. Older cities like Boston and New York had a more medieval aspect: most of their dwellings and shops were wooden structures with tiny windows and low ceilings, rising no higher than two stories to steeply pitched roofs. The narrow cobblestone streets of Boston and New York also challenged pedestrians, who competed for space with livestock being driven to the butcher, roaming herds of swine and packs of dogs, clattering carts, carriages, and horses.

*The commercial classes*

Commerce, the lifeblood of seaport economies, was managed by merchants who tapped the wealth of surrounding regions. Traders in New York and Philadelphia shipped the Hudson and Delaware valleys' surplus of grain and livestock to the West Indies. Boston's merchants sent fish to the Caribbean and Catholic Europe, masts to England, and rum to West Africa. Charlestonians exported indigo to English dyemakers and rice to southern

Europe. Other merchants specialized in the import trade, selling luxuries and manufactured goods produced in England—fine fabrics, ceramics, tea, and farming implements. Wealth brought many merchants political power: they dominated city governments and shared power in colonial assemblies with lawyers and the largest farmers and planters.

Skilled craftworkers or artisans made up the middling classes of colonial cities. The households of master craftworkers usually included a few younger and less skilled journeymen working in other artisans' shops. Unskilled boy apprentices not only worked but also lived under the watchful eye of their masters. Some artisans specialized in the maritime trades as shipbuilders, blacksmiths, and sailmakers. Others, like butchers, millers, and distillers, processed and packed raw materials for export. Still others served the basic needs of city dwellers—the men and, occasionally, women who baked bread, mended shoes, combed and powdered wigs, and tended shops and taverns.

On the lowest rung of a seaport's social hierarchy were free and bound workers. Free laborers were mainly young white men and women—journeymen artisans, sailors, fishermen, domestic workers, seamstresses, and prostitutes. The ranks of unfree workers included apprentices and indentured servants doing menial labor in shops and on the docks. Black men and women also made up a substantial part of the bound labor force of colonial seaports. While the vast majority of African slaves were sold to southern plantations, a smaller number were bought by urban merchants and craftworkers. Laboring as porters at the docks, as assistants in craft shops, or as servants in wealthy households, black residents made up almost 20 percent of the population in New York City and 10 percent in Boston and Philadelphia.

*Free and bound workers*

The character of slavery in northern seaports changed decisively during the mid–eighteenth century. When wars raging in Europe reduced the supply of white indentured servants, colonial cities imported a larger number of Africans. Those newcomers brought to urban black culture a new awareness of a common West African past. The influence of African traditions appeared most vividly in an annual event known as "Negro election day," celebrated in northern seaports. During the festival, similar to ones held in West Africa, some black men and women paraded in their masters' clothes or mounted on their horses. An election followed, to choose black "kings," "governors," and "judges," who then "held court" and settled minor disputes among white and black members of the community. "Negro election day" did not challenge the established racial order with its temporary reversal of roles, but it did allow the black community of seaports to honor their own leaders.

The availability of domestic workers, both black and white, made for leisured lives among women from wealthy white families. Even those city women who could not afford household help spent less time on domestic work than did farming wives and daughters. Although some housewives grew vegetables in backyard gardens or kept a few chickens, large markets stocked by outlying farmers supplied most of the food for urban families.

*Women in cities*

For women who had to support themselves, seaports offered a number of employments. Young single women from poorer families worked in wealthier households as maids, cooks, laundresses, seamstresses, or nurses. The highest-paying occupations for women, midwifery and dressmaking, both required long apprenticeships and expert skills. The wives of artisans and traders sometimes assisted their husbands and, as widows, often continued to manage groceries, taverns, and printshops. But most women were confined to caring for households, husbands, and children; fewer than 1 out of every 10 women in seaports worked outside their own homes.

*Urban diversions and hazards*

All seaport dwellers—perhaps 1 out of every 20 Americans—enjoyed a more stimulating environment than did other colonials. The wealthiest could attend an occasional ball or concert; those living in New York or Charleston might even see a play performed by touring English actors. The middling classes could converse with other tradespeople at private social clubs and fraternal societies. Men of every class found diversion in drink and cockfighting. Crowds of men, women, and children swarmed to tavern exhibitions of trained dogs and horses or the spectacular waxworks of one John Dyer, featuring "a lively Representation of Margaret, Countess of Herrinburg, who had 365 Children at one Birth."

But city dwellers, then as now, paid a price for their pleasures. Commerce was riddled with risk: ships sank and wars disrupted trade. When such disasters struck, the lower classes suffered most. The ups and downs of seaport economies, combined with the influx of immigrants, swelled the ranks of the poor in all cities by the mid–eighteenth century. Furthermore, epidemics and catastrophic fires occurred with greater frequency and produced higher mortality rates in congested seaports than in the countryside.

## Social Conflict in Seaports

The swelling of seaport populations, like the movement of whites to the West, often churned up trouble. English, Scots-Irish, Germans, Swiss, Dutch, French, and Spanish jostled uneasily against one another in the close quarters of Philadelphia and New York. To make matters worse, religious differences heightened ethnic divisions. Jewish funerals in New York, for example, drew crowds of hostile and curious Protestants, who heckled the mourners.

Class resentment also stirred unrest. Some merchant families flaunted their wealth, building imposing town mansions and dressing in the finest imported fashions. During hard times, expensive coaches and full warehouses became targets of mob vandalism. Crowds also gathered to intimidate and punish other groups who provoked popular hostility—unresponsive politicians, prostitutes, and "press gangs." Impressment, attempts to force colonials to serve in the British navy, triggered some of the most violent urban riots.

## SLAVE SOCIETIES IN THE EIGHTEENTH-CENTURY SOUTH

Far starker than the inequalities and divisions among seaport dwellers were those between white and black in the South. By 1775 one out of every five Americans was of African ancestry, and over 90 percent of all black Americans lived in the South, most along the seaboard. Here, on tobacco and rice plantations, slaves fashioned a distinctive African American society and culture. But they were able to build stable families and communities only late in the eighteenth century, and against enormous odds.

Whether a slave was auctioned off to the Chesapeake or to the Lower South shaped his or her future in important ways. Slaves in the low country of South Carolina and Georgia lived on large plantations with as many as 50 other black workers, about half of whom were African-born. They had infrequent contact with either their masters or the rest of the sparse *The Chesapeake versus the Lower South* white population. "They are as 'twere, a Nation within a Nation," observed Francis LeJau, an Anglican priest in the low country. And their work was arduous, for rice required constant cultivation. Black laborers tended young plants and hoed fields in the sweltering summer heat of the mosquito-infested lowlands. During the winter and early spring, they built dams and canals to regulate the flow of water into the rice fields. But the use of the "task system" rather than gang labor widened the window of freedom within slavery. When a slave had completed his assigned task for the day, one planter explained, "his master feels no right to call upon him."

Many Chesapeake slaves, like those in the Lower South, were African-born, but most lived on smaller plantations with fewer than 20 fellow slaves. Less densely concentrated than in the low country, Chesapeake slaves also had more contact with whites. Unlike Carolina's absentee owners, who left white overseers and black drivers to run their plantations, Chesapeake masters actively managed their estates and subjected their slaves to closer scrutiny.

### The Slave Family and Community

After the middle of the eighteenth century, a number of changes fostered the growth of black families and the vitality of slave communities. As slave importations began to taper off, the rate of natural reproduction among blacks started to climb. As the proportion of new Africans dropped and the number of native-born black Americans grew, the ratio of men to women in the slave community became more equal. Those changes and the appearance of more large plantations, even in the Chesapeake, created more opportunities for black men and women to find partners and form families. Elaborate kinship networks gradually developed, often extending over several plantations in a single neighborhood.

Even so, black families remained vulnerable. If a planter fell on hard times, members of black families might be sold off to different buyers to meet his debts.

*The Old Plantation* affords a rare glimpse of life in the slave quarters.
At this festive gathering, both men and women dance to the music
of a molo (a stringed instrument similar to a banjo) and drums.

When a master died, black families might be divided among surviving heirs. Even under the best circumstances, fathers might be hired out to other planters for long periods or sent to work in distant quarters.

Black families struggling with terrible uncertainties were sustained by the distinctive African American culture evolving in the slave community. The high per-

*Influence of African culture*

centage of native Africans among the eighteenth-century American black population made it easier for slaves to retain the ways of their lost homeland. Christianity won few converts, in part because white masters feared that baptizing slaves might make them more rebellious, but also because African Americans preferred their traditional religions. African influence appeared as well in the slaves' agricultural skills and practices, folktales, music, and dances.

## Slavery and Colonial Society in French Louisiana

The experience of Africans unfolded differently in the lower Mississippi valley, France's southernmost outpost in eighteenth-century North America. Louisiana's earliest colonial settlements were begun by a few thousand French soldiers, joined by indentured servants, free settlers straggling down from Canada, and immigrants from France and Germany. When they founded New Orleans in 1718, the colonists, hoping to create prosperous plantations in the surrounding Mississippi Delta, immediately clamored for bound laborers. A year later, French authorities bent to their demands, and the Company of the Indies, which managed France's slave trade, brought nearly 6000 slaves, overwhelmingly men, directly from Africa to Louisiana. Yet even with this influx of new laborers, the search for a cash crop eluded white planters, whose tobacco and, later, indigo proved inferior to the varieties exported from Britain's colonies.

Instead of proving the formula for economic success, the sudden influx of Africans challenged French control. In 1729, with blacks already making up a majority of the population, some newly arrived slaves joined forces with the Natchez Indians who feared the expansion of white settlement. Their rebellion, the Natchez Revolt, left 200 French planters dead—more than 10 percent of the European population of Louisiana. The French retaliated in a devastating counterattack, enlisting both the Choctaw Indians, who were rivals of the Natchez, and other enslaved blacks, who were promised freedom in return for their support.

*Natchez revolt*

The planters' costly victory persuaded French authorities to stop importing slaves into Louisiana, which helped ensure that the colony did not develop a plantation economy until the end of the eighteenth century, when the cotton boom transformed its culture. In the meantime, blacks continued to make up a majority of all Louisianans, and by the middle of the eighteenth century, nearly all were native-born. The vast majority were slaves, but their work routines—tending cattle, cutting timber, producing naval stores, working on boats—afforded them greater freedom of movement than most slaves enjoyed elsewhere in the American South. Louisiana blacks were also encouraged to market the produce of their gardens, hunts, and handicrafts, which became the basis of a thriving trade with both white settlers and the dwindling numbers of Native Americans. But the greatest prize—freedom—was awarded those black men who served in the French militia, defending the colony from the English and Indians as well as capturing slave runaways. The descendants of these black militiamen would become the core of Louisiana's free black population.

*Greater freedom for blacks in Louisiana*

## Slave Resistance in Eighteenth-Century British North America

British North America had no comparable group of black soldiers, but it also had no shortage of African Americans who both resisted captivity and developed strategies for survival. Among newly arrived Africans, collective attempts at escape were most common. Groups of slaves, often made up of newcomers from the same tribe, fled inland and formed "Maroon" communities of runaways. These efforts were usually unsuccessful because the Maroon settlements were large enough to be easily detected.

More acculturated blacks adopted subtler ways of subverting slavery. Domestics and field hands alike faked illness, feigned stupidity and laziness, broke tools, pilfered from storehouses, hid in the woods for weeks at a time, or simply took off to visit other plantations. Other slaves, usually escaping bondage as solitary individuals, found new lives as craftworkers, dock laborers, or sailors in the relative anonymity of colonial seaports.

Less frequently, black rebellion took direct and violent form. Whites in communities with large numbers of blacks lived in dread of arson, poisoning, and

*The Stono Rebellion*  insurrection. Four slave conspiracies were reported in Virginia before 1750. In South Carolina, more than two decades of abortive uprisings and insurrection scares culminated in the Stono Rebellion of 1739, the largest slave revolt of the colonial period. Nearly 100 African Americans, led by a slave

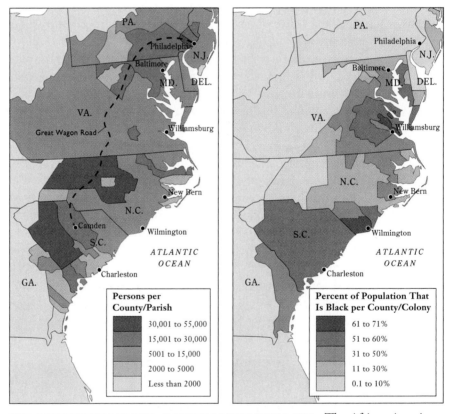

THE DISTRIBUTION OF THE AMERICAN POPULATION, 1775   The African American population expanded dramatically during the eighteenth century, especially in the southern colonies. While the high volume of slave imports accounted for most of the growth in the first half of the century, natural increase was responsible for the rising black population during later decades.

named Jemmy, seized arms from a store in the coastal district of Stono and killed several white neighbors before they were caught and killed by the white militia.

Despite the growing rebelliousness of black slaves, southern planters continued to import Africans throughout the eighteenth century. The practice mystified Franklin, revealing at least one gap in his knowledge: the crucial importance of slavery in the southern economy. But unlike some of his Quaker neighbors in Pennsylvania, who were beginning to object to slavery on moral and humanitarian grounds, Franklin's reservations—like his opposition to German immigration—were overtly racist. "Why increase the sons of Africa by planting them in America," he asked, "where we have so fair an opportunity, by excluding all blacks and tawnys, of increasing the lovely white and red?"

## ENLIGHTENMENT AND AWAKENING IN AMERICA

The differences among eighteenth-century colonials resulted in more than clashes between regions, races, classes, and ethnic groups. Those differences also made for diversity in the ways that Americans thought and believed. City dwellers were more attuned to European culture than were people living in small villages or on the frontier. White males from well-to-do families of English ancestry were far more likely to receive college educations than were those from poorer or immigrant households. White women of every class and background were excluded from higher education, and slaves received no formal education at all. Where they lived, how well they lived, whether they were male or female, native-born or immigrant, slave or free—all these variables fostered among colonials distinctive worldviews, differing attitudes and assumptions about the individual's relationship to nature, society, and God.

### The Enlightenment in America

The diversity of colonials' inner lives became even more pronounced during the eighteenth century because of the Enlightenment, an intellectual movement that started in Europe during the seventeenth century. The leading figures of the Enlightenment, the "philosophes," stressed the power of human reason to promote progress by revealing the laws that governed both nature and society. In the American colonies the Enlightenment influenced some curious artisans in major seaports as well as wealthy merchants, lawyers, and landowners with the leisure and education to read the latest books from Europe.

Like many devotees of the Enlightenment, Franklin was most impressed by its emphasis on useful knowledge and experimentation. He pondered air currents and then invented a stove that heated houses more efficiently. He toyed with electricity and then invented lightning rods to protect buildings in thunderstorms. Other amateur colonial scientists constructed simple telescopes, classified animal species native to North America, or sought to explain epidemics in terms of natural causes.

Some clergy educated at American colleges (six had been established by 1763) were touched by the Enlightenment, adopting a more liberal theology

*Rational versus traditional Christianity*

that stressed the reasonableness of Christian beliefs. By the middle of the eighteenth century this "rational Christianity" commanded a small following among colonials, usually Anglicans or liberal Congregationalists. Their God was not the Calvinists' awesome deity, but a benevolent creator who offered salvation to all, not just to a small, predestined elite. They believed that God's greatest gift to humanity was reason, which enabled all human beings to follow the moral teachings of Jesus. They muted the Calvinist emphasis on human sinfulness and the need for a soul-shattering conversion.

Enlightenment philosophy and rational Christianity did not affect the outlook of most colonials. By the middle of the eighteenth century, over half of all white men (and a smaller percentage of white women) were literate. But most colonial readers were not equipped to tackle the learned writings of Enlightenment philosophes. As a result, the outlook of most colonials contrasted sharply with that of the cosmopolitan few. The great majority of Americans still looked for ultimate truth in biblical revelation rather than human reason and explained the workings of the world in terms of divine providence rather than natural law.

Widespread attachment to traditional Christian beliefs was strengthened by the hundreds of new churches built during the first half of the eighteenth century. Church attendance ran highest in the northern colonies, where some 80 percent of the population turned out for public worship on the Sabbath. In the South, because of the greater distances involved and the shortage of clergy, about half of all colonials regularly attended Sunday services.

Despite the prevalence of traditional religious beliefs, many ministers expressed concern about the dangerous influence of rational Christianity. They also worried that the lack of churches might tempt many frontier families to abandon Christianity altogether. Exaggerated as these fears may have been, the consequence was a major religious revival that swept the colonies during the middle decades of the eighteenth century.

## The First Great Awakening

The Great Awakening, as the revival came to be called, deepened the influence of older forms of Protestant Christianity, and specifically Calvinism, throughout British America. Participation in the revival was the only experience that a large number of people everywhere in the colonies had in common. But the Great Awakening also heightened religious divisions among Americans.

George Whitefield drew critics as well as admirers in both England and America. In this satirical English cartoon, he is depicted as a money-grubbing evangelist, while his audience, which consists mainly of women, is taken in by his pose of sanctity and youthful good looks.

The first stirrings of revival appeared in the 1730s among Presbyterians and Congregationalists in the middle colonies and New England. Many ministers in these churches preached an "evangelical" message, emphasizing the need for individuals to experience "a new birth" through religious conversion. Among them was the Reverend Jonathan Edwards of Northampton, Massachusetts. Edwards's preaching combined moving descriptions of God's grace with terrifying portrayals of eternal damnation. "The God that holds you over the pit of hell, much as one holds a spider or some loathsome insect over the fire, abhors you and is dreadfully provoked," he declaimed to one congregation; ". . . there is no other reason to be given, why you have not dropped into hell since you arise in the morning, but that God's hand has held you up."

These local revivals of the 1730s were mere tremors compared to the earthquake of religious enthusiasm that shook the colonies with the arrival in the fall of 1739 of George Whitefield. This handsome, cross-eyed "boy preacher" from England electrified crowds from Georgia to New Hampshire during his two-year tour of the colonies. He and his many imitators among colonial ministers turned the church into a theater, enlivening sermons with dramatic gestures, flowing tears, and gruesome depictions of hell's *The appeal of George Whitefield* torments. The drama of such performances appealed to people of all classes, ethnic groups, and races. By the time Whitefield sailed back to England in 1741, thousands of awakened souls were joining older churches or forming new ones.

## The Aftermath of the Great Awakening

Whitefield also left behind a raging storm of controversy. Many "awakened" church members now openly criticized their ministers as cold, unconverted, and uninspiring. To supply the missing fire, some laymen—"and even Women

*Religious controversies*
and Common Negroes"—took to "exhorting" any audience willing to listen. The most popular ministers became "itinerants," traveling like Whitefield from one town to another. Throughout the colonies, the more rationalist and moderate clergy questioned the unrestrained emotionalism and the disorder that attended the gatherings of lay exhorters and itinerants.

Although Americans had been fighting over religion well before the Great Awakening, the new revivals left colonials even more divided along religious lines. The largest single group of churchgoers in the northern colonies remained within the Congregational and Presbyterian denominations. But both these groups split into factions that either supported or condemned the revivals. Some conservative Presbyterians and Congregationalists, disgusted with the disorder, defected to the Quakers and the Anglicans, who had shunned the revivals. On the other hand, the most radical converts joined forces with the warmest champions of the Awakening, the Baptists.

While northern churches splintered and bickered, the fires of revivalism spread to the South and its backcountry. From the mid-1740s until the 1770s,

*Evangelicalism on the frontier*
scores of new Presbyterian and Baptist churches were formed, but conflict often accompanied religious zeal. Ardent Presbyterians in the Carolina backcountry disrupted Anglican worship by loosing packs of dogs in local chapels. In northern Virginia, Anglicans took the offensive against the Baptists, whose strict moral code sounded a silent reproach to the hard-drinking, high-stepping, horse-racing, slaveholding gentry. County officials, prodded by resentful Anglican parsons, harassed, fined, and imprisoned Baptist ministers.

And so a diverse lot of Americans found themselves continually at odds with one another. Because of differences in religion and education, colonials quarreled over whether rational Christianity enlightened the world or emotional revivalists destroyed its order. Because of ethnic and racial tensions, Spanish Jews found themselves persecuted, and African Americans searched for ways to resist their white masters. Because of westward expansion, Carolina Regulators waged war against coastal planters, while colonial legislatures from Massachusetts to Virginia quarreled over western boundaries.

Benjamin Franklin surely understood the depth of those divisions as he made his way toward the Albany Congress in the spring of 1754. He himself had brooded over the boatloads of non-English newcomers. He had lived in two booming seaports and felt the explosive force of the frontier. He personified the Enlightenment—and he had heard George Whitefield himself preach from the steps of the Philadelphia courthouse.

How, then, could Franklin, who knew how little held the colonials together, sustain his hopes for political unity? The answer may be that even in 1754, the majority of colonials were of English descent. And these free, white Americans liked being English. That much they had in common.

## Benjamin Franklin Attends the Preaching
## of George Whitefield

 happened . . . to attend one of his Sermons, in the Course of which I perceived he intended to finish with a Collection, and I silently resolved he should get nothing from me. I had in my Pocket a Handful of Copper Money, three or four silver Dollars, and five Pistoles in Gold. As he proceeded I began to soften, and concluded to give the Coppers. Another Stroke of his Oratory made me asham'd of that, and determin'd me to give the Silver; and he finish'd so admirably, that I emptied my Pocket wholly into the Collectors' Dish, Gold and all. . . .

Some of Mr. Whitefield's Enemies affected to suppose that he would apply these Collections to his own private Emolument; but I, who was intimately acquainted with him, (being employ'd in printing his Sermons and Journals, etc.) never had the least Suspicion of his Integrity, but am to this day decidedly of Opinion that he was in all his Conduct a perfectly *honest* Man. And methinks my Testimony in his Favor ought to have the more Weight, as we had no religious Connection. He us'd indeed sometimes to pray for my Conversion, but never had the Satisfaction of believing that his Prayers were heard. Ours was a mere civil Friendship, sincere on both Sides, and lasted to his Death.

He had a loud and clear Voice, and articulated his Words and Sentences so perfectly that he might be heard and understood at a great distance, especially as his Auditors, however numerous, observ'd the most exact Silence. He preach'd one Evening from the Top of the Court House Steps, which are in the Middle of Market Street. . . . I had the Curiosity to learn how far he could be heard by retiring backwards down the Street towards the River. . . . I computed that he might well be heard by more than Thirty Thousand.

Source: Excerpt from *The Autobiography of Benjamin Franklin* (New York: Washington Square Press, 1960), pp. 131–133.

## ANGLO-AMERICAN WORLDS OF THE EIGHTEENTH CENTURY

Most Americans prided themselves on being English. When colonials named their towns and counties, they named them after places in their parent country. When colonials established governments, they turned to England for their political models. They frequently claimed "the liberties of freeborn Englishmen" as their birthright. Even in diet, dress, furniture, architecture, and literature, colonists adopted English standards of taste.

Yet American society had developed in ways significantly different from that of Great Britain.* Some differences made colonials feel inferior, ashamed of their

*When England and Scotland were unified in 1707, the nation as a whole became known officially as Great Britain; its citizens, as British.

simplicity when compared with London's sophistication. But they also came to appreciate the greater equality of colonial society and the more representative character of colonial governments. If it was good to be English, it was better still to be English in America.

## English Economic and Social Development

The differences between England and America began with their economies. Large financial institutions like the Bank of England and influential corporations like the East India Company were driving England's commercial development. New textile factories and mines were deepening its industrial development. Although most English men and women worked at agriculture, it, too, had become a business. Members of the gentry rented their estates to tenants, members of the rural middle class. In turn, these tenants hired workers from the swollen ranks of England's landless to perform the actual farm labor. In contrast, most colonial farmers owned their land, and most family farms were a few hundred acres. The scale of commerce and manufacturing was equally modest.

England's more developed economy fostered the growth of cities, especially London, a teeming colossus of 675,000 inhabitants in 1750. In contrast, 90 percent of all eighteenth-century colonials lived in towns with populations of less than 2000.

## The Consumer Revolution

In another respect, England's more advanced economy drew the colonies and the parent country together as a consumer revolution transformed the everyday lives of people on both sides of the Atlantic. By the beginning of the eighteenth century, small manufacturers throughout England were producing a newly large and enticing array of consumer goods—fine textiles and hats, ceramics and glassware, carpets and furniture. Americans proved as eager as Britons to acquire these commodities— so eager that the per capita consumption of imported manufactures among colonials rose 120 percent between 1750 and 1773. Only the wealthy could afford goods of the highest quality, but people of all classes demanded and indulged in small luxuries like a tin of tea, a pair of gloves, or a bar of Irish soap. In both England and its colonies, the spare and simple material life of earlier centuries was giving way to a new order in which even people of ordinary means owned a wider variety of things.

## Inequality in England and America

The opportunities for great wealth provided by England's more developed economy created deep class distinctions, as did the inherited privileges of its aristocracy. The

*Class distinctions* members of the upper class, the landed aristocracy and gentry, made up less than 2 percent of England's population but owned 70 percent of its land. By right of birth, English aristocrats claimed membership in the House of Lords; by custom, certain powerful gentry families dominated the other branch

This portrait of John Stuart, the third Earl of Bute (1713–1792), wearing the ceremonial robes of the House of Lords, illustrates the opulence of Britain's ruling class in the eighteenth century.

of Parliament, the House of Commons. England's titled gentlemen shared power and wealth and often family ties with the rich men of the city—major merchants, successful lawyers, and lucky financiers. They too exerted political influence through the House of Commons. The colonies had their own prominent families but no titled ruling class holding political privilege by hereditary right. And even the wealthiest colonial families lived in far less magnificence than their English counterparts.

If England's upper classes lived more splendidly, its lower classes were larger and worse off than those in the colonies. Less than a third of England's inhabitants belonged to the "middling sort" of traders, professionals, artisans, and tenant farmers. More than two-thirds struggled for survival at the bottom of society. In contrast, the colonial middle class counted for nearly three-quarters of the white population. With land cheap, labor scarce, and wages for both urban and rural workers 100 percent higher in America than in England, it was much easier for colonials to accumulate savings and then buy farms of their own.

Colonials were both fascinated and repelled by English society. They gushed over the grandeur of aristocratic estates and imported suits of livery for their servants and tea services for their wives. They exported their sons to | *Ambivalent Americans* Britain for college educations at Oxford and Cambridge, medical school at Edinburgh, and legal training at London's Inns of Court.

But colonials recognized that England's ruling classes purchased their luxury and leisure at the cost of the rest of the nation. In his *Autobiography*, Benjamin Franklin painted a devastating portrait of the degraded lives of his fellow workers in a London printshop, who drowned their disappointments by drinking throughout the workday, even more excessively on the Sabbath, and then faithfully observing the holiday of "St. Monday's" to nurse their hangovers. Like Franklin, many colonials believed that gross inequalities of wealth would endanger liberty. They regarded the idle among England's rich and poor alike as ominous signs of a degenerate nation.

### Politics in England and America

Colonials were also of two minds about England's government. While they praised the English constitution as the basis of all liberties, they were alarmed by the actual workings of English politics. In theory, England's "balanced constitution" was designed to give every order of English society some voice in the workings of government. While the Crown represented the monarchy and the House of Lords the aristocracy, the House of Commons represented the democracy, the people of England. In fact, the monarch's executive ministers had become dominant by creating support for their policies in Parliament through patronage—or, put more bluntly, bribery.

*England's balanced constitution*

Over the course of the eighteenth century, a large executive bureaucracy had evolved in order to enforce laws, collect taxes, and wage the nearly constant wars in Europe and America. The power to appoint all military and treasury officials, customs and tax collectors, judges and justices of the peace lay with the monarch and his or her ministers. By the middle of the eighteenth century, almost half of all members of Parliament held such Crown offices or government contracts. Royal patronage was also used to manipulate parliamentary elections. The executive branch used money or liquor to bribe local voters into selecting their candidates. The small size of England's electorate fostered executive influence. Perhaps one-fourth of all adult males could vote, and many electoral districts were not adjusted to keep pace with population growth and resettlement. The notorious "rotten boroughs" each elected a member of Parliament to represent fewer than 500 easily bribable voters, while some large cities like Manchester and Leeds, newly populous because of industrial growth, had no representation in Parliament at all.

*Tools for "managing" Parliament*

Americans liked to think that their colonial governments mirrored the ideal English constitution. In terms of formal structure, there were similarities. Most colonies had a royal governor who represented the monarch in America and a bicameral (two-house) legislature made up of a lower house (the assembly) and an upper house (or council). The democratically elected assembly, like the House of Commons, stood for popular interests, while the council, some of whose members were elected and others appointed, more roughly approximated the House of Lords.

*Colonial governments*

But these formal similarities masked real differences between English and colonial governments. On the face of it, royal governors had much more power than the English Crown. Unlike kings and queens, royal governors could veto laws passed by assemblies; they could dissolve those bodies at will; they could create courts and dismiss judges. However, governors who asserted such powers found that their assemblies protested that popular liberty was being endangered. In most showdowns royal governors had to give way, for they lacked the government offices and contracts that bought loyalty. The colonial legislatures possessed additional leverage, since all of them retained the sole authority to levy taxes.

Even if the governors had enjoyed greater patronage powers, their efforts to influence colonial legislatures would have been frustrated by the sheer size of the American electorate. There were too many voters in America to bribe. Over half and possibly as many as 70 percent of all white adult colonial men were enfranchised. Property requirements were the same in America as in England, but widespread ownership of land in the colonies allowed most men to meet the qualifications easily.

The colonial electorate was also more watchful. Representatives were required to reside in the districts that they served, and a few even received binding instructions from their constituents about how to vote. Representation was also apportioned according to population far more equitably than in England. Since they were so closely tied to their constituents' wishes, colonial legislators were far less likely than members of Parliament to be swayed by executive pressure.

Most Americans were as pleased with their inexpensive and representative colonial governments as they were horrified by the conduct of politics in England. John Dickinson, a young Pennsylvanian training as a lawyer in London, was scandalized by a parliamentary election he witnessed in 1754. The king and his ministers had spent over 100,000 pounds sterling to buy support for their candidates, he wrote his father, and "if a man cannot be brought to vote as he is desired, he is made dead drunk and kept in that state, never heard of by his family and friends, till all is over and he can do no harm."

### The Imperial System before 1760

Colonials like Dickinson thought long and hard about the condition of England's society and politics. Meanwhile, the English thought about their colonies little, understood them less, and wished neither to think about them more nor to understand them better.

That indifference contributed to England's haphazard administration of its colonies. The Board of Trade and Plantations, created in 1696, gathered information about Atlantic trading and fishing, reviewed laws and petitions drawn up by colonial assemblies, and exchanged letters and instructions with royal governors. But the Board of Trade was only an advisory body.

Real authority over the colonies was divided among an array of other agencies. The Treasury oversaw customs and gathered other royal revenues; the Admiralty Board enforced regulations of trade; the War Office orchestrated colonial defense. But these departments spent most of their hours handling more pressing responsibilities. Colonial affairs stood at the bottom of their agendas. Most British officials in America seemed equally indifferent. Often enough, they had been awarded their jobs in return for political support, not in recognition of administrative ability.

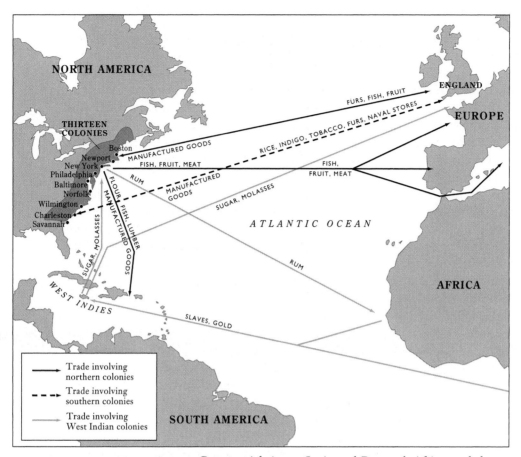

OVERSEAS TRADE NETWORKS   Commercial ties to Spain and Portugal, Africa, and the
Caribbean sustained the growth of both seaports and commercial farming regions
on the British North American mainland and enabled colonials to purchase
an increasing volume of finished goods from England.

But the branch of England's government most indifferent to America was
Parliament. Aside from passing an occasional law to regulate trade, restrict
manufacturing, or direct monetary policy, Parliament made no effort to assert
its authority in America. Its members assumed that Parliament's sovereignty extended over the entire empire, and nothing had occurred to make them think
otherwise.

For the colonies, this chaotic and inefficient system of colonial administration
worked well enough. The very weakness of imperial oversight left Americans with

*The benefits of benign*
*neglect*

a great deal of freedom. Even England's regulation of trade rested
lightly on the shoulders of most Americans. Southern planters were
obliged to send their rice, indigo, and tobacco to Britain only, but they

enjoyed favorable credit terms and knowledgeable marketing from English merchants. Colonials were prohibited from finishing iron products and exporting hats and textiles, but they had scant interest in developing domestic industries. Americans were required to import all manufactured goods through England, but by doing so, they acquired high-quality goods at low prices. At little sacrifice, most Americans obeyed imperial regulations. Only sugar, molasses, and tea were routinely smuggled.

Following this policy of benign neglect the British empire muddled on to the satisfaction of most people on both sides of the Atlantic. Economic growth and political autonomy allowed most Americans to like being English despite their misgivings about their parent nation. The beauty of it was that Americans could be English in America, enjoying greater economic opportunity and political equality. If imperial arrangements had remained as they were in 1754, the empire might have muddled on indefinitely. But because of the French and the Indians on the American frontier, the British empire began to change. And those changes made it increasingly hard for Americans to be English in America.

## TOWARD THE SEVEN YEARS' WAR

In the late spring of 1754, while Benjamin Franklin dreamed of unifying Americans, a young Virginian dreamed of military glory. As Franklin rode toward Albany, the young man, an inexperienced officer, led his company of Virginia militia toward Fort Duquesne, the French stronghold on the forks of the Ohio.

Less than a year earlier, the king's ministers had advised royal governors in America to halt the French advance into the Ohio country. The Virginia government organized an expedition against Fort Duquesne, placing at its head the young man who combined an imposing physique with the self-possession of an English gentleman. He wanted, more than anything, to become an officer in the regular British army.

But events in the Ohio country during that spring and summer did not go George Washington's way. French soldiers easily captured Fort Necessity, his crude outpost near Fort Duquesne. In early July, as the Albany Congress was debating, Washington was surrendering to a French force in the Pennsylvania backcountry and beating a retreat back to Virginia. *Washington at Fort Necessity* By the end of 1754, he had resigned his militia command and retired to his plantation at Mount Vernon. The disaster at Fort Necessity had dashed his dreams of martial glory and a regular army commission. He had no future as a soldier.

With the rout of Washington and his troops, the French grew bolder and the Indians more restless. The renewal of war between England and France was certain by the beginning of 1755. This time the contest between the two powers would decide the question of sovereignty over North America. That, at least, was the dream of William Pitt, who was about to become the most powerful man in England.

Even by the standards of English politicians, William Pitt was an odd character. Subject to bouts of illness and depression and loathed for his opportunism

*The ambitions of William Pitt*

and egotism, Pitt surmounted every challenge, buoyed by a strong sense of destiny—his own and that of England. He believed that England must seize the world's trade, for trade meant wealth and wealth meant power. As early as the 1730s, Pitt recognized that the only obstacle between England and its destiny was France—and that the contest between the two for world supremacy would be decided in America. During King George's War, Pitt had mesmerized the House of Commons and the nation with his spellbinding oratory about England's imperial destiny. But the mounting cost of fighting prompted the government to accept peace with France in 1748. In frustration Pitt retired from public life.

But while Pitt sulked in his library, the rivalry for the American frontier moved toward a showdown. The French pressed their front lines eastward; the English pushed for land westward; the Indians maneuvered for position. Heartened by the news from America, Pitt clung to his dream of English commercial dominion and French defeat. By the late spring of 1754, as Benjamin Franklin and George Washington rode toward their defeats, William Pitt knew that he would have his war with France and his way with the world.

Other dreams would wait longer for fulfillment. The Albany Congress had demonstrated that a few Americans like Franklin had seen beyond the diversity of a divided colonial world to the possibility of union, however unaccustomed and untried. But it would take another war, one that restructured an empire, before some Americans saw in themselves a likeness that was not English.

# chapter summary

Over the course of the eighteenth century, British North Americans grew increasingly diverse, which made the prospect of any future colonial political union appear remote.

- Differences became more pronounced among whites because of the immigration of larger numbers of non-English settlers, the spread of settlement to the backcountry, and the growth of major seaports.

- Although disorder was not uncommon either on the frontier or in cities, the most serious social and political conflict drew its strength from sectional controversies between East and West.

- The South became more embattled, too, as a result of the massive importation of slaves directly from Africa during the first half of the eighteenth century and a rising tide of black resistance to slavery.

- After about 1750 the growth of a native-born population strengthened black communal and family life.

- Religious conflict among colonials was intensified by the spread of Enlightenment ideas and the influence of the first Great Awakening.

- Despite their many differences, a majority of white colonials took pride in their common English ancestry and in belonging to a powerful empire.

# interactive learning

The Primary Source Investigator CD-ROM offers the following materials related to this chapter:

- Interactive maps: **The Atlantic World, 1400–1850** (M2) and **The Settlement of Colonial America, 1700–1763** (M5)

- A collection of primary sources exploring the development of the British empire in North America, such as a diagram of a slave ship, an image of a homespun garment, and a sermon from the famous itinerant preacher George Whitefield. Several sources illustrate the consequences of widespread slavery, including a poem by African American Phyllis Wheatley and a minister's description of racial slavery. In addition, several sources demonstrate how imperial expansion sparked internal problems: disputes with colonial governments and the Carolina Regulators movement, an image dealing with the subject of Iroquois go-between Mary Brant, and a political cartoon from Benjamin Franklin on the difficulties of uniting the colonies.

For quizzes and a variety of interactive resources, visit the book's Online Learning Center at www.mhhe.com/davidsonconcise4.

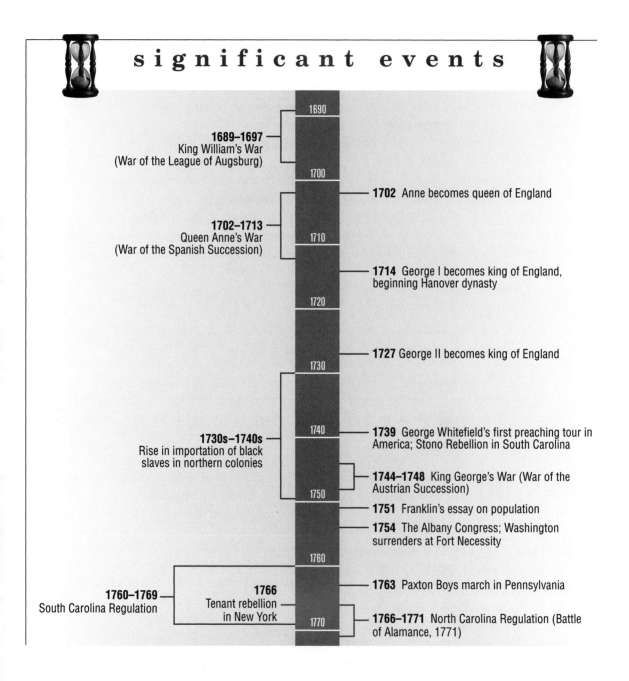

## significant events

**1689–1697**
King William's War
(War of the League of Augsburg)

1690

1700

**1702** Anne becomes queen of England

**1702–1713**
Queen Anne's War
(War of the Spanish Succession)

1710

**1714** George I becomes king of England, beginning Hanover dynasty

1720

**1727** George II becomes king of England

1730

**1730s–1740s**
Rise in importation of black slaves in northern colonies

1740

**1739** George Whitefield's first preaching tour in America; Stono Rebellion in South Carolina

**1744–1748** King George's War (War of the Austrian Succession)

1750

**1751** Franklin's essay on population

**1754** The Albany Congress; Washington surrenders at Fort Necessity

1760

**1760–1769**
South Carolina Regulation

**1766**
Tenant rebellion in New York

**1763** Paxton Boys march in Pennsylvania

**1766–1771** North Carolina Regulation (Battle of Alamance, 1771)

1770

# PART TWO

# The Creation of a New Republic

s Benjamin Franklin had observed in 1751, the population of British North America was doubling approximately every 25 years. This astonishing rate was quite possibly the fastest in the world at the time. Even so, the surge was merely one part of a more general global rise in population during the second half of the eighteenth century. In sheer numbers China led the way. Its population of 150 million in 1700 had doubled to more than 313 million by the end of the century. Europe's total rose from about 118 million in 1700 to about 187 million a century later, the greatest growth coming on its eastern and western flanks, in Great Britain and Russia. African and Indian populations seem to have increased as well.

Climate may have been one reason for the worldwide rise. In Europe, warmer and drier seasons produced generally better harvests. Furthermore, health and nutrition improved globally with the spread of Native American crops. Irish farmers discovered that a single acre planted with the lowly American potato could support an entire family. The tomato added crucial vitamins to the Mediterranean diet, while maize provided more calories per acre than any European or African grain. In China the American sweet potato thrived in hilly regions where rice would not grow.

Not only plants but diseases were carried back and forth by European ships. As we have seen, contact between previously isolated peoples produced extreme mortality from epidemics. But after more than two centuries of sustained contact, Indians developed increased biological resistance to European and African illnesses. The frequent circulation of diseases worldwide led to a more stable environment in which populations began to swell.

am not a Virginian, but an American," Patrick Henry declared in the Virginia House of Burgesses. Most likely he was lying. Certainly no one listening took him seriously, for the newly independent colonists did not identify themselves as members of a nation. They would have said, as did Thomas Jefferson, "Virginia, Sir, is my country." Or as John Adams wrote to another native son, "Massachusetts is our country." Jefferson and Adams were men of wide political vision and experience: both were leaders in the Continental Congress and more inclined than most to think nationally. But like other members of the revolutionary generation, they identified deeply with their home states and even more deeply with their home counties and towns.

# Crisis and Constitution
## 1776–1789

It followed that allegiance to the states, not the Union, determined the shape of the first republican political experiments. For a decade after independence, the revolutionaries were less com-

**Preview** *For a decade after independence, American revolutionaries were less committed to creating a single national republic than to organizing 13 separate state republics, united only loosely under the Articles of Confederation. By the mid-1780s, however, the weakness of the Confederation seemed evident to many Americans. The Constitutional Convention of 1787 produced a new frame of government that was truly national in scope.*

mitted to creating an American nation than to organizing 13 separate state republics. The Declaration of Independence referred explicitly not to *the* United States but to *these* United States. It envisioned not one republic so much as a federation of 13.

Only when peace was restored during the decade of the 1780s were Americans forced to face some unanswered questions raised by their revolution. The Declaration proclaimed that these "free and independent states" had "full power to levy war, conclude peace, contract alliances, establish commerce." Did *How close a union?* that mean that New Jersey, as a free and independent state, could sign a trade agreement with France, excluding the other states? If the United States was to be more than a loose federation, how could it assert power on a national scale? Similarly, American borderlands to the west presented problems. If these territories were settled by Americans, would they eventually join the United States? Go their own ways as independent nations? Become new colonies of Spain or England?

Such problems were more than political; they were rooted in social realities. For a political union to succeed, the inhabitants of 13 separate states had to start thinking of themselves as Americans. When it came right down to it, what united a Vermont farmer working his rocky fields and a South Carolina gentleman presiding over a vast rice plantation? What bonds existed between a Kentuckian rafting the Ohio River and a Salem merchant sailing to China for porcelain?

And in a society where all citizens were said to be "created equal," the inevitable social inequalities had to be confronted. How could women participate in the Revolution's bid for freedom if they were not free to vote or to hold property? How could black Americans feel a bond with white Americans when so often the only existing bonds had been forged with chains? To these questions there were no final answers in 1781. And as the decade progressed, the sense of crisis deepened. Americans worried that factions and selfish interest groups would pull "these" United States apart. The new republican union, which spread out over so many miles, constituted a truly unprecedented venture. A good deal of experimenting would be needed if it was to succeed.

## REPUBLICAN EXPERIMENTS

After independence was declared in July 1776, many of America's best political minds turned to draw up constitutions for their individual states. In truth, the state constitutions were crucial republican experiments, the first efforts at establishing a government of and by the people. All the revolutionaries agreed that the people—not a king or a few privileged aristocrats—should rule. Yet they were

*Belief in the need for small republics*

equally certain that republican governments were best suited to small territories. They believed that the new United States was too sprawling and its people too diverse to be safely consolidated into a single national republic. They feared, too, that the government of a large republic would inevitably grow indifferent to popular concerns, being distant from many of its citizens. Without being under the watchful eye of the people, representatives would become less accountable to the electorate and turn tyrannical. A federation of small state republics, they reasoned, would stand a far better chance of enduring.

### The State Constitutions

The new state constitutions retained the basic form of their old colonial governments, most providing for a governor and a bicameral legislature. But while most states did not alter the basic structure of their governments, they changed dramatically the balance of power among the different branches of government.

Americans responded to independence with rituals of "killing the king," as did this New York crowd in 1776, which is pulling down a statue of George III. Americans also expressed their mistrust of monarchs by establishing state governments with weak executive branches.

From the republican perspective in 1776, the greatest problem of any government lay in curbing executive power. What had driven Americans into rebellion was the abuse of authority by the king and his appointed officials. To ensure that the executive could never again threaten popular liberty, the new states either accorded almost no power to their governors or abolished that office entirely. The governors had no authority to convene or dissolve the legislature. They could not veto the legislatures' laws, grant land, or erect courts. Most important from the republican point of view, governors had few powers to appoint other state officials. All these limits were designed to deprive the executive of any patronage or other form of influence over the legislature.

*Curbing executive power*

What the state governors lost, the legislatures gained. To ensure that those powerful legislatures truly represented the will of the people, the new state constitutions called for annual elections and required candidates for the legislature to live in the district they represented. Many states even asserted the right of voters to instruct the men elected to office how to vote on specific issues. Although no state granted universal manhood suffrage, most reduced the amount of property required of qualified voters. Finally, state supreme courts were also either elected by the legislatures or appointed by an elected governor.

*Strengthening legislative powers*

By investing all power in popular assemblies, Americans abandoned the British system of mixed government. In one sense, that change was fairly democratic. A majority of voters within a state could do whatever they wanted, unchecked by governors or courts. On the other hand, the arrangement opened the door for legislatures to turn as tyrannical as governors. The revolutionaries brushed that prospect aside: republican theory assured them that the people possessed a generous share of civic virtue, the capacity for selfless pursuit of the general welfare.

In an equally momentous change, the revolutionaries insisted on written state constitutions. Whenever government appeared to exceed the limits of its authority,

*Written constitutions*

Americans wanted to have at hand the written contract between rulers and ruled. When eighteenth-century Englishmen used the word *constitution*, they meant the existing arrangement of government—not an actual document but a collection of parliamentary laws, customs, and precedents. But Americans believed that a constitution should be a written code that stood apart from and above government, a yardstick against which the people measured the performance of their rulers. After all, they reasoned, if Britain's constitution had been written down, available for all to consult, would American rights have been violated?

### From Congress to Confederation

While Americans lavished attention on their state constitutions, the national government nearly languished during the decade after 1776. With the coming of independence, the Second Continental Congress conducted the common business of the federated states. It created and maintained the Continental Army, issued currency, and negotiated with foreign powers.

But while Congress acted as a central government by common consent, it lacked any legal basis for its authority. To redress that need, in July 1776 Congress appointed a committee to draft a constitution for a national government. The more urgent business of waging and paying for the war made for delay, as did the consuming interest in framing state constitutions. Congress finally approved the first national constitution in November 1777, but it took four more years for all of the states to ratify these Articles of Confederation.

The Articles of Confederation provided for a government by a national legislature—essentially a continuation of the Second Continental Congress.

*Articles of Confederation*

That body had the authority to declare war and make peace, conduct diplomacy, regulate Indian affairs, appoint military and naval officers, and requisition men from the states. In affairs of finance it could coin money and issue paper currency. Extensive as these responsibilities were, Congress could not levy taxes or even regulate trade. The crucial power of the purse rested entirely with the states, as did the final power to make and execute laws. Even worse, the national government had no distinct executive branch. Congressional committees, constantly changing in their membership, not only had to make laws but had to administer and enforce them as well.

Those weaknesses of the federal government appear more evident in hindsight. Most American leaders of the 1770s had given little thought to federalism, the organization of a United States. Political leaders had not yet recognized the need for dividing power between the states and the national government. With the new nation in the midst of a military crisis, Congress assumed—correctly in most cases—that the states did not have to be forced to contribute men and money to the common defense. Creating a strong national government would have antagonized many Americans, who after all had just rebelled against the distant, centralized authority of Britain's king and Parliament.

Guided by republican political theory and by their colonial experience, American revolutionaries created a loose confederation of 13 independent state republics under a nearly powerless national government. They succeeded so well that the United States almost failed to survive its first decade of independence. The problem was that lessons from the colonial past were not always useful guides to postwar realities. Only when events forced Americans to think nationally did they begin to consider the possibility of reinventing "these United States"—this time under the yoke of a truly federal republic.

## THE TEMPTATIONS OF PEACE

The surrender of Cornwallis at Yorktown in 1781 marked the end of military crisis in America. But as the threat from Britain receded, so did the source of American unity. The many differences among Americans, most of which lay submerged during the struggle for independence, surfaced in full force. Those domestic divisions, combined with challenges to the new nation from Britain and Spain, created conflicts that neither the states nor the national government proved equal to handling.

### *The Temptations of the West*

The greatest opportunities and the greatest problems for postwar Americans awaited in the rapidly expanding West. With the boundary of the new United States now set at the Mississippi River, more settlers spilled across the Appalachians, planting farmsteads and towns throughout Ohio, Kentucky, and Tennessee. By 1790 places that had been almost uninhabited by whites in 1760 held more than 2.25 million people, one-third of the nation's population.

After the Revolution, as before, western settlement fostered intense conflict. American claims that its territory stretched all the way to the Mississippi were by no means taken for granted by European and Indian powers. The West also confronted Americans with questions about their own national identity. Would the newly settled territories enter the nation as states on an equal footing with the original 13 states? Would they be ruled as dependent colonies? The fate of

As the stumps dotting the landscape indicate, western farmers first sought to "improve" their acreage by felling trees. But their dwellings were far less substantial than those depicted in this idealized sketch of an "American New Cleared Farm." And while some Indians guided parties of whites into the West, as shown in the foreground, more often they resisted white encroachment. For that reason, dogs, here perched placidly in canoes, were trained to alert their white masters to the approach of Indians.

the West, in other words, constituted a crucial test of whether "these" United States could grow and still remain united.

## Foreign Intrigues

Both the British from their base in Canada and the Spanish in Florida and Louisiana hoped to chisel away at American borders. Their considerable success in the 1780s exposed the weakness of Confederation diplomacy.

Before the ink was dry on the Treaty of Paris, Britain's ministers were secretly instructing Canadians to maintain their forts and trading posts inside the United States' northwestern frontier. They reckoned—correctly—that with the Continental Army disbanded, the Confederation could not force the British to withdraw.

The British also made mischief along the Confederation's northern borders, mainly with Vermont. For decades, Ethan Allen and his Green Mountain Boys had waged a war of nerves with neighboring New York, which claimed Vermont as part of its territory. After the Revolution the Vermonters petitioned Congress for statehood, demanding independence of both New York and New Hampshire. When Congress dragged its feet, the British tried to woo Vermont into their empire as a province of Canada. That flirtation with the British pressured Congress into granting Vermont statehood in 1791.

The loyalty of the southwestern frontier was even less certain. By 1790 more than 100,000 settlers had poured through the Cumberland Gap to reach Kentucky and Tennessee. But the commercial possibilities of the region depended entirely on access to the Mississippi and the port of New Orleans, since it was far too costly to ship southwestern produce over the rough trails east across the Appalachians. And the Mississippi route was still dominated by the Spanish, who controlled Louisiana as well as forts along western Mississippi shores as far north as St. Louis. The Spanish, seeing their opportunity, closed the Mississippi to American navigation in 1784. That action prompted serious talk among southwesterners about seceding from the United States and joining Spain's empire.

*Spanish designs on the Southwest*

The Spanish also tried to strengthen their hold on North America by making common cause with the Indians. Of particular concern to both groups was protecting Florida, which had reverted to Spain's possession, from the encroachment of American settlers filtering south from Georgia. Florida's governor alerted his superiors back in Spain to the threat posed by those backwoodsmen who were "nomadic like Arabs and . . . distinguished from savages only in their color, language, and the superiority of their depraved cunning and untrustworthiness." So Spanish colonial officials responded eagerly to the overtures of Alexander McGillivray, a young Indian leader whose mother was of French-Creek descent and whose father was a Scots trader. His efforts brought about a treaty of alliance between the Creeks and the Spanish in 1784, quickly followed by similar alliances with the Choctaws and the Chickasaws. What cemented such treaties were the trade goods that the Spanish agreed to supply to the tribes. Securing European gunpowder and guns had become essential to southeastern Indians, because their entire economies now revolved around hunting and selling deerskins to white traders.

## Disputes among the States

As if foreign intrigues were not divisive enough, the states continued to argue among themselves over western land claims. The old royal charters for some colonies had extended their boundaries all the way to the Mississippi and beyond. (See the map, page 180.) But the charters were often vague, granting both Massachusetts and Virginia, for example, undisputed possession of present-day Wisconsin. In contrast, other charters limited state boundaries to within a few hundred miles of the Atlantic coast. "Landed" states like Virginia wanted to secure control over the large territory granted by their charters. "Landless" states (which included Maryland, Delaware, Pennsylvania, Rhode Island, and New Jersey) called on Congress to restrict the boundaries of landed states and to convert western lands into a domain administered by the Confederation.

*Landed versus landless states*

WESTERN LAND CLAIMS, 1782–1802  The Confederation's settlement of conflicting western land claims was an achievement essential to the consolidation of political union. Some states asserted that their original charters extended their western borders to the Mississippi River. A few states, like Virginia, claimed western borders on the Pacific Ocean.

The landless states lost the opening round of the contest over ownership of the West. The Articles of Confederation acknowledged the old charter claims of the landed states. Then Maryland, one of the smallest landless states, retaliated by refusing to ratify the Articles. Since every state had to approve the Articles before they were formally accepted, the fate of the United States hung in the balance. One by one the landed states relented. The last holdout, Virginia, in

January 1781 ceded its charter rights to land north of the Ohio River. Once Virginia ceded, Maryland ratified the Articles in February 1781, four long years after Congress had first approved them.

## The More Democratic West

More bitterly disputed than land claims in the West was the issue concerning the sort of men westerners elected to political office. The state legislatures of the 1780s were both larger and more democratic in their membership than the old colonial assemblies were. Before the Revolution no more than a fifth of the men serving in the assemblies were middle-class farmers or artisans; government was almost exclusively the domain of the wealthiest merchants, lawyers, and planters. After the Revolution twice as many state legislators were men of moderate wealth. The shift was more marked in the North, where middle-class men predominated among representatives. But in every state, some men of modest means, humble background, and little formal education attained political power.

State legislatures became more democratic in membership mainly because as backcountry districts grew, so did the number of their representatives. Since western districts tended to be less developed economically and culturally, their leading men were less rich and cultivated than the seaboard elite. *Changing composition of state legislatures* Wealthy, well-educated gentlemen thus became a much smaller and less powerful group within the legislatures because of greater western representation and influence.

But many republican gentlemen, while endorsing government by popular consent, doubted whether ordinary people were fit to rule. The problem, they contended, was that the new western legislators concerned themselves only with the narrow interests of their constituents, not with the good of the whole state. As Ezra Stiles, the president of Yale College, observed, the new breed of politicians were those with "the all-prevailing popular talent of coaxing and flattering," who "whenever a bill is read in the legislature . . . instantly thinks how it will affect his constituents." And if state legislatures could not rise above petty bickering and narrow self-interest, how long would it be before civic virtue and a concern for the general welfare simply withered away?

## The Northwest Territory

Such fears of "democratic excess" also influenced policy when Congress debated what to do with the Northwest Territory. Carved out of the land ceded by the states to the national government, the Northwest Territory comprised the present-day states of Ohio, Indiana, Illinois, Michigan, and Wisconsin. With so many white settlers moving into these lands, Congress was faced with a crucial test of its federal system. If the Confederation could not expand in an orderly way beyond the original 13 colonies, the new territories might well become independent countries

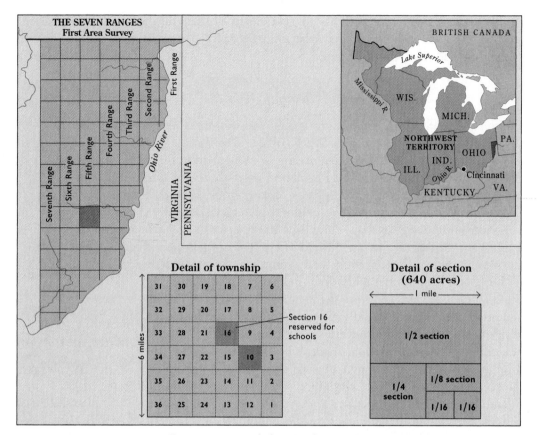

THE ORDINANCE OF 1785   Surveyors entered the Northwest Territory in September of 1785, imposing on the land regular grids of six square miles to define new townships, as shown on this range map of a portion of Ohio. Farmers purchased blocks of land within townships, each one mile square, from the federal government or from land speculators.

or even colonies of Spain or Britain. Congress dealt with the issue of expansion by adopting three ordinances.

The first, drafted by Thomas Jefferson in 1784, divided the Northwest Territory into 10 states, each to be admitted to the Union on equal terms as soon as its

*Jefferson's plan for the Northwest*

population equaled that in any of the existing states. In the meantime, Jefferson provided for democratic self-government of the territory by all free adult males. A second ordinance of 1785 set up an efficient mechanism for dividing and selling public lands. The Northwest Territory was surveyed into townships of six miles square. Each township then was divided into 36 lots of one square mile, or 640 acres.

Congress waited in vain for buyers to flock to the land offices it established. The cost of even a single lot—$640—was too steep for most farmers. Disappointed by the shortage of buyers and desperate for money, Congress finally

## A Traveler from Virginia Considers the Ruins of an Ancient Indian Civilization in the Ohio Valley

 have often observed while travelling thro' this country, a number of round hillocks, raised from 15 feet high and under and from 50 to 100 yards around them. It seems evident that those places are not natural, but are the work of man. The only question seems to be, "What were they made for?" Some have supposed they were once places of defence. But the most probable opinion is, that they are burying places of the former inhabitants of this country. On digging into these, I am informed, great quantities of bones are found, lying in a confus'd promiscuous manner. Some authors inform us that once in ten years the Indians collect the bones of their dead, and bring them all to one place and bury them. Thus they proceed, putting one layer over another till they get them to the height above mentioned.

An object, however, of a different kind now presents itself to our view . . . a neck of land about 4 or 500 yards wide. Across this neck of land lies an old wall, joining the river at each end and enclosing, I suppose, about 100 acres of land. This wall is composed of earth dug from the outside, where a ditch of some depth is still discernible. The wall at present is so mouldered down that a man could easily ride over it. It is however about 10 feet, as near as I can judge, in perpendicular height, and gives growth to a number of large trees. In one place I observe a breach in the wall about 60 feet wide, where I suppose the gate formerly stood through which the people passed in and out of this stronghold. Compared with this, what feeble and insignificant works are those of Fort Hamilton or Fort Washington! They are no more in comparison to it than a rail fence is to a brick wall.

Source: 18 November 1795, Journal of the Reverend James Smith. Richard H. Collins Papers, Durrett Collection, University of Chicago.

accepted a proposition submitted by a private company of land speculators that offered to buy some 6 million acres in present-day southeastern Ohio. That several members of Congress numbered among the company's stockholders no doubt added to enthusiasm for the deal.

The transaction concluded, Congress calmed the speculators' worries that incoming settlers might enjoy too much self-government by scrapping Jefferson's democratic design and substituting the Northwest Ordinance of 1787. That ordinance provided for a period in which Congress held sway in the territory through its appointees—a governor, a secretary, and three judges. When the population reached 5000 free adult males, a legislature was to be established, although its laws required the governor's approval. A representative could sit in Congress but had no vote. When the population reached 60,000, the inhabitants

*Northwest Ordinance*

might apply for statehood, and the whole Northwest Territory was to be divided into not less than three or more than five states. The ordinance also guaranteed basic rights—freedom of religion and trial by jury—and provided for the support of public education.

Congress's plan completely ignored the rights of the Shawnee, Chippewa, and other Indian peoples who lived in the region. To them, it made no difference that the British had ceded their lands to the Americans. And in terms of Jefferson's democratic ideals for white inhabitants, the ordinance of 1787 also fell short. Still, Congress had succeeded in extending republican government to the West and incorporating the frontier into the new nation. Congress also outlawed slavery throughout the territory.

That decision had an unexpected, almost ironic consequence. The Northwest Ordinance went a long way toward establishing a federal system that would minimize tensions between the East and the West, a major source of postwar conflict. The Republic now had a peaceful, orderly way to expand its federation of states. Yet by limiting the spread of slavery in the northern states, Congress deepened the critical social and economic differences between North and South, evident already in the 1780s.

## Slavery and Sectionalism

When white Americans declared their independence, they owned nearly half a million black Americans. African Americans of the revolutionary generation, most of them enslaved, constituted 20 percent of the total population of the colonies in 1775, and nearly 90 percent of them lived in the South. Yet few political leaders directly confronted the issue of whether slavery should be permitted to exist in a truly republican society.

When political discussion did stray toward the subject of slavery, southerners—especially ardent republicans—bristled defensively. Theirs was a difficult position,

*Republicanism and slavery*

riddled with contradictions. On the one hand, they had condemned parliamentary taxation as tantamount to political "slavery" and had rebelled, declaring that all men were "created equal." On the other hand, enslaved African Americans formed the basis of the South's plantation economy. To surrender slavery, southerners believed, would be to usher in economic ruin.

Some planters in the Upper South resolved the dilemma by freeing their slaves. Such decisions were made easier by changing economic conditions in the Chesapeake. As planters shifted from tobacco toward wheat, a crop demanding a good deal less labor, Virginia and Maryland liberalized their manumission statutes, laws providing for freeing slaves. Between 1776 and 1789, most southern states also joined the North in prohibiting the importation of slaves, and a few antislavery societies appeared in the Upper South. But no southern state legally abolished slavery. Masters defended their right to hold human property in the name of republicanism.

*Negro Methodists Holding a Meeting in a Philadelphia Alley* evokes the vibrancy of black religious life in the city that became a haven for free African Americans.

Eighteenth-century republicans regarded property as crucial, for it provided a man and his family with security, status, and wealth. More important, it provided a measure of independence: to be able to act freely, without fear or favor of others. People without property were dangerous, republicans believed, because the poor could never be politically independent. Southern defenders of slavery thus argued that free, propertyless black people would pose a political threat to the liberty of propertied white citizens. Subordinating the human rights of blacks to the property rights of whites, southern republicans reached the paradoxical conclusion that their freedom depended on keeping African Americans in bondage.

The North followed a different course. Because its economy depended far less on slave labor, black emancipation did not run counter to powerful economic interests. Antislavery societies, the first founded by the Quakers in 1775, spread throughout the northern states during the next quarter century. Over the same period the legislatures of most northern states provided for the immediate or gradual abolition of slavery. Freedom for most northern African Americans came slowly, but by 1830 there were fewer than 3000 slaves out of a total northern black population of 125,000.

The Revolution, which had been fought for liberty and equality, did little to change the status of most black Americans. By 1800 more enslaved African

Americans lived in the United States than had lived there in 1776. Slavery continued to grow in the Lower South as the rice culture of the Carolinas and Georgia expanded and as the new cotton culture spread westward.

*Free black sailors*

Still, a larger number of slaves than ever before became free during the war and in the decades following, whether through military service, successful escape, manumission, or gradual emancipation. All these developments fostered the growth of free black communities, especially in the Upper South and in northern cities. By 1810 free African Americans made up 10 percent of the total population of Maryland and Virginia. The composition of the postwar free community changed as well. Before independence most free blacks had been either mulattoes—the offspring of interracial unions—or former slaves too sick or aged to have value as laborers. In contrast, the free population of the 1780s became darker skinned, younger, and healthier. This group injected new vitality into black communal life, organizing independent schools, churches, and mutual benefit societies for the growing number of "free people of color."

*Growth of the free black community*

After the Revolution slavery ceased to be a national institution. It became the "peculiar institution" of a single region, the American South. The isolation of slavery in one section set North and South on radically different courses of social development, sharpening economic and political divisions.

## Wartime Economic Disruption

With the outbreak of the Revolution, Americans had suffered an immediate loss of the manufactured goods, markets, and credit that Britain had formerly supplied. Matters did not improve with the coming of peace. France and Britain flooded the new states with their manufactures, and postwar Americans, eager for luxuries, indulged in a most unrepublican spending spree. The flurry of buying left some American merchants and consumers as deeply in debt as their governments. When loans from private citizens and foreign creditors like France had proved insufficient to finance the fighting, both Congress and the states had printed paper money—a whopping total of $400 million. The paper currency was backed only by the government's promise to redeem the bills with money from future taxes, since legislatures balked at the unpopular alternative of levying taxes during the war. For the bills to be redeemed, the United States had to survive, so by the end of 1776, when Continental forces sustained a series of defeats, paper money started to depreciate dramatically. By 1781 it was virtually without value, and Americans coined the expression "not worth a Continental."

*Public and private debt*

The printing of paper money, combined with a wartime shortage of goods, triggered an inflationary spiral of scarcer and scarcer goods costing more and more worthless dollars. In this spiral, creditors were gouged by debtors, who paid them back with depreciated currency. At the same time, soaring prices for food and manufactured goods eroded the buying power

*Postwar inflation*

of wage earners and small farmers. And the end of the war brought on demands for prompt repayment from the new nation's foreign creditors as well as from soldiers seeking back pay and pensions.

Congress could do nothing. With no power to regulate trade, it could neither dam the stream of imported goods rushing into the states nor stanch the flow of gold and silver to Europe to pay for these items. With no power to prohibit the states from issuing paper money, it could not halt depreciation. With no power to regulate wages or prices, it could not curb inflation. With no power to tax, it could not reduce the public debt. Efforts to grant Congress greater powers met with determined resistance from the states.

Within states, too, economic problems aroused discord. Some major merchants, creditors, and large commercial farmers had profited handsomely during the war by selling supplies to the American, British, and French armies at high prices or by preying on enemy vessels as privateers. Eager to protect their windfall, they lobbied state legislatures for an end to inflationary monetary policies. That meant passing high taxes to pay wartime debts, a paper currency that was backed up with gold and silver, and an active policy to encourage foreign trade.

*Political divisions over economic policy*

Less affluent men fought back, pressing legislatures for programs that met their needs. Western farmers, often in debt, urged the states to print more paper money and to pass laws lowering taxes and postponing the foreclosure of mortgages. Artisans opposed merchants by calling for protection from low-priced foreign imports that competed with the goods they produced. They set themselves against farmers as well by demanding price regulation of the farm products they consumed. In the continuing struggle, the state legislatures became the battleground of competing economic factions.

As the 1780s wore on, conflicts mounted. As long as the individual states remained sovereign, the Confederation was crippled—unable to conduct foreign affairs effectively, unable to set coherent economic policy, unable to deal with discontent in the West. Equally dismaying was the discovery that many Americans, instead of being selflessly concerned for the public good, selfishly pursued their private interests.

## REPUBLICAN SOCIETY

The war for independence transformed not only America's government and economy but also its society and culture. Inspired by the Declaration's ideal of equality, some Americans rejected the subordinate position assigned to them under the old colonial order. Westerners, newly wealthy entrepreneurs, urban artisans, and women all claimed greater freedom, power, and recognition. The authority of the traditional leaders of government, society, and the family came under a new scrutiny; the impulse to defer to social superiors became less automatic. The new assertiveness demonstrated how deeply egalitarian assumptions were taking root in American culture.

## The New Men of the Revolution

The Revolution gave rise to a new sense of social identity and a new set of ambitions among several groups of men who had once accepted a humbler status. The war also offered opportunities to aspiring entrepreneurs everywhere, and often they were not the same men who had prospered before the war. At a stroke, inde-

*Winners and losers* pendence swept away the prominence of loyalists, whose ranks included an especially high number of government officials, large landowners, and major merchants. And while loyalists found their properties confiscated by revolutionary governments, other Americans grew rich. Many northern merchants gained newfound wealth from privateering or military contracts. Commercial farmers in the mid-Atlantic states prospered from the high food prices caused by wartime scarcity and army demand.

The Revolution effected no dramatic redistribution of wealth. Indeed, the gap between rich and poor increased during the 1780s. But those families newly enriched by the Revolution came to demand and receive greater social recognition and political influence. The republican ideal of "an aristocracy of merit" justified their ambitions.

City craftworkers pushed for recognition too. Their experience in organizing boycotts against British goods during the imperial crisis gave artisans a greater taste

*Urban artisans* of politics. With the Revolution accomplished, they clamored for men of their own kind to represent them in government. Their assertiveness came as a rude shock to gentlemen like South Carolina's William Henry Drayton, who balked at sharing power with men "who never were in a way to study" anything except "how to cut up a beast in the market to the best advantage, to cobble an old shoe in the neatest manner, or to build a necessary house."

While master craftworkers competed for political office, the laborers who worked for them also exhibited a new sense of independence. Recognizing that their interests were often distinct from those of masters, journeymen formed new organizations to secure higher wages. Between 1786 and 1816 skilled urban laborers organized the first major strikes in American history.

## The New Women of the Revolution

Not long after the fighting with Britain had broken out, Margaret Livingston of New York wrote to her sister Catherine, "You know that our Sex are doomed to be obedient in every stage of life so that we shant be great gainers by this contest." By war's end, however, Eliza Wilkinson from rural South Carolina was complaining boldly to a woman friend: "The men say we have no business with political matters . . . it's not our sphere. . . . [But] I won't have it thought that because we are the weaker Sex (as to bodily strength my dear) we are Capable of nothing more, than minding the Dairy . . . surely we may have enough sense to give our Opinions."

What separated Margaret Livingston's resignation from Eliza Wilkinson's assertion of personal worth and independence was the Revolution. Eliza Wilkinson had managed her parents' plantation during the war and defended it from British marauders. Other women discovered similar reserves of skill and resourcefulness. When soldiers returned home, some were surprised to find their wives and daughters, who had been running family farms and businesses, less submissive and more self-confident.

But American men had not fought a revolution for the equality of American women. In fact, male revolutionaries gave no thought to the role of women in the new nation, assuming that those of the "weaker sex" were incapable of making informed and independent political decisions. Most women of the revolutionary generation agreed that the proper female domain was the home, not the public arena of politics. Still, the currents of the Revolution occasionally left gaps that allowed women to display their political interests. When a loosely worded provision in the New Jersey state constitution gave the vote to "all free inhabitants" owning a specified amount of property, white widows and single women went to the polls. Only in 1807 did the state legislature close the loophole.

*Exclusion of women from politics*

### *Mary Wollstonecraft's* Vindication

In the wake of the Revolution there also appeared in England a book that would become a classic text of modern feminism, Mary Wollstonecraft's *A Vindication of the Rights of Women* (1792). Attracting a wide, if not widely approving, readership in America as well, it called not only for laws to guarantee women civil and political equality but also for educational reforms to ensure their social and economic equality.

Wollstonecraft dashed off *Vindication* in six short months. She charged that men deliberately conspired to keep women in "a state of perpetual childhood" by giving them inferior, frivolous educations. That encouraged young girls to fixate on fashion and flirtation and made them "only anxious to inspire love, when they ought to cherish a nobler ambition, and by their abilities and virtues exact respect." Girls, she proposed, should receive the same education as boys, including training that would prepare them for careers in medicine, politics, and business. No woman should have to pin her hopes for financial security on making a good marriage, Wollstonecraft argued. On the contrary, well-educated and resourceful women capable of supporting themselves would make the best wives and mothers, assets to the family and the nation.

*Vindication* might have been written in gunpowder rather than ink, given the reaction it aroused on both sides of the Atlantic. Even so, Wollstonecraft at first

This strikingly masculinized portrait in a book published in the United States in 1809 placed Mary Wollstonecraft in the company of "actresses, adventurers, authoresses, fortunetellers, gipsies, dwarfs, swindlers, and vagrants."

won many defenders among both men and women, who sometimes publicly and more often privately expressed their agreement with her views. This favorable reception ended abruptly after her death in childbirth in 1797, when a memoir written by her husband revealed that she had lived out of wedlock with him—and before him, with another lover. Even so, Wollstonecraft's views found some admirers in America. Among them were Aaron Burr, the future vice president, who dubbed *Vindication* "a work of genius" and promised to read it aloud to his wife, and the Philadelphia Quaker Elizabeth Drinker, who confided to her diary that "In very many of her sentiments, she . . . *speaks my mind.*"

### Seduction Literature and the Virtues of Women

English writers like Wollstonecraft influenced attitudes toward women in both Britain and America in another important way. In the last half of the eighteenth century, England's novelists, poets, and moralists—and their many eager imitators in the new republic—drew literary inspiration from the theme of seduction. Books, magazines, and newspapers overflowed with cautionary tales of young white women who were seduced or coerced into surrendering their virginity by unscrupulous "rakes," only to be abandoned by these faithless lovers, disowned by their families for becoming pregnant out of wedlock, and finally reduced to beggary or prostitution. As one popular magazine published in New England warned, "Every town and village affords some instance of a ruined female, who has fallen from the heights of purity to the lowest grade of humanity."

"Seduction literature" sent the unmistakable message that young women must preserve their sexual purity by assuming the responsibility for correct behavior during courtship. Women were equipped with greater self-control by nature, authors advised, and they were obliged to inspire the same restraint in their suitors, for men were naturally passionate and impulsive. Depicting women as the guardians of sexual virtue marked a major shift in cultural attitudes, because for centuries before, most male writers had insisted that women were the more dangerous sex, their insatiable lust and deceitful ways luring men into sin.

## Republican Motherhood and Education for Women

In the new republic, the new image of women as the upholders of private virtue met with an enthusiastic reception, especially among those who believed that wives and mothers had an obligation to encourage republican virtue in their husbands and children. That view, known as "republican motherhood," inspired many educational reformers in the revolutionary generation. Philadelphian Benjamin Rush argued that only educated and independent-minded women could raise the informed and self-reliant citizens that a republican government required, while New Englander Judith Sargent Murray urged the cultivation of women's minds to encourage self-respect. Their efforts contributed to the most dramatic change in the lives of women after the war—the spread of female literacy.

Between 1780 and 1830 the number of American colleges and secondary academies rose dramatically, and some of these new institutions were devoted to educating women. Not only did the number of schools for women increase, but these schools also offered a solid academic curriculum. By 1850— for the first time in American history—there were as many literate women as there were men. To counter popular prejudices, the defenders of female education contended that schooling for women would produce the ideal republican mother. An educated woman, as one graduate of a female academy claimed, would "inspire her brothers, her husband, or her sons with such a love of virtue, such just ideas of the true value of civil liberty . . . that future heroes and statesmen shall exaltingly declare, it is to my mother that I owe this elevation."

*Improved schooling and literacy rates*

The Revolution also prompted some states to reform their marriage laws, making divorce somewhat easier, although it remained extremely rare. But while women won greater freedom to divorce, courts became less concerned with enforcing a widow's traditional legal claim to one-third of her spouse's real estate. And married women still could not sue or be sued, make wills or contracts, or buy and sell property. Any wages that they earned went to their husbands; so did all personal property that wives brought into a marriage; so did the rents and profits of any real estate they owned. Despite the high ideals of "republican motherhood," most women remained confined to the "domestic sphere" of the home and deprived of the most basic legal and political rights.

*Women's legal status*

## The Attack on Aristocracy

Why wasn't the American Revolution more revolutionary? Independence secured the full political equality of white men who owned property, but women were still deprived of political rights, African Americans of human rights. Why did the revolutionaries stop short of extending equality to the most unequal groups in American society—and with so little sense that they were being inconsistent?

In part, the lack of concern was rooted in republican ideas themselves. Republican ideology viewed property as the key to independence and power. Lacking

*Republican view
of equality*

property, women and black Americans were easily consigned to the custody of husbands and masters. Then, too, prejudice played its part: the perception of women and blacks as naturally inferior beings.

But revolutionary leaders also failed to press for greater equality because they conceived their crusade in terms of eliminating the evils of a European past dominated by kings and aristocrats. They believed that the great obstacle to equality was monarchy—kings and queens who bestowed hereditary honors and political office on favored individuals and granted legal privileges and monopolies to favored churches and businesses. These artificial inequalities posed the real threat to liberty, most republicans concluded. In other words, the men of the Revolution were intent on attaining equality by leveling off the top of society. It did not occur to most republicans that the cause of equality could also be served by raising up the bottom—by attacking the laws and prejudices that kept African Americans enslaved and women dependent.

The most significant reform of the republican campaign against artificial privilege was the dismantling of state-supported churches. Most states had a religious

*Disestablishment*

establishment. In New York and the South, it was the Anglican Church; in New England, the Congregational Church. Since the 1740s, dissenters who did not worship at state churches had protested laws that taxed all citizens to support the clergy of established denominations. After the Revolution, as more dissenters became voters, state legislators gradually abolished state support for Anglican and Congregational churches.

Not only in religious life but in all aspects of their culture, Americans rejected inequalities associated with a monarchical past. In that spirit reformers attacked

*Society of Cincinnati*

the Society of Cincinnati, a group organized by former officers of the Continental Army in 1783. The society, which was merely a social club for veterans, was forced to disband for its policy of passing on its membership rights to eldest sons. In this way, critics charged, the Cincinnati was creating artificial distinctions and perpetuating a hereditary warrior nobility.

Today many of the republican efforts at reform seem misdirected. While only a handful of revolutionaries worked for the education of women and the emancipation of slaves, enormous zeal went into fighting threats from a monarchical past that had never existed in America. Yet the threat from kings and aristocrats was real to the revolutionaries—and indeed remained real in many parts of Europe. Their determination to sweep away every shred of formal privilege ensured that these forms of inequality never took root in America.

## FROM CONFEDERATION TO CONSTITUTION

While Americans from many walks of life sought to realize the republican commitment to equality, leaders in Congress wrestled with the problem of preserving the nation itself. With the new republic slowly rending itself to pieces, some political leaders concluded that neither the Confederation nor the state legislatures were able to remedy the basic difficulties facing the nation. But how could the states be convinced to surrender their sovereign powers? The answer came in the wake of two events—one foreign, one domestic—that lent momentum to the cause of strengthening the central government.

## The Jay-Gardoqui Treaty

The international episode that threatened to leave the Confederation in shambles was a debate over a proposed treaty with Spain. In 1785 southwesterners still could not legally navigate the Mississippi and were still threatening to secede from the union and annex their territory to Spain's American empire. To shore up southwestern loyalties, Congress instructed its secretary of foreign affairs, John Jay, to negotiate an agreement with Spain preserving American rights to navigate on the Mississippi River. But the Spanish emissary, Don Diego de Gardoqui, sweet-talked Jay into accepting a treaty by which the United States would give up all rights to the Mississippi for 25 years. In return, Spain agreed to grant trading privileges to American merchants.

Jay, a New Yorker, knew more than a few northern merchants who were eager to open new markets. But when the proposed treaty became public knowledge, southwesterners denounced it as nothing short of betrayal. The treaty was never ratified, but the hostility stirred up during the debate revealed the strength of sectional feelings.

## Shays's Rebellion

On the heels of this humiliation by Spain came an internal conflict that challenged the notion that individual states could maintain order in their own territories. The trouble erupted in western Massachusetts, where many small farmers were close to ruin. Yet they still had to pay mortgages on their farms, still had other debts, and were perpetually short of money. In 1786 the lower house of the Massachusetts legislature obliged the farmers with a package of relief measures. But creditors in eastern Massachusetts, determined to safeguard their own investments, persuaded the upper house to defeat the measures.

In the summer of 1786 western farmers responded, demanding that the upper house of the legislature be abolished and that the relief measures go into effect. That autumn 2000 farmers rose in armed rebellion, led by Captain Daniel Shays, a veteran of the Revolution. They closed the county courts to halt creditors from foreclosing on their farms and marched on the federal arsenal at Springfield. The state militia quelled the uprising by February 1787, but the insurrection left many in Massachusetts and the rest of the country thoroughly shaken.

Alarmed conservatives saw Shays's Rebellion as the consequence of radical democracy. "The natural effects of pure democracy are already produced among us," lamented one republican gentleman. "It is a war against virtue, talents, and property carried on by the dregs and scum of mankind." He was wrong.

Daniel Shays's rebels were no impoverished rabble. They were reputable members of western communities who wanted their property protected and believed
*Response to agrarian unrest* — that government existed to provide that protection. The Massachusetts state legislature had been unable to safeguard the property of farmers from the inroads of recession or to protect the property of creditors from the armed debtors who closed the courts. It had failed, in other words, to fulfill the most basic aim of republican government.

Other states with discontented debtors feared what the example of western Massachusetts might mean for the future of the Confederation itself. But by 1786 Shays's Rebellion supplied only the sharpest jolt to a movement for reform that was already under way. Even before the rebellion, a group of Virginians had proposed a meeting of the states to adopt a uniform system of commercial regulations. Once assembled at Annapolis in September 1786, the delegates from five states agreed to a more ambitious undertaking. They called for a second, broader meeting in Philadelphia, which Congress approved, for the "express purpose of revising the Articles of Confederation."

## Framing a Federal Constitution

It was the wettest spring anyone could remember. The 55 men who traveled over muddy roads to Philadelphia in May 1787 arrived drenched and bespattered. Fortunately, most of the travelers were men in their 30s and 40s, young enough to survive a good soaking. Since most were gentlemen of some means—planters, merchants, and lawyers with powdered wigs and prosperous paunches—they could recover from the rigors of their journey in the best accommodations offered by America's largest city.

James Madison, the scholar and statesman whose ideas and political skill shaped the Constitution.

The delegates came from all the states except Rhode Island. The rest of New England supplied shrewd backroom politicians—Roger Sherman and Oliver Ellsworth from Connecticut and Rufus King and Elbridge Gerry, Massachusetts men who had learned a trick or two from Sam Adams. The middle states marshaled much of the intellectual might: two Philadelphia lawyers, John Dickinson and James Wilson; one Philadelphia financier, Robert Morris; and the aristocratic Gouverneur Morris. From New York there was Alexander Hamilton, the mercurial and ambitious young protégé of Washington. South Carolina provided fiery orators Charles Pinckney and John Rutledge.

It was "an assembly of the demi-gods," gushed Thomas Jefferson, who, along with John Adams, was serving as a diplomat in Europe when the convention met. In fact, the only delegate who looked even remotely divine was the convention's presiding deity. Towering a full half foot taller than most of his colleagues, George Washington displayed his usual self-possession from a chair elevated on the speaker's platform where the delegates met, in the Pennsylvania State House. At first glance, the delegate of least commanding presence was Washington's fellow Virginian, James Madison. Short and slightly built, the 36-year-old Madison had no profession except hypochondria. But he was an astute politician and a brilliant political thinker who, more than anyone else, shaped the framing of the federal Constitution.

*James Madison*

The delegates from 12 different states had two things in common. They were all men of considerable political experience, and they all recognized the need for a stronger national union. So when the Virginia delegation introduced Madison's outline for a new central government, the convention was ready to listen.

### The Virginia and New Jersey Plans

What Madison had in mind was a truly national republic, not a confederation of independent states. His "Virginia Plan" proposed a central government with three branches: legislative, executive, and judicial. Furthermore, the legislative branch, Congress, would possess the power to veto all state legislation. In place of the Confederation's single assembly, Madison substituted a bicameral legislature, with a lower house elected directly by the people and an upper house chosen by the lower from nominations made by state legislatures. Representatives to both houses would be apportioned according to population—a change from practice under the Articles, in which each state had a single vote in Congress. Madison also revised the structure of government that had existed under the Articles by adding an executive, who would be elected by Congress, and an independent federal judiciary.

*Madison's Virginia Plan*

After two weeks of debate over the Virginia Plan, William Paterson, a lawyer from New Jersey, presented a less radical counterproposal. While his "New Jersey Plan" increased Congress's power to tax and to regulate trade, it kept the national government as a unicameral assembly, with each state receiving one vote in Congress under the policy of equal representation. The delegates took just four days to reject Paterson's plan. Most endorsed Madison's design for a stronger central government.

*Paterson's New Jersey Plan*

Even so, the issue of apportioning representation continued to divide the delegates. While smaller states pressed for each state having an equal vote in Congress, larger states backed Madison's provision for basing representation on population. Underlying the dispute over representation was an even deeper rivalry between southern and northern states. While northern and southern populations were nearly equal in the 1780s, and the South's population was growing more rapidly, the northern states were more numerous. Giving the states equal votes would put the South at a disadvantage. Southerners feared being outvoted in Congress by the northern states and felt that only proportional representation would protect the interests of their section.

That division turned into a deadlock as the wet spring burned off into a blazing summer. Delegates suffered the daily torture of staring at a large sun painted on the speaker's chair occupied by Washington. The stifling heat was made even worse because the windows remained shut, to keep any news of the proceedings from drifting out onto the Philadelphia streets.

### The Deadlock Broken

Finally, as the heat wave broke, so did the political stalemate. On July 2 a committee headed by Benjamin Franklin suggested a compromise. States would be equally represented in the upper house of Congress, each state legislature appointing two senators to six-year terms. That satisfied the smaller states. In the lower house of Congress, which alone could initiate money bills, representation was to be apportioned according to population. Every 30,000 inhabitants would entitle a state to send one representative for a two-year term. A slave was to count as three-fifths of a free person in the calculation of population, and the slave trade was to continue until 1808. That satisfied the larger states and the South.

*Compromise over representation*

By the end of August the convention was prepared to approve the final draft of the Constitution. The delegates agreed that the executive, now called the president, would be chosen every four years. Direct election seemed out of the question—after all, how could citizens in South Carolina know anything about a presidential candidate who happened to live in distant Massachusetts, or vice versa? But if each state chose presidential electors, either by popular election or by having the state legislature name them, those eminent men would likely have been involved in national politics, have known the candidates personally, and be prepared to vote wisely. Thus the Electoral College was established, with each state's total number of senators and representatives determining its share of electoral votes.

*Electoral College*

An array of other powers ensured that the executive would remain independent and strong: the president would have command over the armed forces, authority to conduct diplomatic relations, responsibility to nominate judges and officials in the executive branch, and the power to veto congressional legislation. Just as the executive branch was made independent, so too the federal judiciary was separated from the other two branches of government. Madison believed that this clear separation of powers was essential to a balanced republican government.

*Separation of powers*

Madison's only real defeat came when the convention refused to give Congress veto power over state legislation. Still, the new bicameral national legislature enjoyed much broader authority than Congress had under the Confederation, including the power to tax and to regulate commerce. The Constitution also limited the powers of state legislatures, prohibiting them from levying duties on trade, coining money or issuing paper currency, and conducting foreign relations. The Constitution and the acts passed by Congress were declared the supreme law of the land, taking precedence over any legislation passed by the states. And changing the Constitution would not be easy. *Amending the Constitution* Amendments could be proposed only by a two-thirds vote of both houses of Congress or in a convention requested by two-thirds of the state legislatures. Ratification of amendments required approval by three-quarters of the states.

On September 17, 1787, 39 of the 42 delegates remaining in Philadelphia signed the Constitution. Charged only with revising the Articles, the delegates had instead written a completely new frame of government. And to speed up ratification, the convention decided that the Constitution would go into effect after only nine states had approved it. They further declared that the people themselves—not the state legislatures—would pass judgment on the Constitution in special ratifying conventions. To serve final notice that the new central government was a republic of the people and not merely another confederation of states, Gouverneur Morris of Pennsylvania hit on a happy turn of phrase to introduce the Constitution. "We the People," the document begins, "in order to form a more perfect union . . ."

## Ratification

With grave misgivings on the part of many, the states called for conventions to decide whether to ratify the new Constitution. Those with the gravest misgivings—the Anti-Federalists, as they came to be called—voiced familiar republican fears. Older and less cosmopolitan than their Federalist opponents, the Anti-Federalists drew upon their memories of the struggle with England to frame their criticisms of the Constitution. Expanding the power of the central government at the expense of the states, they warned, would lead to corrupt and arbitrary rule by new aristocrats. Extending a republic over a large territory, they cautioned, would separate national legislators from the interests and close oversight of their constituents. *The Anti-Federalists*

Madison responded to these objections in *The Federalist Papers*, a series of 85 essays written with Alexander Hamilton and John Jay during the winter of 1787–1788. He countered Anti-Federalist concerns over the centralization of power by pointing out that each separate branch of the national government would keep the others within the limits of their legal authority. That mechanism of checks and balances would prevent the executive from oppressing the people while preventing the people from oppressing themselves. **The Federalist Papers**

To answer Anti-Federalist objections to a national republic, Madison drew on the ideas of an English philosopher, David Hume. In his famous 10th essay in *The Federalist Papers*, Madison argued that in a great republic, "the Society becomes broken into a greater variety of interests, of pursuits, of passions, which check each other." The larger the territory, the more likely it was to contain multiple political interests and parties, so that no single faction could dominate. Instead, each would cancel out the others.

The one Anti-Federalist criticism Madison could not get around was the absence of a national bill of rights. Opponents insisted on an explicit statement

*Bill of Rights* of rights to prevent the freedoms of individuals and minorities from being violated by the federal government. Madison finally promised to place a bill of rights before Congress immediately after the Constitution was ratified.

Throughout the early months of 1788, Anti-Federalists continued their opposition. But they lacked the articulate and influential leadership that rallied behind the Constitution and commanded greater access to the public press. In the end, too, Anti-Federalist fears of centralized power proved less compelling than Federalist prophecies of the chaos that would follow if the Constitution were not adopted.

By June 1788 all but three states had voted in favor of ratification. The last holdout—to no one's surprise Rhode Island—finally came aboard in May 1790, after Madison had carried through on his pledge to submit a bill of rights to the new Congress. Indeed, these 10 amendments proved to be the Anti-Federalists' most impressive legacy.

### Changing Revolutionary Ideals

Within the life span of a single generation, Americans had declared their independence twice. In many ways the political freedom claimed from Britain in 1776 was less remarkable than the intellectual freedom that Americans achieved by agreeing to the Constitution. The Constitution represented both a triumph of imagination and common sense and a rejection of some older, long-cherished republican beliefs.

Americans thought long and hard before changing their minds, but many did. Committed at first to limiting executive power by making legislatures supreme, they at last ratified a constitution that provided for an independent executive and a balanced government. Committed at first to preserving the sovereignty of the states, they at last established a national government with authority independent of the states. Committed at first to the proposition that a national republic was impossible, they at last created an impossibility that still endures.

What, then, became of the last tenet of the old republican creed—the belief that civic virtue would sustain popular liberty? The hard lessons of the war and the crises of the 1780s withered confidence in the capacity of Americans to

## Isaac Clark Is Impressed by the British Navy

 , Isaac Clark, of Salem . . . Massachusetts, on solemn oath declare . . . that on the 14th day of June, 1809, I was impressed and forcibly taken from the ship *Jane* of Norfolk, by the sailing master . . . of his majesty's ship *Porcupine*, Robert Elliot, commander. I had a protection [i.e., passport] from the Customhouse in Salem, which I showed to captain Elliot: he swore that I was an Englishman, tore my protection to pieces before my eyes, and threw it overboard, and ordered me to go to work—I told him I did not belong to his flag, and I would do no work under it. He then ordered my legs to be put in irons, and the next morning ordered the master at arms to . . . give me two dozen lashes; after receiving them, he ordered him to keep me in irons, and give me one biscuit and one pint of water for 24 hours. After keeping me in this situation for one week, I was . . . asked by captain Elliot if I would go to my duty—on my refusing, he . . . gave me two dozen more [lashes] and kept me on the same allowance another week—then . . . asked if I would go to work; I still persisted . . . [and he] gave me the third two dozen lashes, ordered a very heavy chain put round my neck . . . and that no person . . . give me any thing to eat or drink, but my one biscuit and pint of water for 24 hours, until I would go to work. I was kept in this situation for nine weeks, when being exhausted by hunger and thirst, I was obliged to yield. After being on board the ship more than two years and a half . . . [t]he American consul received a copy of my protection from Salem, and procured my discharge on the 29th of April [1812].

Source: Clement Cleveland Sawtell, "Impressment of American Seamen by the British," *Essex Institute Historical Collections*, v. 76 (October 1940), pp. 318–319. Reprinted by permission by Peabody Essex Museum, Salem, MA.

### Madison and the Young Republicans

Following Washington's example, Jefferson did not seek a third term. A caucus of Republican members of Congress selected James Madison to run against Federalist Charles Cotesworth Pinckney. Madison triumphed easily.

Few men have assumed the presidency with more experience than James Madison. A leading nationalist in the 1780s, the father of the Constitution, a key floor leader in Congress, the founder of the Republican party, Jefferson's secretary of state and closest adviser, Madison had spent over a quarter of a century in public life. Yet as president he lacked the force of leadership and the inner strength to impose his will on less capable individuals.

With a president reluctant to fight for what he wanted, leadership passed to a new generation of Republicans in Congress. Much more nationalistic, they advocated an ambitious program of economic development and were aggressive expansionists, especially those from frontier districts. Their | *War Hawks* feisty willingness to go to war earned them the name of War Hawks, and they quickly became the driving force in the Republican party.

## The Decision for War

During Jefferson's final week in office in early 1809, Congress repealed the Embargo Act and reopened trade except with Britain and France. The following year it authorized trade with France and England but decreed that if one of the two belligerents agreed to stop interfering with American shipping, trade with the other would be prohibited.

*Growing conflict with Great Britain*

In this situation, Napoleon outmaneuvered the British by announcing that he would set aside the French trade regulations. Madison eagerly took the French emperor at his word and reimposed a ban on trade with England. It soon became clear that Napoleon's words were not matched by French deeds. Madison refused to rescind his order unless the British revoked the Orders in Council. In the ensuing disputes, American anger focused on the British, who seized many more ships than the French and continued to impress American sailors.

*Debate over going to war*

When the British ministry finally suspended the Orders in Council on June 16, 1812, it was too late. Two days earlier, unaware of the change in policy, Congress had granted Madison's request for a declaration of war against Britain. The vote of 79 to 49 in the House and 19 to 13 in the Senate mostly followed party lines, with every Federalist voting against war. As the representatives of commercial interests, particularly in New England, Federalists were convinced that war would ruin American commerce. They also still identified with Britain as the champion of order and conservatism. The handful of Republicans who joined the Federalists represented coastal districts, which were most vulnerable to the Royal Navy.

Clearly, the vote for war could not be explained as a matter of outraged Americans protecting neutral rights. The coastal areas, which were most affected, preferred trade over high principle. On the other hand, members of Congress from the South and the West, regions that had a less direct interest in the issue, clamored most strongly for war. Their constituents were eager to seize territory in Canada or in Florida (owned by Britain's ally Spain) and accused the British of stirring up hostility among the Indian tribes.

Perhaps most important, the War Hawks were convinced that Britain had never truly accepted the verdict of the American Revolution. To them, American independence—and with it republicanism—hung in the balance. For Americans hungering for acceptance in the community of nations, nothing rankled more than being treated by the British as colonials. John Quincy Adams expressed this point of view when he declared: "In this question something besides dollars and cents is concerned and no alternative [is] left but war or the abandonment of our rights as an independent nation."

## National Unpreparedness

With Britain preoccupied with Napoleon, the War Hawks expected that the United States would win an easy victory. In truth, the nation was totally unprepared for war. Crippled by Jefferson's cutbacks, the navy could not break the British blockade of the American coast. The army was small and poorly led, and volunteering lagged, even in states where sentiment for war was highest. Congress was also reluctant to levy taxes to finance the war.

A three-pronged American invasion of Canada failed dismally in 1812. The Americans fared better in 1813, when Commander Oliver Hazard Perry won a decisive victory on Lake Erie. Perry's triumph gave the United States control of Lake Erie and greatly strengthened the American position in the Northwest.

*Battle of Lake Erie*

## "A Chance Such as Will Never Occur Again"

As the United States struggled to organize its forces, Tecumseh saw his long-awaited opportunity to drive Americans out of the western territories. "Here is a chance . . . such as will never occur again," he told a war council, "for us Indians of North America to form ourselves into one great combination." Joining up with the British, Tecumseh traveled south in the fall to coordinate a concerted offensive with his Creek allies for the following summer. He left a bundle of red sticks with eager Creek soldiers, who were to remove one stick each day from the bundle and attack when the sticks had run out.

A number of the older Creeks were more acculturated and preferred an American alliance. But about 2000 younger "Red Stick" Creeks launched a series of attacks. Once again, the Indians' lack of unity was a serious handicap, as warriors from the Cherokee, Choctaw, and Chickasaw tribes, traditional Creek enemies, allied with the Americans. At the Battle of Horseshoe Bend in March 1814, General Andrew Jackson soundly defeated the Creeks. Jackson promptly dictated a peace treaty under which the Creeks ceded 22 million acres of land in the Mississippi Territory. They and the other southern tribes still retained significant landholdings, but Indian military power had been broken in the Old Southwest.

*Defeat of the Creeks*

Farther north, in October 1813 American forces under General William Henry Harrison defeated the British and their Indian allies at the Battle of the Thames. In the midst of heavy fighting Tecumseh was slain—and with him died any hope of a Pan-Indian movement.

*Tecumseh's death*

## The British Invasion

As long as the war against Napoleon continued, the British were unwilling to divert army units to North America. But in 1814 Napoleon was at last defeated.

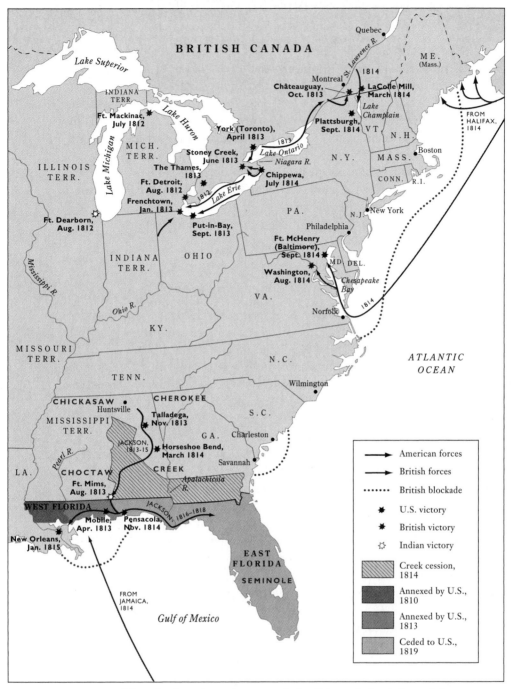

THE WAR OF 1812 After the American victory on Lake Erie and the defeat of the western Indians at the Battle of the Thames, the British adopted a three-pronged strategy to invade the United States, culminating in an attack on New Orleans. But they met their match in Andrew Jackson, whose troops marched to New Orleans after fighting a series of battles against the Creeks and forcing them to cede a massive tract of land.

Free to concentrate on America, the British devised a coordinated strategy to invade the United States in the northern, central, and southern parts of the country. The main army headed south from Montreal but was checked when Captain Thomas Macdonough destroyed the British fleet on Lake Champlain.

Meanwhile, a smaller British force captured Washington and burned several public buildings, including the Capitol and the president's home. The British withdrew, however, after they failed to capture Baltimore, their principal objective. Witnessing the unsuccessful British attack on Fort McHenry in the city's harbor, Francis Scott Key penned the verses of "The Star Spangled Banner," which was eventually adopted as the national anthem.

The third British target was New Orleans, where a formidable army of 7500 British troops was opposed by a hastily assembled American force commanded by Major General Andrew Jackson. Jackson's outnumbered and ill-equipped forces won a stunning victory, which made Jackson an overnight hero. The Battle of New Orleans enabled Americans to *Jackson's victory at New Orleans* forget the war's many failures and to boast that once again the United States had humbled the world's greatest military power.

### The Hartford Convention

In December 1814, while Jackson was organizing the defense of New Orleans, New England Federalists met in Hartford to voice their grievances. Rejecting calls for secession, the delegates proposed a series of amendments to the Constitution that demonstrated their displeasure with the government's economic policies and their resentment of the South's national political power. The burst of national pride following Jackson's victory, however, badly undercut the Hartford Convention, as did news from Ghent, Belgium, that a peace treaty had been signed.

Like the war itself, the Treaty of Ghent accomplished little. All the major issues between the two countries were either ignored or referred to future commissions for settlement. As John Quincy Adams commented, "Nothing was adjusted, nothing was settled. . . ." Both sides were simply *Treaty of Ghent* relieved to end the conflict.

### AMERICA TURNS INWARD

Adams was right in concluding that in international relations the war had settled nothing. Psychologically, however, the nation's mood had perceptibly changed. "Let any man look at the degraded condition of this country before the war," declaimed young Henry Clay, a leading War Hawk. "The scorn of the universe, the contempt of ourselves. . . . What is our present situation? Respectability and character abroad—security and confidence at home." Indeed, the return of peace brought with it an outburst of American nationalism. Jackson's drubbing of the British at New Orleans in particular strengthened Americans' confidence in their country's destiny.

The surge in nationalism sounded the death knell of the Federalist party, whose members had flirted with secession at the Hartford Convention. Although

*Death of the Federalist party*

the party had made its best showing in years in 1812, when Madison narrowly won reelection, its support collapsed in the 1816 election. Madison's secretary of state, James Monroe, resoundingly defeated Federalist Rufus King of New York. Four years later Monroe ran for reelection unopposed.

The spirit of postwar harmony produced the so-called Era of Good Feelings, presided over by James Monroe, the last president of the revolutionary generation. Monroe, like Jefferson before him, hoped to eliminate political parties, which he considered unnecessary in a free government. Like Washington, he thought of himself as the head of the nation rather than of a party.

## The Missouri Crisis

The optimism of the era, however, was suddenly undercut by sectional rivalries that flared up in 1819 when the Missouri Territory applied for admission as a slave state.

Congress had prohibited the African slave trade in 1808, the earliest year this could be done under the Constitution, but before now, slavery had not been a major issue in American politics. In the absence of any federal legislation, slavery had crossed the Mississippi River into the Louisiana Purchase. Louisiana entered the Union in 1812 as a slave state, and in 1818 Missouri, which had about 10,000 slaves in its population, asked permission to come in, too.

At this time, there were 11 free and 11 slave states. The North's greater population gave it a majority in the House of Representatives, but the Senate was evenly balanced, since each state had two senators regardless of population. Then Maine, previously part of Massachusetts, requested admission as a free state. That would upset the balance unless Missouri came in as a slave state.

Representative James Tallmadge of New York disturbed this delicate state of affairs when in 1819 he introduced an amendment designed to establish a program of gradual emancipation in Missouri. The debate that followed was bitter, as for the first time Congress directly debated the morality of slavery. The House approved the Tallmadge amendment, but the Senate refused to accept it, and the two houses deadlocked.

When Congress reconvened in 1820, Henry Clay of Kentucky promoted what came to be known as the Missouri Compromise. Under its terms Missouri

*Missouri Compromise*

was admitted as a slave state and Maine as a free state. In addition, slavery was forever prohibited in the remainder of the Louisiana

out the various parts of a shoe, and could stitch and glue those parts together. He then sold the shoes in the same shop where he and his apprentices made them. Unlike the textile industry, shoemaking was not rapidly transformed in this period by a shift to heavy machinery. Even so, expanding transportation networks and national markets fundamentally altered this business.

Micajah Pratt, a cobbler from Lynn, Massachusetts, realized that there were ready markets for cheap shoes in the South and West. So he hired workers to produce shoes in larger and larger central shops. Pratt cut costs further by using new production techniques, such as standardized patterns and sole-cutting machines. Pratt eventually employed as many as 500 men and women.

*Lynn, center of shoe manufacturing*

Unable to keep up with demand, he and other manufacturers hired farmers, fishermen, and their families in surrounding towns to do part-time work at home. Women and girls sewed the upper parts of a shoe; men and boys attached the bottoms. While slow, this mode of production allowed wages to be reduced still further. A few highly paid workers performed critical tasks like cutting the leather, but most work was done either in large central shops or in homes. With workers no longer able to make an entire shoe, in little more than a generation shoemaking ceased to be a craft. Though not organized in a factory setting, it had become essentially an assembly-line process.

### The Labor Movement

In this newly emerging economic order, workers sometimes organized to protect their rights and traditional ways of life. Craftworkers such as carpenters, printers, and tailors formed unions, and in 1834 individual unions came together in the National Trades' Union.

Union leaders argued that labor was degraded in America: workers endured long hours, low pay, and low status. Unlike most American social thinkers of the day, they accepted the idea of conflict between different classes. They did not believe that the interests of workers and employers could be reconciled, and they blamed the plight of labor on monopolies, especially banking and paper money, and on machines and the factory system.

If the unions' rhetoric sounded radical, the solutions they proposed were moderate. Reformers agitated for public education, abolition of imprisonment for debt, political action by workers, and effective unions as the means to guarantee social equality and restore labor to its former honored position. Proclaiming the republican virtues of freedom and equality, they attacked special privilege, denounced the lack of equal opportunity, and decried workers' loss of independence.

The labor movement gathered some momentum in the decade before the Panic of 1837, but in the depression that followed, labor's strength collapsed.

During hard times, few workers were willing to strike or engage in collective action. Nor did skilled craftworkers, who spearheaded the union move-

*Difficulties of the union movement*

ment, feel a particularly strong bond with semiskilled factory workers and unskilled laborers. More than a decade of agitation did finally win the 10-hour day for some workers by the 1850s, and the courts also recognized workers' right to strike, but these gains had little immediate impact.

Workers were united in resenting the industrial system and their loss of status, but they were divided by ethnic and racial antagonisms, gender, conflicting religious perspectives, occupational differences, party loyalties, and disagreements over tactics. For them, the factory and industrialism were not agents of opportunity but reminders of their loss of independence and a measure of control over their lives.

### Sam Patch and a Worker's "Art"

Some fought against the loss of independence in unusual ways. The waterfalls that served as a magnet for capitalists building mills also attracted their workers. Such cascades were places to visit during off-hours to picnic, swim, fish, or laze about. And for those with nerve, the falls provided a place to show off skills in a different way. Every mill town had its waterfall jumpers, with their own techniques to survive the plunge (knees bent, chest thrust forward). No jumper won more fame than Sam Patch, a young man who had begun working at the Pawtucket mills at the age of 7. By the time he was in his 20s, Patch was working at the mills around Paterson, New Jersey, along the Passaic River.

Patch attracted attention in 1827, when he became disgusted by the conduct of a sawmill owner who had bought land around Passaic Falls and was set to charge admission to the scenic views in a new private "Forest Garden." The fee was meant to keep out "the lazy, idle, rascally, drunken vagabonds" who might spoil the pleasure of more refined folk. Workers who resented this fencing out rejoiced when Patch vowed to spoil Forest Garden's opening-day party. Constables locked him in a cellar to prevent any mischief, but a sympathizer set him free. And as proper folk gathered at the garden, thousands of ordinary laborers gathered on the opposite riverbank to see Patch jump 70 feet straight down. When he bobbed to the surface, raucous cheering broke out.

Patch's fame led him eventually to the biggest challenge of all: Niagara Falls. Twice he leapt more than 80 feet into the cascade's churning waters. But he drowned a month later when he dared Genesee Falls in another mill town along the Erie Canal—Rochester, New York. Still, his fame persisted for decades. Leaping waterfalls was "an art which I have knowledge of and courage to perform," he once declared defiantly. In a market economy where skilled "arts"

Waterfalls at mill towns, like this one in Pawtucket, Rhode Island, were places to swim, fish, and relax, as the people do in the foreground. Jumpers like Sam Patch leaped off the Pawtucket bridge and also off the roof of a nearby building into the foamy froth.

were being replaced by machine labor, Sam Patch's acts were a defiant protest against the changing times.

## SOCIAL STRUCTURES OF THE MARKET SOCIETY

Thousands of miles beyond Lowell's factory gates a different sort of American roamed, who at first appeared unconnected to the bustle of urban markets. These were the legendary mountain men, who flourished from the mid-1820s through the mid-1840s. Traveling across the Great Plains, along upland streams, and over the passes of the Rockies, outdoorsmen like Jim Bridger, Jedediah Smith, and James Walker wore buckskin hunting shirts, let their hair grow to their shoulders, and stuck pistols and tomahawks in their belts. Wild and exotic, the mountain men became romantic symbols of the American quest for individual freedom.

Yet these wanderers, too, were tied to the emerging market society. The mountain men hunted beaver pelts and shipped them east, to be turned into fancy hats for gentlemen. The fur trade was not a sporting event but a business, dominated by organizations like John Jacob Astor's American Fur Company, and the trapper was the agent of an economic structure that stretched from the mountains to eastern cities and even to Europe. Most of these men went into the wilderness not to flee civilization but to make money—to accumulate capital in order to set themselves up in society. Of those who survived the fur trade, almost none remained permanently outside civilization; most returned and took up new careers as shopkeepers, traders, ranchers, politicians, and even bankers. Far from rejecting society's values, the mountain men sought respectability. They, like farmers, were expectant capitalists for whom the West was a land of opportunity.

*The mountain men tied to market society*

The revolution in markets, in other words, affected Americans from all walks of life: mountain men as well as merchants, laborers as well as farmers. Equally critical, it restructured American society as a whole.

## Economic Specialization

To begin with, the spread of the market produced greater specialization. As we have seen, transportation networks made it possible for farmers to concentrate on producing certain crops, while factories could focus on making a single item such as cloth or shoes. Within factories, the division of labor meant that the process of manufacturing an item became more specialized. No longer did cobblers produce a pair of shoes from start to finish; the operation was broken down into more specialized (and less skilled) tasks.

This process evolved at different rates. Textiles and milling were completely mechanized, while other sectors of the economy, such as shoes and men's clothing, depended little on machinery. Moreover, large factories were the exception rather than the rule. Still, the tendency was toward more technology, greater efficiency, and increasing specialization.

Specialization had consequences at home as well as in the workplace. The average eighteenth-century American woman produced items like thread, cloth, clothing, and candles in the home for family use. As factories spread, however, household manufacturing all but disappeared, and women lost many of the economic functions they had previously performed in the family unit. Again, textiles are a striking example. Between 1815 and 1860, the price of cotton cloth fell from 18 to 2 cents a yard, and because it was also smoother and more brightly colored than homespun, most women purchased cloth rather than making it themselves. Similarly, the development of ready-made men's clothing reduced the amount of sewing women did, especially in urban centers. As Chapter 12 will make clearer, the growth of industry led

*Decline of women's traditional work*

to an economic reorganization of the family and a new definition of women's role in society.

## Materialism

European visitors were struck during these years by how much Americans were preoccupied with material goods. The new generation did not invent materialism, but the spread of the market after 1815 made it much more evident. "I know of no country, indeed," Tocqueville commented, "where the love of money has taken stronger hold on the affections of men."

In a nation that had no legally recognized aristocracy, no established church, and class lines that were only informally drawn, wealth became the most obvious symbol of status. Dismissing birth as "a mere idea," one magazine explained, "Wealth is something substantial. Everybody knows that and feels it." Materialism reflected more than a desire for goods and physical comfort. It represented a quest for respect and recognition. "Americans boast of their skill in money making," one contemporary observed, "and as it is the only standard of dignity and nobility and worth, they endeavor to obtain it by every possible means." *Wealth and status*

The emphasis on money and material goods left its mark on the American character. Often enough, it encouraged sharp business practices and promoted a greater tolerance of wealth acquired by questionable means. Americans also emphasized practicality over theory. The esteem of the founding generation for intellectual achievement was mostly lost in the scramble for wealth that seemed to consume the new generation.

## The Emerging Middle Class

In the years after 1815, a new middle class took shape in American society. A small class of shopkeepers, professionals, and master artisans had existed earlier, but the creation of a national market economy greatly expanded its size and influence. As specialization increased, office work and selling were more often physically separated from the production and handling of merchandise. Businesspeople, professionals, storekeepers, clerks, office workers, and supervisors began to think of themselves as a distinct social group. Members of the growing middle class had access to more education and enjoyed greater social mobility. They were paid not only more but differently. A manual worker might earn $300 a year, paid as wages computed on an hourly basis. Professionals received a yearly salary and might make $1000 a year or more. *Separation of middle class from manual laborers*

Middle-class neighborhoods, segregated along income and occupational lines, also began to develop in towns and cities. In larger cities improved transportation enabled middle-class residents to move to surrounding suburbs and commute to work. Leisure also became segregated, as separate working-class and middle-class social organizations and institutions emerged.

As middle-class Americans accumulated greater wealth, they were able to consume more. Thus material goods became emblems of success and status—as *Material goods as emblems of middle-class success* clockmaker Chauncey Jerome sadly discovered when his business failed and his wealth vanished. Indeed, this materialistic ethos was most apparent in the middle class, as they strove to set themselves apart from other groups in society. The middle class also came to embrace a new concept of marriage, the family, and the home, as we will see in Chapter 12. Along with occupation and income, moral outlook also marked class boundaries during this period.

## The Distribution of Wealth

As American society became more specialized, greater extremes of wealth appeared. As the new markets created fortunes for the few, the factory system lowered the wages of workers by dividing labor into smaller, less skilled tasks.

Indeed, local tax records reveal a growing concentration of wealth at the top of the social pyramid after 1815. Wealth was most highly concentrated in *Growing inequality of wealth* large eastern cities and in the cotton kingdom of the South, but everywhere the tendency was for the rich to get richer and own a larger share of the community's total wealth. By 1860, 5 percent of American families owned more than 50 percent of the nation's wealth. In villages where the market revolution had not penetrated, wealth tended to be less concentrated.

In a market society, the rich were able to build up their assets because those with capital were in a position to increase it dramatically by taking advantage of new investment opportunities. Although a few men, such as Cornelius Vanderbilt and John Jacob Astor, vaulted from the bottom ranks of society to the top, most of the nation's richest individuals came from wealthy families.

## Social Mobility

The existence of great fortunes is not necessarily inconsistent with the idea of social mobility or property accumulation. Although the gap between the rich and the poor widened after 1820, even the incomes of most poor Americans rose, because the total amount of wealth produced in America had become much larger. From about 1825 to 1860 the average per capita income almost doubled, to $300. Voicing the popular belief, a New York judge proclaimed, "In this favored land of liberty, the road to advancement is open to all."

Social mobility existed in these years, but not as much as contemporaries boasted. Most laborers—or more often their sons—did manage to move up the social ladder, but only a rung or two. Few unskilled workers rose higher than to a semiskilled occupation. Even the children of skilled workers normally did not escape the laboring classes to enter the middle-class ranks of clerks, managers, or lawyers. For most workers improved status came in the form of a savings account or home ownership, which gave them some security during economic downswings and in old age.

*Limits to social mobility*

## A New Sensitivity to Time

It was no accident that Chauncey Jerome's clocks spread throughout the nation along with the market economy. The new methods of doing business involved a new and stricter sense of time. Factory life necessitated a more regimented schedule, where work began at the sound of a bell, workers kept machines going at a constant pace, and the day was divided into hours and even minutes.

Clocks began to invade private as well as public space. With mass production ordinary families could now afford clocks, and even farmers became more sensitive to time as they were integrated into the market. As one frontier traveler reported in 1844, "In Kentucky, in Indiana, in Illinois, in Missouri, and here in every dale in Arkansas, and in cabins where there was not a chair to sit on, there was sure to be a Connecticut clock."

## PROSPERITY AND ANXIETY

As Americans watched their nation's frontiers expand and its economy grow, many began to view history in terms of continuous improvement. The path of commerce, however, was not steadily upward. Rather, it advanced in a series of wrenching boom-bust cycles: accelerating growth, followed by a crash, and then depression.

The country remained extraordinarily prosperous from 1815 until 1819, only to sink into a depression that lasted from 1819 to 1823. During the next cycle, the economy expanded slowly during the 1820s, followed by almost frenzied speculation in the 1830s. Then came the inevitable contraction in 1837, and the country suffered an even more severe depression from 1839 to 1843. The third cycle followed the familiar pattern: gradual economic growth during the 1840s, frantic expansion in the 1850s, and a third depression, which began in 1857 and lasted until the Civil War. In each of these depressions, thousands of workers were thrown out of work, overextended farmers lost their farms, and many businesses closed their doors.

*Boom-bust cycle*

The impact of the boom-bust cycle can be seen in the contrasting fates of two Americans who moved west in search of opportunity. In 1820, 17-year-old Benjamin Remington left Hancock, Massachusetts, for western New York, which was just being opened to white settlement. After working at several jobs, he managed to purchase on credit a 150-acre farm near the growing city of Rochester. Remington's timing was ideal. In 1823, two years after his arrival, the new Erie Canal came through town. Wheat prices rose, flour shipments from the region shot up, and Remington prospered supplying food for eastern markets. Over the years, he added to his acreage, built a comfortable family home, and was elected town supervisor. For Remington, the West was indeed a land of opportunity.

Somewhat younger, Addison Ward left Virginia for Indiana when he came of age in 1831. Unfortunately, by the time Ward arrived in Greene County, the best land had already been claimed. All he could afford was 80 acres of rough government land, which he bought in 1837 largely on credit. The region lacked adequate transportation to outside markets, but the economy was booming, and the state had begun an ambitious internal improvements program. Ward's timing, however, could not have been worse. Almost immediately the country entered a depression, driving farm prices and land values downward. Overwhelmed by debts, Ward sold his farm and fell into the ranks of tenant farmers. He continued to struggle until his death around 1850. Catching the wrong end of the boom-bust cycle, Ward never achieved economic success and social respectability.

In such an environment, prosperity, like personal success, seemed all too fleeting. Because Americans believed the good times would not last—that the bubble would burst and another "panic" set in—their optimism was often tinged *Popular anxiety* by insecurity and anxiety. They knew too many individuals like Chauncey Jerome, who had been rich and then lost all their wealth in a downturn.

## The Panic of 1819

The initial shock of this boom-and-bust psychology came with the Panic of 1819, the first major depression in the nation's history. From 1815 to 1818 cotton had commanded truly fabulous prices on the Liverpool market, reaching 32.5 cents a pound in 1818. In this heady prosperity, the federal government extended liberal credit for land purchases, and the new national bank encouraged merchants and farmers to borrow in order to catch the rising tide.

But in 1819 the price of cotton collapsed and took the rest of the economy with it. As the inflationary bubble burst, land values, which had been driven to *National depression* new heights by the speculative fever, plummeted 50 to 75 percent almost overnight. As the economy went slack, so did the demand for western foodstuffs and eastern manufactured goods and services, sending the nation reeling into a severe depression.

Because the market economy had spread to new areas, this downturn affected not only urban Americans but those living in the countryside as well. Many farmers, especially in newly settled regions, had bought their land on credit, and others in established areas had expanded their operations in anticipation of future returns. When prices fell, both groups were hard-pressed to pay their debts. New cotton planters in the Southwest, who were especially vulnerable to fluctuations in the world market, were particularly hard-hit.

In the wake of the Panic of 1819, the new nationalism's spirit of cooperation gave way to jealousy and conflict between competing interests and social groups. One consequence was an increase in sectional tensions, but the panic affected political life in even more direct ways. As the depression deepened and hardship spread, Americans viewed government policies as at least partly to blame. The postwar nationalism, after all, had been based on the belief that government should stimulate economic development through a national bank and protective tariff, by improving transportation, and by opening up new lands. As Americans struggled to make sense of their new economic order, they looked to take more direct control of the government that was so actively shaping their lives. During the 1820s, the popular response to the market and the Panic of 1819 produced a strikingly new kind of politics in the Republic.

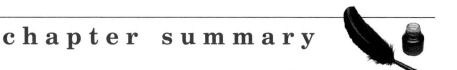

# chapter summary

By uniting the country in a single market, the market revolution transformed the United States during the quarter century after 1815.

- The federal government promoted the creation of a market through a protective tariff, a national bank, and internal improvements.

- The development of new forms of transportation, including canals, steamboats, and eventually railroads, allowed goods to be transported cheaply on land.

- The Supreme Court adopted a pro-business stance that encouraged investment and risk-taking.

- Economic expansion generated greater national wealth, but it also brought social and intellectual change.

 – Americans pursued opportunity, embraced a new concept of progress, viewed change as normal, developed a strong materialist ethic, and considered wealth the primary means to determine status.

 – Entrepreneurs reorganized their operations to increase production and sell in a wider market.

- The earliest factories were built to serve the textile industry, and the first laborers in them were young women from rural families.

 – Factory work imposed on workers a new discipline based on time and strict routine.

 – Workers' declining status led them to form unions and resort to strikes, but the depression that began in 1837 destroyed these organizations.

- The market revolution distributed wealth much more unevenly and left Americans feeling alternatively buoyant and anxious about their social and economic status.
  - Social mobility existed, but it was more limited than popular belief claimed.
- The economy lurched up and down in a boom-bust cycle.
- In hard times, Americans looked to the government to relieve economic distress.

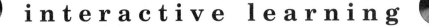

# interactive learning

The Primary Source Investigator CD-ROM offers the following materials related to this chapter:

- Interactive maps: **Slavery and the Cotton Kingdom** (M11) and **The Transportation Revolution, 1830–1890** (M12)
- A collection of primary sources, including many exploring the massive economic expansion that occurred in this period. Other documents demonstrate social changes connected to the rise of the cotton kingdom, including patent diagrams of the cotton gin and advertisements selling western land investment opportunities. Also read about the building of the National Road.

 For quizzes and a variety of interactive resources, visit the book's Online Learning Center at www.mhhe.com/davidsonconcise4.

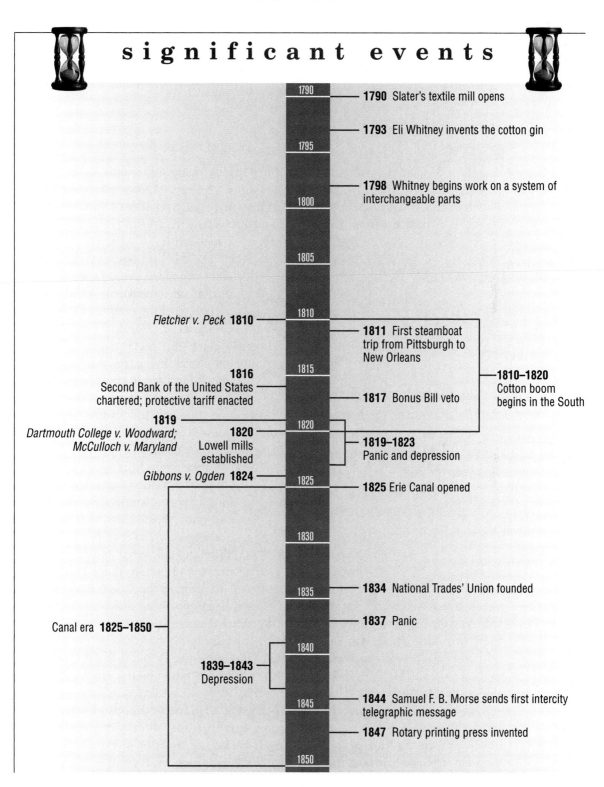

# significant events

**1790** Slater's textile mill opens

**1793** Eli Whitney invents the cotton gin

**1798** Whitney begins work on a system of interchangeable parts

*Fletcher v. Peck* **1810**

**1811** First steamboat trip from Pittsburgh to New Orleans

**1816** Second Bank of the United States chartered; protective tariff enacted

**1817** Bonus Bill veto

**1810–1820** Cotton boom begins in the South

**1819**
*Dartmouth College v. Woodward; McCulloch v. Maryland*

**1820** Lowell mills established

**1819–1823** Panic and depression

*Gibbons v. Ogden* **1824**

**1825** Erie Canal opened

Canal era **1825–1850**

**1834** National Trades' Union founded

**1837** Panic

**1839–1843** Depression

**1844** Samuel F. B. Morse sends first intercity telegraphic message

**1847** Rotary printing press invented

out of Missouri in 1839. In response, Smith established a new holy city, Nauvoo, along the Mississippi River in Illinois.

At Nauvoo, Smith introduced the most distinctive features of Mormon theology, including baptism for the dead, eternal marriage, and polygamy, or plural marriage. As a result, Mormonism increasingly diverged from traditional Christianity and became a distinct new religion. Neighboring *City of Zion: Nauvoo* residents, alarmed by the Mormons' growing political power and reports that church leaders were practicing polygamy, demanded that Nauvoo's charter be revoked and the church suppressed. In 1844 Smith was murdered by an anti-Mormon mob. The Mormons abandoned Nauvoo in 1846, and the following year Brigham Young, Smith's successor, led them westward to Utah (page 388). Nauvoo ceased to be a holy city.

## Socialist Communities

The hardship and poverty that accompanied the growth of industrial factories inspired utopian communities based on science and reason rather than religion. Robert Owen, a Scottish industrialist, came to the United States in 1824 and founded the community of New Harmony in Indiana. Owen *Owen's New Harmony* believed that the character of individuals was shaped by their surroundings, and that by changing those surroundings, one could change human character. Unfortunately, most of the 900 or so volunteers who flocked to New Harmony lacked the skills and commitment needed to make the community a success, and bitter factions soon split the settlement.

The experience of New Harmony and other communities demonstrated that the United States was poor soil for socialistic experiments. Wages were too high and land too cheap to interest most Americans in collectivist ventures. And individualism was too strong to create a commitment to cooperative action.

## The Temperance Movement

The most significant reform movements of the period sought not to withdraw from society but to change it directly. One of the most determined of these was the temperance movement.

The origins of the campaign lay in the heavy drinking of the early nineteenth century. Alcohol consumption soared after the Revolution, so that by 1830 the average American consumed four gallons of absolute alcohol a year, the highest level in American history and nearly triple present-day levels. Anne Royale, whose travels took her cross-country by stage, reported, "When I was in Virginia, it was too much whiskey—in Ohio, too much whiskey—in Tennessee, it is too, too much whiskey!" The social costs for such habits were high: broken families, abused and neglected wives and children, sickness and disability, poverty, and crime. The temperance movement undertook to eliminate these problems by curbing drinking.

Led largely by clergy, the movement at first focused on drunkenness and did not oppose moderate drinking. But in 1826 the American Temperance Society was founded, taking voluntary abstinence as its goal. During the next decade approximately 5000 local temperance societies were founded. As the movement gained momentum, annual per capita consumption of alcohol dropped sharply, so that by 1845 it had fallen below two gallons a year.

*The move toward abstinence*

The temperance movement was more sustained and more popular than other reforms. It appealed to young and old, to urban and rural residents, to workers and businesspeople. And it was the only reform movement with significant support in the South. Its success came partly for social reasons. Democracy necessitated sober voters; factories required sober workers. Temperance attracted the upwardly mobile—professionals and skilled artisans anxious to improve their social standing. Finally, temperance advocates stressed the suffering that men inflicted on women and children, and thus the movement appealed to women as a means to defend the home and carry out their domestic mission.

## Educational Reform

In 1800 Massachusetts was the only state requiring free public schools supported by community funds. The call for tax-supported education arose first among workers, as a means to restore their deteriorating position in society. But middle-class

Prison reformers believed that rigid discipline, extensive rules, and (in some programs) solitary confinement were necessary to rehabilitate criminals. Prisoners often had to march lockstep under strict supervision and wear uniforms such as those seen in this photograph from the 1870s.

reformers quickly took control of the movement, looking to uplift common citizens and make them responsible. Reformers appealed to business leaders by arguing that the new economic order needed educated workers.

Under Horace Mann's leadership, Massachusetts adopted a minimum-length school year, provided for training of teachers, and expanded the curriculum to include subjects such as history, geography, and various applied skills. Still, outside of Massachusetts there were only a few high schools. Moreover, attendance was rarely compulsory, and many poor parents sent their children to work instead of school. Nevertheless, by the 1850s the number of schools, attendance figures, and school budgets had all increased sharply. School reformers enjoyed their greatest success in the Northeast and the least in the South, where planters opposed paying taxes to educate poorer white children.

Educational opportunities for women also expanded. Teachers like Catharine Beecher and Emma Hunt Willard established a number of private girls' schools, putting to rest the objection of many male educators that fragile female minds could not absorb large doses of mathematics, physics, or geography. In 1833 Oberlin became the nation's first coeducational college. Four years later Mary Lyon founded Mount Holyoke, the first American college for women.

*Female education*

## The Asylum Movement

After 1820 there was also a dramatic increase in the number of asylums of every sort—orphanages, jails, and hospitals. Advocates of asylums called for isolating and separating the criminal, the insane, the ill, and the dependent from outside society. The goal of care in asylums, which earlier had focused on confinement, shifted to the reform of personal character.

Dorothea Dix, a Boston schoolteacher, took the lead in advocating state-supported asylums for the mentally ill. She attracted much attention to the movement by her report detailing the horrors to which the mentally ill were subjected, including being chained, kept in cages and closets, and beaten with rods. In response to her efforts, 28 states maintained mental institutions by 1860.

Like other reform movements, the push for new asylums and better educational facilities reflected overtones of both liberation and control. Asylums freed prisoners and the mentally ill from the harsh punishments of the past, but the new techniques of "rehabilitation" forced prisoners to march in lockstep. Education brought with it the freedom to question and to acquire knowledge, but some reformers hoped that schools would become as orderly as prisons. Louis Dwight, who advocated solitary confinement for prisoners at night and total silence by day, suggested eagerly that such methods "would greatly promote order, seriousness, and purity in large families, male and female boarding schools, and colleges."

*Order and social control*

## ABOLITIONISM

In the fall of 1834, Lyman Beecher, as president of Lane Seminary in Cincinnati, was continuing his efforts to "overturn and overturn" on behalf of the kingdom of God. The school had everything needed by an institution for training ministers to convert the West—everything, that is, except students. In October all but 8 of Lane's 100 students had departed after months of bitter controversy with Beecher and the trustees over the issue of abolition.

Beecher knew the source of his troubles: a scruffy yet magnetic student named Theodore Dwight Weld. Weld had been firing up his classmates over the need to immediately free the slaves. Beecher was not surprised, for Weld had been converted by that incendiary Finney. He knew, too, that Weld was a follower of William Lloyd Garrison, whose abolitionist writings had sent shock waves across the entire nation. Indeed, Beecher's troubles at Lane Seminary provided only one example of how the flames of reform, when fanned, could spread along paths not anticipated by those who first kindled them.

### *The Beginnings of the Abolitionist Movement*

William Lloyd Garrison symbolized the transition from a moderate antislavery movement to the more militant abolitionism of the 1830s. A deeply religious young man, Garrison endorsed the colonization movement, which advocated sending blacks to Africa, and went to Baltimore in 1829 to work for Benjamin Lundy, who edited the leading antislavery newspaper in the country.

It was in Baltimore that Garrison first encountered the opinions of free African Americans, who played a major role in launching the abolitionist movement. To Garrison's surprise, most of them strongly opposed the colonization movement as proslavery and antiblack. "This is our home, and this is our country," a free black convention proclaimed in 1831. "Here we were born, and here we will die." Under their influence, Garrison soon developed views far more radical than Lundy's, and within a year of moving to Baltimore, the young firebrand was convicted of libel and imprisoned.

Upon his release Garrison hurried back to Boston, determined to publish a new kind of antislavery journal. On January 1, 1831, the first issue of *The Liberator*

*Garrison's immediatism*

appeared, and abolitionism was born. In appearance, the bespectacled Garrison seemed frail, almost mousy, but in print he was abrasive, withering, and uncompromising. "On this subject, I do not wish to think, or speak, or write with moderation," he proclaimed. "I am in earnest—I will not equivocate—I will not excuse—I will not retreat a single inch—AND I WILL BE HEARD." Repudiating gradual emancipation and embracing "immediatism," Garrison insisted that slavery end at once. He denounced colonization as a racist movement and upheld the principle of racial equality. To those who suggested that slaveowners should be compensated for freeing their slaves, Garrison was firm.

Southerners ought to be convinced by "moral suasion" to renounce slavery as a sin. Virtue was its own reward.

Garrison attracted the most attention, but other abolitionists spoke with equal conviction. Wendell Phillips, from a socially prominent Boston family, held listeners spellbound with his speeches. Lewis Tappan and his brother Arthur, two New York City silk merchants, boldly placed their wealth behind various humanitarian causes, including abolitionism. James G. Birney, an Alabama slaveholder, converted to abolitionism after wrestling with his conscience, and Angelina and Sarah Grimké, the daughters of a South Carolina planter, left their native state to speak against the institution. And there was Angelina's future husband, Theodore Weld, the restless student at Lane Seminary who had fallen so dramatically under Garrison's influence.

To abolitionists, slavery was a moral, not an economic, question. The institution seemed a contradiction of the principle of the American Revolution that all human beings had been created with natural rights. Abolitionists condemned slavery because of the breakup of marriages and families by sale, the harsh punishment of the lash, slaves' lack of access to education, and the sexual abuse of black women. But most of all, abolitionists denounced slavery as outrageously contrary to Christian teaching. As one Ohio antislavery paper declared, "We believe slavery to be a sin, always, everywhere, and only, sin—sin, in itself." Abolitionism forced the churches to face the question of slavery head-on, and in the 1840s the Methodist and Baptist churches each split into northern and southern organizations over the issue.

## The Spread of Abolitionism

After helping organize the New England Anti-Slavery Society in 1832, Garrison joined with Lewis Tappan and Theodore Weld the following year to establish a national organization, the American Anti-Slavery Society. During the years before the Civil War, perhaps 200,000 northerners belonged to an abolitionist society.

Abolitionists were concentrated in the East, especially New England, and in areas that had been settled by New Englanders, such as western New York and northern Ohio. The movement was not strong in cities or among businesspeople and workers. Most abolitionists were young, being generally in their 20s and 30s when the movement began, and had grown up in rural areas and small towns in middle-class families. Intensely religious, many had been profoundly affected by the revivals of the Second Great Awakening.

*Support for abolitionism*

Certainly Theodore Weld was cut from this mold. After enrolling in Lane Seminary in 1833, he promoted immediate abolitionism among his fellow students. Unlike some abolitionists, who opposed slavery but disdained blacks as inferior, Lane students mingled freely with Cincinnati's free black population. In the summer of 1834, Beecher and Lane's trustees forbade any discussion of slavery on campus and ordered students to return to their studies. All but a handful left the school and enrolled at Oberlin College, where Charles Finney was professor of theology.

Black abolitionist Frederick Douglass (second from left at the podium) was only one of nearly 50 runaway slaves who appeared at an abolitionist convention held in August 1850 in Cazenovia, New York. Other runaways included Emily and Mary Edmonson (both in plaid dresses). When the Edmonsons' attempt at escape failed, Henry Ward Beecher (Lyman Beecher's son) rallied his congregation in Brooklyn to raise the money to purchase the girls' freedom.

Free African Americans, who made up the majority of subscribers to Garrison's *Liberator*, provided important support and leadership for the movement. Frederick Douglass assumed the greatest prominence. Having escaped from slavery in Maryland, he became an eloquent critic of its evils. Initially a follower of Garrison, Douglass eventually broke with him and started his own newspaper in Rochester. Other important black abolitionists included Martin Delany, William Wells Brown, William Still, and Sojourner Truth. Most black Americans endorsed peaceful means to end slavery, but David Walker in his *Appeal to the Colored Citizens of the World* (1829) urged slaves to use violence to end bondage.

*African American abolitionists*

A network of antislavery sympathizers developed in the North to convey runaway slaves to Canada and freedom. While not as extensive or as tightly organized as contemporaries claimed, the Underground Railroad hid fugitives and transported them northward from one station to the next. Free African Americans, who were more readily trusted by wary slaves, played a leading role in the Underground Railroad. One of its most famous conductors was Harriet Tubman, an escaped slave who repeatedly returned to the South and eventually escorted more than 200 slaves to freedom.

## Opponents and Divisions

The drive for immediate abolition faced massive obstacles, no matter how fervent its advocates. With slavery increasingly important to the South's economic life, the abolitionist cause encountered extreme hostility there. And in the North, where racism was equally entrenched, abolitionism provoked bitter resistance. Even abolitionists like Garrison treated blacks paternalistically, contending that they should occupy a subordinate place in the antislavery movement.

*Hostility toward abolitionists*

On occasion, northern resistance turned violent. An anti-abolitionist mob burned down the headquarters of the American Anti-Slavery Society in Philadelphia, and in 1837 in Alton, Illinois, Elijah Lovejoy was murdered when he tried to protect his printing press from an angry crowd. The leaders of these mobs were not from the bottom of society but, as one of their victims noted, were "gentlemen of property and standing." Prominent leaders in the community, they reacted vigorously to the threat that abolitionists posed to their power and prosperity and to the established order.

But abolitionists were also hindered by divisions among reformers. At Oberlin College Finney, too, ended up opposing Theodore Weld's fervent abolitionism. More conservative than Finney, Lyman Beecher saw his son Edward stand guard over Elijah Lovejoy's printing press the evening before the editor's murder. Within another decade, Beecher would see his daughter Harriet Beecher Stowe write the most successful piece of antislavery literature in the nation's history, *Uncle Tom's Cabin* (page 411). Even the abolitionists themselves splintered. More conservative reformers wanted to work within established institutions, using churches and political action to end slavery. But for Garrison and his followers, the mob violence demonstrated that slavery was only part of a deeper national disease, whose cure required the overthrow of American institutions and values.

*Divisions among reformers*

By the end of the decade, Garrison had worked out a program for the total reform of society. He embraced perfectionism, denounced the clergy, and urged members to leave the churches. Condemning the Constitution as proslavery—"a covenant with death and an agreement with hell"—he argued that no person of conscience could participate in the corrupt political system. This platform was radical enough on all counts, but the final straw for Garrison's opponents was his endorsement of women's rights as an inseparable part of abolitionism.

## The Women's Rights Movement

Women faced many disadvantages in American society. They were kept out of most jobs, denied political rights, and given only limited access to education beyond the elementary grades. When a woman married, her husband became the legal representative of the marriage and gained complete control of her property. Any unmarried woman was made the ward of a male relative.

When abolitionists divided over the issue of female participation, women found it easy to identify with the situation of slaves, since both were victims of male tyranny. Sarah and Angelina Grimké took up the cause of women's rights after they were criticized for speaking to audiences that included men as well as women. Sarah, who had wanted to be a lawyer, responded with *Letters on the Condition of Women and the Equality of the Sexes* (1838), a pioneering feminist tract that argued that women deserved the same rights as men. Abby Kelly, another abolitionist, remarked that women "have good cause to be grateful to the slave," for in "striving to strike his irons off, we found most surely, that we were manacled *ourselves.*"

Two abolitionists, Elizabeth Cady Stanton and Lucretia Mott, launched the women's rights movement after they were forced to sit behind a cur-

*Seneca Falls convention*

tain at a world antislavery convention in London. In 1848 Stanton and Mott organized a conference in Seneca Falls, New York, that attracted about a hundred supporters. The meeting issued a Declaration of Sentiments, modeled after the Declaration of Independence, that began, "All men and women are created equal." The Seneca Falls convention approved resolutions calling for educational and professional opportunities for women, control by women of their property, recognition of legal equality, and repeal of laws awarding the father custody of the children in divorce. The most controversial proposal, and the only resolution that did not pass unanimously, was one demanding the right to vote. The Seneca Falls convention established the arguments and the program for the women's rights movement for the remainder of the century.

Elizabeth Cady Stanton, one of the instigators and guiding spirits at the Seneca Falls convention, photographed with two of her children about that time.

The women's rights movement won few victories before 1860. Several states gave women greater control over their property, and a few made divorce easier or granted women the right to sue in courts. But disappointments and defeats outweighed these early victories. Still, many of the important leaders in the crusade for women's rights that emerged after the Civil War had already taken their places at the forefront of the movement. They included Stanton, Susan B. Anthony, Lucy Stone, and—as

Lyman Beecher by now must have expected—one of his daughters, Isabella Beecher Hooker.

## The Schism of 1840

It was Garrison's position on women's rights that finally split antislavery ranks asunder. The showdown came in 1840 at the national meeting of the American Anti-Slavery Society, when delegates debated whether women could hold office in the organization. Garrison's opponents feared that this issue would drive off potential supporters, but Garrison carried the day. His opponents, led by Lewis Tappan, resigned to found the rival American and Foreign Anti-Slavery Society.

The schism of 1840 lessened the influence of abolitionism as a benevolent reform movement in American society. Although abolitionism heightened moral concern about slavery, it failed to convert the North to its program, and its supporters remained a tiny minority. For all the considerable courage they showed, their movement suffered from the lack of a realistic, long-range plan for eliminating so deeply entrenched an institution. Garrison even boasted that "the genius of the abolitionist movement is to have *no* plan." Abolitionism demonstrated the serious limitations of moral suasion and individual conversions as a solution to deeply rooted social problems.

## REFORM SHAKES THE PARTY SYSTEM

"What a fog-bank we are in politically! Do you see any head-land or light—or can you get an observation—or soundings?" The words came from a puzzled Whig politician writing a friend after the Massachusetts state elections of 1853. He was in such a confused state because reformers were increasingly entering the political arena to achieve their goals.

The crusading idealism of revivalists and reformers inevitably collided with the hard reality that society could not be perfected by converting individuals. In America's democratic society, politics and government coercion promised a more effective means to impose a new moral vision on the nation.

Politicians did not particularly welcome the new interest. Because the Whig and Democratic parties both drew on evangelical and nonevangelical voters, heated moral debates over the harmful effects of drink or the evils of slavery threatened to detach regular party members from their old loyalties.

## Women and the Right to Vote

As the focus of change and reform shifted toward the political arena, women in particular lost influence. As major participants in the benevolent organizations of the 1820s and 1830s, they had used their efforts on behalf of "moral suasion." But since women could not vote, they felt excluded when the temperance and abolitionist movements turned to electoral action to accomplish their goals. By the 1840s female reformers increasingly demanded the right to vote as the means to reform society.

Previously, many female reformers had accepted the right of petition as their most appropriate political activity. But *The Lily*, a women's rights paper, soon changed its tack. "Why shall [women] be left only the poor resource of petition?" it asked. "For even petitions, when they are from women, without the elective franchise to give them backbone, are of but little consequence."

### The Maine Law

Although drinking had significantly declined in American society by 1840, it had hardly been eliminated. After 1845 the arrival of large numbers of German and Irish immigrants, who were accustomed to consuming alcohol, made voluntary prohibition even more remote. In response, temperance advocates proposed state laws that would outlaw the manufacture and sale of alcoholic beverages. If liquor was unavailable, reformers reasoned, the attitude of drinkers was unimportant: they would be forced to reform whether they wanted to or not.

The issue of prohibition cut across party lines, with large numbers of Whigs and Democrats on both sides of the question. When party leaders tried to dodge the issue, the temperance movement adopted the strategy of endorsing the legislative candidates who pledged to support a prohibitory law. To win additional recruits, temperance leaders took up techniques used in political campaigns, including house-to-house canvasses, parades and processions, bands and singing, banners, picnics, and mass rallies.

The temperance movement's first major triumph came in 1851 in Maine. The Maine Law, as it was known, authorized search and seizure of private property and provided stiff penalties for selling liquor. In the next few years a number of states enacted similar laws, although most were struck down by the courts or later repealed.

Even though prohibition had been temporarily defeated, the issue badly disrupted the unity of the Whig and Democratic parties. It detached a number

*Effect on the party system*

of voters from both coalitions, greatly increased the extent of party switching, and brought to the polls a large number of new voters, including many "wets" who wanted to preserve their right to drink. By dissolving the ties between so many voters and their parties, the temperance issue played a major role in the eventual collapse of the Jacksonian party system in the 1850s.

### Abolitionism and the Party System

Abolition was the most divisive issue to come out of the benevolent movement. In 1835 abolitionists distributed over a million pamphlets through the post office to southern whites. A wave of excitement swept the South when the first batches arrived. Former senator Robert Hayne led a Charleston mob that burned sacks of U.S. mail containing abolitionist literature, and postmasters in other southern cities refused to deliver the material. When the Jackson administration acquiesced in this censorship, abolitionists protested that their civil rights had been violated. In reaction, the number of antislavery societies in the North nearly tripled.

*Censorship of the mails*

With access to the mails impaired, abolitionists began flooding Congress with petitions against slavery. Asserting that Congress had no power over the institution, angry southern representatives persuaded the House to adopt the so-called gag rule in 1836. It tabled without consideration any petition dealing with slavery. Claiming that the right of petition was also under attack by slavery's champions, abolitionists gained new supporters. In 1844 the House finally repealed the controversial rule.

*The gag rule*

Many abolitionists outside Garrison's extreme circle were increasingly convinced that an antislavery third party offered a more effective means of attacking slavery. In 1840 these political abolitionists founded the Liberty party and nominated for president James Birney, a former slaveholder who had converted to abolitionism. Birney received only 7000 votes, but the Liberty party was the seed from which a stronger antislavery political movement would grow. In the next two decades, abolitionism's greatest importance would be in the political arena rather than as a voluntary reform organization.

After two decades of fiery revivals, benevolent crusades, utopian experiments, and Transcendental philosophizing, the ferment of reform had spread through urban streets, canal town churches, frontier clearings, and the halls of Congress. Abolition, potentially the most dangerous issue, seemed still under control in 1840. Birney's small vote, coupled with the disputes between the two national antislavery societies, encouraged political leaders to believe that the party system had turned back this latest threat of sectionalism.

But the growing northern concern about slavery highlighted differences between the two sections. Despite the strength of evangelicalism in the South, the reform impulse spawned by the revivals found little support there, since reform movements were discredited by their association with abolitionism. The party system confronted the difficult challenge of holding together sections that, although sharing much, were also diverging in important ways. To the residents of both sections, the South increasingly seemed to be a unique society with its own distinctive way of life.

# chapter summary

The Jacksonian era produced the greatest number of significant reform movements in American history.

- The movements grew out of the revivals of the Second Great Awakening, which emphasized emotion and preached the doctrines of good works and salvation available to all.
  - Evangelical Protestantism also endorsed the ideals of perfectionism and millennialism.
  - The revival theology helped people adjust to the pressures in their daily lives created by the new market economy.
- Romanticism, which emphasized the unlimited potential of each individual, also strengthened reform.
- Women's role in society was now defined by the ideal of domesticity—that women's lives should center on the home and the family.

- Middle-class women turned to religion and reform as ways to shape society.
- Utopian communities sought to establish a model society for the rest of the world to follow.
- Humanitarian movements combated a variety of social evils.
  - Crusades for temperance, educational reform, and the establishment of asylums all gained significant support.
  - Abolitionism precipitated both strong support and violent opposition, and the movement itself split in 1840.
- Temperance, abolitionism, and women's rights movements all turned to political action to accomplish their goals.
- Although it survived, the party system was seriously weakened by these reform movements.

# interactive learning

The Primary Source Investigator CD-ROM offers the following materials related to this chapter:

- A collection of primary sources exploring the growing fever for reform in the United States, including Abraham Lincoln's discussion of the Declaration of Independence and the Constitution in regard to slavery and the Declaration of Sentiments, an appeal to Americans for equal treatment of women. Other sources include a certificate of freedom for Harriet Bolling in Petersburg, Virginia; a newspaper produced for a nineteenth-century factory; and an image of a homespun stocking.

For quizzes and a variety of interactive resources, visit the book's Online Learning Center at www.mhhe.com/davidsonconcise4.

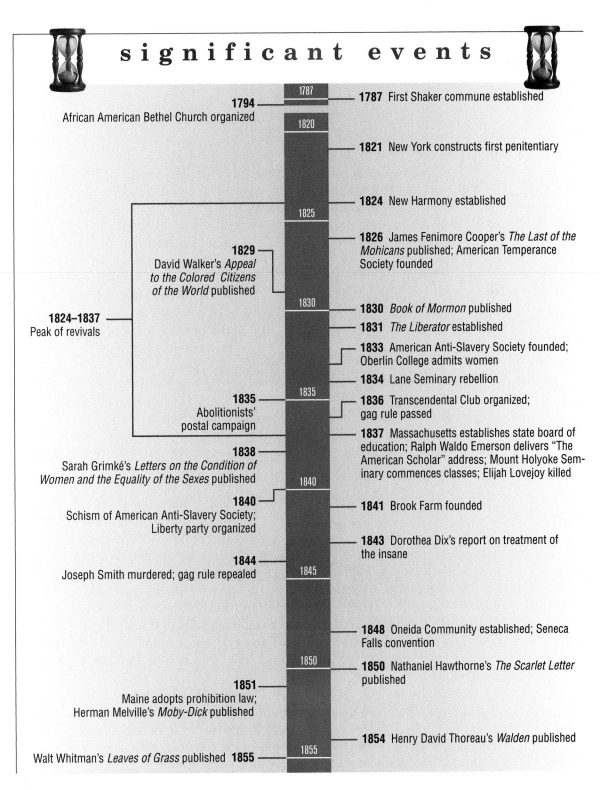

# significant events

**1787** First Shaker commune established

**1794**
African American Bethel Church organized

1787

1820

**1821** New York constructs first penitentiary

**1824** New Harmony established

1825

**1826** James Fenimore Cooper's *The Last of the Mohicans* published; American Temperance Society founded

**1829**
David Walker's *Appeal to the Colored Citizens of the World* published

1830

**1824–1837**
Peak of revivals

**1830** *Book of Mormon* published

**1831** *The Liberator* established

**1833** American Anti-Slavery Society founded; Oberlin College admits women

**1834** Lane Seminary rebellion

1835

**1835**
Abolitionists' postal campaign

**1836** Transcendental Club organized; gag rule passed

**1837** Massachusetts establishes state board of education; Ralph Waldo Emerson delivers "The American Scholar" address; Mount Holyoke Seminary commences classes; Elijah Lovejoy killed

**1838**
Sarah Grimké's *Letters on the Condition of Women and the Equality of the Sexes* published

1840

**1840**
Schism of American Anti-Slavery Society; Liberty party organized

**1841** Brook Farm founded

**1843** Dorothea Dix's report on treatment of the insane

**1844**
Joseph Smith murdered; gag rule repealed

1845

**1848** Oneida Community established; Seneca Falls convention

1850

**1850** Nathaniel Hawthorne's *The Scarlet Letter* published

**1851**
Maine adopts prohibition law; Herman Melville's *Moby-Dick* published

**1854** Henry David Thoreau's *Walden* published

1855

Walt Whitman's *Leaves of Grass* published **1855**

# CHAPTER 13

**T**he impeccably dressed Colonel Daniel Jordan, master of 261 slaves at Laurel Hill, strolls down his oak-lined lawn to the dock along the Waccamaw River, a day's journey north of Charleston, to board the steamship *Nina*. On Fridays, it is Colonel Jordan's custom to visit the exclusive Hot and Hot Fish

# The Old South
## 1820–1860

**Preview** *In the decades before the Civil War, the rural South depended on the export of staple crops like rice, tobacco, sugar, and cotton—and the slave labor used to produce them. Though most southern whites did not own slaves, those who did reaped prestige, political influence, and wealth. Excluded from white society, enslaved African Americans resisted bondage and developed their own culture, whose religion, songs, and shared experiences helped them survive a cruel and arbitrary regime.*

Club, founded by his fellow low-country planters, to play a game of lawn bowling or billiards and be waited on by black servants in livery as he sips an iced mint julep in the refined atmosphere that for him is the South.

Several hundred miles to the west another steamboat, the *Fashion*, makes its way along the Alabama River. One of the passengers is upset by the boat's slow pace. He has been away from his plantation in the Red River country of Texas and is eager to get back. "Time's money, time's money!" he mutters. "Time's worth more'n money to me now; a hundred percent more, 'cause I left my niggers all alone; not a damn white man within four mile on 'em." When asked what they are doing, since the cotton crop has already been picked, he says, "I set 'em to clairin', but they ain't doin' a damn thing. . . . But I'll make it up, I'll make it up when I get thar, now you'd better believe." For this Red River planter, time is money and cotton is his world—indeed, cotton is what the South is all about. "I am a cotton man, I am, and I don't car who knows it," he proclaims. "I know cotton, I do. I'm dam' if I know anythin' but cotton."

At the other end of the South, the slave Sam Williams works in the intense heat of Buffalo Forge, an iron-making factory nine miles from Lexington, Virginia, in the Shenandoah Valley. As a refiner, Williams has the most important job at the forge, alternately heating pig iron in the white-hot coals, then slinging the ball of glowing metal onto an anvil, where he pounds it with huge, water-powered hammers to remove the impurities. Ambitious and hardworking, he earns extra money (at the same rate paid to whites) for any iron he produces beyond his weekly quota. His wife, Nancy, who is in charge of the dairy, earns extra money as well, and their savings at the local bank total more than $150. The additional income helps them keep their family intact in an unstable environment: they know that their owner is unlikely to sell away slaves who work so hard. For Sam and Nancy Williams, family ties, worship at the local Baptist church, and socializing with their fellow slaves are what make life important.

In the bayous of the Deep South, only a few miles from where the Mississippi Delta meets the Gulf, Octave Johnson hears the dogs coming. For over a year now Johnson has been a runaway slave. He fled from a Louisiana plantation in St. James Parish when the overseer threatened to whip him for staying in bed. To survive, he hides in the swamps four miles behind the plantation—stealing turkeys, chickens, and pigs and trading with other slaves. As uncertain as this life is, nearly 30 other slaves have joined him over the past year.

This time when the pack of hounds bursts upon them, the slaves do not flee but kill as many dogs as possible. Then they plunge into the bayou. For Octave Johnson the real South is a matter of weighing one's prospects between

*Plantation Burial*, painted about 1860 by John Antrobus, portrays the black slave community from a Louisiana plantation burying a loved one. Religion played a central role in the life of slaves.

the uncertainties of alligators and the overseer's whip—and deciding when to say no.

Ferdinand Steel and his family are not forced, by the flick of the lash, to rise at five in the morning. They rise because the land demands it. Steel, in his 20s, owns 170 acres of land in Carroll County, Mississippi. His life is one of continuous hard work, caring for the animals and tending the crops. His mother, Eliza, and sister, Julia, have plenty to keep them busy: making soap, fashioning dippers out of gourds, sewing.

The Steel family grows cotton, too, but not with the single-minded devotion of the planter aboard the *Fashion*. Self-sufficiency and family security always come first, and Steel's total crop amounts to only five or six bales. His profit is never enough for him to consider buying even one slave. In fact, he would prefer not to raise any cotton—"We are to[o] weak handed," he explains—but the cotton means cash, and cash means that he can buy things he needs in nearby Grenada. Though fiercely independent, Steel and his scattered neighbors help each other raise houses, clear fields, shuck corn, and quilt. They depend on one another and are bound together by blood, religion, obligation, and honor. For small farmers like Ferdinand Steel, these ties constitute the real South.

The portraits could go on: different people, different Souths, all of them real. Such contrasts underscore the difficulty of trying to define a regional identity. Encompassing in 1860 the 15 slave states plus the District of Columbia, the South was a land of great social and geographic diversity.

Yet despite its many differences of people and geography, the South was bonded by ties so strong, they eventually outpulled those of the nation itself.

*Factors unifying the South* | At the heart of this unity was an agricultural system that took advantage of the region's warm climate and long growing season. Most important, this rural agricultural economy was based on the institution of slavery, which had far-reaching effects on all aspects of southern society. It shaped not only the culture of the slaves themselves but the lives of their masters and mistresses, and even of farm families and herders in the hills and backwoods, who saw few slaves from day to day. To understand the Old South, then, we must understand how the southern agricultural economy and the institution of slavery affected the social class structure of both white and black southerners.

## THE SOCIAL STRUCTURE OF THE COTTON KINGDOM

We have already seen (in Chapter 10) that the spread of cotton stimulated the nation's remarkable economic growth after the War of 1812. Demand spurred by the textile industry sent the price of cotton soaring on the international market, and white southerners scrambled into the fresh lands of the old Southwest to reap the profits to be made in the cotton sweepstakes.

## Deep South, Upper South

As Indian lands were opened to white settlement, word spread of the "black belt" region of central Alabama (map, below), where the dark, rich soil was particularly suited to growing cotton, and of the tremendous yields from the soils along the Mississippi River's broad reaches. "The Alabama Feaver rages here with great violence and has carried off vast numbers of our Citizens," a North Carolinian wrote in 1817. A generation later, in the 1830s, immigrants were still "pouring in with a ceaseless tide," an Alabama observer reported. But the booming frontier in the

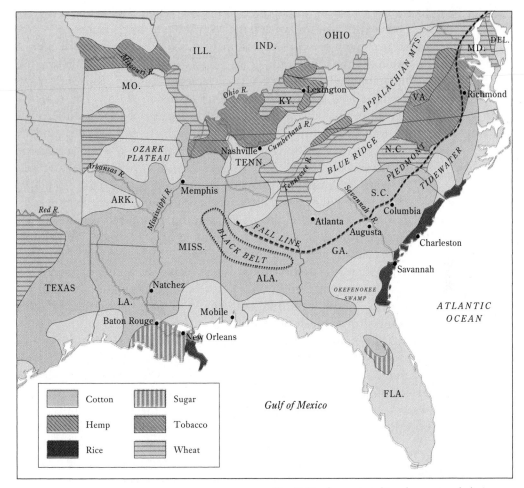

COTTON AND OTHER CROPS OF THE SOUTH  By 1860, the cotton kingdom extended across the Lower South into the Texas prairie and up the Mississippi River valley. Tobacco and hemp were the staple crops of the Upper South, where they competed with corn and wheat. Rice production was concentrated in the swampy coastal region of South Carolina and Georgia as well as the lower tip of Louisiana. The sugar district was in southern Louisiana.

Deep South pushed even farther west. By the 1840s residents were leaving Alabama and Mississippi and heading for fresher cotton lands along the Red River and up into Texas. Amazingly, by the eve of the Civil War nearly a third of the total cotton crop came from west of the Mississippi River.

As Senator James Henry Hammond of South Carolina boasted in 1858, cotton was king in the Old South. True, the region devoted more acreage to corn, but cotton was the primary export and the major source of southern wealth. Indeed, by 1860 the United States produced three-fourths of the world's supply of cotton. Per capita income among southern whites actually exceeded that of the free states, though wealth was not so evenly distributed in the plantation South as in northern agricultural areas.

*Cotton and southern prosperity*

This prosperity, however, masked basic problems in the economy—problems that would become more apparent after the Civil War. Much of the South's new wealth resulted from migration of its population to more productive western lands. The amount of prime agricultural land was limited, and once it was settled, the South could not sustain its rate of expansion.

Furthermore, the single-crop agriculture practiced by southern farmers (especially in tobacco and corn) rapidly wore out the soil. Planters and farmers in the Upper South increasingly shifted to wheat production to restore their soils, but because they now plowed fields rather than using the hoe, this shift accelerated soil erosion. So did destruction of the forests, particularly in the Piedmont, where commercial agriculture now took hold. In addition, reliance on a single crop increased toxins and parasites in the soil, making southern agriculture more vulnerable than diversified agriculture was.

*Environmental impact of single-crop agriculture*

Only the South's low population density eased such environmental damage. More remote areas remained heavily forested, wetlands were still extensive, and as late as 1860 eighty percent of the region was uncultivated. (Cattle and hogs, however, ranged over much of this acreage.)

Perhaps the most striking environmental consequence of the expansion of southern society was the increase in disease. Epidemic diseases such as malaria, yellow fever, and cholera were brought to the area by Europeans. The clearing of land—which increased runoff, precipitated floods, and produced pools of stagnant water—encouraged their spread, especially in the Lower South.

As cotton transformed the boom country of the Deep South, agriculture in the Upper South also adjusted.* Scientific agricultural practices reversed the decline in tobacco, which had begun in the 1790s. More important, farmers in the Upper South made wheat and corn their

*The Upper South's new orientation*

---

*The Upper South included the border states (Delaware, Maryland, Kentucky, and Missouri) and Virginia, North Carolina, Tennessee, and Arkansas. The states of the Deep South were South Carolina, Georgia, Florida, Alabama, Mississippi, Louisiana, and Texas.

major crops. Because the new crops required less labor, slaveholders in the Upper South sold their surplus slaves to planters in the Deep South. There, eager buyers paid as much as $1500 in the late 1850s for a prime field hand.

## The Rural South

The Old South, then, was expanding, dynamic, and booming economically. But the region remained overwhelmingly rural, with 84 percent of its labor force engaged in agriculture in 1860, compared with 40 percent in the North. Conversely, the South produced only 9 percent of the nation's *Lack of manufacturing* manufactured goods. Efforts to diversify the South's economy made little headway in the face of the high profits from cotton. With so little industry, few cities developed in the South. Only 1 in 10 southerners lived in cities and towns in 1860, compared with 1 out of 3 persons in the North. North Carolina, Florida, Alabama, Mississippi, Arkansas, and Texas did not contain a single city with a population of 10,000.

As a rural society, the South evidenced far less interest in education. Most wealthy planters opposed a state-supported school system, because they hired tutors or sent their children to private academies. Thus free public *White illiteracy* schools were rare: Georgia in 1860 had only one county with a free school system, and Mississippi had no public schools outside its few cities. The 1850 census showed that among native-born white citizens, 20 percent were unable to read and write. In the middle states the figure was 3 percent; in New England, only 0.4 percent.

## Distribution of Slavery

Even more than agrarian ways, slavery set the South apart. Whereas in 1776 slavery had been a national institution, by 1820 it was confined to the states south of Pennsylvania and the Ohio River. The South's "peculiar institution" bound white and black southerners together in a multitude of ways.

Slaves were not evenly distributed throughout the region. More than half lived in the Deep South, where African Americans outnumbered white southerners in both South Carolina and Mississippi by the 1850s. Elsewhere in the Deep South, the black population exceeded 40 percent in all states except Texas. In the Upper South, on the other hand, whites greatly outnumbered blacks. Only in Virginia and North Carolina did the slave population top 30 percent.

The distribution of slaves showed striking geographic variations within individual states as well. In areas of fertile soil, flat or rolling countryside, and good transportation, slavery and the plantation system dominated. In the pine barrens, areas isolated by lack of transportation, and hilly and mountainous regions, small family farms and few slaves were the rule.

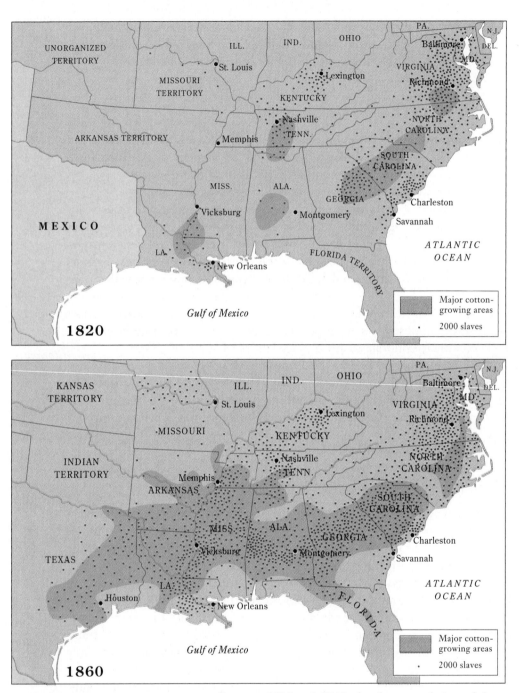

THE SPREAD OF SLAVERY, 1820–1860   Between 1820 and 1860, the slave population of the South shifted south and westward, concentrating especially heavily in coastal South Carolina and Georgia, in the black belt of central Alabama and Mississippi (so named because of its rich soil), and in the Mississippi valley.

Almost all enslaved African Americans, male and female, worked in agricultural pursuits, with only about 10 percent living in cities and towns. On large plantations, a few slaves were domestic servants, and others were skilled artisans— *Slave occupations* blacksmiths, carpenters, or bricklayers—but most toiled in the fields.

### Slavery as a Labor System

Slavery was, first and foremost, a system to manage and control labor. The plantation system, with its extensive estates and large labor forces, could never have developed without slavery. Slaves represented an enormous capital *Profitability of slavery* investment, worth more than all the land in the Old South. Furthermore, slavery remained a highly profitable investment. The average slaveowner spent perhaps $30 to $35 a year to support an adult slave; some expended as little as half that. Even at the higher cost of support, a slaveowner took about 60 percent of the annual wealth produced by a slave's labor. For those who pinched pennies and drove slaves harder, the profits were even greater.

By concentrating wealth and power in the hands of the planter class, slavery shaped the tone of southern society. Planters were not aristocrats in the European sense of having special legal privileges or formal titles of rank. Still, *Slavery and aristocratic values* the system encouraged southern planters to think of themselves as a landed gentry upholding the aristocratic values of pride, honor, family, and hospitality.

Public opinion in Europe and in the North grew increasingly hostile to the peculiar institution, causing white southerners to feel like an isolated minority defending an embattled position. Yet they clung tenaciously to slavery, for it was the base on which the South's economic growth and way of life rested. As one Georgian observed on the eve of the Civil War, slavery was "so intimately mingled with our social conditions that it would be impossible to eradicate it."

## CLASS STRUCTURE OF THE WHITE SOUTH

Once a year around Christmastime, James Henry Hammond gave a dinner for his neighbors at his South Carolina plantation, Silver Bluff. The richest man for miles around as well as an ambitious politician, the aristocratic Hammond used these dinners to put his neighbors under personal obligation to him as well as to receive the honor and respect he believed his due. Indeed, Hammond's social and political ambitions caused him to carefully cultivate his neighbors, despite his low opinion of them, by hiring them to perform various tasks and by providing them a variety of services such as ginning their cotton and allowing them to use his grist mill. These services enhanced his ethic of paternalism, but his less affluent neighbors also displayed a strong personal pride. After he ungraciously complained about the inconvenience of these services, only three of his neighbors came to his Christmas dinner in 1837, a snub that enraged him. As Hammond's

page 392). The arrangement gave the United States Puget Sound, which had been the president's objective all along.

## The Mexican War

The Oregon settlement left Polk free to deal with Mexico. In 1845 Congress admitted Texas to the Union as a slave state, but Mexico had never formally recognized Texas's independence. Mexico insisted, moreover, that Texas's southern boundary was the Nueces River, not the Rio Grande, 130 miles

*Disputed boundary of Texas*

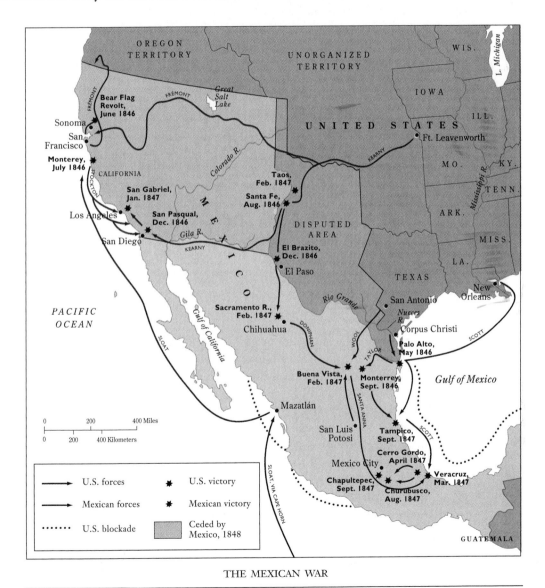

THE MEXICAN WAR

to the south, as claimed by Texas. In reality, Texas had never controlled the disputed region, but Polk, already looking toward the Pacific, supported the Rio Grande boundary.

Knowing that the Mexican government desperately needed money, the president attempted to buy New Mexico and California. But the Mexican public overwhelmingly opposed ceding any more territory to the land-hungry Yankees. Blocked on the diplomatic front, Polk ordered General Zachary Taylor to proceed south with American troops to the Rio Grande. From the Mexican standpoint, the Americans had invaded their country and occupied their territory. On April 25 Mexican forces clashed with Taylor's troops.

Polk had already resolved to send Congress a war message citing Mexico's refusal to negotiate when word arrived of the fighting along the Rio Grande. The president quickly revised his war message, placing the entire blame for the war on Mexico. "Mexico has passed the boundary of the United States, has invaded our territory, and shed American blood upon American soil," he told Congress on May 11. "War exists, and notwithstanding all our efforts to avoid it, exists by the act of Mexico herself." The administration sent a bill to Congress calling for volunteers and requesting money to supply American troops.

The war with Mexico posed a dilemma for Whigs. They were convinced (correctly) that Polk had provoked it in order to acquire more territory from Mexico, *Opposition to the war* and many northern Whigs accused the president of seeking to extend slavery. But they also feared that if they opposed the war, they would ruin their party. Therefore, they voted for military supply bills but, at the same time, strenuously attacked the conduct of "Mr. Polk's War" and, in an effort to curb sectional rivalries, opposed the acquisition of any territory from Mexico.

## The Price of Victory

Even before word of hostilities arrived in California, a group of impetuous American settlers around Sacramento launched the "Bear Flag Revolt." In June 1846 they proclaimed California an independent republic. American forces in the area soon put down any Mexican resistance, and by the following January California was safely in American hands.

Meanwhile, Taylor moved south from the Rio Grande and won several decisive battles, ending the war in the northern provinces. Polk had gained the territory he sought to reach the Pacific; now he wanted only peace. But *Conquest of Mexico* the Mexican people refused to support any government that sued for peace, so Polk ordered an invasion into the heart of the country. Only after an American army commanded by General Winfield Scott captured Mexico City on September 14, 1847, did Mexico surrender.

The war had cost $97 million and 13,000 American lives, mostly as a result of disease. Yet the real cost was even higher. By bringing vast new territories into the Union, the war forced the explosive slavery issue to the center of national politics and threatened to upset the balance of power between North and South.

Ralph Waldo Emerson had been prophetic when he declared that the conquest of Mexico "will poison us."

## The Rise of the Slavery Issue

The annexation of so much southwestern territory left not only northern Whigs but also many northern Democrats embittered. They complained that Polk, a Tennessee slaveholder, had compromised with the British on Oregon at the same time that he used military force to defend the absurd boundary claims of Texas. This discontent finally erupted in August 1846 when Polk requested $2 million from Congress. On August 8 David Wilmot, an obscure Pennsylvania congressman, startled Democratic leaders by introducing an amendment to the bill barring slavery from any territory acquired from Mexico. The Wilmot Proviso, as the amendment became known, passed the House of Representatives several times with strong northern support, only to be rejected in the Senate, where the South had greater power.

*Wilmot Proviso*

Wilmot was hardly an abolitionist. Indeed, he hoped to keep not only slaves but all black people out of the territories. "I would preserve for white free labor a fair country," he explained, ". . . where the sons of toil, of my own race and color, can live without the disgrace which association with negro slavery brings upon free labor." The Wilmot Proviso aimed not to destroy slavery in the South but to confine the institution to those states where it already existed.

The status of slavery in the territories became more than an abstract question when the Senate in 1848 ratified the Treaty of Guadalupe Hidalgo. Under its terms the United States acquired Mexico's provinces of New Mexico and Upper California in return for approximately $18 million. With the United States in control of the Pacific Coast from San Diego to Puget Sound, Polk's continental vision had become a reality.

*Peace treaty with Mexico*

## NEW SOCIETIES IN THE WEST

As Hispanic, Indian, Asian, and Anglo-American cultures mixed, the patterns of settlement along the frontier varied widely. In California the new settlements were overwhelmingly shaped by the rush for gold after 1848. And in the Great Basin around Salt Lake, the Mormons established a society whose sense of religious mission was as strong as that of the Puritans.

## Farming in the West

The overlanders expected to replicate the societies they had left behind. By the time a wagon train arrived at its destination, members had usually exhausted their resources, and they thus quickly scattered in search of employment or a good farm site.

In a process repeated over and over, settlers in a new area set up the machinery of government. Churches took longer to establish, for ministers were hard to

*Evolution of western society*

recruit and congregations were often not large enough to support a
church. As the population grew, however, a more conventional society evolved. Towns and a middle class developed, the proportion of
women increased, schools were established, and the residents became less mobile.

Although opportunity was greater on the frontier and early arrivals had a special advantage, more and more the agricultural frontier of the West resembled
the older society of the East. With the development of markets and transportation, wealth became concentrated; some families fell to the lower rungs of society, and those who were less successful left, seeking yet another fresh start.

## The Gold Rush

In January 1848, while constructing a sawmill along the American River, James
Marshall noticed gold flecks in the millrace. More discoveries followed, and when
the news reached the East, it spread like wildfire. The following spring the Overland Trail was jammed with eager "forty-niners." In only two years, from 1848
to the end of 1849, California's population jumped from 14,000 to 100,000. By
1860 it stood at 380,000.

Those intent on making a fortune and returning home gave no thought to
putting down roots. Mining camps literally appeared and died overnight, as word

*Life in the mining camps*

of a new strike sent miners racing off to another canyon, valley, or
streambed. More than 80 percent of the prospectors who poured into
the gold country were Americans, including free blacks. Mexicans,
Australians, Hawaiians, Chinese, French, English, and Irish also came. Whatever
their nationality, the new arrivals were overwhelmingly unmarried men in their
20s and 30s.

The constant movement, the hard labor of mining, the ready cash, and the
rootlessness all made camp society unstable. "There is an excitement connected
with the pursuit of gold which renders one restless and uneasy—ever hoping to
do something better," explained one forty-niner. Removed from the traditional
forms of social control, miners engaged in gambling, swearing, drinking, and
fighting. As a Denver paper complained during that territory's gold rush a few
years later, as soon as "men of decent appearance" reached a mining camp, they
"sang low songs, walked openly with the painted courtesans with whom the town
teems, and generally gave themselves up to what they term, 'a time!'"

Only about 5 percent of gold rush emigrants were women or children; given
this scarcity, men were willing to pay top dollar to women to cook, sew, and wash.

*Women in the camps*

Other women ran hotels and boardinghouses. "A smart woman can do
very well in this country," one woman informed a friend in the East.
"It is the only country I ever was in where a woman received anything like a just
compensation for work." Likewise, they suffered no shortage of suitors. "I had men

## Disappointment in the Gold Diggings

My expectations are not realized. We have been unlucky—or rather, by being inexperienced, we selected a poor spot for a location and staked all on it, and it has proved worth nothing. Had it proved as it was expected when we took it up . . . I should have today been on my way to the bosom of my family in possession of sufficient means to have made them and me comfortable through life. . . . I mostly regret the necessity of staying here longer.

I was in hopes to have sent home a good pile of money before this time, but I am not able to at present. Still, my expectations are high, and in my opinion the excitement about the gold mines was not caused by exaggeration. In fact, I believe that greater amounts of gold have been and will be taken from the mines this summer than the gold news have told. . . . But I am of the opinion that the gold will soon be gathered from these washings and then will come the hardest part of this gold fever. I therefore would advise no one to come here. . . . But were I to be unfortunate in all my business here and arrive at last at home without *one cent*, I should ever be glad that I have taken the trip to California. It has learnt me to have confidence in myself, has disciplined my impetuous disposition and has learnt me to think and act for myself and to look upon men and things in a true light. Notwithstanding all these favorable circumstances, it is a fact that no energy or industry can secure certain success in the business of mining.

Source: Excerpt from "The California Gold Rush Experience" in *The World Rushed In* by J. S. Holliday. Copyright © 1981 by J. S. Holliday. Reprinted by permission of J. S. Holliday.

come forty miles over the mountains, just to look at me," Eliza Wilson recalled, "and I never was called a handsome woman, in my best days, even by my most ardent admirers." The class of women most frequently seen in the diggings was prostitutes, who numbered perhaps 20 percent of female Californians in 1850.

Violence was common in the mining districts, so when a new camp opened, miners adopted a set of rules and regulations. Justice was dispensed promptly, either by a vote of all the miners or by an elected jury. While effective when administered fairly, the system at times degenerated into lynch law. In addition, American miners frustrated by a lack of success often directed their hostility toward foreigners. The miners ruthlessly exterminated the Indians in the area, mob violence drove Mexicans out of nearly every camp, and the Chinese were confined to claims abandoned by Americans as unprofitable. The state eventually enacted a foreign miners' tax that fell largely on the Chinese. Free African Americans felt the sting of discrimination as well. White American miners proclaimed that "colored men were not privileged to work in a country intended only for American citizens."

*Nativist and racial prejudices*

Before long, the most easily worked claims had been played out, and competition steadily drove down the average earnings from $20 a day in 1848 to $6 in 1852. As gold became increasingly difficult to extract, corporations using heavy equipment and employing miners working for wages came to dominate the industry. As the era of the individual miner passed, so too did mining camps and the unique society they spawned.

The damage mining did to the land endured longer. Abandoned diggings pockmarked the gold fields and created piles of debris that heavy rains washed down the valley, choking streams and rivers and ruining lands below.

*Environmental impact of mining*

Excavation of hillsides, construction of dams to divert rivers, and the destruction of the forest cover to meet the heavy demand for lumber and firewood caused spring floods and serious erosion of the soil. The attitude of the individual miners differed little from that of the capitalists who succeeded them: both sought to exploit the environment as rapidly as possible with little thought to long-term consequences. Untempered by any sense of restraint, the quest for rapid wealth left long-lasting scars on the landscape of the gold country.

## Instant City: San Francisco

When the United States assumed control of California, San Francisco had a population of perhaps 200. But thousands of emigrants took the water route west, passing through San Francisco's harbor on their way to the diggings. By 1856 the city's population had jumped to an astonishing 50,000. In a mere 8 years the city had attained the size New York had taken 190 years to reach.

The product of economic self-interest, San Francisco developed in helter-skelter fashion. Since the city government took virtually no role in directing

*San Francisco's chaotic growth*

development, almost no land was reserved for public use. Property owners defeated a proposal to widen the streets, prompting the city's leading newspaper to complain, "To sell a few more feet of lots, the streets were compressed like a cheese, into half their width."

The gold rush that swelled San Francisco's streets was a global phenomenon. Americans predominated in the mining population, but Latin Americans, Europeans, Australians, and the Chinese swarmed into California. An amazing assortment of languages could be heard on the city's streets: indeed, in 1860 the population of San Francisco was 50 percent foreign-born.

The most distinctive of the ethnic groups was the Chinese. They had come to *Gum San*, the land of the golden mountain. Those who arrived in California overwhelmingly hailed from the area of southern China around Canton—

*Migration from China*

and not by accident. Canton, like other provinces of China, suffered

from economic distress, population pressures, social unrest, and political upheaval. But Canton had a large European presence, because it was the only port open to outsiders. That situation changed after the first Opium War (1839–1842), when Britain forced China to open other ports to trade. For Cantonese, the sudden loss

San Francisco in 1852

of this trade monopoly produced widespread economic hardship. At the same time, a series of religious and political revolts in the region led to severe fighting that devastated the countryside. A growing number of residents concluded that emigration was the only way to survive, and the presence of western ships in the harbors of Canton and nearby Hong Kong (a British possession since 1842) made it easier for Cantonese to migrate to California rather than to southeast Asia.

Between 1849 and 1854, some 45,000 Chinese went to California. Among those who did was 16-year-old Lee Chew, who left for California after a man from his village returned with great wealth from the "country of the American wizards." Like the other gold seekers, the Chinese newcomers were overwhelmingly young and male, and they wanted only to accumulate savings and return home to their families. (Indeed, only 16 Chinese women arrived before 1854.)

When the Chinese were harassed in the mines, many opened laundries in San Francisco and elsewhere, since little capital was required. Other Chinese around San Francisco set up restaurants or worked in the fishing industry. In these early years they found Americans less hostile, as long as they stayed away from the gold fields. As immigration and the competition for jobs increased, however, anti-Chinese sentiment intensified.

Gradually, San Francisco took on the trappings of a more orderly community. The city government established a public school system, erected streetlights, created a municipal water system, and halted further filling in of the bay. Fashionable neighborhoods sprouted on several hills, as high rents drove many residents from the developing commercial center. Churches and families became more common. By 1856, the city of the gold rush had been replaced by a new city whose stone and brick buildings gave it a newfound sense of permanence.

## The Mormons in Utah

The makeshift, often chaotic society spawned by the gold rush was a product of largely uncontrolled economic forces. In contrast, an entirely different society evolved in the Great Basin of Utah under the control of the Church of Jesus Christ of Latter-day Saints.

After Joseph Smith's death in 1844 (page 327), the Mormon church was led by Brigham Young, who lacked Smith's religious mysticism but was a brilliant organizer. Young decided to move his followers to the Great Basin, an isolated area a thousand miles from settled regions of the United States, where they could live and worship without interference. In 1847 the first thousand settlers arrived, the vanguard of thousands more who extended Mormon settlement throughout the valley of the Great Salt Lake and the West. The Mormons' success rested on a community-oriented effort firmly controlled by church elders. Families were given only as much farmland as they could use, and church officials, headed by Young, exercised supreme power in legislative, executive, and judicial matters as well as religious affairs.

The most controversial church teaching was the doctrine of polygamy, or plural marriage, which Young finally sanctioned publicly in 1852. Visitors reported with

*Polygamy* surprise that few Mormon wives seemed to rebel against the practice. If the wives lived together, the system allowed them to share domestic work. When the husband established separate households, wives enjoyed greater freedom, since he was not constantly present. Moreover, because polygamy distinguished Mormonism from other religions, plural wives saw it as an expression of their religious faith. "I want to be assured of *my position in God's estimation,*" one such wife explained. "If polygamy is the Lord's order, we must carry it out."

The Mormons connected control of water to their sense of mission. The Salt Lake valley, where the Mormons established their holy community, lacked sig-

*Irrigation and community* nificant rivers or abundant sources of water. Thus their success depended on irrigating the region, something never before attempted. By constructing a coordinated series of dams, aqueducts, and ditches, they brought life-giving water to the valleys of the region. By 1850, there were more than 16,000 irrigated acres in what would become Utah.

Manipulation of water reinforced the Mormons' sense of hierarchy and group discipline. Centralization of authority in the hands of church officials made possible an overall plan of development, allowed for maximum exploitation of resources, and freed communities from the disputes over water rights that plagued many settlements in the arid West. In a radical departure from American ideals, church leaders insisted that water belonged to the community, not individuals, and vested this authority in the hands of the local bishop. Control of vital water resources reinforced the power of the church hierarchy over not just the faithful but dissidents as well. Thus irrigation did more than make the desert bloom. By checking the Jeffersonian ideal of an independent, self-sufficient farmer, it also sustained a centralized, well-regulated society under the firm control of the church.

## Temple City: Salt Lake City

In laying out the Mormons' "temple city" of Salt Lake, Young was also determined to avoid the commercial worldliness and competitive individualism that had plagued Joseph Smith's settlement at Nauvoo. City lots, which were distributed by lottery, could not be subdivided for sale, and real estate speculation was forbidden.

The city itself was laid out in a checkerboard grid well suited to the level terrain. Streets were 132 feet wide (compared with 60 feet in San Francisco), and a square block contained eight home lots of 1.25 acres each. Unlike in early San Francisco, in Salt Lake City the family was the basic social unit, and almost from the beginning the city had an equal balance of men and women. The planners also provided for four public squares in various parts of the city. The city was divided into 18 wards, each under the supervision of a bishop who held civil as well as religious power.

*Salt Lake City's orderly growth*

As the city expanded, the original plan had to be modified to accommodate the developing commercial district by dividing lots into sizes more suitable for stores. Experience and growth also eventually dictated smaller blocks and narrower streets, but the city still retained its spacious appearance and regular design. Through religious and economic discipline church leaders succeeded in preserving a sense of common purpose.

## Shadows on the Moving Frontier

Transformations like Salt Lake City and San Francisco were truly remarkable. But it is important to remember that Americans were not coming into a trackless, unsettled wilderness. As frontier lines crossed, 75,000 Mexicans had to adapt to American rule.

The Treaty of Guadalupe Hidalgo guaranteed Mexicans in the ceded territory "the free enjoyment of their liberty and property." As long as Mexicans continued to be a sizable majority in a given area, such as New Mexico, their influence was strong. But wherever Anglos became more numerous, they demanded conformity to American customs. When Mexicans remained faithful to their heritage, language, and religion, these cultural differences worked to reinforce Hispanic powerlessness, social isolation, and economic exploitation.

The rush of American emigrants quickly overwhelmed Hispanic settlers in California. Even in 1848, before the discovery of gold, Americans in California outnumbered Mexicans two to one, and by 1860 Hispanics amounted to only 2 percent of the population. Changes in California

*Hispanic-Anglo conflict*

land law required verification of the *rancheros'* original land grants by a federal commission. Since the average claim took 17 years to complete and imposed complex procedures and hefty legal fees, many *rancheros* lost large tracts of land to Americans. Lower-class Mexicans scratched out a bare existence on ranches and farms or in the growing cities and towns.

Mexicans in Texas were also greatly outnumbered: they totaled only 6 percent of the population in 1860. Stigmatized as inferior, they were the poorest group in free society. One response to this dislocation, an option commonly taken by persecuted minorities, was social banditry. An example was the folk hero Juan Cortina. A member of a displaced landed family in southern Texas, Cortina in the 1850s began stealing from wealthy Anglos to aid poor Mexicans, proclaiming, "To me is entrusted the breaking of the chains of your slavery." He continued to raid Texas border settlements until finally imprisoned by Mexican authorities. While failing to produce any lasting change, Cortina demonstrated the depth of frustration and resentment among Hispanics over their abuse at the hands of the new Anglo majority.

## ESCAPE FROM CRISIS

With the return of peace, Congress confronted the problem of whether to allow slavery in the newly won territories. David Wilmot, in his controversial proviso, had already proposed to outlaw slavery throughout the Mexican cession. John C. Calhoun, representing the extreme southern position, countered that slavery was legal in all territories. The federal government had acted as the agent of all the states in acquiring the land, he argued, and southerners had a right to take their property there, including slaves. Only when the residents of a territory drafted a state constitution could they decide the question of slavery.

*Constitution and extension of slavery*

Between these extremes were two moderate positions. One proposed extending the Missouri Compromise line of 36°30′ to the Pacific, which would have continued the earlier policy of dividing the national domain between the North and the South. The other proposal, championed by Senator Lewis Cass of Michigan and Senator Stephen A. Douglas of Illinois, was to allow the people of the territory rather than Congress to decide the status of slavery. This solution, which became known as popular sovereignty, was deliberately ambiguous, since its supporters refused to specify whether the residents could make this decision at any time or only when drafting a state constitution, as Calhoun insisted.

Senator John C. Calhoun

When Congress organized the Oregon Territory in 1848, it prohibited slavery there, since even southerners admitted that the region was too far north to grow the South's staple crops. But this seemingly straightforward decision made it impossible to apply the Missouri Compromise line to the other territories. Without Oregon as a part of the package, the bulk of the remaining land would be open to slavery, something at which the North balked. Almost inadvertently, one of the two moderate solutions had been discarded by the summer of 1848.

## A Two-Faced Campaign

In the election of 1848 both major parties tried to avoid the slavery issue. The Democrats nominated Lewis Cass, a supporter of popular sovereignty, while the Whigs bypassed all their prominent leaders and selected General Zachary Taylor of Louisiana, who had taken no position on any public issue.

But the slavery issue would not go away. A new antislavery coalition, the Free Soil party, brought together northern Democrats who had rallied to the Wilmot Proviso, Conscience Whigs who disavowed Taylor's nomination because he was a slaveholder, and political abolitionists in the Liberty party. To gain more votes, the Free Soil platform focused on the dangers of extending slavery rather than on the evil of slavery itself. Ironically, the party nominated Martin Van Buren—the man who for years had struggled to keep the slavery issue out of national politics.

*Free Soil party*

Both the Whigs and the Democrats ran different campaigns in the North and the South. To southern audiences, each party promised it would protect slavery in the territories; to northern voters, each claimed it would keep the territories free. In this two-faced, sectional campaign, the Whigs won their second national victory. Taylor held on to the core of Whig voters in both sections (Van Buren as well as Cass, after all, had long been a Democrat). But in the South, where the contest pitted a southern slaveholder against two northerners, Taylor won many more votes than Clay had in 1844. As one southern Democrat complained, "We have lost hundreds of votes, solely on the ground that General Cass was a Northerner and General Taylor a Southern man." Furthermore, Van Buren polled five times as many votes as the Liberty party had four years earlier. Increasingly the two national political parties were being pulled apart along sectional lines.

## The Compromise of 1850

Once he became president, Taylor could no longer remain silent. The territories gained from Mexico had to be organized; furthermore, by 1849 California had gained enough residents to be admitted as a state. In the Senate the balance of power between North and South stood at 15 states each. California's admission would break the sectional balance.

Called "Old Rough and Ready" by his troops, Taylor was a forthright man of action, but he was politically inexperienced and oversimplified complex problems. Since even Calhoun conceded that entering states had the right to ban slavery, Taylor proposed that the way to end the sectional crisis was to skip the territorial stage by combining all the Mexican cession into two huge states, New Mexico and California.

*Taylor's plan* | Even more shocking to southern Whigs, he proposed to apply the Wilmot Proviso to the entire area, since he was convinced that slavery would never flourish there. When Congress convened in December 1849, Taylor recommended that California and New Mexico be admitted as free states. The president's plan touched off the most serious sectional crisis the Union had yet confronted.

Into this turmoil stepped Henry Clay, now 73 years old and nearing the end of his career. A savvy card player all his life, Clay loved the bargaining, the wheeling and dealing, the late-night trade-offs eased along by a bottle of bourbon that were part of politics. Clay decided that a grand compromise was needed to end

TERRITORIAL GROWTH AND THE COMPROMISE OF 1850

all disputes between the North and South and save the Union. Already, Mississippi had summoned a southern convention to meet at Nashville to discuss the crisis, and extremists were pushing for secession.

Clay's compromise, submitted in January 1850, addressed all the major controversies between the two sections. California, he proposed, should be admitted as a free state, which represented the clear wishes of most settlers there. The rest of the Mexican cession would be organized as two territories, New Mexico and Utah, under the doctrine of popular sovereignty. Thus slavery would not be prohibited in these regions. Clay also proposed that Congress abolish the slave trade but not slavery itself in the District of Columbia and that a new, more rigorous fugitive slave law be passed to enable southerners to reclaim runaway slaves. To reinforce the idea that both North and South were yielding ground, Clay combined those provisions that dealt with the Mexican cession (and several others adjusting the Texas–New Mexico border) into a larger package known as the Omnibus Bill.

*Clay's compromise*

With the stakes so high, the Senate debated the bill for six months. Clay, wracked by a hacking cough, spent long hours trying to line up the needed votes. But for once, the great whist enthusiast had misplayed his hand. The Omnibus Bill required that the components of the compromise be approved as a package. Extremists in Congress from both regions, however, combined against the moderates and rejected the bill.

With Clay exhausted and his strategy in shambles, Democrat Stephen A. Douglas assumed leadership of the pro-compromise forces. The sudden death in July of President Taylor, who had threatened to veto Clay's plan, aided the compromise movement. One by one, Douglas submitted the individual measures for a vote. Northern representatives provided the necessary votes to admit California and abolish the slave trade in the District of Columbia, while southern representatives supplied the edge needed to organize the Utah and New Mexico territories and pass the new fugitive slave law. On the face of it, everyone had compromised. But in truth, only 61 members of Congress, or 21 percent of the membership, had not voted against some part of the Compromise.

*Compromise of 1850 passed*

By September 17 all the separate parts of the Compromise of 1850 had passed and been signed into law by the new president, Millard Fillmore. The Union, it seemed, was safe.

### Away from the Brink

The general public, both North and South, rallied to the Compromise. At the convention of southern states in Nashville, the fire-eaters—the radical proponents of states' rights and secession—found themselves voted down by more moderate voices. Even in the Deep South, coalitions of pro-compromise Whigs and Democrats soundly defeated secessionists in state elections. Nevertheless, most southerners felt that a firm line had been drawn. With California's admission, they were now outnumbered in the Senate, so it was critical that slaveholders be

*Rejection of secession*

there). This act effectively repealed the Missouri Compromise.

- Popular sovereignty failed in the Kansas Territory, where fighting broke out between proslavery and antislavery partisans.

- Sectional violence reached a climax in May 1856 with the proslavery attack on Lawrence, Kansas, and the caning of Senator Charles Sumner of Massachusetts by Representative Preston S. Brooks of South Carolina.

• Sectional tensions sparked the formation of a new antislavery Republican party, and the party system realigned along sectional lines.

- The Supreme Court's *Dred Scott* decision, the Panic of 1857, the congressional strug-

gle over the proslavery Lecompton constitution, and John Brown's attack on Harpers Ferry in 1859 strengthened the two sectional extremes.

• In 1860 Abraham Lincoln became the first Republican to be elected president.

- Following Lincoln's triumph, the seven states of the Deep South seceded.

- When Lincoln sent supplies to the Union garrison in Fort Sumter in Charleston harbor, Confederate batteries bombarded the fort into submission.

- The North rallied to Lincoln's decision to use force to restore the Union, and in response the four states of the Upper South seceded.

# interactive learning

The Primary Source Investigator CD-ROM offers the following materials related to this chapter:

• Interactive maps: **Election of 1860** (M7) and **The Transportation Revolution, 1830–1890** (M12)

• A collection of primary sources illuminating the political and social strife of the

1850s, including the First and Second Confiscation Acts. Other sources capture the anxiety of the age, such as a letter written by John Boston proclaiming his freedom and a letter regarding how to handle contraband slaves.

For quizzes and a variety of interactive resources, visit the book's Online Learning Center at www.mhhe.com/davidsonconcise4.

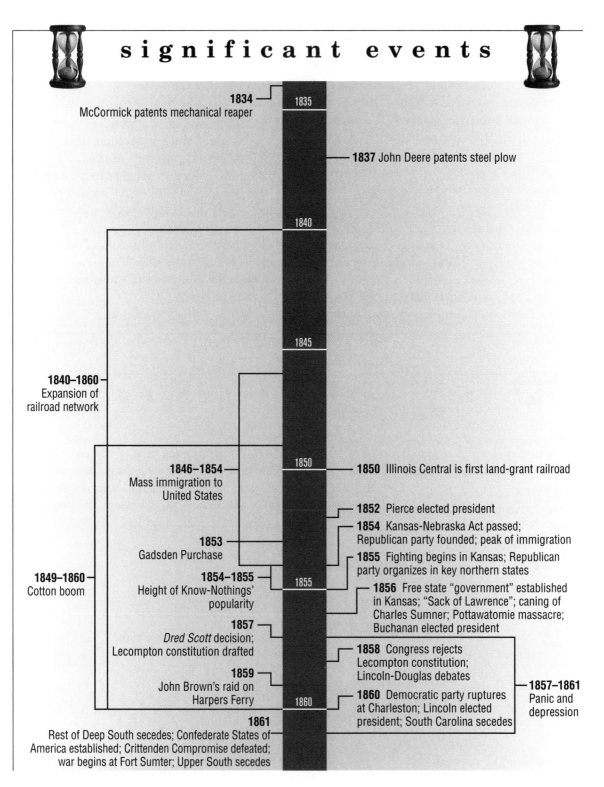

# significant events

**1834** McCormick patents mechanical reaper

1835

**1837** John Deere patents steel plow

1840

1845

**1840–1860** Expansion of railroad network

**1846–1854** Mass immigration to United States

1850

**1850** Illinois Central is first land-grant railroad

**1852** Pierce elected president

**1854** Kansas-Nebraska Act passed; Republican party founded; peak of immigration

**1853** Gadsden Purchase

**1855** Fighting begins in Kansas; Republican party organizes in key northern states

**1849–1860** Cotton boom

**1854–1855** Height of Know-Nothings' popularity

1855

**1856** Free state "government" established in Kansas; "Sack of Lawrence"; caning of Charles Sumner; Pottawatomie massacre; Buchanan elected president

**1857** *Dred Scott* decision; Lecompton constitution drafted

**1858** Congress rejects Lecompton constitution; Lincoln-Douglas debates

**1859** John Brown's raid on Harpers Ferry

1860

**1857–1861** Panic and depression

**1860** Democratic party ruptures at Charleston; Lincoln elected president; South Carolina secedes

**1861** Rest of Deep South secedes; Confederate States of America established; Crittenden Compromise defeated; war begins at Fort Sumter; Upper South secedes

# CHAPTER 16

# Total War and the Republic
## 1861–1865

**Preview** *As the first total war in history, the Civil War was fought not just by armies but through the mobilization of each society's human and economic resources. Lincoln's leadership was key. He moved slowly at first, to keep the border slave states within the Union, but later accepted the destruction of slavery as a war aim. Indeed, the freeing of 4 million slaves was only the most monumental of the war's many transformations, in both the South and the North.*

T he war won't last sixty days!" Of that Jim Tinkham was confident. With dreams of a hero's return, Tinkham enlisted for three months in a Massachusetts regiment. Soon he was transferred to Washington as part of the Union army being assembled under the command of General Irvin McDowell to crush the rebellion. Tinkham was elated when in mid-July the army was finally ordered to march toward the Confederates concentrated at Manassas Junction, 25 miles away.*

The battle began at dawn on July 21, with McDowell commanding 30,000 troops against General Pierre Beauregard's 22,000. Tinkham did not arrive on the field until early afternoon. As his regiment pushed toward the front, he felt faint at his first sight of the dead and wounded, some mangled horribly. But he was soon caught up in the excitement of battle as he charged up Henry Hill. Suddenly the Confederate ranks broke and exuberant Union troops shouted, "The war is over!"

The timely arrival of fresh troops, however, enabled the Confederates to regroup and resume the fight. Among the reinforcements who rushed to Henry Hill was 19-year-old Randolph McKim of Baltimore. A student at the University of Virginia when the war began, McKim joined the First Maryland Infantry as a private when Abraham Lincoln imposed martial law in his home state. "The cause of the South had become identified with liberty itself," he explained. After only a week of drill, McKim boarded a train on July 21 bound for Manassas. The arrival of the First Maryland and other reinforcements in

---

*The Union and the Confederacy often gave different names to a battle. The Confederates called the first battle Manassas; the Union, Bull Run.

the late afternoon turned the tide of battle. The faltering Confederate line held, and Union troops began to withdraw.

Once McDowell ordered a retreat, discipline dissolved, the army degenerated into a mob, and a stampede began. As they fled, terrified troops threw away their equipment, shoved aside officers who tried to stop them, and raced frantically past the wagons and artillery pieces that clogged the road. Joining the stampede was Jim Tinkham, who confessed he would have continued on to Boston if he had not been stopped by a guard in Washington.

All the next day in a drizzling rain, mud-spattered troops straggled into the capital in complete disorder. William Russell, an English reporter, asked one pale officer where they were coming from. "Well, sir, I guess we're all coming out of Virginny as far as we can, and pretty well whipped too," he replied. "I know I'm going home. I've had enough of fighting to last my lifetime."

The rout at Bull Run sobered the North. Gone were dreams of ending the war with one glorious battle. Gone was the illusion that 75,000 volunteers serving three months would be sufficient. As one perceptive observer noted, "We have undertaken to make war without in the least knowing how." Having cast off his earlier misconceptions, a newly determined Jim Tinkham reenlisted for a three-year hitch.

Still, it was not surprising that both sides underestimated the magnitude of the conflict. Previous warfare as it had evolved in Europe consisted largely of *Meaning of total war* maneuverings that took relatively few lives, respected private property, and left civilians largely unharmed. The Civil War, on the other hand, was the first war whose major battles routinely involved more than 100,000 troops. So many combatants could be equipped only through the use of factory-produced weaponry, they could be moved and supplied only with the help of railroads, and they could be sustained only through the concerted efforts of civilian society as a whole. The morale of the population, the quality of political leadership, and the utilization of industrial and economic might were all critical to the outcome. Quite simply, the Civil War was the first total war in history.

## THE DEMANDS OF TOTAL WAR

When the war began, the North had an enormous advantage in manpower and industrial capacity. The Union's population was 2.5 times larger; it contained more railroad track and rolling stock and possessed more than 10 times the industrial capacity.

From a modern perspective, the South's attempt to defend its independence against such odds seems hopeless. Yet this view indicates how much the conception of war has changed. European observers, who knew the strength and resources of the two sides, believed that the Confederacy could never be conquered. Indeed, the South enjoyed definite strategic advantages. To
*Southern advantages*

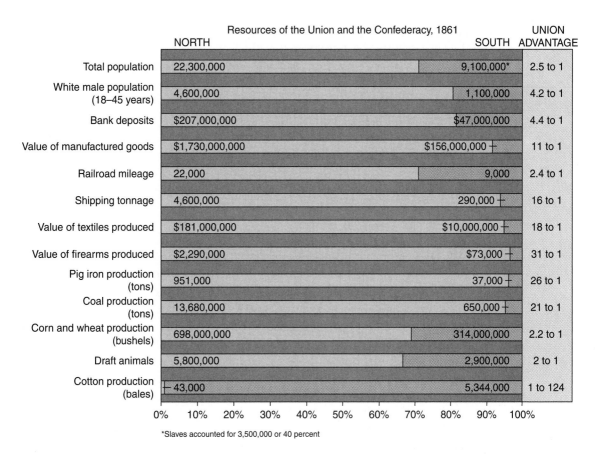

| | NORTH | SOUTH | UNION ADVANTAGE |
|---|---|---|---|
| Total population | 22,300,000 | 9,100,000* | 2.5 to 1 |
| White male population (18–45 years) | 4,600,000 | 1,100,000 | 4.2 to 1 |
| Bank deposits | $207,000,000 | $47,000,000 | 4.4 to 1 |
| Value of manufactured goods | $1,730,000,000 | $156,000,000 | 11 to 1 |
| Railroad mileage | 22,000 | 9,000 | 2.4 to 1 |
| Shipping tonnage | 4,600,000 | 290,000 | 16 to 1 |
| Value of textiles produced | $181,000,000 | $10,000,000 | 18 to 1 |
| Value of firearms produced | $2,290,000 | $73,000 | 31 to 1 |
| Pig iron production (tons) | 951,000 | 37,000 | 26 to 1 |
| Coal production (tons) | 13,680,000 | 650,000 | 21 to 1 |
| Corn and wheat production (bushels) | 698,000,000 | 314,000,000 | 2.2 to 1 |
| Draft animals | 5,800,000 | 2,900,000 | 2 to 1 |
| Cotton production (bales) | 43,000 | 5,344,000 | 1 to 124 |

Resources of the Union and the Confederacy, 1861

0%  10%  20%  30%  40%  50%  60%  70%  80%  90%  100%

*Slaves accounted for 3,500,000 or 40 percent

*Source:* U.S. Census 1860 and E. B. Long, *The Civil War Day by Day* (New York: Doubleday, 1971), p.723.

be victorious, it did not need to invade the North—only to defend its own land and prevent the North from destroying its armies. Southern soldiers knew the topography of their home country better, and a friendly population regularly supplied them with intelligence about Union troop movements.

The North, in contrast, had to invade and conquer the Confederacy and destroy the southern will to resist. To do so, it would have to deploy thousands of soldiers to defend long supply lines in enemy territory, a situation that significantly reduced the northern advantage in manpower. Yet by 1865 Union forces had penetrated virtually every part of the 500,000 square miles of the Confederacy and were able to move almost at will. The Civil War demonstrated the capacity of a modern society to overcome the problems of distance and terrain with technology.

## Political Leadership

To sustain a commitment to total war required effective political leadership. This task fell on Abraham Lincoln and Jefferson Davis, presidents of the rival governments.

Jefferson Davis grew up in Mississippi accustomed to life's advantages. Educated at West Point, he fought in the Mexican War, served as Franklin Pierce's secretary of war, and became one of the South's leading advocates in the Senate. Although he was hardworking and committed to the cause he led, his temperament was not well suited to his new post: he was quarrelsome, resented criticism, and refused to work with those he disliked. "He cannot brook opposition or criticism," one member of the Confederate Congress testified, "and those who do not bow down before him have no chance of success with him."

*Davis's character*

Yet for all Davis's personal handicaps, he faced an institutional one even more daunting. The Confederacy had been founded on the ideology of states' rights. Yet to meet the demands of total war, Davis would need to increase the authority of the central government beyond anything the South had ever experienced.

When Lincoln took the oath of office, his national experience consisted of one term in the House of Representatives. But Lincoln was a shrewd judge of character and a superb politician. To achieve a common goal, he willingly overlooked withering criticism and personal slights. He was not easily humbugged, overawed, or flattered and never allowed personal feelings to blind him to his larger objectives. "No man knew better how to summon and dispose of political ability to attain great political ends," commented one associate.

*Lincoln's leadership*

"This is essentially a People's contest," Lincoln asserted at the start of the war, and few presidents have been better able to communicate with the average citizen. He regularly visited Union troops in camp, in the field, and in army hospitals. "The boys liked him," wrote Joseph Twichell, from a Connecticut regiment, "in fact his popularity with the army is and has been universal." Always Lincoln reminded the public that the war was being fought for the ideals of the Revolution and the Republic. It was a test, he remarked in his famous address at Gettysburg, of whether a nation "conceived in Liberty, and dedicated to the proposition that all men are created equal" could "long endure."

He also proved the more effective military leader. Jefferson Davis took his title of commander in chief literally, constantly interfering with his generals, but he failed to formulate an overarching strategy. In contrast, Lincoln clearly grasped the challenge confronting the Union. He accepted General Winfield Scott's proposal to blockade the Confederacy, cut off its

Jefferson Davis

supplies, and slowly strangle it into submission. But unlike Scott, he realized that this plan was not enough. The South would also have to be invaded and defeated, not only on an eastern front in Virginia but in the West, where Union control of the Mississippi would divide the Confederacy. Lincoln understood that the Union's superior manpower and matériel would become decisive only when the Confederacy was simultaneously threatened along a broad front. It took time before the president found generals able to execute this novel strategy.

## The Border States

When the war began, only Delaware of the border slave states was certain to remain in the Union. Lincoln's immediate political challenge was to retain the loyalty of Maryland, Kentucky, and Missouri. Maryland especially was crucial, for if it was lost, Washington itself would have to be abandoned.

Lincoln moved vigorously—even ruthlessly—to secure Maryland. He suppressed pro-Confederate newspapers and suspended the writ of habeas corpus, the right under the Constitution of an arrested person either to be charged with a specific crime or to be released. That done, he held without trial prominent Confederate sympathizers. Intervention by the army ensured that Unionists won a complete victory in the fall state election. The election ended any possibility that Maryland would join the Confederacy.

*Suppression in Maryland*

At the beginning of the conflict, Kentucky officially declared its neutrality. Union generals requested permission to occupy the state, but the president refused, preferring to act cautiously and wait for Unionist sentiment to assert itself. After Unionists won control of the legislature in the summer election, a Confederate army entered the state, giving Lincoln the opening he needed. He quickly sent in troops, and Kentucky stayed in the Union.

*Kentucky's neutrality*

In Missouri, skirmishing broke out between Union and Confederate sympathizers. Only after the Union victory at the Battle of Pea Ridge in March 1862 was Missouri secure from any Confederate threat. Even so, guerrilla warfare continued in the state throughout the remainder of the war.

In Virginia, internal divisions led to the creation of a new border state, as the hilly western counties where slavery was weak refused to support the Confederacy. After adopting a congressionally mandated program of gradual emancipation, West Virginia was formally admitted to the Union in June 1863.

The Union scored an important triumph in holding the border states. The population of all five equaled that of the four states of the Upper South that had joined the Confederacy, and their production of military supplies— food, animals, and minerals—was greater. Furthermore, Maryland and West Virginia contained key railroad lines and were critical to the defense of Washington, while Kentucky and Missouri gave the Union army access to the major river systems of the western theater, down which it launched the first successful invasions of the Confederacy.

*Importance of the border states*

## OPENING MOVES

As with so many Civil War battles, the Confederate victory at Bull Run achieved no decisive military results. But Congress authorized a much larger army of long-term volunteers, and Lincoln named 34-year-old George McClellan, a West Point graduate and former railroad executive, to be the new commander. Energetic and ambitious, he spent the next eight months directing the much-needed task of organizing and drilling the Army of the Potomac.

### Blockade and Isolate

Although the U.S. Navy began the war with only 42 ships available to blockade 3550 miles of Confederate coastline, by the spring of 1862 it had taken control of key islands off the coasts of the Carolinas and Georgia, to use as supply bases. The navy also began building powerful gunboats to operate on the rivers. In April 1862 Flag Officer David G. Farragut ran a gauntlet of Confederate shore batteries to capture New Orleans, the Confederacy's largest port. Memphis, another important river city, fell to Union forces in June.

The blockade was hardly leakproof, and small, fast ships continued to slip through it. Still, southern trade suffered badly. In hopes of lifting the blockade, *Ironclads* the Confederacy converted the wooden USS *Merrimack*, which was rechristened the *Virginia*, into an ironclad gunboat. In March 1862 a Union ironclad, the *Monitor*, battled it to a standoff, and the Confederates scuttled the *Virginia* when they evacuated Norfolk in May. After that, the Union's naval supremacy was secure.

The Confederacy looked to diplomacy as another means to lift the blockade. With cotton so vital to European economies, especially Great Britain's, south-*King cotton diplomacy* erners believed Europe would formally recognize the Confederacy and come to its aid. The British government favored the South, but it hesitated to act until Confederate armies demonstrated that they could win the war. Meanwhile, new supplies of cotton from Egypt and India enabled the British textile industry to recover. In the end, Britain and the rest of Europe refused to recognize the Confederacy, and the South was left to stand or fall on its own resources.

### Grant in the West

In the western war theater, the first decisive Union victory was won by a short, shabbily dressed, cigar-chomping general named Ulysses S. Grant. An undistinguished student at West Point, Grant eventually had resigned his commission. He had failed at everything he tried in civilian life, and when the war broke out, he was a store clerk in Galena, Illinois. Almost 39, he promptly volunteered, and two months later became a brigadier general.

Grant's quiet, self-effacing manner gave little indication of his military ability or iron determination. He had a flair for improvising, was alert to seize any opening, and remained extraordinarily calm and clear-headed in battle. Most important, Grant grasped that hard fighting, not fancy maneuvering, would bring victory. "The art of war is simple," he once explained. "Find out where your enemy is, get at him as soon as you can and strike him as hard as you can, and keep moving on."

*Grant's character*

Grant realized that rivers were avenues into the interior of the Confederacy, and in February 1862, supported by Union gunboats, he captured Fort Henry on the Tennessee River and Fort Donelson on the Cumberland. These victories forced the Confederates to withdraw from Kentucky and middle Tennessee. Grant continued south with 40,000 men, but he was surprised on April 6 by General Albert Johnston at Shiloh, just north of the Tennessee-Mississippi border. Johnston was killed in the day's fierce fighting, but by nightfall his army had driven the Union troops back to the Tennessee River, where they huddled numbly as a cold rain fell. William Tecumseh Sherman, one of Grant's subordinates, found the general standing under a dripping tree, his coat collar drawn up against the damp, puffing on a cigar. Sherman was about to suggest retreat, but something in Grant's eyes, lighted by the glow of his stogie, made him hesitate. So he said only, "Well, Grant, we've had the devil's own day, haven't we?" "Yes," the Union commander replied quietly. "Lick 'em tomorrow, though." And he did. With the aid of reinforcements, which he methodically ferried across the river all night, Grant counterattacked the next morning and drove the Confederates from the field.

*Shiloh*

But victory came at a high price, for Shiloh inflicted more than 23,000 casualties. Grant, who previously had doubted the commitment of Confederate troops, came away deeply impressed with their determination. "At Shiloh," he wrote afterward, "I gave up all idea of saving the Union except by complete conquest."

### Eastern Stalemate

Grant's victories did not silence his critics, who charged he drank too much. But Lincoln was unmoved. "I can't spare this man. He fights." That was a quality in short supply in the East, where General McClellan directed operations.

McClellan looked like a general, but beneath his arrogance and bravado lay a self-doubt that rendered him excessively cautious. As the months dragged on and McClellan did nothing but train and plan, Lincoln's frustration grew. "If General McClellan does not want to use the army I would like to *borrow* it," he remarked sarcastically. In the spring of 1862 the general finally transported his 130,000 troops to the Virginia coast and began inching toward Richmond, the Confederate capital. In May General Joseph Johnston suddenly attacked him near Fair Oaks, from which he barely escaped. Worse for

*"McClellan has the slows"*

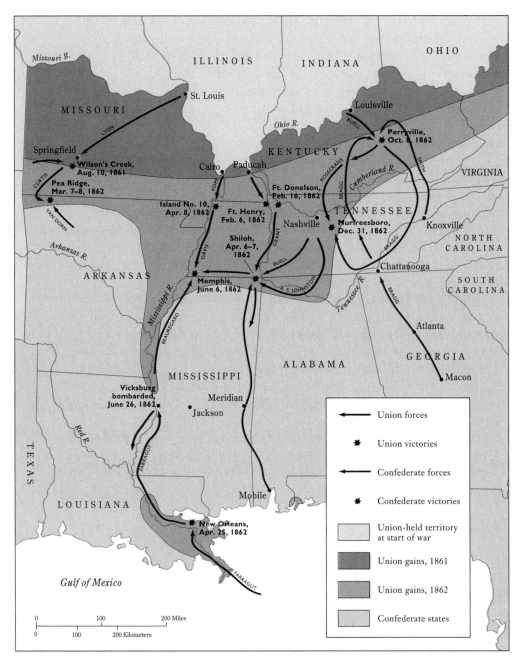

**THE WAR IN THE WEST, 1861–1862** Grant's push southward stalled after his costly victory at Shiloh; nevertheless, by the end of 1862 the Union had secured Kentucky and Missouri, as well as most of Confederate Tennessee and the upper and lower stretches of the Mississippi River.

McClellan, when Johnston was badly wounded, the formidable Robert E. Lee took command of the Army of Northern Virginia.

Where McClellan was cautious and defensive, the aristocratic Lee was daring and ever alert to assume the offensive. His first name, one of his colleagues commented, should have been Audacity: "He will take more chances, and take them quicker than any other general in this country." In the | *Lee's generalship* Seven Days' battles, McClellan successfully parried the attacks of Lee and Thomas "Stonewall" Jackson but stayed on the defensive. As McClellan retreated to the protection of the Union gunboats, Lincoln ordered the Peninsula campaign abandoned and formed a new army under John Pope. After Lee badly mauled Pope at the second Battle of Bull Run in August, Lincoln restored McClellan to command.

Realizing that the Confederacy needed a decisive victory, Lee invaded the North, hoping to detach Maryland and isolate Washington. Learning that he greatly outnumbered Lee, McClellan launched a series of badly coor- | *Antietam* dinated assaults near Antietam Creek on September 17 that Lee barely repulsed. The bloody exchanges horrified both sides for their sheer carnage. Nearly 5000 soldiers were killed and another 18,000 wounded, making it the bloodiest single day in American history. When McClellan allowed Lee's army to escape back into Virginia, an exasperated Lincoln permanently relieved him of command in November.

The winter of 1862 was the North's Valley Forge, as morale sank to an all-time low. It took General Ambrose Burnside, who assumed McClellan's place, little more than a month to demonstrate his utter incompetence at the Battle of Fredericksburg. The Union's disastrous defeat there prompted Lincoln to put "Fighting Joe" Hooker in charge. In the West, Grant had emerged as the dominant figure, but the Army of the Potomac still lacked a capable commander, the deaths kept mounting, and no end to the war was in sight.

## EMANCIPATION

In 1858 Abraham Lincoln had proclaimed that the United States must eventually become either all slave or all free. When the war began, however, the president refused to make emancipation a Union war aim. | *Crittenden Resolution* He perceived, accurately, that most white northerners were not deeply committed to emancipation. He feared the social upheaval that such a revolutionary step would cause, and he did not want to alarm the wavering border slave states. Thus when Congress met in special session in July 1861, Lincoln fully supported a resolution offered by John J. Crittenden of Kentucky, which declared that the war was being fought solely to save the Union. The Crittenden Resolution passed the House 117 to 2 and the Senate by 30 to 5.

Lee surrendered at Appomattox Courthouse. As the vanquished foe mounted his horse, Grant saluted by raising his hat; Lee raised his respectfully and rode off at a slow trot. The guns were quiet.

Remaining resistance throughout the Confederacy collapsed within a matter of weeks. Visiting the captured city of Richmond on April 4, Lincoln was enthusiastically greeted by the black population. He looked "pale, haggard, utterly worn out," noted one observer. The lines in his face showed how much the war had aged him in only four years. Often his friends had counseled rest, but Lincoln had observed that "the tired part of me is *inside* and out of reach." The burden, he confessed, was almost too much to bear.

Back in Washington the president received news of Lee's surrender with relief. The evening of April 14, Lincoln, seeking a welcome escape, went to a comedy at Ford's Theater. In the midst of the performance John Wilkes Booth, a famous actor and Confederate sympathizer, slipped into the presidential box and shot him. Lincoln died the next morning. As he had called upon his fellow citizens to do in his Gettysburg Address, the sixteenth president had given his "last full measure of devotion" to the Republic.

*Lincoln's assassination*

## THE IMPACT OF WAR

The assassination left a tiredness in the nation's bones—a tiredness *"inside"* and not easily within reach. In every way the conflict had produced fundamental, often devastating changes. There was, of course, the carnage. Approximately 620,000 men on both sides lost their lives, almost as many as in all the other wars the nation has fought from the Revolution through Vietnam combined. In material terms, the conflict cost an estimated $20 billion, more than 11 times the total amount spent by the federal government from 1789 to 1861. Even without adding the market value of freed slaves, southern wealth declined 43 percent, transforming what had been the richest section in the nation (on a white per capita basis) into the poorest.

*Cost of war*

The effects of total war, however, went well beyond upheaval and destruction. The Civil War rearranged and reordered not only the national economy but also economic relations worldwide. In the nation, demand for the machines of war stimulated industrialization, especially in the heavy industries of iron and coal, machinery, and agricultural implements. Manufacturers were forced to supply the army on an unprecedented scale over great distances. One consequence was the creation of truly national industries in flour milling, meat packing, clothing and shoe manufacture, and machinery making.

People across the globe felt the effects of the war, particularly due to changes in the cotton trade. By 1860 the South was supplying more than three-quarters of all cotton imported by Britain, France, Germany, and Russia. When the war cut off that supply, manufacturers scrambled to find new sources. India, Egypt, and Brazil all improved their railroad facilities and ports in order to encourage planters to open new cotton fields. The Indian city of Bombay experienced explosive growth handling the flood of new cotton. The effect of the trade on Egypt was so great, historians of that nation rank the American Civil War and the construction of the Suez Canal as the most crucial events in its nineteenth-century history. In the end, the efforts of cotton merchants, textile operators, and European governments marked the first steps by European powers toward a more aggressive imperialism that flourished in the late nineteenth century.

*The war's effects on the cotton trade worldwide*

Politically, the war dramatically changed the balance of power. The South lost its substantial influence, as did the Democratic party, while the Republicans emerged in a dominant position. The Union's military victory also signaled the triumph of nationalism. The war destroyed the idea that the Union was a voluntary confederacy of sovereign states, which theorists like John C. Calhoun had argued, and that the states had the right to secede.

In the short run, the price was disillusionment and bitterness. The South had to live with the humiliation of military defeat and occupation, while former slaves anxiously waited to see what their situation would be in freedom. The war's corrosive effect on morals corrupted American life and politics, destroyed idealism, and severely crippled humanitarian reform. Millennialism and perfectionism were victims of the war's appalling slaughter, forsaken for a new emphasis on practicality, order, materialism, and science. As the war unfolded, the New York *Herald* recognized the deep changes: "All sorts of old fogy ideas, manners, and customs have gone under, and all sorts of new ideas, modes, and practices have risen to the surface and become popular."

*Spiritual toll of war*

George Ticknor, a prominent author and critic who was sensitive to shifting intellectual and social currents, reflected on the changes that had shaken the nation in only a few short years. The war, it seemed to him, had left "a great gulf between what happened before it in our century and what has happened since. . . . It does not seem to me as if I were living in the country in which I was born."

 **c h a p t e r    s u m m a r y**

As the first total war in history, the Civil War's outcome depended not just on armies but also on the mobilization of society's human, economic, and intellectual resources.

- Confederate president Jefferson Davis's policy of concentrating power in the government at Richmond, along with the resort to a draft and impressment of private property, provoked strong protests from many southerners.

- Abraham Lincoln's policies, especially his suspension of the writ of habeas corpus and his interference with civil liberties, were equally controversial.

- But Lincoln skillfully handled the delicate situation of the border states in the first year of the war, keeping them in the Union.
- Lincoln at first resisted pressure to make emancipation a Union war aim, but he eventually issued the Emancipation Proclamation, which transformed the meaning of the war.
- African Americans helped undermine slavery in the Confederacy and made a vital contribution to the Union's military victory.
- The war had a powerful impact on the home front.
  - Women confronted new responsibilities and enjoyed new occupational opportunities.
  - In the Confederacy, hardship and suffering became a fact of life.
  - The Confederate government's financial and tax policies and the tightening Union blockade increased this suffering.
- Both societies also experienced the ravages of moral decay.
- The Civil War changed the nature of warfare.
  - Technology, particularly the use of rifles and rifled artillery, revolutionized tactics and strategy.
  - The Union eventually adopted the strategy of attacking the civilian population of the South.
  - Soldiers in both armies suffered from disease and inadequate medical care, poor food, moral corruption, and the mounting death toll.
- The war altered the nation's political institutions, its economy, and its values.

# interactive learning

The Primary Source Investigator CD-ROM offers the following materials related to this chapter:

- Interactive maps: **Slavery and the Cotton Kingdom** (M11) and **Civil War, 1861–1864** (M15)
- A short documentary movie on the process of emancipation during the Civil War (D9)
- A collection of primary sources exploring the course of America's first "total war." Several

documents reveal African Americans' role in the war: a photograph of contrabands crossing a river, a map of the distribution of slaves, and an image of the 6th Colored Regiment's flag. Other documents explore how the international community reacted to America's Civil War: a political cartoon illustrating England's concerns over its cotton supply and an English cartoon depicting Lincoln asking slaves for help in the war.

 For quizzes and a variety of interactive resources, visit the book's Online Learning Center at www.mhhe.com/davidsonconcise4.

# significant events

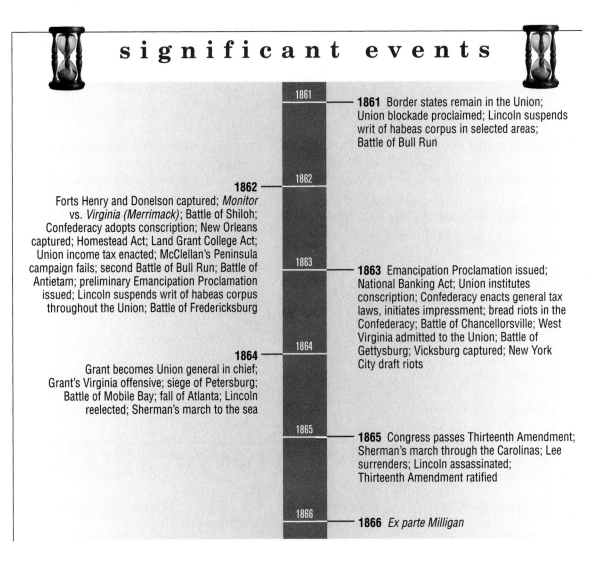

**1861** Border states remain in the Union; Union blockade proclaimed; Lincoln suspends writ of habeas corpus in selected areas; Battle of Bull Run

**1862** Forts Henry and Donelson captured; *Monitor* vs. *Virginia (Merrimack)*; Battle of Shiloh; Confederacy adopts conscription; New Orleans captured; Homestead Act; Land Grant College Act; Union income tax enacted; McClellan's Peninsula campaign fails; second Battle of Bull Run; Battle of Antietam; preliminary Emancipation Proclamation issued; Lincoln suspends writ of habeas corpus throughout the Union; Battle of Fredericksburg

**1863** Emancipation Proclamation issued; National Banking Act; Union institutes conscription; Confederacy enacts general tax laws, initiates impressment; bread riots in the Confederacy; Battle of Chancellorsville; West Virginia admitted to the Union; Battle of Gettysburg; Vicksburg captured; New York City draft riots

**1864** Grant becomes Union general in chief; Grant's Virginia offensive; siege of Petersburg; Battle of Mobile Bay; fall of Atlanta; Lincoln reelected; Sherman's march to the sea

**1865** Congress passes Thirteenth Amendment; Sherman's march through the Carolinas; Lee surrenders; Lincoln assassinated; Thirteenth Amendment ratified

**1866** *Ex parte Milligan*

# CHAPTER 17

J oseph Davis had had enough. Well on in years and financially ruined by the war, he decided to quit farming. So, on November 19, 1866, he sold his Mississippi plantations Hurricane and Brierfield to Benjamin Montgomery and his sons. The sale of southern plantations was common enough after the war, but

this transaction was bound to attract attention, since Joseph Davis was the elder brother of Jefferson Davis. Indeed, before the war the ex-Confederate president had operated Brierfield as his own plantation, even though his brother retained legal title to it. But the sale was unusual for another reason—so unusual that the parties involved agreed to keep it secret. The plantation's new owners were black, and Mississippi law prohibited African Americans from owning land.

Though a slave, Benjamin Montgomery had been the business manager of the two Davis plantations before the war. He had also operated a store on Hurricane Plan-

# Reconstructing the Union
## 1865–1877

**Preview** *Reconstruction became the battleground of attempts to define the new shape of the Union. Congress rejected Andrew Johnson's lenient terms for the South's reentry and enacted a program that included the principle of black suffrage. African Americans asserted their freedom by uniting divided families, establishing churches, and seeking education and land. But when northern whites became disillusioned with reform, the ideology of white supremacy brought Reconstruction to an end.*

tation with his own line of credit in New Orleans. In 1863 Montgomery fled to the North, but when the war was over, he returned to Davis Bend, where the federal government had confiscated the Davis plantations and was leasing plots of the land to black farmers. Montgomery quickly emerged as the leader of the African American community at the Bend.

Then, in 1866, President Andrew Johnson pardoned Joseph Davis and restored his lands. Davis was now over 80 years old and lacked the will and stamina to rebuild, yet unlike many ex-slaveholders, he felt bound by obligations to his former slaves. Convinced that with proper encouragement African Americans could succeed economically in freedom, he sold his land secretly to Benjamin Montgomery. Only when the law prohibiting African Americans from owning land was overturned in 1867 did Davis publicly confirm the sale to his former slave.

For his part, Montgomery undertook to create a model society at Davis Bend based on mutual cooperation. He rented land to black farmers, hired others to work his own fields, sold supplies on credit, and ginned and marketed the crops. To the growing African American community, he preached the gospel of hard work, self-reliance, and education.

Various difficulties dogged these black farmers, including the destruction caused by the war, several disastrous floods, insects, droughts, and declining cotton prices. Yet before long, cotton production exceeded that of the prewar years, and in 1870 the black families at Davis Bend produced 2500 bales. The Montgomerys eventually acquired 5500 acres, which made them reputedly the third largest planters in the state, and they won national and international awards for the quality of their cotton. Their success demonstrated what African Americans, given a fair chance, might accomplish.

The experiences of Benjamin Montgomery during the years after 1865 were not those of most black southerners, who did not own land or have a powerful white benefactor. Yet Montgomery's dream of economic independence was shared by all African Americans. As one black veteran noted, "Every colored man will be a slave, and feel himself a slave until he can raise him own *bale of cotton* and put him own mark upon it and say dis is mine!" Blacks could not gain effective freedom simply through a proclamation of emancipation. They also needed economic power, including their own land that no one could unfairly take away.

For nearly two centuries the laws had prevented slaves from possessing such economic power. If these conditions were to be overturned, black Americans needed political power too. Thus the Republic would have to be reconstructed to give African Americans political power that they had been previously denied.

War, in its blunt way, had roughed out the contours of a solution, but only in broad terms. Clearly, African Americans would no longer be enslaved. The North, with its industrial might, would be the driving force in the nation's economy and retain the dominant political voice. But beyond that, the outlines of a reconstructed Republic remained vague. Would African Americans receive effective power? How would North and South readjust their economic and political relations? These questions lay at the heart of the problem of Reconstruction.

## PRESIDENTIAL RECONSTRUCTION

Throughout the war Abraham Lincoln had considered Reconstruction his responsibility. Elected with less than 40 percent of the popular vote in 1860, he was acutely aware that once the states of the Confederacy were restored to the Union, the Republicans would be weakened unless they ceased to be a sectional party. By a generous peace, Lincoln hoped to attract former Whigs in the South, who supported many of the Republicans' economic policies, and build up a southern wing of the party.

## Lincoln's 10 Percent Plan

Lincoln outlined his program in a Proclamation of Amnesty and Reconstruction, issued in December 1863. When a minimum of 10 percent of the qualified voters from 1860 took a loyalty oath to the Union, they could organize a state government. The new state constitution had to abolish slavery and provide for black education, but Lincoln did not insist that high-ranking Confederate leaders be barred from public life.

Lincoln indicated that he would be generous in granting pardons to prominent Confederate leaders and did not rule out compensation for slave property. Moreover, while he privately advocated limited black suffrage in the disloyal southern states, he did not demand social or political equality for black Americans, and he recognized pro-Union governments in Louisiana, Arkansas, and Tennessee that allowed only white men to vote.

The Radical Republicans found Lincoln's approach much too lenient. Strongly antislavery, Radical members of Congress had led the struggle to make emancipation a war aim. Now they led the fight to guarantee the rights of former slaves, or freedpeople. The Radicals believed that it was the duty of Congress, not the president, to set the terms under which states would regain their rights in the Union. Though the Radicals often disagreed on other matters, they were united in a determination to readmit southern states only after slavery had been ended, black rights protected, and the power of the planter class destroyed. | *Radical Republicans*

Under the direction of Senator Benjamin Wade of Ohio and Representative Henry Winter Davis of Maryland, Congress formulated a much stricter plan of Reconstruction. It required half the white adult males to take an oath of allegiance before drafting a new state constitution, and it restricted political power to the hard-core Unionists. When the Wade-Davis bill passed on the final day of the 1864 congressional session, Lincoln exercised his right of a pocket veto.* Still, his own program could not succeed without the assistance of Congress, which refused to recognize his governments in Louisiana and Arkansas. As the war drew to a close, Lincoln appeared ready to make concessions to the Radicals, and at his final cabinet meeting he approved placing the defeated South temporarily under military rule. But only a few days later Booth's bullet found its mark, and Lincoln's final approach to Reconstruction would never be known. | *Wade-Davis bill*

## The Mood of the South

In the wake of defeat, the immediate reaction among white southerners was one of shock, despair, and hopelessness. Some former Confederates were openly antagonistic. A North Carolina innkeeper remarked bitterly that Yankees had

---

*If a president does not sign a bill after Congress has adjourned, it has the same effect as a veto.

The mood of white southerners at the end of the war was mixed. Many, like the veteran caricatured here by northern cartoonist Thomas Nast, remained hostile. Others, like Texas captain Samuel Foster, came to believe that the institution of slavery "had been abused, and perhaps for that abuse this terrible war . . . was brought upon us as a punishment."

stolen his slaves, burned his house, and killed all his sons, leaving him only one privilege: "To hate 'em. I git up at half-past four in the morning, and sit up till twelve at night, to hate 'em." Most Confederate soldiers were less defiant, having had their fill of war. Even among hostile civilians the feeling was widespread that the South must accept northern terms. A South Carolina paper admitted that "the conqueror has the right to make the terms, and we must submit."

This psychological moment was critical. To prevent a resurgence of resistance, the president needed to lay out in unmistakable terms what white southerners had to do to regain their old status in the Union. Perhaps even a clear and firm policy would not have been enough. But with Lincoln's death, the executive power came to rest in far less capable hands.

## Johnson's Program of Reconstruction

Andrew Johnson, the new president, had been born in North Carolina and eventually moved to Tennessee, where he worked as a tailor. Barely able to read and write when he married, he rose to political power by portraying himself as the champion of the people against the wealthy planter class. "Some day I will show the stuck-up aristocrats who is running the country," he vowed as he began his political career. He had not opposed slavery before the war, and although he accepted emancipation as one consequence of the war, Johnson remained a confirmed racist with no concern for the welfare of African Americans. "Damn the negroes," he said during the war, "I am fighting these traitorous aristocrats, their masters."

*Johnson's character and values*

During the war he had joined the Radicals in calling for stern treatment of southern rebels. "Treason must be made odious and traitors must be punished and impoverished," he proclaimed in 1864. After serving in Congress and as military governor of Tennessee following its occupation by Union forces, Johnson, a Democrat, was tapped by Lincoln in 1864 as his running mate on the rechristened "Union" ticket.

The Radicals expected Johnson to uphold their views on Reconstruction, and upon assuming the presidency he spoke of trying Confederate leaders and breaking up planters' estates. Unlike most Republicans, however, Johnson strongly supported states' rights and opposed government aid to business. Given such differences, conflict between the president and the majority in Congress was inevitable, but Johnson's political shortcomings made the situation worse. Scarred by his humble origins, he became tactless and inflexible when challenged or criticized, and he alienated even those who sought to work with him.

Johnson moved to quickly return the southern states to their place in the Union. He prescribed a loyalty oath white southerners would have to take to regain their civil and political rights and to have their property, except for slaves, restored. Excluded were high Confederate officials and those with property worth over $20,000, who had to apply for individual pardons. Johnson announced that once a state had drafted a new constitution and elected state officers and members of Congress, he would revoke martial law and recognize the new state government. Suffrage was limited to white citizens who had taken the loyalty oath. This plan was similar to Lincoln's, though more lenient. Only informally did Johnson stipulate that the southern states were to renounce their ordinances of secession, repudiate the Confederate debt, and ratify the proposed Thirteenth Amendment abolishing slavery.

*Johnson's program*

## The Failure of Johnson's Program

The southern delegates who met to construct new governments soon demonstrated that they were in no frame of mind to follow Johnson's recommendations. Several states merely repealed instead of repudiating their ordinances of secession, rejected the Thirteenth Amendment, or refused to repudiate the Confederate debt.

Nor did any of the new governments allow African Americans any political rights or provide in any effective way for black education. In addition, each state passed a series of laws, often modeled on its old slave code, that applied only to African Americans. These "black codes" did give African Americans some rights that had not been granted to slaves. They legalized marriages from slavery and allowed black southerners to hold and sell property and to sue and be sued in state courts. Yet their primary intent was to keep African Americans as propertyless agricultural laborers with inferior legal rights. The new freedpeople could not serve on juries, testify against whites, or work as they pleased. Mississippi prohibited them from buying or renting farmland, and most states ominously provided that black people who were vagrants could be arrested and hired out to landowners. Many northerners were incensed by the restrictive black codes, which violated their conception of freedom.

*Black codes*

Andrew Johnson was a staunch Unionist, but his contentious personality and inflexibility soured his relationship with Congress.

Southern voters under Johnson's plan also defiantly elected prominent Confederate military and political leaders to office. At this point, Johnson could have called for new elections or admitted that a different program of Reconstruction was needed. Instead he caved in. For all his harsh rhetoric, he shrank from the prospect of social upheaval, and as the lines of ex-Confederates waiting to see him lengthened, he began issuing special pardons almost as fast as they could be printed. Publicly Johnson put on a bold face, announcing that Reconstruction had been successfully completed. But many members of Congress were deeply alarmed, and the stage was set for a serious confrontation.

*Elections in the South*

## Johnson's Break with Congress

The new Congress was by no means of one mind. A small number of Democrats and a few conservative Republicans backed the president's program of immediate and unconditional restoration. At the other end of the spectrum, a larger group of Radical Republicans, led by Thaddeus Stevens, Charles Sumner, Benjamin Wade, and others, was bent on remaking southern society in the image of the North. Reconstruction must "revolutionize Southern institutions, habits, and manners," thundered Representative Stevens, ". . . or all our blood and treasure have been spent in vain."

As a minority, the Radicals needed the aid of the moderate Republicans, the largest bloc in Congress. Led by William Pitt Fessenden and Lyman Trumbull, the moderates hoped to avoid a clash with the president, and they had no desire to foster social revolution or promote racial equality in the South. But they wanted to keep Confederate leaders from reassuming power, and they were convinced that the former slaves needed federal protection. Otherwise, Trumbull declared, the freedpeople would "be tyrannized over, abused, and virtually reenslaved."

The central issue dividing Johnson and the Radicals was the place of African Americans in American society. Johnson accused his opponents of seeking "to Africanize the southern half of our country," while the Radicals championed civil and political rights for African Americans. The only way to maintain loyal governments and develop a Republican party in the South, Radicals argued, was to give black men the ballot. Moderates agreed that the new southern governments were too harsh toward African Americans, but they feared that too great an emphasis on black civil rights would alienate northern voters.

*Issue of black rights*

In December 1865, when southern representatives to Congress appeared in Washington, a majority in Congress voted to exclude them. Congress also appointed a joint committee, chaired by Senator Fessenden, to look into Reconstruction.

The growing split with the president became clearer when Congress passed a bill extending the life of the Freedmen's Bureau. Created in March 1865, the bureau provided emergency food, clothing, and medical care to war refugees (including white southerners) and took charge of settling freedpeople on abandoned lands. The new bill gave the bureau the added responsibilities of supervising special courts to resolve disputes involving freedpeople and establishing schools for black southerners. Although this bill passed with virtually unanimous Republican support, Johnson vetoed it.

Johnson also vetoed a civil rights bill designed to overturn the more flagrant provisions of the black codes. The law made African Americans citizens of the United States and granted them the right to own property, make con- *Johnson's vetoes* tracts, and have access to courts as parties and witnesses. For most Republicans Johnson's action was the last straw, and in April 1866 Congress overrode his veto. Congress then approved a slightly revised Freedmen's Bureau bill in July and promptly overrode the president's veto. Johnson's refusal to compromise drove the moderates into the arms of the Radicals.

## The Fourteenth Amendment

To prevent unrepentant Confederates from taking over the reconstructed state governments and denying African Americans basic freedoms, the Joint Committee on Reconstruction proposed an amendment to the Constitution, which passed both houses of Congress with the necessary two-thirds vote in June 1866.

The amendment guaranteed repayment of the national war debt and prohibited repayment of the Confederate debt. To counteract the president's wholesale pardons, it disqualified prominent Confederates from holding office *Provisions of the* and provided that only Congress by a two-thirds vote could remove *amendment* this penalty. Because moderates balked at giving the vote to African Americans, the amendment merely gave Congress the right to reduce the representation of any state that did not have impartial male suffrage. The practical effect of this provision, which Radicals labeled a "swindle," was to allow northern states to retain white suffrage, since unlike southern states they had few African Americans in their populations and thus would not be penalized.

The amendment's most important provision, Section 1, defined an American citizen as anyone born in the United States or naturalized, thereby automatically making African Americans citizens. Section 1 also prohibited states from abridging "the privileges or immunities" of citizens, depriving "any person of life, liberty, or property, without due process of law," or denying "any person . . . equal protection of the laws." The framers of the amendment probably intended to prohibit laws that applied to one race only, such as the black codes, or that made certain acts felonies when committed by black but not white people, or that decreed different penalties for the same crime when committed by white and black lawbreakers. The framers probably did not intend to prevent segregation (the legal separation of the races) in schools and public places.

Johnson denounced the proposed amendment and urged southern states not to ratify it. Ironically, of the seceded states only the president's own state ratified the amendment, and Congress readmitted Tennessee with no further restrictions. The telegram sent to Congress by a longtime foe of Johnson officially announcing Tennessee's approval ended, "Give my respects to the dead dog in the White House."

## The Election of 1866

When Congress blocked his policies, Johnson undertook a speaking tour of the East and Midwest in the fall of 1866 to drum up popular support. But Johnson found it difficult to convince northern audiences that white southerners were fully repentant. Only months earlier white mobs in Memphis and New Orleans had attacked black residents and killed nearly 100 in two major race riots. "The negroes now know, to their sorrow, that it is best not to arouse the fury of the white man," boasted one Memphis newspaper. When the president encountered hostile audiences during his northern campaign, he only made matters worse by trading insults and proclaiming that the Radicals were traitors.

Not to be outdone, the Radicals vilified Johnson as a traitor aiming to turn the country over to former rebels. Resorting to the tactic of "waving the bloody shirt," they appealed to voters by reviving bitter memories of the war. In a classic example of such rhetoric, Governor Oliver Morton of Indiana proclaimed that "every bounty jumper, every deserter, every sneak who ran away from the draft" was a Democrat; every "New York rioter in 1863 who burned up little children in colored asylums called himself a Democrat. In short, the Democratic party may be described as a common sewer."

*Repudiation of Johnson*

Voters soundly repudiated Johnson, as the Republicans won more than a two-thirds majority in both houses of Congress. The Radicals had reached the height of their power, propelled by genuine alarm among northerners that Johnson's policies would lose the fruits of the Union's victory. Johnson was a president virtually without a party.

## CONGRESSIONAL RECONSTRUCTION

With a clear mandate in hand, congressional Republicans passed their own program of Reconstruction, beginning with the first Reconstruction Act in March 1867. Like all later pieces of Reconstruction legislation, it was repassed over Johnson's veto.

Placing the 10 unreconstructed states under military commanders, the act provided that in enrolling voters, officials were to include black adult males but not former Confederates who were barred from holding office under the Fourteenth Amendment. Delegates to the state conventions were to frame constitutions that provided for black suffrage and disqualified prominent ex-Confederates from office. The first state legislatures to meet under the new constitution were required to ratify the Fourteenth Amendment. Once these steps were completed and Congress approved the new state constitution, a state could send representatives to Congress.

White southerners found these requirements so obnoxious that officials took no steps to register voters. Congress then enacted a second Reconstruction Act, also in March, ordering the local military commanders to put the machinery of Reconstruction into motion. Johnson's efforts to limit the power of military commanders produced a third act, passed in July, that upheld their superiority in all matters. When the first election was held in Alabama to ratify the new state constitution, whites boycotted it in sufficient numbers to prevent a majority of voters from participating. Undaunted, Congress passed the fourth Reconstruction Act (March 1868), which required ratification of the constitution by only a majority of those voting rather than those who were registered.

*Resistance of white southerners*

By June 1868 Congress had readmitted the representatives of seven states. Texas, Virginia, and Mississippi did not complete the process until 1869. Georgia finally followed in 1870.

## Post-emancipation Societies in the Americas

With the exception of Haiti's revolution (1791–1804), the United States was the only society in the Americas in which the destruction of slavery was accomplished by violence. But the United States, uniquely among these societies, enfranchised former slaves almost immediately after the emancipation. Thus in the United States former masters and slaves battled for control of the state in ways that did not occur in other post-emancipation societies. In most of the Caribbean, property requirements for voting left the planters in political control. Jamaica, for example, with a population of 500,000 in the 1860s, had only 3000 voters.

Moreover, in reaction to political efforts to mobilize disfranchised black peasants, Jamaican planters dissolved the assembly and reverted to being a Crown colony governed from London. Of the sugar islands, all but Barbados adopted the same policy, thereby blocking the potential for any future black peasant democracy. Nor did any of these societies have the counterparts of the Radical Republicans, a group of outsiders with political power that promoted the fundamental transformation of the post-emancipation South. These comparisons highlight the radicalism of Reconstruction in the United States, which alone saw an effort to forge an interracial democracy.

## The Land Issue

While the political process of Reconstruction proceeded, Congress debated whether land should be given to former slaves to foster economic independence. At a meeting with Secretary of War Edwin Stanton near the end of the war, African American leaders declared, "The way we can best take care of ourselves is to have land, and till it by our own labor." The Second Confiscation Act of 1862 had authorized the government to seize and sell the property of supporters of the rebellion. In June 1866, however, President Johnson ruled that confiscation laws applied only to wartime.

For over a year Congress debated land confiscation off and on, but in the end it rejected all proposals to give land to former slaves. Even some Radicals were opposed. Given Americans' strong belief in self-reliance, little sympathy existed for the idea that government should support any group. In addition, land redistribution represented an attack on property rights, another cherished American

*Failure of land redistribution*

value. "A division of rich men's lands amongst the landless," argued the *Nation*, a Radical journal, "would give a shock to our whole social and political system from which it would hardly recover without the loss of liberty." By 1867 land reform was dead.

Few freedpeople acquired land after the war, a development that severely limited African Americans' economic independence and left them vulnerable to white coercion. It is doubtful, however, that this decision was the basic cause of the failure of Reconstruction. In the face of white hostility, African Americans probably would have been no more successful in protecting their property than they were in maintaining the right to vote.

## Impeachment

Throughout 1867 Congress routinely overrode Johnson's vetoes, but the president had other ways of undercutting congressional Reconstruction. He interpreted the new laws as narrowly as possible and removed military commanders who vigorously enforced them. Congress responded by restricting his power to issue orders to mil-

*Tenure of Office Act*

itary commanders in the South. It also passed the Tenure of Office Act, which forbade Johnson to remove any member of the cabinet without the Senate's consent. The intention of this law was to prevent him from firing Secretary of War Edwin Stanton, the only remaining Radical in the cabinet.

When Johnson tried to dismiss Stanton in February 1868, the House of Representatives angrily approved articles of impeachment. The articles focused on the violation of the Tenure of Office Act, but the charge with the most substance was that Johnson had acted to systematically obstruct Reconstruction legislation.

*Johnson's acquittal*

In the trial before the Senate, his lawyers argued that a president could be impeached only for an indictable crime, which Johnson clearly had not committed. The Radicals countered that impeachment applied to political offenses and not merely criminal acts. In May 1868 the Senate voted 35 to 19 to convict, one vote short of the two-thirds majority needed. The seven Republicans who joined the Democrats in voting for acquittal were uneasy about using impeachment as a political weapon.

## RECONSTRUCTION IN THE SOUTH

The waning power of the Radicals in Congress, evident in the failure to remove Johnson, meant that the success or failure of Reconstruction increasingly hinged on developments in the southern states themselves. Power in these states rested with the new Republican parties, representing a coalition of black and white southerners and transplanted northerners.

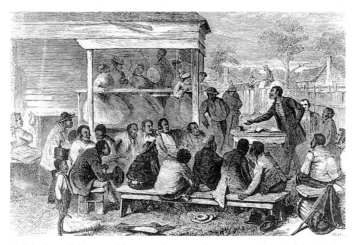

A black politician addresses former slaves at a political meeting in the South during the 1868 presidential campaign. Although only men could vote, black women are also in the audience.

### Black Officeholding

Almost from the beginning of Reconstruction, African Americans had lobbied for the right to vote. After they received the franchise, black men constituted as much as 80 percent of the Republican voters in the South. They steadfastly opposed the Democratic party with its appeal to white supremacy. As one Tennessee Republican explained, "The blacks know that many conservatives [Democrats] hope to reduce them again to some form of peonage. Under the impulse of this fear they will roll up their whole strength and will go entirely for the Republican candidate whoever he may be."

Throughout Reconstruction, African Americans never held office in proportion to their voting strength. No African American was ever elected governor, and only in South Carolina, where more than 60 percent of the population was black, did they control even one house of the legislature. During Reconstruction between 15 and 20 percent of the state officers and 6 percent of members of Congress (2 senators and 15 representatives) were black. Only in South Carolina did black officeholders approach their proportion of the population.

Those who held office came from the top levels of African American society. Among state and federal officeholders, perhaps four-fifths were literate, and over a quarter had been free before the war, both marks of distinction in the black community. Their occupations also set them apart: two-fifths were professionals (mostly clergy), and of the third who were farmers, nearly all owned land. In their political and social values, African American leaders were more conservative than the rural black population, and they showed little interest in land reform.

*Black political leadership*

## White Republicans in the South

Black citizens were a majority of the voters only in South Carolina, Mississippi, and Louisiana. Thus in most of the South the Republican party had to secure

*Scalawags*

white votes to stay in power. Opponents scornfully labeled white southerners who allied with the Republican party scalawags, yet an estimated quarter of white southerners at one time voted Republican. They were primarily Unionists from the upland counties and hill areas who were largely yeoman farmers. Such voters were attracted by Republican promises to rebuild the South, restore prosperity, create public schools, and open isolated areas to the market with railroads.

The other group of white Republicans in the South were known as carpetbaggers. Originally from the North, they allegedly had arrived with all their

*Carpetbaggers*

worldly possessions stuffed in a carpetbag, ready to loot and plunder the defeated South. Some did, certainly, but northerners moved south for a variety of reasons. Though carpetbaggers made up only a small percentage of Republican voters, they controlled almost a third of the offices. More than half of all southern Republican governors and nearly half of Republican members of Congress were originally northerners.

The Republican party in the South had difficulty maintaining unity. Scalawags were especially susceptible to the race issue and social pressure. "Even my own kinspeople have turned the cold shoulder to me because I hold office under a Republican administration," testified a Mississippi white Republican. As black southerners pressed for greater recognition, white southerners increasingly defected to the Democrats. Carpetbaggers, in contrast, were less sensitive to race, although most felt that their black allies should be content with minor offices. The animosity between scalawags and carpetbaggers, which grew out of their rivalry for party honors, was particularly intense.

## Reforms under the New State Governments

The new southern state constitutions enacted several significant reforms. They devised fairer systems of legislative representation and made many previously

*Reconstruction state constitutions*

appointive offices elective. The Radical state governments also assumed some responsibility for social welfare and established the first statewide systems of public schools in the South. Although the Fourteenth Amendment prevented high Confederate officials from holding office, only Alabama and Arkansas temporarily prohibited some ex-Confederates from voting.

All the new constitutions proclaimed the principle of equality and granted

*Race and social equality*

black adult males the right to vote. On social relations they were much more cautious. No state outlawed segregation, and South Carolina and Louisiana were the only ones that required integration in public schools (a mandate that was almost universally ignored). Sensitive to status, mulattoes pushed for prohibition of social discrimination, but white Republicans refused to adopt such a radical policy.

### Economic Issues and Corruption

With the southern economy in ruins at the end of the war, problems of economic reconstruction were severe. The new Republican governments sought to encourage industrial development by providing subsidies, loans, and even temporary exemptions from taxes. These governments also largely rebuilt the southern railroad system, often offering lavish aid to railroad corporations. In the two decades after 1860, the region doubled its manufacturing establishments, yet the South steadily slipped further behind the booming industrial economy of the North.

The expansion of government services offered temptations for corruption. In many southern states, officials regularly received bribes and kickbacks for their award of railroad charters, franchises, and other contracts. *Corruption* By 1872 the debts of the 11 states of the Confederacy had increased $132 million, largely because of railroad grants and new social services such as schools. The tax rate grew as expenditures went up, so that by the 1870s it was four times the rate of 1860.

Corruption, however, was not only a southern problem: the decline in morality affected the entire nation. During these years, the Democratic Tweed Ring in New York City alone stole more money than all the Radical Republican governments in the South combined. Moreover, corruption in the South was hardly limited to Republicans. Many Democrats and white business leaders participated in these corrupt practices, both before and after the Radical governments were in power. Louisiana governor Henry Warmoth, a carpetbagger, told a congressional committee, "Everybody is demoralizing down here. Corruption is the fashion."

Corruption in Radical governments undeniably existed, but southern Democrats exaggerated its extent for partisan purposes. They opposed honest Radical regimes just as bitterly as notoriously corrupt ones. In the eyes of most white southerners, the real crime of the Radical governments was that they allowed black citizens to hold some offices and tried to protect the civil rights of black Americans. Race was white conservatives' greatest weapon. And it would prove the most effective means to undermine Republican power in the South.

## BLACK ASPIRATIONS

Emancipation came to slaves in different ways and at different times. Betty Jones's grandmother was told about the Emancipation Proclamation by another slave while they were hoeing corn. Mary Anderson received the news from her master near the end of the war when Sherman's army invaded North Carolina. And for Louis Napoleon, emancipation arrived after the war when Union troops occupied Tallahassee, Florida. Whatever the timing, freedom meant a host of precious blessings to people who had been in bondage all their lives.

## Experiencing Freedom

The first impulse was to think of freedom as a contrast to slavery. Emancipation immediately released slaves from the most oppressive aspects of bondage—the whippings, the breakup of families, the sexual exploitation. Freedom also meant movement, the right to travel without a pass or white permission. Above all, freedom meant that African Americans' labor would be for their own benefit. One Arkansas freedman, who earned his first dollar working on a railroad, recalled that when he was paid, "I felt like the richest man in the world."

*Meaning of freedom*

Freedom included finding a new place to work. Changing jobs was one concrete way to break the psychological ties of slavery. Even planters with reputations for kindness sometimes found that most of their former hands had departed. The cook who left a South Carolina family, even though they offered her higher wages than her new job did, explained, "I must go. If I stays here I'll never know I'm free."

Symbolically, freedom meant having a full name. African Americans now adopted last names, most commonly the name of the first master in the family's oral history as far back as it could be recalled. Most, on the other hand, retained their first name, especially if the name had been given to them by their parents (as most often had been the case). Whatever name they took, it was important to black Americans that they made the decision themselves.

## The Black Family

African Americans also sought to strengthen the family in freedom. Since slave marriages had not been recognized as legal, thousands of former slaves insisted on being married again by proper authorities, even though this was not required by law. Those who had been forcibly separated in slavery and later remarried confronted the dilemma of which spouse to take. Laura Spicer, whose husband had been sold away in slavery, wrote him after the war seeking to resume their marriage. In a series of wrenching letters, he explained that he had thought her dead, had remarried, and had a new family. "You know it never was our wishes to be separated from each other, and it never was our fault. I had rather anything to had happened to me most than ever have been parted from you and the children," he wrote. "As I am, I do not know which I love best, you or Anna." Declining to return, he closed, "Laura, truly, I have got another wife, and I am very sorry."

*Upholding the family*

As in white families, black husbands deemed themselves the head of the family and acted legally for their wives. They often insisted that their wives would not work in the fields as they had in slavery. "The [black] women say they never mean to do any more outdoor work," one planter reported, "that white men support their wives and they mean that their husbands shall support them." In negotiating contracts, a father also demanded the right to control his children and their labor. All these changes were designed to insulate the black family from white control.

### The Schoolhouse and the Church

In freedom, the schoolhouse and the black church became essential institutions in the black community. "My Lord, Ma'am, what a great thing learning is!" a South Carolina freedman told a northern teacher. "White folks can do what they likes, for they know so much more than we." At first, northern churches and missionaries, working with the Freedmen's Bureau, set up black schools in the South. Tuition at these schools represented 10 percent or more of a laborer's monthly wages, yet these schools were full. Eventually, states established public school systems, which by 1867 enrolled 40 percent of African American children.

*Black education*

Black adults, who often attended night classes, had good reasons for seeking literacy. They wanted to be able to read the Bible, to defend their newly gained civil and political rights, and to protect themselves from being cheated. Both races saw that education would undermine the old servility that slavery had fostered.

The teachers in the Freedmen's Bureau schools were primarily northern middle-class white women sent south by northern missionary societies. "I feel that it is a precious privilege," Esther Douglass wrote, "to be allowed to do something for these poor people." Many saw themselves as peacetime soldiers, struggling to make emancipation a reality. Indeed, hostile white southerners sometimes destroyed black schools and threatened and even murdered white teachers. Then there were the everyday challenges: low pay, dilapidated buildings, insufficient books, classes of 100 or more children, and irregular attendance. Meanwhile, the Freedmen's Bureau undertook to train black teachers, and by 1869 a majority of the teachers in these schools were black.

*Teachers in black schools*

Most slaves had attended white churches or services supervised by whites. Once free, African Americans quickly established their own congregations led by black preachers. Mostly Methodist and Baptist, black churches were the only major organizations in the African American community controlled by blacks themselves. A white missionary reported that "the Ebony preacher who promises perfect independence from White control and direction carried the colored heart at once." Just as in slavery, religion offered

*Independent black churches*

African Americans a place of refuge in a hostile white world and provided them with hope, comfort, and a means of self-identification.

## New Working Conditions

As a largely propertyless class, blacks in the postwar South had no choice but to work for white landowners. Except for paying wages, whites wanted to retain the old system of labor, including close supervision, gang labor, and physical punishment. Determined to remove all emblems of servitude, African Americans refused to work under these conditions, and they demanded time off to devote to their own interests. Because of shorter hours and the withdrawal of children and women from the fields, blacks' output declined by an estimated 35 percent in freedom. They also refused to live in the old slave quarters located near the master's house and instead erected cabins on distant parts of the plantation. Wages initially were $5 or $6 a month plus provisions and a cabin; by 1867, they had risen to an average of $10 a month.

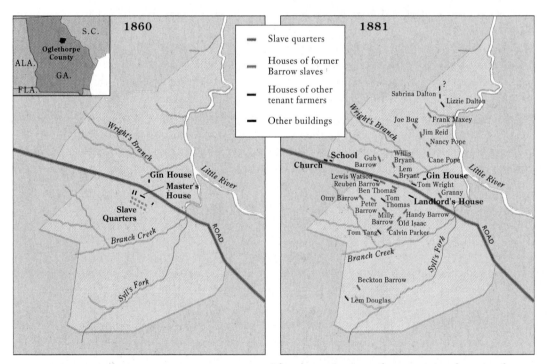

A GEORGIA PLANTATION AFTER THE WAR   After emancipation, sharecropping became the dominant form of agricultural labor in the South. Black families no longer lived in the old slave quarters but dispersed themselves to separate plots of land that they farmed themselves. At the end of the year each sharecropper turned over part of the crop to the white landowner.

These changes eventually led to the rise of sharecropping. Under this arrangement African American families farmed separate plots of land and then at the end of the year divided the crop, normally on an equal basis, with the white landowner. Sharecropping had higher status and offered *Sharecropping* greater personal freedom than being a wage laborer. "I am not working for wages," one black farmer declared in defending his right to leave the plantation at will, "but am part owner of the crop and as [such,] I have all the rights that you or any other man has." Although black per capita agricultural income increased 40 percent in freedom, sharecropping was a harshly exploitative system in which black families often sank into perpetual debt.

## The Freedmen's Bureau

The task of supervising the transition from slavery to freedom on southern plantations fell to the Freedmen's Bureau, a unique experiment in social policy supported by the federal government. Assigned the task of protecting freedpeople's economic rights, approximately 550 local agents regulated working conditions in southern agriculture after the war. The racial attitudes of Bureau agents varied widely, as did their commitment and competence. Then, too, they had to depend on the army to enforce their decisions.

Most agents required written contracts between white planters and black laborers, specifying not only wages but also the conditions of employment. Although agents sometimes intervened to protect freedpeople from un- *The Bureau's mixed* fair treatment, they also provided important help to planters. They *record* insisted that black laborers not leave at harvesttime, they arrested those who violated their contracts or refused to sign new ones at the beginning of the year, and they preached the gospel of hard work and the need to be orderly and respectful. Given such attitudes, freedpeople increasingly complained that Bureau agents were mere tools of the planter class. One observer reported, "Doing justice seems to mean seeing that the blacks don't break contracts and compelling them to submit cheerfully."

The primary means of enforcing working conditions were the Freedmen's Courts, which Congress created in 1866 in order to avoid the discrimination African Americans received in state courts. These new courts functioned as military tribunals, and often the agent was the entire court. The sympathy black laborers received varied from state to state. In 1867 one agent summarized the Bureau's experience with the labor contract system: "It has succeeded in making the freedman work and in rendering labor secure and stable—but it has failed to secure to the Freedman his just dues or compensation."

Opposed to any permanent welfare agency, Congress in 1869 decided to shut down the Bureau, and by 1872 it had gone out of business. Despite its mixed record, it was the most effective agency in protecting blacks' civil and political rights. Its disbanding signaled the beginning of the northern retreat from Reconstruction.

## Planters and a New Way of Life

Planters and other white southerners faced emancipation with dread. "All the traditions and habits of both races had been suddenly overthrown," a Tennessee planter recalled, "and neither knew just what to do, or how to accommodate themselves to the new situation."

The old ideal of a paternalistic planter, which required a facade of black subservience and affection, gave way to an emphasis on strictly economic relationships. When two black laborers falsely accused her of trickery and hauled her into court, Mary Jones, a Georgia slaveholder before the war, told her assembled employees that she had previously "considered them friends and treated them as such but now they were only laborers under contract, and only the law would rule between us." Only with time did planters develop new norms to judge black behavior. What in 1865 had seemed insolence was viewed by the 1870s as the normal attitude of freedom.

Slavery had been a complex institution that welded black and white southerners together in intimate relationships. After the war, however, planters increasingly *Planters' new values* embraced the ideology of segregation. Since emancipation significantly reduced the social distance between the races, white southerners sought psychological separation and kept dealings with African Americans to a minimum. By the time Reconstruction ended, white planters had developed a new way of life based on the institutions of sharecropping and segregation and undergirded by a militant white supremacy.

While most planters kept their land, they did not regain the economic prosperity of the prewar years. Cotton prices began a long decline, and southern per capita income suffered as a result. By 1880 the value of southern farms had slid 33 percent below the level of 1860.

## THE ABANDONMENT OF RECONSTRUCTION

On Christmas Day 1875 a white acquaintance approached Charles Caldwell in Clinton, Mississippi, and invited him to have a drink. A former slave, Caldwell was a state senator and the leader of the Republican party in Hinds County. But the black leader's fearlessness made him a marked man. Only two months earlier, Caldwell had fled the county to escape an armed white mob. Despite threats against him, he had returned home to vote in the November state election. Now, as Caldwell and his "friend" raised their glasses in a holiday toast, a gunshot exploded through the window and Caldwell collapsed, mortally wounded. He was taken outside, where his assassins riddled his body with bullets. He died alone in the street.

Charles Caldwell shared the fate of a number of black Republican leaders in the South during Reconstruction. Resorting to violence and terror, southern whites challenged the commitment of the federal government to sustaining Reconstruction. But following Johnson's acquittal, the Radicals' influence waned, and the Republican party was increasingly drained of its crusading idealism. Ulysses S. Grant was hardly the cause of this change, but he certainly came to symbolize it.

## The Election of Grant

In 1868 Republicans nominated Grant for president. Although he was elected, Republicans were shocked that despite his status as a great war hero, his popular margin was only 300,000 votes and that, with an estimated 450,000 black Republican votes cast in the South, a majority of whites had voted Democratic. The 1868 election helped convince Republican leaders that an amendment securing black suffrage throughout the nation was necessary.

In February 1869 Congress sent the Fifteenth Amendment to the states for ratification. It forbade any state to deny the right to vote on grounds of race, color, or previous condition of servitude. It did not forbid literacy and property requirements, as some Radicals wanted, because the moderates feared that only a conservative version could be ratified. *Fifteenth Amendment ratified* As a result, the final amendment left loopholes that eventually allowed southern states to disfranchise African Americans. Furthermore, advocates of women's suffrage like Lucy Stone and Susan B. Anthony were bitterly disappointed when Congress refused to prohibit voting discrimination on the basis of sex as well as race. The amendment was ratified in March 1870, aided by the votes of the four southern states that had not completed the process of Reconstruction and thus were also required to endorse this amendment before being readmitted to Congress.

## The Grant Administration

Ulysses S. Grant was ill at ease with the political process: his simple, quiet manner, while superb for commanding armies, did not serve him as well in public life, and his well-known resolution withered when he was uncertain of his goal.

A series of scandals wracked Grant's presidency, so much so that "Grantism" soon became a code word in American politics for corruption, cronyism, and venality. Although Grant did not profit personally, he remained loyal to his friends and displayed little zeal to root out wrongdoing. James W. *Corruption under Grant* Grimes, one of the party's founders, denounced the Republican party under Grant as "the most corrupt and debauched political party that has ever existed."

Nor was Congress immune from the lowered tone of public life. In such a climate ruthless state machines, led by men who favored the status quo, came to dominate the party. Office and power became ends in themselves, and party leaders worked in close cooperation with northern industrial interests.

New Anglos frequently fought Hispanos. But it was western lawyers and politicians, using legal tactics, who deprived Hispanos of most of their property. Thomas Catron, an ambitious New Mexico lawyer, squeezed out many Hispanos by contesting land titles so aggressively that his holdings grew to 3 million acres. In those areas of New Mexico and California where they remained a majority, Hispanos continued to play a role in public life. During the early 1890s Herrera and his allies formed a "People's Party," swept local elections, and managed to defeat a bid by Catron to represent the territory in Congress.

With the railroads came more white settlers as well as Mexican laborers from south of the border. Just as the southern economy depended on African American labor, the Southwest grew on the labor of Mexicans. Mexican immigrants worked mostly as contract and seasonal laborers for railroads *Mexican immigrants* and large farms. Many of them settled in the growing cities along the rail lines: El Paso, Albuquerque, Tucson, Phoenix, and Los Angeles. They lived in segregated barrios, Spanish towns, where their cultural traditions persisted. But by the late nineteenth century, most Hispanics, whether in barrios or on farms and ranches, had been excluded from power.

Yet to focus on cities alone would distort the experience of most southwesterners of Spanish descent, who lived in small villages like those in northern New Mexico and southern Colorado. There a pattern of adaptation and resistance to Anglo penetration developed. As the market economy advanced, Hispanic villagers turned to migratory labor to adapt. While women continued to work in the old villages, men traveled from job to job in mining, in farming, and on the railroads. The resulting "regional communities" of village and migrant workers allowed Hispanic residents to preserve the communal culture of the village, incorporating those aspects of Anglo culture—like the sewing machine—that suited their needs. At the same time, the regional community also sustained migrant workers with a base of operations and a haven to which they could return in protest against harsh working conditions.

### Ethno-Racial Identity in the New West

The New West met the Old South in the diamond-shaped Blackland Prairie of central Texas. Before the Civil War, King Cotton had thrived in its rich soil. Afterward, Texas became the leading cotton-producing state in the country. Having embraced the slave system of the Old South, Texas also adopted the New South's system of crop liens and segregation, with its racial separation, restrictions on black voting, and biracial labor force of African Americans and poor whites.

Yet Texas was also part of the borderlands of the American West, where the Anglo culture of European Americans met the Latino culture of Mexicans and Mexican Americans. Many Mexicanos had lived in Texas since before the 1840s, when it had been part of Mexico. In the late nineteenth and early twentieth centuries, more newcomers crossed the Rio Grande in search of work. Between 1890 and 1910, the Spanish-speaking population of the Southwest nearly doubled.

In central Texas, the presence of this large and growing force of Mexicano laborers complicated racial matters. The black-and-white poles of European and African Americans that had defined identity in the Old South were now replaced by a new racial triad of black, white, and brown who negotiated identity and status among themselves.

*A new racial triad*

Like African Americans, Mexican Americans and Mexican immigrants in Texas were separated from Anglos by a color line and were considered inferior by most whites. Unlike African Americans, however, Texans of Mexican descent sometimes found themselves swinging between the white world of privilege and the black world of disadvantage. In 1914, for example, Mexicans gained status by joining Anglos in the Land League, a radical organization of Texas renters dedicated to land reform. Its secretary, frustrated over the reluctance of whites to sign on, extolled the virtues of Mexican members who would "starve before they will submit to a higher rent than the League and the law says is just."

And whites could lose status, as had the many Texans who sank into landlessness and poverty on the eve of the First World War. White landowners disdained them as "white trash" and a "white scourge." As small white operators lost their farms and ranches to large corporations they saw the social distance shrink between themselves and black and brown laborers, sharecroppers, and tenants. By the 1920s, a multiracial labor force of landless wage earners worked on giant ranches and large farms across the Southwest. In Texas, the labor force was tri-racial, but in California it also included Asian Americans and, elsewhere, American Indians as well. Thus racial identity in the New West would be more complicated and, for Mexicans and Mexican Americans, more fluid.


BOOM AND BUST IN THE WEST

Opportunity in the West lay in land and resources, but wealth also accumulated in the towns. Each time a speculative fever hit a region, new communities sprouted to serve those who rushed in. The western boom began in mining—with the California Gold Rush of 1849 and the rise of San Francisco. In the decades that followed, new hordes threw up towns in Park City, Utah; Tombstone, Arizona; Deadwood in the Dakota Territories; and other promising sites. All too often, busts followed booms, transforming boom towns into ghost towns.

## Mining Sets a Pattern

The gold and silver strikes of the 1840s and 1850s set a pattern followed by other booms. Stories of easy riches attracted single prospectors with their shovels and wash pans. Almost all were male and nearly half foreign-born. Muddy mining camps sprang up, where a prospector could register a claim, get provisions, bathe, and buy a drink or a companion. Outfitting these boom societies siphoned riches into the pockets of storeowners and other suppliers. Once the quick profits were gone, a period of consolidation brought more order to towns and larger scale to regional businesses.

In the mine fields, that meant corporations with the capital for hydraulic water jets to blast ore loose and other heavy equipment to crush rock and extract silver and gold from deeper veins. In their quest for quick profits, such oper- *Environmental costs* ations often led to environmental disaster. Floods, mud slides, and dirty streams threatened the livelihood of farmers in the valleys below.

In corporate mining operations, paid laborers replaced the independent prospectors of earlier days. As miners sought better wages and working conditions, along with shorter hours, management fought back. In Coeur d'Alene, Idaho, troops crushed a strike in 1892, killing seven miners. The miners, in turn, created the Western Federation of Miners. In the decade after 1893 the union attracted some 50,000 members and gained a reputation for militancy. Across the West, the rowdy mining frontier of small-scale prospectors was integrated into the industrial system of wage labor, large-scale resource extraction, and high-finance capital.

### The Transcontinental Railroad

As William Gilpin predicted in 1849, the development of the West awaited the railroads. Before the Central and Union Pacific railroads were joined in 1869, travel across the West was slow and dusty. Vast distances and sparse population gave entrepreneurs little chance to follow the eastern practice of building local railroads from city to city.

In 1862 Congress granted the Central Pacific Railroad the right to build the western link of the transcontinental railroad eastward from Sacramento. To the Union Pacific Corporation fell responsibility for the section from *Railroad land grants* Omaha westward. Generous loans and gifts of federal and state lands made the venture wildly profitable. For every mile of track completed, the rail companies received between 200 and 400 square miles of land—some 45 million acres by the time the route was completed. Fraudulent stock practices, corrupt accounting, and wholesale bribery (involving a vice president of the United States and at least two members of Congress) swelled profits even more. More than 75 western railroads eventually benefited from such government generosity before the lines were linked at Promontory Summit, Utah, on May 10, 1869.

General Grenville Dodge, an army engineer on leave to the Union Pacific, recruited his immense labor force from Irish and other European immigrants. Charles Crocker of the Central Pacific relied on some 10,000 Chinese laborers. With wheelbarrows, picks, shovels, and baskets they inched eastward, building trestles like the one at Secrettown (page 510) and chipping away at the Sierras' looming granite walls.

As the railroads pushed west in the 1860s, they helped to spawn cities like Denver and later awakened sleepy communities such as Los Angeles. Railroads opened the Great Plains to cattle drives that in the 1870s brought great herds to "cow towns" like Sedalia, Missouri, and Cheyenne, Wyoming, where cattle could be shipped to market. The rail companies recognized the strategic position they held. Just by threatening to bypass a town, a railroad could extract concessions on rights of way, taxes, and loans. If a key to profiting from the gold rush was supplying miners, one way to prosper from the West was to control transportation. That was why westerners developed such mixed feelings toward the railroads.

*The power of the railroads*

## Cattle Kingdom

Westerners recognized that railroads were keys to the cattle kingdom. Cow towns like Abilene, Denver, and Cheyenne flourished from the business of the growing cattle kingdom. By 1860, some five million head of longhorn cattle were wandering the grassy plains of Texas. Ranchers allowed their herds to roam the unbroken or "open" range freely, identified only by a distinctive brand. Each spring cowboys rounded up the herds, branded the calves, and selected the steers to send to market.

Trestles for the transcontinental railroad at Secrettown. Nearly 10,000 Chinese laborers, some pictured above, chipped away with picks and shovels at the granite walls of the Sierra Nevada.

Anglo-Americans who came to Texas readily adopted the Mexican equipment: the tough mustangs and broncos (horses suited to managing mean-spirited longhorns), the branding iron for marking the herds, the corral for holding cattle, and the riata, or lariat, for roping. The cowboys also wore Mexican chaps, spurs, and the broad-brimmed sombrero, or "hat that provides shade." After the Civil War, veterans of the Confederate army made up the majority of the cowhands in Texas. But at least a third of all cowboys were Mexicans and black freedmen.

*Mexican ranching techniques*

In 1866, as rail lines swept west, Texas ranchers began driving their herds north to railheads for shipment to market. These "long drives" lasted two to three months and might cover more than 1000 miles. When early routes to Sedalia, Missouri, proved unfriendly, ranchers scouted alternatives. The Chisholm Trail led from San Antonio to Abilene and Ellsworth in Kansas. More westerly routes ran to Dodge City and even Denver and Cheyenne.

Since cattle grazed on the open range, early ranches were primitive. Most had a house for the rancher and his family, a bunkhouse for the hired hands, and about 30 to 40 acres per animal. Women were scarce in the cattle kingdom. Most were ranchers' wives, who cooked, nursed the sick, and helped run things. Some women ranched themselves. When Helen Wiser Stewart of Nevada learned that her husband had been murdered, she took over the ranch— buying and selling cattle, managing the hands, and tending to family and crops.

*Home on the range*

Farmers looking for their own homesteads soon became rivals to the cattle ranchers. The "nesters," as ranchers disdainfully called them, fenced off their lands, thus shrinking the open range. Vast grants to the railroads also limited the area of free land, while ranchers intent on breeding heavier cattle with more tender beef began to fence in their stock to prevent them from mixing with inferior strays. Conflicts also arose between cattle ranchers and herders of another animal introduced by the Mexicans: sheep. Sheep cropped grasses so short that they ruined land for cattle grazing. On one occasion enraged cattlemen clubbed 8000 sheep to death along the Green River in Wyoming. The feuds often burst into range wars, some more violent than those between farmers and ranchers.

Ranchers came to expect profits of 25 to 40 percent a year. As in all booms, however, forces were at work bringing the inevitable bust. High profits soon swelled the size of the herds and led to overproduction. Increased competition from cattle producers in Canada and Argentina caused beef prices to fall. And in the end, nature imposed its own limits on the boom. There was simply not enough grass along the trails to support the millions of head on their way to market. Then in 1886 and 1887 came two of the coldest winters in recorded history. The winds brought blizzards that drove wandering herds up against fences, where they froze or starved to death. Summer brought no relief. Heat and drought scorched the grasslands and dried up waterholes. In the Dakotas, Montana, Colorado, and Wyoming, losses ran as high as 90 percent.

*Western boom and bust*

By the 1890s the open range and the long drives had largely vanished. What prevailed were the larger cattle corporations like the King Ranch of Texas. Only they had enough capital to acquire and fence vast grazing lands, hire ranchers to manage herds, and pay for feed during winter months. As for the cowboys, most became wage laborers employed by the ranching corporations. Like the mining industry, the cattle industry in the West was succumbing to the eastern pattern of economic concentration and labor specialization. See Interactive Map 4 in the color section for a depiction of the mining and cattle frontiers.

## THE FINAL FRONTIER

In the 1860s they had come in a trickle; in the 1870s they became a torrent. They were farmers from the East and Midwest, black freedpeople from the rural South, and peasant-born immigrants from Europe. What bound them together was a craving for land. They had read railroad and steamship advertisements and heard stories from friends about millions of free acres in the plains west of the 98th meridian. Hardier strains of wheat like the "Turkey Red" (imported from Russia), improved machinery, and new farming methods made it possible to raise crops in what once had been called the "Great American Desert." The number of farms in the United States jumped from around two million on the eve of the Civil War to almost six million in 1900.

### Farming on the Plains

Farmers looking to plow the plains faced a daunting task. Under the Homestead Act, government land could be bought for $1.25 an acre, or claimed free if a homesteader worked it for five years. But the best parcels—near a railroad line, with access to eastern markets—were owned by the railroads themselves or by speculators, and sold for around $25 an acre. Furthermore, successful farming on the plains demanded expensive machinery. Steel-tipped plows and harrows (which left a blanket of dust to keep moisture from evaporating too quickly) permitted "dry farming" in arid climates. Threshers, combines, and harvesters brought in the crop, while steam tractors pulled the heavy equipment.

With little rain, many farmers had to install windmills and pumping equipment to draw water from deep underground. The threat of cattle trampling the fields forced farmers to erect fences. Lacking wood, they found the answer in barbed wire, first marketed in 1874. When all was said and done, the average farmer spent what was for the poor a small fortune, about $785 on machinery and another $500 for land. Bigger operators invested 10 or 20 times as much.

Tracts of 160 acres granted under the Homestead Act might be enough for eastern farms, but in the drier West more land was needed to produce the same harvest. Farms of more than 1000 acres, known as "bonanza farms," were most common in the wheatlands of the northern plains. A steam tractor working a bonanza farm could plow, harrow, and seed up to 50 acres a day—20 times more than a single person could do without machinery. Against such com- | *Bonanza farms* petition, small-scale farmers could scarcely survive. As in the South, many workers in the West became tenants on land owned by others. Bonanza farmers hired as many as 250 laborers to work each 10,000 acres in return for room, board, and 50 cents a day in wages.

## *A Plains Existence*

For poor farm families, life on the plains meant sod houses or dugouts carved from hillsides for protection against the wind. Tough, root-bound sod was cut into bricks a foot wide and three feet long and laid edgewise to create walls; sod bricks covered rafters for a roof. The average house was seldom more than 18 by 24 feet and in severe weather had to accommodate animals as well as people. One door and a single window provided light and air. The thick walls kept the house warm in winter and cool in summer, but a heavy, soaking rain or snow could bring the roof down, or drip mud and water into the living area.

The heaviest burdens fell to women. With stores and supplies scarce, they spent long days over hot tubs preparing tallow wax for candles or soaking ashes and boiling lye with grease and pork rinds to make soap. In the early | *Plains women* years of settlement wool was in such short supply that resourceful women used hair from wolves and other wild animals to make cloth. Buttons had to be fashioned from old wooden spoons. Without doctors, women learned how to care for the hurt and sick, treating anything from frostbite to snakebite to burns and rheumatism.

Nature imposed added hardships. Blizzards piled snow to the rooftops and halted all travel. Weeks could pass before farm families saw an outsider. In the summers, searing winds blasted the plains for weeks. Grasses grew so dry that a single spark could ignite thousands of acres. Farmers in the Southwest lived in dread of stinging centipedes and scorpions that inhabited wall cracks. From Missouri to Oregon, nothing spelled disaster like locusts. They descended without warning in swarms 100 miles long. Beating against houses like hailstones, they stripped all vegetation, including the bark of trees. An entire year's labor might be destroyed in a day.

In the face of such hardships many westerners found comfort in religion. Indians turned to traditional spiritualism, Hispanics to the Catholic Church, as a means of coping with nature and change. Though Catholics and Jews | *Religion* came west, evangelical Protestants dominated the Anglo frontier in the mining towns and in other western communities. Worship offered an emotional outlet, intellectual stimulation, a means of preserving old values and sustaining hope. In the West, as in the rural South, circuit riders compensated for the shortage of preachers, while camp meetings offered the chance to socialize.

Both brought contact with a world beyond the prairie. In many communities it was the churches that first instilled order on public life, addressing local problems like the need for schools or charity for the poor.

## The Urban Frontier

Not all westerners lived in such isolation. By 1890, the percentage of those living in cities of 10,000 or more was greater than in any other section of the country except the Northeast.

Some western cities—San Antonio, El Paso, Los Angeles—were old Spanish towns whose growth had been reignited by the westward march of Anglo migrants, the northward push of Mexican immigrants, and the spread of railroads. Other cities, like Portland near the Columbia River in Oregon, blossomed because they stood astride commercial routes. Still others, such as Witchita, Kansas, arose to serve the cattle and mining booms. As technology freed people from the need to produce their own food and clothing, westerners turned to the business of supplying goods and services, enterprises that required the labor of densely populated cities.

Denver was typical. Founded in 1859, the city profited from the discovery of gold in nearby Cherry Creek. The completion of the Denver Pacific and Kansas Pacific railroads sparked a second growth spurt in the 1870s. By the 1890s, with a population of over 100,000, it ranked behind only Los Angeles and Omaha among western cities. Like much of the urban West, Denver grew outward rather than upward, breaking the pattern set by the cramped cities of the East. In the West, such urban sprawl produced cities with sharply divided districts for business, government, and industry. Workers lived in one section of town, managers, owners, and wealthier citizens in another.

## The West and the World Economy

In its cities or on its open ranges, deep in its mine shafts or on the sun-soaked fields of its bonanza farms, the West was being linked to the world economy. Longhorn cattle that grazed on Texas prairies fed city dwellers in the eastern United States and in Europe as well. Wood from the forests of the Pacific Northwest found its way into the hulls of British schooners and the furniture that adorned the parlors of Paris. Wheat grown on the Great Plains competed with grain from South America and Australia. Gold and silver mined in the Rockies were minted into coins around the world.

The ceaseless search for western resources depended ultimately on money. As raw materials flowed out of the region capital flowed in, most of it from the East and from Europe. Foreign investment varied from industry to industry but generally came in two forms: direct stock purchases and loans to western corporations and individuals. The great open-range cattle boom of the 1870s and 1880s, for example, brought an estimated $45 million into the western livestock industry from Great Britain alone. By 1887, Congress had become so alarmed at foreign ownership of western land that it enacted the Alien Land Law, which prohibited the purchase of any land in western territories by foreign corporations or by individuals who did not intend to become citizens. Capital-hungry westerners paid little attention. A decade later, there had been virtually no forfeitures of land under the law.

Westerners were becoming part of a vast network of production and trade that spanned the globe. Between 1865 and 1915, world population increased by more than 50 percent, and demand mushroomed. Better and cheaper transportation, fed by a new industrial order, allowed westerners to supply raw materials and agricultural goods to places they knew only as exotic names on a map. Still, global reach came at a price. Decisions made elsewhere—in London and Paris, in Tokyo and Buenos Aires—now determined the prices that westerners charged and the profits they made.

### Packaging and Exporting the "Wild West"

No one linked the West to the wider world and shaped perceptions of the region more than William F. ("Buffalo Bill") Cody. In 1883, trading on his fame as an army scout and buffalo hunter, Cody packaged the West in his "Wild West, Rocky Mountain, and Prairie Exhibition." Rope-twirling cowboys, fierce-looking Indians, and Annie Oakley, celebrated as much for her beauty as for her aim with a gun, entertained audiences across the continent. For many Americans, Buffalo Bill's "Wild West" *was* the West, where six-shooters administered justice, where Indians lived in tepees and made war on whites, where romance and adventure obscured the realities of conquest, exploitation, and corporate control. Cowboys and Indians had been commercialized and packaged, to be marketed across the globe—for Cody took his troupe London, Paris, and even Outer Mongolia.

Examining the returns from 1890, the superintendent of the census noted that landed settlements stretched so far that "there can hardly be said to be a frontier line." One after another, territories became

By the 1880s, when Buffalo Bill Cody created his Wild West show, Americans were already longing for the "vanishing frontier." Buffalo Bill provided it for them, complete with mythical stereotypes that reinforced the image of the West as a savage land in need of taming but also an Eden of boundless opportunity and adventure. The reach of such fantasies was truly global, and cultural exchange flowed in both directions, as the poster for the grand opening of the Wild West's new amphitheater suggests. Note the Arabs and cowboys on horseback and exotic camels.

centuries. They began as fraternal and charitable organizations. Over the years they became centers of political power. In New York the machine was Democratic; in Philadelphia, Republican. Machines could even be found in rural areas such as Duval County, Texas, where the Spanish-speaking Anglo boss Archie Parr molded a powerful alliance with Mexican American landowners.

In an age of enterprise, the boss operated his political machine like a corporation. His office might be a saloon, a funeral home, or, like George Washington Plunkitt's, a shoeshine stand. His managers were party activists, *The boss as* connected in a corporate-like chain of command. Local committeemen *entrepreneur* reported to district captains, captains to district leaders, district leaders to the boss or bosses who directed the machine.

The goods and services of the machine were basics: a Christmas turkey, a load of coal for the winter, jobs for the unemployed, English-language classes for recent immigrants. Bosses sponsored fun too: sports teams, glee clubs, balls and barbecues.

This system, rough and uneven as it was, served as a form of public welfare at a time when private charity could not cope with the crush of demands. To the unskilled, the boss doled out jobs in public construction. For bright, *Crude welfare system* ambitious young men, he had places in city offices or in the party. These represented the first steps into the middle class.

In return, citizens expressed their gratitude at the ballot box. Sometimes the votes of the grateful were not enough. "Little Bob" Davies of Jersey City was adept at mobilizing the "graveyard vote." He drew names from tombstones to pad lists of registered voters and hired "repeaters" to vote under the phony names. When reformers introduced the Australian (secret) ballot in the 1880s to prevent fraud, bosses pulled the "Tasmanian dodge" by premarking election tickets. Failing that, they dumped whole ballot boxes into the river or used hired thugs to scare unpersuaded voters away from the polls.

### Rewards, Accomplishments, and Costs

Why did bosses go to such lengths? Some simply loved the game of politics. More often bosses loved money. Their ability to get it was limited only by their ingenuity or the occasional success of an outraged reformer. The record *Boss William Tweed* for brassiness must go to Boss William Tweed. During his reign in the 1860s and 1870s, Tweed swindled New York City out of a fortune. His masterpiece of graft was a chunky three-story courthouse in lower Manhattan originally budgeted at $250,000. When Tweed was through, the city had spent more than $13 million, over 60 percent of which lined the pockets of Tweed and his cronies. Tweed died in prison, but with such profits to be made, it was small wonder that bosses rivaled the pharaohs of Egypt as builders.

In their fashion bosses played a vital role in the industrial city. Rising from the bottom ranks, they guided immigrants into American life and helped some of the underprivileged up from poverty. They changed the urban landscape with a massive construction program. They modernized city government by uniting it and making it perform. Choosing the aldermen, municipal judges, mayors, and administrative officials, bosses exerted new control to provide the contracts and franchises to run cities. Such accomplishments fostered the notion that government could be called on to help the needy. The welfare state, still decades away, had some roots here.

The toll was often outrageous. Inflated taxes, extorted revenue, unpunished vice and crime were only the obvious costs. A woman whose family enjoyed Plunkitt's Christmas turkey might be widowed by an accident to her husband in a sweatshop kept open by timely bribes. Filthy buildings might claim her children as corrupt inspectors ignored serious violations. Buying votes and selling favors, bosses turned democracy into a petty business—as much a "business," said Plunkitt, "as the grocery or dry-goods or the drug business." Yet they were the forerunners of the new breed of professional politicians who would soon govern the cities and the nation as well.

## Nativism, Revivals, and the Social Gospel

Urban blight and the condition of the poor inspired social as well as political activism, especially within churches. Not all of it was constructive. The popular Congregationalist minister Josiah Strong concluded that the city was "a menace to society." Along with anxious economists and social workers, he blamed everything from corruption to unemployment on immigrant city dwellers and urged restricting their entry.

In the 1880s and 1890s, two depressions sharpened such anxieties. Nativism, a defensive and fearful nationalism, peaked as organizations like the new Immigration Restriction League attacked Catholics and foreigners. Already the victims of racial prejudice, the Chinese were an easy target. In 1882 Congress enacted the Chinese Exclusion Act. It banned the entry of Chinese laborers and represented an important step in the drive to restrict immigration. In 1897 the first bill requiring literacy tests for immigrants passed Congress, but President Grover Cleveland vetoed it.

*Nativist restrictions*

Some clergy took their missions to the slums to bridge the gap between the middle class and the poor. Beginning in 1870 Dwight Lyman Moody, a 300-pound former shoe salesman, won armies of lowly converts with revivals in Boston, Chicago, and other cities. Evangelists helped to found American branches of the British Young Men's Christian Association and the Salvation Army. By the end of the century the Salvation Army had grown to 700 corps staffed by some 3000 officers. They ministered to the needy with food, music, shelter, and simple good fellowship.

A small group of ministers rejected the traditional notion that weak character explained sin and that society would be perfected only as individual sinners were converted. They spread a new "Social Gospel" that focused on improving the conditions of society in order to save individuals. In *Applied Christianity* (1886), the influential Washington Gladden preached that the church must be responsible for correcting social injustices, including dangerous working conditions and unfair labor practices. Houses of worship, such as William Rainford's St. George's Episcopal Church in New York, became centers of social activity, with boys' clubs, gymnasiums, libraries, glee clubs, and industrial training programs.

*The Social Gospel*

### The Social Settlement Movement

Church-sponsored programs sometimes repelled the immigrant poor, especially when they saw them as thinly disguised missionary efforts. Immigrants and other slum dwellers were more receptive to a bold experiment called the settlement house. Situated in the worst slums, often in renovated old houses, these early community centers were run by middle-class women and men to help the poor and foreign-born. At the turn of the century there were more than 100 of them, the most famous being Jane Addams's Hull House in Chicago. In 1898 the Catholic Church sponsored its first settlement house in New York, and in 1900 Bronson House opened its doors to the Latino community in Los Angeles.

*The settlement house*

High purposes inspired settlement workers, who actually lived in the settlement houses. They left comfortable middle-class homes and dedicated themselves

*Billy Sunday* (1923), by George Bellows, depicts a revival meeting of William Ashley "Billy" Sunday. Sunday, a hard-drinking professional baseball player turned evangelist, began his religious revivals in the 1890s and drew thousands.

(like the "early Christians," said one) to service and sacrifice. They aimed to teach immigrants American ways and to create a community spirit that would foster "right living through social relations." But immigrants were also encouraged to preserve their heritages through festivals, parades, and museums. Like political bosses, settlement reformers furnished help, from day nurseries to English-language and cooking classes to playgrounds and libraries. Armed with statistics and personal experiences, they also lobbied for social legislation to improve housing, women's working conditions, and public schools.

## CITY LIFE

City life reflected the stratified nature of American society in the late nineteenth century. Every city had its slums and tenements but also its fashionable avenues, where many-roomed mansions housed the rich. The rich constituted barely 1 percent of the population but owned a fourth of all wealth. In between tenement and mansion lived the broad middle of urban society, which made up nearly a third of the population and owned about half of the nation's wealth. With more money and leisure time, the middle class was increasing its power and influence.

In the impersonal city of the late nineteenth century, class distinctions, as ever, continued to be based on wealth and income. But no longer were

*Urban social stratification*

dress and manners enough to distinguish one class from another. Such differences were reflected in where people lived, what they bought, which organizations they joined, and how they spent their leisure time.

### The Immigrant in the City

When they put into port, the first thing immigrants were likely to see was a city. Perhaps it was Boston or New York or Galveston, Texas, where an overflow of Jewish immigrants was directed after the turn of the century. Most immigrants, exhausted physically and financially, settled in cities.

Cities developed a well-defined mosaic of ethnic communities, since immigrants usually clustered together on the basis of their villages or provinces. But

*Ethnic neighborhoods*

these neighborhoods were in constant flux. As many as half the residents moved every 10 years, often because they got better-paying jobs or had more of their family working.

Ethnic communities served as havens from the strangeness of American society and springboards to a new life. From the moment they stepped off the boat,

*Adapting to America*

newcomers felt pressed to learn English, don American clothes, and drop their "greenhorn" ways. Yet in their neighborhoods they also found comrades who spoke their language, theaters that performed their plays and music, restaurants that served their food. Foreign-language newspapers reported events from both the Old World and the New in a tongue that first-generation immigrants could understand. Meanwhile, immigrant aid societies

Entertainment in immigrant neighborhoods often resulted in a cross-fertilization
of cultures. The Cathay Boys Club Band (pictured above), a marching band of
Chinese Americans, was formed in San Francisco's Chinatown in 1911. It was
inspired by the Columbia Park Boys Band of Italians from nearby
North Beach and played American music only.

furnished assistance with housing and jobs and sponsored baseball teams, insurance programs, and English-language classes.

Sometimes immigrants combined the old and the new in creative ways. Italians developed a pidgin dialect called Italglish. It permitted them to communicate quickly with Americans and to absorb American customs. So the Fourth of
July became "Il Forte Gelato" (literally "The Great Freeze"), a play on the sound
of the words. Other immigrant groups invented similar idioms, like Chuco, a
dialect that developed among border Mexicans in El Paso.

Houses of worship were always at the center of immigrant life. They often
catered to the practices of individual towns or provinces. Occasionally they
changed their ways under the cultural pressures of American life. Where the Irish
dominated the American Catholic Church, other immigrants formed new churches
with priests from their homelands. Eastern European Jews began to break the
old law against men sitting next to their wives and daughters in synagogues. The
Orthodox churches of Armenians, Syrians, Romanians, and Serbians gradually lost
their national identifications.

The backgrounds and cultural values of immigrants influenced their choice
of jobs. Because Chinese men did not scorn washing or ironing, more than 7500
of them could be found in San Francisco laundries by 1880. Sewing ladies'
garments seemed unmanly to many native-born Americans but not to Russian and

## A Chinese Immigrant Names
## His Children

As we children arrived, Father was confronted with a vexatious problem. It perplexed not only him, but every other Chinatown father. What names should he give us children born in this country? . . . He winced at the prospect of saddling his children with names which could be ridiculously distorted into pidgin English. He had had enough, he said, of Sing High, Sing Low, Wun Long Hop, Ching Chong, Long Song.

. . . For him the problem, when I arrived, was immensely simplified. According to the Barbarian calender, I was born on "The Double Ninth," or the ninth day of the ninth month . . . a holiday commemorating California's admission into the Union. "Why not," suggested Dr. [Mabel] LaPlace [who delivered his daughter and for whom she was named] . . . , "name your son after the Governor?" . . . At that time the Governor of California bore the name of Dr. George C. Pardee. . . . I was named for a fellow Republican.

I doubt whether Father ever quite realized the tremendous burden he placed upon our shoulders. Sister Mabel . . . never had to live up to her name in school, although she did have to live down among her playmates the discreditable fact that her brothers and sisters bore the socially forbidding names of George C. Pardee, Alice Roosevelt, Helen Taft, Woodrow Wilson, and Thomas Riley Marshall.

. . . As we grew up, our Chinese names were used less and less. When we visited Chinatown and were addressed, as always happened, by these Chinese names, it gave us a weird, uncomfortable feeling as though someone other than ourselves were being addressed. . . . Our lives never seemed to be ours to do with as we saw fit. . . . In our Chinese world we had to order our lives for the happiness of our parents and the dignity of our clan; while in the American one it was no different. It was obvious that we not only had to "make a name" for ourselves, but acquit with distinction our namesakes as well.

Source: Excerpt from Lowe, *Father and Glorious Descendant* (Boston: Little, Brown, and Company, 1943), pp. 12–25. Copyright renewed in 1971 by Pardee Lowe. All rights reserved.

Italian tailors. Slavs tended to be physically robust and valued steady income over education. They pulled their children out of school, sent them to work, and worked themselves in the mines for better pay than in factories.

On the whole, immigrants married later and had more children than the native-born. Greeks and eastern European Jews prearranged marriages according to tradition. They imported "picture brides," betrothed by mail with a photograph. After marriage men ruled the household, but women managed it. Although child-rearing practices varied, immigrants resisted the relative permissiveness of American parents. Youngsters were expected to contribute like little adults to the welfare of the family.

*Family life*

In these "family economies" of working-class immigrants, key decisions—over whether and whom to marry, over work and education, over when to leave home—were made on the basis of collective rather than individual needs. Though immigrant boys were more likely to work outside the home than girls, daughters often went to work at an early age so sons could continue their education. It was customary for one daughter to remain unmarried so she could care for younger siblings or aged parents.

The Chinese were an exception to the pattern. The ban on the immigration of Chinese laborers in the 1880s had frozen the gender ratio of Chinese communities into a curious imbalance. Like other immigrants, most Chinese newcomers had been single men. In the wake of the ban, those in the United States could not bring over their wives and families. Nor by law in 13 states could they marry white Americans. With few women, Chinese communities suffered from high rates of prostitution, large numbers of gangs and secret societies, and low birth totals. When the San Francisco earthquake and fire destroyed birth records in 1906, resourceful Chinese immigrants created "paper sons" (and less often "paper daughters") by forging birth certificates and claiming their China-born children as American citizens.

Caught between past and present, immigrants clung to tradition and assimilated slowly. Their children adjusted more quickly. They soon spoke English like natives, married whomever they pleased, and worked their way out of old neighborhoods. Yet the process was not easy. Children faced heartrending clashes with parents and rejection from peers.

*Acculturation*

## Urban Middle-Class Life

Life for the urban middle class revolved around home and family. By the turn of the century just over a third of middle-class urbanites owned their homes. Often two or three stories, made of brick or brownstone, these houses were a measure of their owners' social standing. The plush furniture, heavy drapes, antiques, and curios all signaled status and refinement.

Such homes, usually on their own lots, also served as havens to protect and nourish the family. Seventeenth-century notions of children as inherently sinful had given way to more modern theories about the shaping influence of environment. Calm and orderly households with nurturing mothers would launch children on the right course. "A clean, fresh, and well-ordered house," stipulated a domestic adviser in 1883, "exercises over its inmates a moral, no less than physical influence, and has a direct tendency to make members of the family sober, peaceable, and considerate of the feelings and happiness of each other."

*The home as haven and status symbol*

A woman was judged by the state of her home. The typical homemaker prepared elaborate meals, cleaned, laundered, and sewed. Each task took time. Baking a loaf of bread required nearly 24 hours, and in 1890, four of five loaves were still made at home. Perhaps 25 percent of

*The middle-class homemaker*

Newly developed "electroplating," which deposited a thin layer of silver or gold over less expensive material, allowed manufacturers to sell to middle-class consumers wares previously reserved for the wealthy. Pictured here are a silver- and gold-plated card receiver and a calling card, once part of the courtly culture of elites and by the 1880s found in more and more middle-class homes. This "downward mobility" of manners and material culture allowed the middle class to ape the conventions of their social superiors, in this case by using calling cards to reinforce social networks and to serve as social barriers should personal contact be unwanted.

urban households had live-in servants to help with the work. They were on call about 100 hours a week, were off but one evening and part of Sunday, and averaged $2 to $5 a week in salary.

By the 1890s a wealth of new consumer products eased the burdens of housework. Brand names trumpeted a new age of commercially prepared food—Campbell's soup, Quaker oats, Pillsbury flour, Jell-O, and Cracker Jacks, to name a few. New appliances, such as "self-working" washers, offered mechanical assistance, but shredded shirts and aching arms testified to how far short mechanization still fell.

Toward the end of the century, Saturday became less of a workday and more of a family day. Sunday mornings remained a time for church, still an important center of family life. Afternoons had a more secular flavor. There were shopping trips (city stores often stayed open) and visits to lakes, zoos, and amusement parks (usually built at the end of trolley lines to attract more riders). Outside institutions—fraternal organizations, uplift groups, athletic teams, and church groups—were becoming part of middle-class urban family life.

## Victorianism and the Pursuit of Virtue

Middle-class life reflected a rigid social code called Victorianism, named for Britain's long-reigning Queen Victoria. It emerged in the 1830s and 1840s as part of an effort to tame the turbulent urban-industrial society developing in Europe.

Victorianism dictated that personal conduct be based on orderly behavior and disciplined moralism. It stressed sobriety, industriousness, self-control, and sexual modesty and taught that demeanor, particularly proper manners, was the backbone of society. According to its sexual precepts, women were "pure vessels," devoid of carnal desire. Their job was to control the "lower natures" of their husbands by withholding sex except for procreation.

Women's fashion mirrored Victorian values. Strenuously laced corsets ("an instrument of torture," according to one woman) pushed breasts up, stomachs in, and rear ends out. The resulting wasplike figure accentuated the breasts and hips, promoting the image of women as child bearers. Ankle-length skirts were draped over bustles, hoops, and petticoats to make hips look even larger and suggest fertility. Such elegant dress set off middle- and upper-class women from those below, whose plain clothes signaled lives of drudgery and want.

When working-class Americans failed to follow Victorian cues, reformers helped them to pursue virtue. In 1879 Frances Willard, fearing the ill effects of alcohol on the family, became the second president of the newly formed Woman's Christian Temperance Union (WCTU; 1874). *WCTU* Under her leadership the WCTU worked relentlessly to stamp out alcohol and promote sexual purity and other middle-class virtues. By the turn of the century it was the largest women's organization in the country, with 500,000 members.

Initially the WCTU focused on temperance—the movement, begun in the 1820s, to stamp out the sale of alcoholic beverages and to end drunkenness. For these women, the campaign seemed a way not merely to reform society but to protect their homes and families from abuse at the hands of drunken husbands and fathers. And in attacking the saloon, Willard also sought to spread democracy by storming these all-male bastions, where political bosses conducted so much political business and where women were refused entry. Soon, under the slogan of "Do Everything," the WCTU was also promoting "woman" suffrage, prison reform, better working conditions, and an end to prostitution. Just as important, it offered talented, committed women an opportunity to move out of their homes and churches and into the public arena of lobbying and politics.

Anthony Comstock crusaded with equal vigor against what he saw as moral pollution, ranging from pornography and gambling to the use of nude art models. In 1873 President Ulysses S. Grant signed the so-called Comstock Law, a statute banning from the mails all materials "designed to incite *Comstock Law* lust." Two days later Comstock went to work as a special agent for the Post Office. In his 41-year career, he claimed to have made more than 3000 arrests and destroyed 160 tons of vice-ridden books and photographs.

Victorian crusaders like Comstock were not simply missionaries of a stuffy morality. They were apostles of a middle-class creed of social control, responding to an increasing incidence of alcoholism, venereal disease, gambling debts, prostitution, and unwanted pregnancies. No doubt they overreacted in warning that the road to ruin lay behind the door of every saloon, gambling parlor, or bedroom. Yet the new urban environment did indeed reflect the disorder of a rapidly industrializing society.

The insistence with which moralists warned against "impropriety" suggests that many people did not heed their advice. Three-quarters of the women surveyed toward the turn of the century reported that they enjoyed sex. The growing variety of contraceptives—including spermicidal douches, sheaths made of animal intestines, rubber condoms, and forerunners of the diaphragm—testified to the desire for pregnancy-free intercourse. Abortion, too, was available. According to one estimate, a third of all pregnancies were aborted, usually with the aid of a midwife. (By the 1880s abortion had been made illegal in most states following the first antiabortion statute in England in 1803.) Despite Victorian marriage manuals, middle-class Americans became more conscious of sexuality as an emotional dimension of a satisfying union.

## Challenges to Convention

A few bold men and women challenged conventions of gender and propriety. Victoria Woodhull, publisher of *Woodhull & Claflin's Weekly*, divorced her husband,

*Victoria Woodhull* ran for president in 1872 on the Equal Rights party ticket, and pressed the case for sexual freedom. "I am a free lover!" she shouted to a riotous audience in New York. "I have the inalienable, constitutional, and natural right to love whom I may, to love as long or as short a period as I can, to change that love every day if I please!" Woodhull made a strong public case for sexual freedom. In private, however, she believed in strict monogamy and romantic love for herself.

The same cosmopolitan conditions that provided protection for Woodhull's unorthodox beliefs also made possible the growth of self-conscious communities

*Urban homosexual communities* of homosexual men and women. Earlier in the century, Americans had idealized romantic friendships among members of the same sex, without necessarily attributing to them sexual overtones. But for friendships with an explicitly sexual dimension, the anonymity of large cities provided new meeting grounds. Single factory workers and clerks, living in furnished rooms rather than with their families in small towns and on farms, were freer to seek others who shared their sexual orientation. Homosexual men and women began forming social networks: on the streets where they regularly met, at specific restaurants and clubs, which, to avoid controversy, sometimes passed themselves off as athletic associations or chess clubs. Such places could be found in New York City's Bowery, around the Presidio military base in San Francisco, and at Lafayette Square in Washington, D.C.

Only toward the end of the century did physicians begin to notice homosexual behavior, usually to condemn it as a disease or an inherited infirmity. Indeed, not until the turn of the century did the term *homosexual* come into existence. Certainly homosexual love itself was not new. But for the first time in the United States, the conditions of urban life allowed gays and lesbians to define themselves in terms of a larger, self-conscious community, even if they were stoutly condemned by the prevailing Victorian morality.

## CITY CULTURE

"We cannot all live in cities," the reformer Horace Greeley lamented just after the Civil War, "yet nearly all seemed determined to do so." Economic opportunity drew people to the teeming industrial city. But so, too, did a vibrant urban culture.

By the 1890s, cities had begun to clean up downtown business districts, pave streets, widen thoroughfares, erect fountains and buildings of marble. This "city beautiful" movement aimed also to elevate public tastes and, like Victorian culture itself, refine the behavior of urbanites. Civic leaders built museums, libraries, and parks to uplift unruly city masses. Public parks followed the model of New York's Central Park. When it opened in 1858, Central Park was meant to serve as a pastoral retreat from the turbulent industrial city. Its rustic paths, woodsy views, and tranquil lakes, said designer Frederick Law Olmsted, would have "a distinctly harmonizing and refining influence" on even the rudest fellow.

For those in search of lower-brow entertainment, cities offered dance halls and sporting events, amusement parks and vaudeville shows, saloons and arcades. In the beckoning cities of the late nineteenth century, Americans sought to realize their dreams of fun and success.

### Public Education in an Urban Industrial World

Those at the bottom and in the middle of city life found in public education one key to success. Although the campaign for public education began in the Jacksonian era, it did not make much headway until after the Civil War, when industrial cities began to mushroom. As late as 1870 half the children in the country received no formal education at all, and one American in five could not read.

Between 1870 and 1900, an educational awakening occurred. As more and more businesses required better-educated workers, attendance in public schools more than doubled. The length of the school term rose from 132 to 144 days. Illiteracy fell by half. By the turn of the century, nearly all the states outside the South had enacted mandatory education laws. Almost three of every four school-age children were enrolled. Even so, the average American adult still attended school for only about five years, and less than 10 percent of those eligible continued beyond the eighth grade.

The average school day started early, but by noon most girls were released under the assumption that they needed less formal education. Curricula stressed the fundamentals of reading, writing, and arithmetic. Courses in manual training, science, and physical education were added as the demand for technical knowledge grew and opportunities to exercise shrank. Students learned by memorization, sitting in silent study with hands clasped or standing erect while they repeated phrases and sums. Few schools encouraged creative thinking. "Don't stop to think," barked a Chicago teacher to a class of terrified youngsters in the 1890s, "tell me what you know!"

A strict social philosophy underlay the harsh routine. In an age of industrialization, massive immigration, and rapid change, schools taught conformity and values as much as facts and figures. Teachers acted as drillmasters, shaping their charges for the sake of society. "Teachers and books are better security than handcuffs and policemen," wrote a New Jersey college professor in 1879.

*African Americans*

As Reconstruction faded, so did the impressive start made in black education. Most of the first generation of former slaves had been illiterate. So eager were they to learn that by the end of the century nearly half of all African Americans could read. But discrimination soon took its toll. For nearly 100 years after the Civil War, the doctrine of "separate but equal," upheld by the Supreme Court in *Plessy v. Ferguson* (1896), kept black and white students apart but scarcely equal (page 497). By 1882 public schools in a half dozen southern states were segregated by law, the rest by practice. Underfunded and ill-equipped, black schools served dirt-poor families whose every member had to work.

*Immigrant education*

Like African Americans, immigrants saw education as a way of getting ahead. Some educators saw it as a means of Americanizing newcomers. They assumed that immigrant and native-born children would learn the same lessons in the same language and turn out the same way. Only toward the end of the century, as immigration mounted, did eastern cities begin to offer night classes that taught English, along with civics lessons, for foreigners. When public education proved inadequate, immigrants established their own schools. Catholics, for example, started an elaborate expansion of their parochial schools in 1884.

By the 1880s educational reforms were helping schools respond to the needs of an urban society. Opened first in St. Louis in 1873, American versions of innovative German "kindergartens" put four- to six-year-olds in orderly classrooms while parents went off to work. "Normal schools" multiplied to provide teachers with more professional training. And in the new industrial age, science and manual training supplemented more conventional subjects in order to supply industry with educated workers.

## Higher Learning and the Rise of the Professional

Colleges served the urban industrial society, too, not by controlling mass habits but by providing leaders and managers. Early in the nineteenth century, most Americans had regarded higher learning as unmanly and irrelevant. The few who sought it often preferred the superior universities of Europe to those in the United States.

*Postgraduate education*

As American society grew more organized, mechanized, and complex, the need for professional, technical, and literary skills brought greater respect for college education. The Morrill Act of 1862 generated a dozen new state colleges and universities, eight mechanical and agricultural colleges, and six black colleges. Private charity added more. Railroad barons like

Johns Hopkins and Leland Stanford used parts of their fortunes to found colleges named after them (Hopkins in 1873, Stanford in 1890). The number of colleges and universities nearly doubled between 1870 and 1910, though less than 5 percent of college-age Americans enrolled in them.

A practical impulse inspired the founding of several black colleges. In the late nineteenth century, few institutions mixed races. Church groups and private foundations, such as the Peabody and Slater funds (supported by white donors from the North), underwrote black colleges after Reconstruction. By 1900, a total of 700 black students were enrolled. About 2000 had graduated. Through hard work and persistence, some even received degrees from institutions reserved for whites.

In keeping with the new emphasis on practical learning, professional schools multiplied to provide training beyond a college degree. American universities adopted the German model, requiring young scholars to perform research as part of their education. The number of law and medical schools more than doubled between 1870 and 1900; medical students almost tripled. Ten percent of them were women, though their numbers shrank as physicians became more organized and exclusive.

Professionals of all kinds—in law, medicine, engineering, business, academics—swelled the ranks of the middle class. Slowly they were becoming a new force in urban America, replacing the ministers and gentlemen freeholders of an earlier day as community leaders.

## Higher Education for Women

Before the Civil War women could attend only three private colleges. After the war they had new ones all their own, including Smith (1871), Wellesley (1875), and Bryn Mawr (1885). Such all-women schools, with their mostly female faculties and administrators, deepened an emerging sense of membership in a special community of women. Many land-grant colleges, chartered to serve all people, also admitted women. By 1910 some 40 percent of college students were women, almost double the 1870 figure. Only one college in five refused to accept them.

Potent myths of gender continued to plague women in college. As Dr. Edward Clarke of the Harvard Medical School told thousands of students in *Sex in Education* (1873), the rigors of a college education could lead the "weaker sex" to physical or mental collapse, infertility, and early death. Women's colleges therefore included a program of physical activity to keep students healthy. Many offered an array of courses in "domestic science"—cooking, sewing, and other such skills—to counter the claim that higher education would be of no value to women.

College students, together with office workers and female athletes, became role models for ambitious young women. These "new women," impatient with custom, cast off Victorian restrictions. Fewer of them married, and more—perhaps 25 percent—were self-supporting. They shed their corsets and bustles and donned lighter, more comfortable clothing, such as "shirtwaist" blouses (styled after men's shirts) and lower-heeled shoes. And they showed that women could move beyond the domestic sphere of home and family.

## A Culture of Consumption

The city spawned a new material culture built around consumption. As standards of living rose, American industries began providing "ready-made" clothing to replace garments that had once been made at home. Similarly, food and furniture were mass-produced in greater quantities. The city became a giant market for these goods, the place where new patterns of mass consumption took hold. Radiating outward to more rural areas, this urban consumer culture helped to level American society. Increasingly, city businesses sold the same goods to farmer and clerk, rich and poor, native-born and immigrant.

Well-made, inexpensive merchandise in standard sizes and shapes found outlets in new palaces of consumption known as "department stores," so called because

*Department stores* they displayed their goods in separate sections or departments. Unlike the small exclusive shops of Europe, department stores were palatial, public, and filled with inviting displays of furniture, housewares, and clothing.

The French writer Emile Zola claimed that department stores "democratized luxury." Anyone could enter free of charge, handle the most elegant and expensive goods, and buy whatever was affordable. When consumers found goods too pricey, department stores pioneered layaway plans with deferred payments. The department store also educated people by showing them what "proper" families owned and the correct names for things like women's wear and parlor furniture. This process of socialization was occurring not only in cities but in towns and villages across America. Mass consumption was giving rise to a mass culture.

"Chain stores" (a term coined in America) spread the culture of consumption without frills. They catered to the working class, who could not afford department

*Chain stores and mail-order houses* stores, and operated on a cash-and-carry basis. Owners kept their costs down by buying in volume to fill the small stores in growing neighborhood chains. Founded in 1859, the Great Atlantic and Pacific Tea Company (later to become A&P supermarkets) was the first of the chain stores. By 1876 its 76 branch stores had added groceries to the original line of teas.

Far from department and chain stores, rural Americans joined the community of consumers by mail. In 1872, Aaron Montgomery Ward sent his first price sheet to farmers from a livery stable loft in Chicago. Ward avoided the intermediaries and promised savings of 40 percent on fans, needles, trunks, harnesses, and scores of other goods. By 1884, his catalog boasted 10,000 items, each illustrated by a lavish woodcut. Similarly, Richard W. Sears and Alvah C. Roebuck built a $500 million mail-order business by 1907. Schoolrooms that had no encyclopedia used a Montgomery Ward or Sears catalog instead. When asked the source of the Ten Commandments, one farm boy replied that they came from Sears, Roebuck.

## Leisure

As mechanization gradually reduced the number of hours on the job, factory workers found themselves with more free time. So did the middle class, with free weekends, evenings, and vacations. A new, stricter division between work and play developed in the more disciplined society of industrial America. City dwellers turned leisure into a consumer item that often reflected differences in class, gender, and ethnicity.

Sports, for example, had been a traditional form of recreation for the rich. They continued to play polo, golf, and the newly imported English game of tennis. Croquet had more middle-class appeal. It required less skill and special equipment. Perhaps as important, it could be enjoyed in mixed company, like the new craze of bicycling. Bicycles evolved from unstable contraptions with large front wheels into "safety" bikes with equal-sized wheels, a dropped middle bar, pneumatic tires, and coaster brakes. A good one cost about $100, far beyond the reach of a factory worker. On Sunday afternoons city parks became crowded with cyclists. Women rode the new safety bikes too, although social convention prohibited them from riding alone. But cycling broke down conventions too. It required looser garments, freeing women from corsets. And lady cyclists demonstrated that they were hardly too fragile for physical exertion.

*Sports and class distinctions*

Organized spectator sports attracted crowds from every walk of life. Baseball overshadowed all others. For city dwellers with dull work, cramped quarters, and isolated lives, baseball offered the chance to join thousands of others for an exciting outdoor spectacle. The first professional teams appeared in 1869, and slowly the game evolved. Umpires began to call balls and strikes, the overhand replaced the underhand pitch, and fielders put on gloves. Teams from eight cities formed the National League of Professional Baseball Clubs in 1876, followed by the American League in 1901. League players were distinctly working class. At first, teams featured some black players. When African Americans were barred in the 1880s, black professionals formed their own team, the Cuban Giants of Long Island, New York, looking to play anyone they could.

*Spectator sports for the urban masses*

Horse racing, bicycle tournaments, and other sports of speed and violence helped to break the monotony, frustration, and routine of the industrial city. Bare-knuckled prizefighting, illegal in some states, gave young men from the streets the chance to stand out from the crowd, win some cash, and prove their masculinity. In 1869, without pads or helmets, Rutgers beat Princeton in the first intercollegiate football match. College football soon attracted crowds of 50,000 or more.

## Arts and Entertainment

Other forms of city entertainment also divided along lines of class. For the wealthy and middle class there were symphonies, operas, and theater. High-brow productions of Shakespearean plays catered to the aspirations of American upper classes for culture and European refinement. Popular melodramas gave middle-class audiences the chance to ignore the ambiguities of modern life, if only for an evening. They booed villains and cheered heroes, all the while marveling at the tricky stage mechanics that made ice floes move and players float heavenward. By 1900, people were bringing their entertainment home, snapping up some three million new phonograph recordings a year.

Workingmen found a haven from the drudgery of factory, mill, and mine in the saloon. It was an all-male preserve—a workingman's club—where one could drink and talk free from Victorian finger-wagging. Young working women found escape alone or with dates at vaudeville shows, dance halls, and the new amusement parks with their mechanical "thrill rides." In the all-black gaming houses and honky-tonks of St. Louis and New Orleans, the syncopated rhythms of African American composer Scott Joplin's "Maple Leaf Rag" (1899) and other ragtime tunes heralded the coming of jazz.

As much as any form of entertainment, the traveling circus embodied the changes of the new urban, industrial world. Moving outward from their city bases, circuses rode the new rail system across the country (after the first transcontinental tour in 1869) and, with the advent of steamships, crisscrossed the globe. The mammoth New York–based Barnum and, Bailey Circus carried dozens of gilded show wagons, scores of animals, tons of equipment, and hundreds of performers, work hands, and animal tenders to the faraway capitals of Europe and Asia. At home, the shows drew patrons from every class, ethnicity, and race,

From balconies at theaters (like the one depicted in Charles Dana Gibson's pen-and-ink drawing *The Villain Dies*) rowdy patrons cheered, whistled, and booed at performers. Around the turn of the century, theater owners imposed strict rules of behavior on audiences in an effort to attract middle-class families.

sometimes numbering in the tens of thousands. Circus workers erected huge "big-top" tents with the factorylike precision of modern industry. And like the city itself, circuses both supported and subverted social conventions. When owners reassured customers that their scantily clad dancers came from respectable families or their muscular lady acrobats prized the Victorian values of motherhood and domesticity, they winked slyly because they knew that the very appearance of these women, let alone their talents, defied the Victorian ideal of dainty and demure femininity.

As the nineteenth century drew to a close, the city was reshaping the country, just as the industrial system was creating a more specialized, diversified, and interlocking economy. Cities beckoned migrants from the countryside and immigrants from abroad with unparalleled opportunities for work and pleasure. The playwright Israel Zangwill celebrated the city's transforming power in his 1908 Broadway hit *The Melting Pot*. "The real American," one of his characters explained, "is only in the Crucible, I tell you—he will be the fusion of all the races, the coming superman."

Where Zangwill saw a melting pot with all its promise for a new super race, champions of traditional American values like the widely read Protestant minister Josiah Strong saw "a commingled mass of venomous filth and seething sin, of lust, of drunkenness, of pauperism, and crime of every sort." Both the champions and the critics of the late nineteenth century had a point. Corruption, crudeness, and disorder were no more or less a part of the cities than the vibrancy, energy, and opportunities that drew people to them. The gap between rich and poor yawned most widely in cities. As social critic Henry George observed, progress and poverty seemed to go hand in hand.

In the end moral judgments, whether pro or con, missed the point. Cities stood at the nexus of the new industrial order. All Americans, whatever they thought about the new urban world, had to search for ways to make that world work.

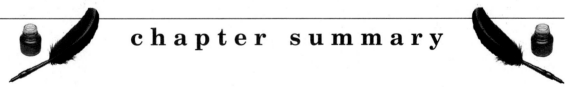

# chapter summary

The modern city was the product of industrialization, lying at the center of the new integrated systems of transportation, communications, manufacturing, marketing, and finance.

- Fed by a great global migration of laborers, cities began to grow and to assume their modern shape of ringed residential patterns around central business districts and strict divisions among different classes, races, and ethnic groups.

- The challenge for the political system was to find within its democratic traditions a way to bring order out of the seeming chaos of unchecked urban growth.

- The urban boss and the urban political machine met the needs of cities for centralized authority but at a terrible cost in corruption, while social settlement houses, the Salvation Army, and the Social Gospel churches represented only a start at coping with the problems of poverty and urban blight.

- As cities grew, the middle-class code of behavior—called Victorianism by historians—spread, teaching the values of sobriety, hard work, self-control, and modesty. Such traits served the needs of new industrial society for efficiency and order and the middle-class need for protection against the turbulence of city life.

- Yet for all the emphasis on skills, discipline, and order, the vibrancy of city culture remained attractive. It drew millions in search of education, entertainment, and opportunity, and it radiated outward to almost every corner of the country.

# interactive learning

The Primary Source Investigator CD-ROM offers the following materials related to this chapter:

- Interactive map: **Streetcar Suburbs in 19th-Century New Orleans** (M17)

- A collection of primary sources demonstrating the rise of urban order in the United States. Sources include a video clip of immigrants arriving at Ellis Island. An advertisement in Godey's Lady's Book illustrates some fashions among middle-class Victorian women.

 For quizzes and a variety of interactive resources, visit the book's Online Learning Center at www.mhhe.com/davidsonconcise4.

# chapter summary

The last third of the nineteenth century witnessed the culmination of years of political stalemate at home and the realization of dreams of empire abroad.

- Republicans and Democrats ground politics into near gridlock over the well-worn issues of regional conflict, tariff, and monetary reform.

- Discontented Americans often fashioned political instruments of their own, whether for woman suffrage, temperance, monetary change, antilynching and civil rights, or farm issues.

- The political deadlock came finally to an end in the turbulent 1890s, when depression-spawned labor strife and a revolt of farmers produced the People's, or Populist, party and a political realignment that left the Republicans in control of national politics.

- By the 1890s, too, the tradition of Manifest Destiny combined powerfully with the needs of the new industrial order for raw materials

and markets and the closing of the American frontier to produce a powerful drive toward empire, which rested on these two principles of American foreign policy:

- The old Monroe Doctrine (1823), which warned European powers to stay out of the Americas.
- The newer open-door notes of Secretary of State John Hay (1899–1900), which stressed the importance of equal commercial access to the markets of Asia.

- Most Americans favored an overseas empire for the United States but disagreed over whether it should be territorial or commercial.

- In the end America's overseas empire was both territorial and commercial. A victory in the Spanish-American War (1898) capped an era of territorial and commercial expansion by furnishing colonial possessions in the Caribbean and the Pacific and at the same time providing more stepping-stones to the markets of Asia.

# interactive learning

The Primary Source Investigator CD-ROM offers the following materials related to this chapter:

- Interactive maps: **Election of 1896** (M7) and **The Spanish-American War in Cuba, 1898** (M20)

- A collection of primary sources exploring the American political system under strain in the

industrial age, including a cartoon of Theodore Roosevelt and reforms passed by Congress, the Sherman Antitrust Act, and the Great Seal of the United States. Other documents illuminate U.S. territorial expansion: the joint resolution annexing Hawaii, for example.

 For quizzes and a variety of interactive resources, visit the book's Online Learning Center at www.mhhe.com/davidsonconcise4.

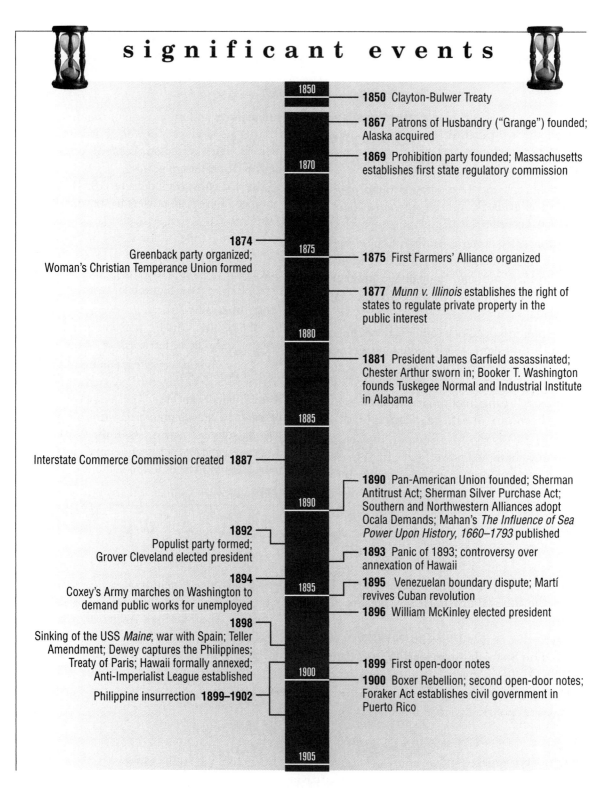

# significant events

**1850** Clayton-Bulwer Treaty

**1867** Patrons of Husbandry ("Grange") founded; Alaska acquired

**1869** Prohibition party founded; Massachusetts establishes first state regulatory commission

**1874** Greenback party organized; Woman's Christian Temperance Union formed

**1875** First Farmers' Alliance organized

**1877** *Munn v. Illinois* establishes the right of states to regulate private property in the public interest

**1881** President James Garfield assassinated; Chester Arthur sworn in; Booker T. Washington founds Tuskegee Normal and Industrial Institute in Alabama

Interstate Commerce Commission created **1887**

**1890** Pan-American Union founded; Sherman Antitrust Act; Sherman Silver Purchase Act; Southern and Northwestern Alliances adopt Ocala Demands; Mahan's *The Influence of Sea Power Upon History, 1660–1793* published

**1892** Populist party formed; Grover Cleveland elected president

**1893** Panic of 1893; controversy over annexation of Hawaii

**1894** Coxey's Army marches on Washington to demand public works for unemployed

**1895** Venezuelan boundary dispute; Martí revives Cuban revolution

**1896** William McKinley elected president

**1898** Sinking of the USS *Maine*; war with Spain; Teller Amendment; Dewey captures the Philippines; Treaty of Paris; Hawaii formally annexed; Anti-Imperialist League established

**1899** First open-door notes

**1900** Boxer Rebellion; second open-door notes; Foraker Act establishes civil government in Puerto Rico

Philippine insurrection **1899–1902**

# CHAPTER 22

Quitting time, March 25, 1911. The long day had almost come to an end at the Triangle Shirtwaist Company in New York City. The deafening whir of some 1500 sewing machines would soon be silenced as hundreds of workers—mostly young immigrant women—were set free. To some, quitting time seemed like an emancipation. Twelve-hour days in stifling, unsafe workrooms, weekly paychecks of only $3 to $15, fines for the tiniest mistakes, deductions for needle and thread—even for electricity—made seamstresses angry. Two years earlier, their frustrations had boiled over into an industrywide strike for better wages and working conditions. Despite a union victory, the only change visible at Triangle was that every morning the doors were locked to keep workers in and labor organizers out.

The fire started in the lofts as the workers were leaving their ma-

# The Progressive Era
## 1890–1920

**Preview** *The first truly broad-based, national reform movement, progressivism addressed problems arising out of industrialization, urbanization, and immigration. Led by members of the urban middle class—many of them women—progressives were moderate modernizers who looked to bring order and efficiency as well as social justice to economic and political life. During the presidencies of Theodore Roosevelt and Woodrow Wilson, they established the modern, activist state.*

chines. In minutes the top stories were ablaze. Terrified seamstresses groped through the black smoke, only to find exits locked or clogged with bodies. All but one of the few working fire escapes collapsed. When the fire trucks arrived, horrified firefighters discovered that their ladders could not reach the top stories. "Spectators saw again and again pitiable companionships formed in the instant of death—girls who placed their arms around each other as they leaped," read one news story. Their bodies hit the sidewalk with a sickening thud or were spiked on the iron guard rails. One hundred forty-six people died, most of them young working-class women.

A few days later 80,000 New Yorkers joined the silent funeral procession snaking slowly up Fifth Avenue in the rain. A quarter of a million watched. At the Metropolitan Opera House, union leader Rose Schneiderman told a rally, "This is not the first time that girls have been burned alive in the city. Every year thousands of us are maimed." A special state commission investigated the tragedy.

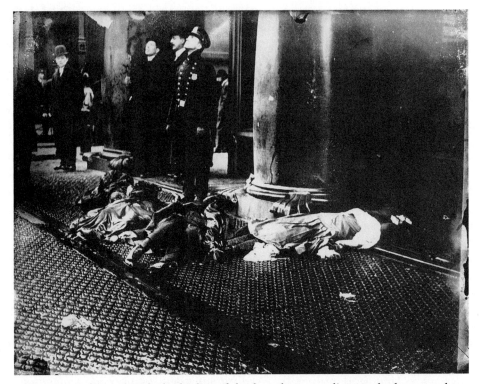

On a street littered with the bodies of dead workers, a policeman looks up at the blazing Triangle Shirtwaist factory, unable to stop more people from jumping. Firefighters arrived within minutes, but their ladders could not reach the top stories.

Over the next four years its recommendations produced 56 state laws regulating fire safety, hours, machinery, and homework. They amounted to the most far-reaching labor code in the country.

The Triangle fire shocked the nation and underscored a growing fear: modern industrial society had created profound strains, widespread misery, and deep class divisions. Corporations grew to unimagined size, bought and sold legislators, dictated the terms of their own profit. Men, women, and children worked around the clock in dangerous factories for wages that barely supported them. In cities across America, tenement-bred disease took innocent lives, criminals threatened people and property, saloons tied the working poor to dishonest political bosses. Even among the middle class, inflation was shrinking their wallets at the rate of 3 percent a year. "It was a world of greed," concluded one garment worker; "the human being didn't mean anything."

But human beings did mean something to followers of an influential reform

*The rise of progressivism*

movement sweeping the country. Progressivism had emerged in the mid-1890s and would last through World War I. The movement sprang from many impulses, mixing a liberal concern for the poor and working class with conservative efforts to stabilize business and avoid social chaos. Liberal or conservative, most progressives shared a desire to soften the harsh impact of industrialization, urbanization, and immigration.

Progressivism thus began in the cities, where those forces converged. It was organized by an angry, idealistic middle class and percolated up from neighborhoods to city halls, state capitals, and, finally, Washington. Though usually pursued through politics, the goals of progressives were broadly social—to create a "good society," where people could live decently, harmoniously, and prosperously, along middle-class guidelines.

Unlike earlier reformers, progressives saw government as a protector, not an oppressor. Only government possessed the resources for the broad-based reforms they sought. Progressivism spawned the modern activist state, with its capacity to regulate the economy and manage society. And because American society had become so interdependent, progressivism became the first nationwide reform movement. No political party monopolized it; no single group controlled it. It flowered in the presidencies of Republican Theodore Roosevelt and Democrat Woodrow Wilson. In 1912 it even spawned its own party, the Progressive, or "Bull Moose," party. By then progressivism had filtered well beyond politics into every realm of American life.

## THE ROOTS OF PROGRESSIVE REFORM

Families turned from their homes; an army of unemployed on the roads; hunger, strikes, and bloody violence across the country—the wrenching depression of 1893 forced Americans to take a hard look at their new industrial order. They found common complaints that cut across region, class, religion, and ethnicity. If streetcar companies raised fares while service deteriorated, if food processors doctored their canned goods with harmful additives, if politicians skimmed money from the public till, everyone suffered. And no one alone could stop it.

The result was not a coherent progressive movement but a set of loosely connected goals. Some progressives fought for efficient government and honest politics. Others called for greater regulation of business and a more orderly economy. Some sought social justice for the urban poor; others, *Aims of progressives* social welfare to protect children, women, workers, and consumers. Still other progressives looked to purify society by outlawing alcohol and drugs, stamping out prostitution and slums, and restricting the flood of new immigrants. And all tried to make business and government more responsive to the democratic will of the people.

Paternalistic by nature, progressives often imposed their solutions no matter what the less "enlightened" poor or oppressed saw as their own best interests. Progressives acted partly out of nostalgia. They wanted to redeem such traditional American values as democracy, opportunity for the individual, and the spirit of public service. Yet if their ends were traditional, their means were distinctly modern. They used the systems and methods of the new industrial order—the latest techniques of organization, management, and science—to fight its excesses.

## Progressive Beliefs

Progressives were moderate modernizers. They accepted the American system as sound, only in need of adjustment. Many drew on the increasingly popular Darwinian theories of evolution to buttress this gradual approach to change. With its notion of slowly changing species, evolution undermined the acceptance of fixed principles that had guided social thought in the Victorian era. Progressives saw an evolving landscape of shifting values. They denied the old Calvinist doctrine of inborn sinfulness and instead saw people as having a greater potential for good than for evil.

Progressives still had to explain the existence of evil and wrongdoing. Most agreed that they were "largely, if not wholly, products of society or environment." People went wrong, wrote one progressive, because of "what happens to them." If what happened changed, the human potential for good could be released.

With an eye to results, progressives asked not "Is it true?" but "Does it work?" Philosopher Charles Peirce called this new way of thinking "pragmatism." *Pragmatism* William James, the Harvard psychologist, became its most famous popularizer. For James, pragmatism meant "looking towards last things, fruits, consequences, facts."

## The Pragmatic Approach

Pragmatism led educators, social scientists, and lawyers to adopt new approaches to reform. John Dewey, the master educator of the progressive era, believed that environment shaped the patterns of human thought. Instead of demanding mindless memorization of abstract and unconnected facts, Dewey tried to "make each one of our schools an embryonic community life." At his School of Pedagogy, founded in 1896, he let students unbolt their desks from the floor, move about, and learn by doing so that they could train for real life.

Psychologist John B. Watson believed that human behavior could be shaped at will. Give him control of an infant's world from birth, Watson boasted, "and *Behaviorism* I'll guarantee to take any one at random and train him to become any specialist I might select, doctor, lawyer, artist, merchant, chief, and yes, even beggarman and thief." "Behaviorism" swept the social sciences and, later, advertising, where Watson himself eventually landed.

Lawyers and legal theorists applied their own blend of pragmatism and behaviorism. Justice Oliver Wendell Holmes Jr., appointed to the Supreme Court in 1902, rejected the idea that the traditions of law were constant and universal. Law was a living organism to be interpreted according to experience and the needs of a changing society.

This environmental view of the law, known as "sociological jurisprudence," found a skilled practitioner in Louis Brandeis. Shaken by the brutal suppression of the Homestead steel strike of 1892, Brandeis quit his corporate practice and proclaimed himself the "people's lawyer." The law must "guide by the light of reason," he wrote, which meant bringing everyday life to bear in any court case. When laundry owner Curt Muller challenged an Oregon *Brandeis Brief* law limiting his laundresses to a 10-hour workday, Brandeis defended the statute before the Supreme Court in 1908. His famous brief contained 102 pages describing the damaging effects of long hours on working women and only 15 pages of legal precedents. In *Muller v. Oregon*, the Supreme Court upheld Oregon's right to limit the working hours of laborers and thus legitimized the "Brandeis Brief."

## The Progressive Method

Seeing the nation torn by conflict, progressives tried to restore a sense of community through the ideal of a single public interest. Christian ethics were their guide, applied after using the latest scientific methods to gather and analyze data about a social problem. The modern corporation furnished an appealing model for organization. Like corporate executives, progressives relied on careful management, coordinated systems, and specialized bureaucracies to carry out reforms.

Between 1902 and 1912 a new breed of journalists provided the necessary evidence and fired public indignation. They investigated wrongdoers, named them in print, and described their misdeeds in vivid detail. Most exposés began as articles in mass-circulation magazines such as *McClure's*. It stirred controversy (and boosted circulation) when publisher Samuel McClure sent reporter Lincoln Steffens to uncover the crooked ties between business and politics. "Tweed Days in St. Louis," which *McClure's* published in October 1902, was followed in the November issue by the first of Ida M. Tarbell's stinging, well-researched indictments of John D. Rockefeller's oil empire, collected later as *The History of the Standard Oil Company* (1904). Soon a full-blown literature of exposure was covering every ill from unsafe food to child labor.

A disgusted Theodore Roosevelt thought the new reporters had gone too far and called them "muckrakers," after the man who raked up filth in the seventeenth-century classic *Pilgrim's Progress*. But by documenting dishonesty and *Muckrakers* blight, muckrakers not only aroused people but also educated them. No broad reform movement of American institutions would have taken place without them.

To move beyond exposure to solutions, progressives stressed volunteerism and collective action. They drew on the organizational impulse that seemed everywhere to be bringing people together in new interest groups. Between 1890 and 1920 nearly 400 organizations were founded, many to combat the ills *Voluntary* of industrial society. Some, like the National Consumers' League, *organizations* grew out of efforts to promote general causes—in this case protecting consumers and workers from exploitation. Others, such as the National Tuberculosis Association, aimed at a specific problem.

When voluntary action failed, progressives looked to government to protect the public welfare. They mistrusted legislators, who might be controlled by corporate interests or political machines. So they strengthened the executive branch by increasing the power of individual mayors, governors, and presidents. Then they watched those executives carefully.

Progressives also drew on the expertise of the newly professionalized middle class. Doctors, engineers, psychiatrists, and city planners mounted campaigns to

*Professionals* | stamp out venereal disease and dysentery, to reform prisons and asylums, and to beautify cities. At local, state, and federal levels, new agencies and commissions staffed by experts began to investigate and regulate lobbyists, insurance and railroad companies, public health, even government itself.

## THE SEARCH FOR THE GOOD SOCIETY

If progressivism ended in politics, it began with social reform: the need to reach out, to do something to bring the "good society" a step closer. Ellen Richards had just such ends in mind in 1890 when she opened the New England Kitchen in downtown Boston. Richards, a chemist and home economist, designed the kitchen to sell cheap, wholesome food to the working poor. For a few pennies, customers could choose from a nutritious menu, every dish of which had been tested in Richards's laboratory at the Massachusetts Institute of Technology.

The New England Kitchen promoted social as well as nutritional reform. Women freed from the drudgery of cooking could seek gainful employment. And as a "household experiment station" and center for dietary information, the kitchen tried to educate the poor and Americanize immigrants by showing them how the middle class prepared meals. According to philanthropist Pauline Shaw, it was also a "rival to the saloon." A common belief was that poor diets fostered drinking, especially among the lower classes.

In the end, the New England Kitchen served more as an inexpensive eatery for middle-class working women and students than as a resource for the poor or

*Pattern of reform* | an agency of Americanization. Still, Ellen Richards's experiment reflected a pattern typical of progressive social reform: the mix of professionalism with uplift, socially conscious women entering the public arena, the hope of creating a better world along middle-class lines.

### Poverty in a New Light

During the 1890s crime reporter and photographer Jacob Riis introduced middle-class audiences to urban poverty. Writing in vivid detail in *How the Other Half Lives* (1890), he brought readers into the teeming tenement. Accompanying the text were shocking photos of poverty-stricken Americans—Riis's "other half." He also used lantern slide shows to publicize their plight. His pictures of slum life appeared artless, merely recording the desperate poverty before the camera. But Riis used them to tell a moralistic story, as the earlier English novelist Charles Dickens had used his melodramatic tales to attack the abuses of industrialism in England. People began to see poverty in a new, more sympathetic light—the fault less of the individual than of social conditions.

A haunting naturalism in fiction and painting followed Riis's gritty photographic essays. In *McTeague* (1899) and *Sister Carrie* (1900), novelists Frank Norris and Theodore Dreiser spun dark tales of city dwellers struggling to keep body and soul intact. The "Ashcan school" painted urban life in all its grimy realism. Photographer Alfred Stieglitz and painters John Sloan and George Bellows chose slums, tenements, and dirty streets as subjects. Poverty began to look less ominous and more heartrending. | *Naturalism*

A new profession—social work—proceeded from this new view of poverty. Social work developed out of the old settlement house movement (pages 561–562). Like the physicians from whom they drew inspiration, social workers studied hard data to diagnose the problems of their "clients" and worked with them to solve their problems. A social worker's "differential case-work" attempted to treat individuals case by case, each according to the way the client had been shaped by environment. | *Social work*

In reality poverty was but a single symptom of deep-rooted personal and social ills. Most progressives, however, continued to see it as a by-product of political and corporate greed, slum neighborhoods, and "institutions of vice" such as the saloon.

### Expanding the "Woman's Sphere"

Progressive social reform attracted a great many women seeking what Jane Addams called "the larger life" of public affairs. In the late nineteenth century, women found that protecting their traditional sphere of home and family forced them to move beyond it. Bringing up children, making meals, keeping house, and caring for the sick now involved community decisions about schools, public health, and countless other matters.

Many middle- and upper-middle-class women received their first taste of public life from women's organizations, including mothers' clubs, temperance societies, and church groups. By the turn of the century, some 500 women's clubs boasted over 160,000 members. Through the General Federation of Women's Clubs, they funded libraries and hospitals and supported schools, settlement houses, compulsory education, and child labor laws. Eventually they reached outside the home and family to endorse such controversial causes as woman suffrage and unionization. To that list the National Association of Colored Women added the special concerns of race, none more urgent than the fight against lynching. | *Women's organizations*

The dawn of the century saw the rise of a new generation of women. Longer lived, better educated, and less often married than their mothers, they were also willing to pursue careers for fulfillment. Usually they turned to professions that involved the traditional female role of nurturer—nursing, library work, teaching, and settlement house work. Custom and prejudice still restricted these new women. The faculty at the Massachusetts Institute of Technology, for example, refused to allow Ellen Richards to pursue a doctorate. Instead they hired her to run the gender-segregated "Woman's Laboratory" for training public school teachers. At the turn of the century, only about 1500 female lawyers practiced in the United States, and in 1910 women made up barely 6 percent of licensed physicians. That figure rapidly declined as male-dominated medical associations grew in power and discouraged the entry of women.

*New woman*

Despite the often bitter opposition of families, some feminists tried to destroy the boundaries of the woman's sphere. In *Women and Economics* (1898) Charlotte Perkins Gilman condemned the conventions of womanhood—femininity, marriage, maternity, domesticity—as enslaving and obsolete. She argued for a radically restructured society with large apartment houses, communal arrangements for child rearing and housekeeping, and cooperative kitchens to free women from economic dependence on men.

Margaret Sanger sought to free women from chronic pregnancy. Sanger, a visiting nurse on the Lower East Side of New York, had seen too many poor women overburdened with children, pregnant year after year, with no hope of escaping the cycle. The consequences were crippling. "Women cannot be on equal footing with men until they have complete control over their reproductive functions," she argued.

*Margaret Sanger*

The insight came as a revelation one summer evening in 1912 when Sanger was called to the home of a distraught immigrant family on Grand Street. Sadie Sachs, mother of three, had nearly died a year earlier from a self-induced abortion. In an effort to terminate another pregnancy, she had killed herself. Sanger vowed that night "to do something to change the destiny of mothers whose miseries were as vast as the sky." She became a crusader for what she called "birth control." By distributing information on contraception, she hoped to free women from unwanted pregnancies and the fate of Sadie Sachs.

Single or married, militant or moderate, professional or lay, white or black, more and more middle-class urban women thus became "social housekeepers." From their own homes they turned to the homes of their neighbors and from there to all of society.

## Social Welfare

In the "bigger family of the city," as one woman reformer called it, settlement house workers found that they alone could not care for the welfare of the poor. If industrial America, with its sooty factories and overcrowded slums, was to be transformed into the good society, individual acts of charity would have to be supplemented by

## Jane Addams Fights Child Labor

Our very first Christmas at Hull-House, when we as yet knew nothing of child labor, a number of little girls refused the candy which was offered them as part of the Christmas good cheer, saying simply that they "worked in a candy factory and could not bear the sight of it." We discovered that for six weeks they had worked from seven in the morning until nine at night, and they were exhausted as well as satiated. The sharp consciousness of stern economic conditions was thus thrust upon us in the midst of the season of good will. . . .

The visits we made in the neighborhood constantly discovered women sewing upon sweatshop work, and often they were assisted by incredibly small children. I remember a little girl of four who pulled out basting threads hour after hour, sitting on a stool at the feet of her Bohemian mother, a little bunch of human misery. But even for that there was no legal redress, for the only child-labor law in Illinois with any provision for enforcement had been secured by the coal miners' unions, and was confined to children employed in mines. . . .

While we found many pathetic cases of child labor and hard-driven victims of the sweating system who could not possibly earn enough in the short busy season to support themselves during the rest of the year, it became evident that we must add carefully collected information to our general impression of neighborhood conditions if we would make it of genuine value.

There was at the time no statistical information on Chicago industrial conditions, and Mrs. Florence Kelley, an early resident of Hull-House, suggested to the Illinois State Bureau of Labor that they investigate the sweating system in Chicago with its attendant child labor. The head of the Bureau adopted this suggestion and engaged Mrs. Kelley to make the investigation. When the report was presented to the Illinois Legislature, a special committee was appointed to look into the Chicago conditions. . . .

As a result of its investigations, this committee recommended to the Legislature the provisions which afterward became those of the first factory law of Illinois, regulating the sanitary conditions of the sweatshop and fixing fourteen as the age at which a child might be employed. . . .

Although this first labor legislation was but bringing Illinois into line with the nations in the modern industrial world, which "have long been obliged for their own sakes to come to the aid of the workers by which they live—that the child, the young person and the woman may be protected from their own weakness and necessity—" nevertheless from the first it ran counter to the instinct and tradition, almost to the very religion of the manufacturers, who were for the most part self-made men.

Source: Jane Addams, *Twenty Years at Hull-House* (New York: The Macmillan Company, 1910), pp. 148–153.

government. Laws had to be passed and agencies created to promote social welfare, including improved housing, workplaces, parks, and playgrounds, the abolition of child labor, and the enactment of eight-hour-day laws for working women.

By 1910 the more than 400 settlement houses across the nation had organized into a loose affiliation, with settlement workers ready to help fashion government policy. With greater experience than men in the field, women led the way. Julia Lathrop, a Vassar College graduate, spent 20 years at Jane Addams's Hull House before becoming the first head of the new federal Children's Bureau in 1912. By then two-thirds of the states had adopted some child labor legislation, although loopholes exempted countless youngsters from coverage. Under Lathrop's leadership, Congress was persuaded to pass the Keating-Owen Act (1916), forbidding goods manufactured by children to cross state lines.*

*Keating-Owen Act*

Florence Kelley, who had also worked at Hull House, spearheaded a similar campaign in Illinois to protect women workers by limiting their workday to eight hours. As general secretary of the National Consumers' League, she also organized boycotts of companies that treated employees inhumanely. Eventually most states enacted laws restricting the number of hours women could work.

## Woman Suffrage

The movement for woman suffrage

Ever since the conference for women's rights held at Seneca Falls in 1848, women reformers had pressed for the right to vote on the grounds of simple justice and equal opportunity. They adopted the slogan "*woman* suffrage" to emphasize the solidarity of women, regardless of class, ethnicity, or race. Progressives embraced woman suffrage by stressing what they saw as the practical results: protecting the home and increasing the voting power of native-born whites. The "purer sensibilities" of women—an ideal held by Victorians and progressives alike—would help cleanse the political process of selfishness and corruption.

*Catt's "winning plan"*

The suffrage movement benefited, too, from new leadership. In 1900 Carrie Chapman Catt became president of the National American Woman Suffrage Association, founded by Susan B. Anthony in 1890. Politically astute and a skilled organizer, Catt mapped a grassroots strategy of education and persuasion from state to state. She called it "the winning plan." As the map (page 626) shows, victories came first in the West, where women and men had already forged a more equal partnership to overcome the hardships of frontier life. By 1914, 10 western states (and Kansas) had granted women the vote in state elections, as Illinois had in presidential elections.

*Militant suffragists*

The slow pace of progress drove some suffragists to militancy. The shift in tactics had its origins abroad. In England, the campaign for woman suffrage had peaked after 1900, when Emmeline Pankhurst and her daughters Christabel and Sylvia turned to violence to make their point that women should be given the right to vote. They and their followers chained themselves to the visitors' gallery in the House of Commons and slashed paintings in museums. When those tactics failed, they invaded the time-honored

---

*The Supreme Court struck down the law in 1918 as an improper regulation of local labor; nonetheless, it focused greater attention on the abuses of child labor.

In this cartoon from a 1914 issue of *Life* magazine, a burly feminist catcher tells a suffragist pitcher to "bean" the male batter at the plate.

"BEAN HIM!"*

*Note for ignorami—Hit him in the head

bastion of British manhood—the golf course—and scrawled "VOTES FOR WOMEN" in acid on the greens. They smashed the windows of department stores, broke up political meetings, even burned the houses of members of Parliament.

British authorities responded to the violence by arresting suffragists and throwing them in jail, Emmeline Pankhurst included. When the women went on hunger strikes in prison, wardens tied them down, held their mouths open with wooden clamps, and fed them by force through tubes placed down their throats and noses. Rather than permit the protesters to die as martyrs, Parliament passed the Cat and Mouse Act, a statute of doubtful constitutionality that allowed officials to release starving prisoners, then rearrest them once they returned to health.

Among the British suffragists was a small American with large, determined eyes. In 1907, barely out of her teens, Alice Paul had gone to England to join the suffrage crusade. When asked why she had enlisted, she recalled her Quaker upbringing. "One of their principles . . . is equality of the sexes," she explained. Paul marched arm-in-arm with British suffragists through the streets of London and more than once was imprisoned and refused to eat. In 1910, she returned to the United States and brought the aggressive tactics with her, inspiriting American suffragists with new vigor.

Three years later, in 1913, Paul organized 5000 women to parade in protest at President Woodrow Wilson's inauguration. Wilson himself was skeptical of women voting and favored a state-by-state approach to the issue. Half a million people watched as a near-riot ensued. Paul and other suffragists were hauled to jail, stripped naked, and thrown into cells with prostitutes.

In 1914, Paul broke with the more moderate National American Woman Suffrage Association and formed the Congressional Union, dedicated to enacting national woman suffrage at any cost through a constitutional amendment. She soon allied her organization with western women voters in the militant National Woman's party in 1917. On October 20, 1917, Paul was arrested for protesting in favor of a constitutional ammendment at the gates of the White House. She received a seven-month sentence. Guards dragged her off to a cell block in the Washington jail, where she and others refused to eat. Prison officials declared her insane, but a public outcry over her treatment soon led to her release.

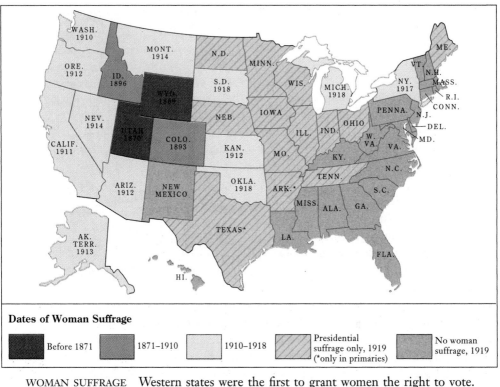

**Dates of Woman Suffrage**

| | | | | |
|---|---|---|---|---|
| Before 1871 | 1871–1910 | 1910–1918 | Presidential suffrage only, 1919 (*only in primaries) | No woman suffrage, 1919 |

WOMAN SUFFRAGE  Western states were the first to grant women the right to vote. Sparsely populated and more egalitarian than the rest of the nation, the West was used to women participating more fully in settlement and work.

Such repression only widened public support for woman suffrage in the United States and elsewhere. So did the contributions of women to the First World War at home and abroad (see Chapter 23). In the wake of the war, Great Britain granted women (over age 30) the right to vote in 1918, Germany and Austria in 1919, and the United States in 1920 through the Nineteenth Amendment. Overnight the number of eligible voters in the country doubled.

*Nineteenth Amendment*

## CONTROLLING THE MASSES

"Observe immigrants," wrote one American in 1912. "You are struck by the fact that from ten to twenty percent are hirsute, low-browed, big-faced persons of obviously low mentality. . . . They clearly belong in skins, in wattled huts at the close of the Ice Age." The writer was neither an uneducated fanatic nor a stern opponent of change. He was Professor Edward A. Ross, a progressive from Madison, Wisconsin, who prided himself on his scientific study of sociology.

Faced with the chaos of urban life, more than a few progressives feared they were losing control of their country. Saloons and dance halls lured youngsters and impoverished laborers; prostitutes walked the streets; vulgar amusements pandered to the uneducated. And worse—strange Old World cultures clashed with "all-American" customs, and races jostled uneasily. The city challenged middle-class reformers to convert this riot of diverse customs into a more uniform society. To maintain control they sometimes moved beyond education and regulation and sought restrictive laws to control the new masses.

## Stemming the Immigrant Tide

A rising tide of new immigrants with darker complexions and non-Protestant religions from southern and eastern Europe especially chilled native-born Americans, including reformers anxious over the changing ethnic complexion of the country. In northern cities progressives often succeeded in reducing the voting power of these new immigrants by increasing residency requirements.

The now-discredited science of "eugenics" lent respectability to the idea that the newcomers were biologically inferior. Eugenicists believed that heredity determined everything and advocated selective breeding for human improvement. By 1914 magazine articles discussed eugenics more than slums, tenements, and living standards combined. In *The Passing of the Great Race* (1916), upper-crust New Yorker and amateur zoologist Madison Grant helped to popularize the notion that the "lesser breeds" threatened to "mongrelize" America. So powerful was the pull of eugenics that it captured the support of some progressives, including birth control advocate Margaret Sanger.

*Eugenics*

Most progressives, however, believed in the shaping power of environment and so favored either assimilating immigrants into American society or restricting their entry into the country. Jane Addams, for one, stressed the "gifts" immigrants brought: folk rituals, dances, music, and handicrafts. With characteristic paternalism, she and other reformers hoped to "Americanize" the foreign-born (the term was newly coined) by teaching them middle-class ways. Education was one key. Progressive educator Peter Roberts, for example, developed a lesson plan for the Young Men's Christian Association that taught immigrants how to dress, tip, buy groceries, and vote.

*Americanization*

Less tolerant citizens (usually native-born and white) sought to restrict immigration as a way of reasserting control and achieving social harmony. Usually not progressives themselves, they employed progressive methods of organization, investigation, education, and legislation. Active since the 1890s, the Immigration Restriction League pressed Congress in 1907 to require a literacy test for admission into the United States. Presidents Taft and Wilson

*Literacy test*

vetoed it in 1913 and 1915, but Congress overrode Wilson's second veto in 1917 as war fever raised fears of foreigners to a new peak.

## The Curse of Demon Rum

Tied closely to concern over immigrants was an attack on saloons. Part of a broader crusade to clean up cities, the antisaloon campaign drew strength from the century-old drive to lessen the consumption of alcohol. Women made up a disproportionate number of alcohol reformers. In some ways, the temperance movement reflected their growing campaign to storm male domains, in this case the saloon, and to contain male violence, particularly the wife and child abuse associated with drinking.

Reformers considered a national ban on drinking unrealistic and intrusive. Instead they concentrated on prohibiting the sale of alcohol at local and state lev-

*Anti-Saloon League*  els. Led by the Anti-Saloon League (1893), a massive publicity campaign bombarded citizens with pamphlets and advertisements. Doctors cited scientific evidence linking alcohol to cirrhosis, heart disease, and insanity. Social workers connected drink to the deterioration of the family; employers, to accidents on the job and lost efficiency.

By 1917 three out of four Americans lived in dry counties. Nearly two-thirds of the states had adopted laws outlawing the manufacture and sale of alcohol. Not all progressives were prohibitionists, but by curtailing the liquor business those who were breathed a sigh of relief at having taken some of the profit out of human pain and corruption.

## Prostitution

No urban vice worried reformers more than prostitution. In their eyes it was a "social evil" that threatened young city women. The Chicago Vice Commission of 1910 estimated that 5000 full-time and 10,000 occasional prostitutes plied their trade in the city. Other cities, small and large, reported similar findings.

An unlikely group of reformers united to fight the vice: feminists who wanted husbands to be as chaste as their wives, social hygienists worried about the spread of venereal disease, immigration restrictionists who regarded the growth of prostitution as yet another sign of corrupt newcomers. Progressives condemned prostitution but saw the problem in economic and environmental terms. "Poverty causes prostitution," concluded the Illinois Vice Commission in 1916.

Some reformers saw more active agents at work. Rumors spread of a vast and profitable "white slave trade." Men armed with hypodermic needles were said to

*White slave trade*  be lurking about streetcars, amusement parks, and dance halls in search of young women. Although the average female rider of the streetcar was hardly in danger of villainous abduction, every city had locked pens where women were held captive and forced into prostitution. By conservative estimates they constituted some 10 percent of all prostitutes.

As real abuses blended with sensationalism, Congress passed the Mann Act (1910), prohibiting the interstate transport of women for immoral purposes. By 1918 reformers succeeded in banning previously tolerated "red-light" districts in most cities. As with the liquor trade, progressives went after those who made money from misery.

### "For Whites Only"

Most progressives paid little attention to the suffering of African Americans. The 1890s had been a low point for black citizens, most of whom still lived in the rural South. Across the region, the lynching of African Americans increased dramatically, as did restrictions on black voting and the use of segregated facilities. Signs decreeing "For Whites Only" appeared on drinking fountains and restrooms and in other public places.

A few progressives, such as muckraker Ray Stannard Baker, condemned racial discrimination, but most ignored it—or used it to political advantage. Throughout the South, white progressives and old-guard politicians used the rhetoric of reform to support white supremacy. Such "reformers" won office by promising to disfranchise African Americans to break the power of corrupt political machines that marshaled the black vote in the South, much as northern machines did with immigrant voters.

In the face of such discrimination, African Americans fought back. After the turn of the century, some black critics rejected the accommodation of Booker T. Washington's "Atlanta Compromise." Washington's cautious approach counseled African Americans to accept segregation and work their way *W. E. B. Du Bois* up the economic ladder by learning a vocational trade such as carpentry or mechanics (page 597). W. E. B. Du Bois, a professor at Atlanta University, leveled the most stinging attack in *The Souls of Black Folk* (1903). He saw no benefit for African Americans in sacrificing intellectual growth for narrow vocational training. Nor was he willing to abide the humiliating stigma that came from the discriminatory caste system of the South. A better future would come only if black citizens struggled politically to achieve suffrage and equal rights.

Instead of exhorting African Americans to pull themselves up slowly from the bottom, Du Bois called on the "talented tenth," a cultured black vanguard, to blaze a trail of protest against segregation, disfranchisement, and *NAACP* discrimination. In 1905, he founded the Niagara movement for political and economic equality. Four years later, in 1909, a coalition of blacks and white reformers transformed the Niagara movement into the National Association for the Advancement of Colored People (NAACP). As with other progressive organizations, its membership was largely limited to the middle class. It worked to extend the principles of tolerance and equal opportunity in a color-blind fashion by mounting legal challenges to segregation and bigotry. By 1914, the NAACP had some 6000 members in 50 branches across the country.

Accommodation was giving way to new combative organizations and new forms of protest.

## THE POLITICS OF MUNICIPAL AND STATE REFORM

Reform the system. In the end, so many urban problems came back to overhauling government. Jane Addams learned as much outside the doors of her beloved Hull House in Chicago. For months during the early 1890s, garbage had piled up in the streets. The filth and stench drove Addams and her fellow workers to city hall in protest—700 times in one summer—but to no avail. In Chicago, as elsewhere, a corrupt band of city bosses had made garbage collection a plum to be awarded to the company that paid the most for it.

Jane Addams founded her settlement at Hull House in Chicago because she was convinced, like many progressives, that reform must be practical, arising out of the needs of individuals within a community. As Addams continued her campaigns, she also looked beyond the local neighborhood to reform political structures of municipal and state governments.

In desperation, Addams submitted a bid for garbage removal in the ward. When it was thrown out on a technicality, she won an appointment as garbage inspector. For almost a year she dogged collection carts, but boss politics kept things dirty. So Addams ran candidates in 1896 and 1898 against the local ward boss. They lost, but Addams kept up the fight for honest government and social reform—at city hall, in the Illinois legislature, and finally in Washington. Politics turned out to be the only way to clean things up.

### The Reformation of the Cities

In the smokestack cities of the Midwest, where the frustrations of industrial and agricultural America fed each other, the urban battleground furnished the middle class with the first test of political reform. A series of colorful and independent mayors demonstrated that cities could be run humanely without changing the structure of government.

In Detroit, shoe magnate Hazen Pingree turned the mayor's office into an agency of reform when elected in 1889. By the end of his fourth term, Detroit had new parks and public baths, fairer taxes, ownership of the local light plant, and a work-relief program for victims of the depression of 1893. In 1901, Cleveland mayor Tom Johnson launched a similar reform campaign. Before he was through, municipal franchises had been limited to a fraction of their previous 99-year terms, and the city ran the utility company. By 1915 nearly two out of three cities in the nation had copied some form of this "gas and water socialism" to control the runaway prices of utility companies.

*Gas and water socialism*

Tragedy sometimes dramatized the need to alter the very structure of government. On a hot September night in 1900 a tidal wave from the Gulf of Mexico smashed the port city of Galveston, Texas. Floods killed one of every six residents. The municipal government sank into confusion. Business leaders stepped in with a new charter that replaced the mayor and city council with a powerful commission. Each of five commissioners controlled a municipal department, and together they ran the city. Nearly 400 cities had adopted the plan by 1920. Expert commissioners enhanced efficiency and helped to check party rule in municipal government.

*Commission plan*

In other cities, elected officials appointed an outside expert or "city manager" to run things, the first in Staunton, Virginia, in 1908. Within a decade, 45 cities had them. At lower levels experts took charge of services: engineers oversaw utilities; accountants, finances; doctors and nurses, public health; specially trained firefighters and police, the safety of citizens.

*City manager plan*

### Progressivism in the States

"Whenever we try to do anything, we run up against the charter," complained the reform-minded mayor of Schenectady, New York. Charters granted by state governments defined the powers of cities. The rural interests that generally dominated state legislatures rarely gave cities adequate authority to levy taxes, set voting requirements, draw up budgets, or legislate reforms. State legislatures, too, found themselves under the influence of business interests, party machines, and county courthouse rings. Reformers therefore tried to place their candidates where they could do some good: in the governors' mansions.

State progressivism, like urban reform, enjoyed its earliest success in the Midwest, under the leadership of Robert La Follette of Wisconsin. La Follette first won election to Congress in 1885 by toeing the Republican line of high tariffs and the gold standard. When a Republican boss offered him a bribe in a railroad case, La Follette pledged to break "the power of this corrupt influence." In 1900 he won the governorship of Wisconsin as an uncommonly independent Republican.

Over the next six years "Battle Bob" La Follette made Wisconsin, in the words of Theodore Roosevelt, "the laboratory of democracy." La Follette's "Wisconsin idea" produced the most comprehensive set of state reforms in American history. There were new laws regulating railroads, controlling corruption, and expanding the civil service. His direct primary

*La Follette's Wisconsin idea*

weakened the hold of party bosses by transferring nominations from the party to the voters. Among La Follette's notable "firsts" were a state income tax, a state commission to oversee factory safety and sanitation, and a Legislative Reference Bureau at the University of Wisconsin. University-trained experts poured into state government.

Other states copied the Wisconsin idea or hatched their own. All but three had direct primary laws by 1916. To cut the power of party organizations and make officeholders directly responsible to the public, progressives worked for three additional reforms: initiative (voter introduction of legislation), referendum (voter enactment or repeal of laws), and recall (voter-initiated removal of elected officials). By 1912 a dozen states had adopted initiative and referendum; seven, recall. A year later the Seventeenth Amendment to the Constitution permitted the direct election of senators. Previously they had been chosen by state legislatures, where political machines and corporate lobbyists controlled the selections.

*Reforming politics*

Almost every state established regulatory commissions with the power to hold public hearings, examine company books, and question officials. Some could set maximum prices and rates. Yet it was not always easy to define, let alone serve, the "public good." All too often commissioners found themselves refereeing battles within industries—between carriers and shippers, for example—rather than between what progressives called "the interests" and "the people." Regulators had to rely on the advice of experts drawn from the business community itself. Many commissions thus became captured by the industries they regulated.

*Regulating business*

Social welfare received special attention from the states. The lack of workers' compensation for injury, illness, or death on the job had long drawn fire from reformers and labor leaders. American courts still operated on the common-law assumption that employees accepted the risks of work. Workers or their families could collect damages only if they proved employer negligence. Most accident victims received nothing. In 1902 Maryland finally adopted the first workers' compensation act. By 1916 most states required insurance for factory accidents, and over half had employer liability laws. Thirteen states also provided pensions for widows with dependent children.

*Seeds of the welfare state*

More and more it was machine politicians and women's organizations that pressed for working-class reforms. Despite the progressive attack on machine politics, political bosses survived, in part by adapting the climate of reform to the needs of their working-class constituents. After the Triangle fire of 1911, for example, it was Tammany Democrats Robert F. Wagner and Alfred E. Smith who led the fight for a new labor code.

This working-class "urban liberalism" also found advocates among women's associations, especially those concerned with mothers, children, and working women. The Federation of Women's Clubs opened a crusade for mothers' pensions (a forerunner of Aid to Mothers with Dependent Children). When in 1912 the National Consumers' League and other women's groups succeeded in establishing the Children's Bureau, it was the first federal welfare agency and the only female-run national bureau in the world. At a time when women lacked the vote, they nonetheless sowed the seeds of the welfare state and helped to make urban liberalism a powerful instrument of social reform.

## PROGRESSIVISM GOES TO WASHINGTON

On September 6, 1901, at the Pan-American Exposition in Buffalo, New York, Leon Czolgosz stood nervously in line. He was waiting among well-wishers to meet President William McKinley. Unemployed and bent on murder, Czolgosz shuffled toward McKinley. As the president reached out, Czolgosz fired two bullets into his chest. McKinley slumped into a chair. Eight days later the president was dead. The mantle of power passed to Theodore Roosevelt. At 42 he was the youngest president ever to hold the office.

Roosevelt's succession was a political accident. Party leaders had seen the weak office of vice president as a way of removing him from power, but the tragedy in Buffalo foiled their plans. "It is a dreadful thing to come into the presidency this way," Roosevelt remarked, "but it would be a far worse thing to be morbid about it." Surely progressivism would have come to Washington without him, and while there, he was never its most daring advocate. In many ways he was quite conservative. He saw reform as a way to avoid more radical change. Yet without Theodore Roosevelt, progressivism would have had neither the broad popular appeal nor the buoyancy he gave it.

## TR

TR, as so many Americans called him, was the scion of seven generations of wealthy, aristocratic New Yorkers. A sickly boy, he built his body through rigorous exercise, sharpened his mind through constant study, and pursued a life so strenuous that few could keep up. He learned to ride and shoot, roped cattle in the Dakota Badlands, mastered judo, and later in life climbed the Matterhorn, hunted African game, and explored the Amazon.

In 1880, driven by an urge to lead and serve, Roosevelt won election to the New York State Assembly. In rapid succession he became a civil service commissioner in Washington, New York City police commissioner, assistant secretary of the navy, and the Rough Rider hero of the Spanish-American War. At the age of 40 he won election as reform governor of New York and two years later as vice president. Through it all, TR remained a loyal Republican, personally flamboyant but committed to mild change only.

To the Executive Mansion (he renamed it the "White House"), Roosevelt brought a passion for order, a commitment to the public, and a sense of presidential possibilities. Most presidents believed that the Constitution set specific limits on

Bullnecked and barrel-chested, Theodore Roosevelt was "pure act," said one admirer. Critics, less enthused with his perpetual motion, charged him with having the attention span of a golden retriever.

their power. Roosevelt thought that the president could do anything not expressly forbidden in the document. Recognizing the value of publicity, he gave reporters the first press room in the White House. He was the first president to ride in an automobile, fly in an airplane, and dive in a submarine—and everyone knew it.

To dramatize racial injustice, Roosevelt invited black educator Booker T. Washington to lunch at the White House in 1901. White southern journalists called such mingling with an African American treason, but for Roosevelt the gesture served both principle and politics. His lunch with Washington was part of a "black and tan" strategy to build a biracial coalition among southern Republicans. He denounced lynching and appointed black southerners to important federal offices in Mississippi and South Carolina.

Sensing the limits of political possibility, Roosevelt went no further. Perhaps his own racial narrowness stopped him too. In 1906, when Atlanta exploded in a race riot that left 12 people dead, he said nothing. Later that year he discharged "without honor" three entire companies of African American troops because some of the soldiers were unjustly charged with having

*Brownsville incident*

"shot up" Brownsville, Texas. All lost their pensions, including six winners of the Medal of Honor. The act stained Roosevelt's record. (Congress acknowledged the wrong in 1972 by granting the soldiers honorable discharges.)

## A Square Deal

Roosevelt could not long follow the cautious course McKinley had charted. He had more energetic plans in mind for the country. He accepted growth—whether of business, labor, or agriculture—as natural. In his pluralistic system, big labor would counterbalance big capital, big farm organizations would offset big food processors, and so on. Standing astride them all, mediating when needed, was a big government that could ensure fairness. Later, as he campaigned for a second term in 1904, Roosevelt named his program the "Square Deal." *Philosophy of the Square Deal*

In a startling display of presidential initiative, Roosevelt in 1902 intervened in a strike that idled 140,000 miners and paralyzed the anthracite (hard) coal industry. As winter approached, public resentment with the operators mounted when they refused even to recognize the miners' union, let alone negotiate. Roosevelt summoned both sides to the White House. John A. Mitchell, the young president of the United Mine Workers, agreed to arbitration, but mine owners balked. Roosevelt leaked word to Wall Street that the army would take over the mines if management did not yield. *Anthracite coal strike*

Seldom had a recent president acted so decisively, and never had one acted on behalf of strikers. In late October 1902 the owners settled by granting miners a 10 percent wage hike and a nine-hour day in return for increases in coal prices and no recognition of the union. Roosevelt was equally prepared to intervene on the side of management, as he did when he sent federal troops to end strikes in Arizona in 1903 and Colorado in 1904. His aim was to establish a vigorous presidency ready to deal squarely with both sides.

Roosevelt especially needed to face the issue of economic concentration. Financial power had become consolidated in giant trusts following a wave of mergers at the end of the century. As large firms swallowed smaller ones, Americans feared that such consolidation would destroy individual enterprise and free competition. A series of government investigations revealed rampant corporate abuses: rebates, collusion, "watered" stock, payoffs to government officials. The conservative courts showed little willingness to break up the giants or blunt their power. In *United States v. E. C. Knight* (1895), the Supreme Court had crippled the Sherman Antitrust Act by ruling that the law applied narrowly to commerce and not to manufacturing. The decision left the American Sugar Refining Company in control of 98 percent of the nation's sugar factories. **United States v. E. C. Knight**

In his first State of the Union message, Roosevelt told Congress that he did not oppose business concentration. As he saw it, large corporations were not only inevitable but more productive than smaller operations. He wanted to regulate them to make them fairer and more efficient. Only then would the economic order be humanized, its victims protected, and class violence avoided. Like individuals, trusts had to be held to strict standards of morality. Conduct, not size, was the yardstick TR used to measure "good" and "bad" trusts.

With a progressive's faith in the power of publicity and a regulator's need for the facts, Roosevelt moved immediately to strengthen the federal power of investigation. He called for the creation of a Department of Labor and Commerce with a Bureau of Corporations that could force companies to hand over their records. Congressional conservatives shuddered at the prospect of putting corporate books on display. Finally, after Roosevelt charged that John D. Rockefeller was orchestrating the opposition, Congress enacted the legislation and provided the Justice Department with additional staff to prosecute antitrust cases.

In 1902, to demonstrate the power of government, Roosevelt had his attorney general file an antitrust suit against the Northern Securities Company. The

*Northern Securities* | mammoth holding company virtually monopolized railroads in the Northwest. Worse still, it had bloated its stock with worthless certificates. Here, clearly, was a symbol of the "bad" trust. A trust-conscious nation cheered as the Supreme Court ordered the company to dissolve in 1904. Ultimately, the Roosevelt administration brought suit against 44 giants, including Standard Oil Company, American Tobacco Company, and Du Pont Corporation.

Despite his reputation for trust-busting, Roosevelt always preferred regulation. The problems of the railroads, for example, were newly underscored by a recent

*Railroad regulation* | round of consolidation that had contributed to higher freight rates. Roosevelt pressed Congress to revive the ineffective Interstate Commerce Commission (ICC). In 1903 Congress passed the Elkins Act, which gave the ICC power to end rebates. Even the railroads supported the act because it saved them from the costly practice of granting special reductions to large shippers.

By the election of 1904 the president's initiatives had won him broad popular support. He trounced his two rivals, Democrat Alton B. Parker, a jurist from New York, and Eugene V. Debs of the Socialist party. No longer was he a "political accident," Roosevelt boasted.

Conservatives in his own party opposed Roosevelt's meddling in the private sector. But progressives demanded still more regulation of the railroads, in particular a controversial proposal for disclosing the value of all rail property or the cost of services as a means of evaluating rate making. In 1906, the president finally reached a compromise typical of his restrained approach to reform. The Hepburn Railway Act allowed the ICC to set maximum rates and to regulate sleeping car companies, ferries, bridges, and terminals. Progressives did not gain the provision for disclosure of company value or service costs, but the Hepburn Act drew Roosevelt nearer to his goal of continuous regulation of business.

### Bad Food and Pristine Wilds

Extending the umbrella of federal protection to consumers, Roosevelt belatedly threw his weight behind two campaigns for healthy foods and drugs. In 1905

Samuel Hopkins Adams of *Collier's Weekly* wrote that in its patent medicines "Gullible America" would get "huge quantities of alcohol, an appalling amount of opiates and narcotics," and worse—axle grease, acid, and glue. Adams sent the samples he collected to Harvey Wiley, chief chemist at the Agriculture Department. Wiley's "Poison Squad" produced scientific evidence of Adams's charges.

Several pure food and drug bills had already died at the hands of lobbyists, despite a presidential endorsement. The appearance of Upton Sinclair's *The Jungle* in 1906 spurred Congress to act. Sinclair intended to recruit people to socialism by exposing the plight of workers in the meatpacking industry. The novel contained a brief but dramatic description of the slaughter of cattle infected with tuberculosis, of meat covered with rat dung, and of men falling into cooking vats. Readers paid scant attention to the workers, but their stomachs turned at what they might be eating for breakfast. The Pure Food and Drug Act of 1906 sailed through Congress, and the Meat Inspection Act soon followed.

Roosevelt came late to the consumer cause, but on conservation he led the nation. An outdoors enthusiast, he galvanized public concern over the reckless use of natural resources. His chief forester, Gifford Pinchot, persuaded him that planned management under federal guidance was needed to protect the natural domain. Cutting trees must be synchronized with tree plantings, oil needed to be pumped from the ground under controlled conditions, and so on.

*Conservation through planned management*

In the western states water was the problem. Economic growth, even survival, depended on it. As uneven local and state water policies sparked controversy, violence, and waste, many progressives campaigned for a federal program to replace the chaotic web of rules. Democratic senator Frederick Newlands of Nevada introduced the Reclamation Act of 1902 to set aside proceeds from the sale of public lands for irrigation projects. The Reclamation Act signaled a progressive step toward the conservationist goal of rational resource development.

Conservation often conflicted with the more radical vision of preservationists, led by naturalist and wilderness philosopher John Muir. Muir founded the Sierra Club (1892) in hopes of maintaining such natural wonders as Yosemite and its neighboring Hetch-Hetchy valley in a state "forever wild" to benefit future generations. Many conservationists saw such valleys as

*John Muir and preservation*

sites for dams and reservoirs to manage and control water. Controversy flared after 1900, when San Francisco announced plans to create a city reservoir flooding the Hetch-Hetchy valley. For 13 years Muir waged a publicity campaign against the reservoir and its "devotees of ravaging commercialism." Pinchot enthusiastically backed San Francisco's claim. Roosevelt, torn by his friendship with Muir, did so less loudly. Not until 1913 did President Woodrow Wilson finally decide the issue in favor of San Francisco. Conservation had won over preservation.

Roosevelt nonetheless advanced many of Muir's goals. Over the protests of cattle and timber interests, he added nearly 200 million acres to government forest reserves; placed coal and mineral lands, oil reserves, and water-power sites in

The Sierra Club, founded by naturalist John Muir, believed in the importance of preserving wilderness in its natural state. Muir helped to persuade President Theodore Roosevelt to double the number of national parks. Here a group of Sierra Club members lounge at the base of a giant redwood in Big Basin in 1905.

Edward Curtis and documenting Native American culture

the public domain; and enlarged the national park system. When Congress balked, he appropriated another 17 million acres of forest before the legislators could pass a bill limiting him. Roosevelt also set in motion national congresses and commissions on conservation and mobilized governors across the country. Like a good progressive, he sent hundreds of experts to work applying science, education, and technology to environmental problems.

As Roosevelt acted more forcefully, conservatives lashed back. So far his record had been modest, but his chief accomplishment—invigorating the presidency—could lead to deeper reform. When another spike in the business cycle produced financial panic on Wall Street in 1907, business leaders and conservative politicians blamed the president. An angry Roosevelt blamed the "speculative folly and the flagrant dishonesty of a few men of great wealth."

Clearly shaken, however, Roosevelt assured business leaders that he would do nothing to interfere with their efforts at recovery. That included a pledge not to file an antitrust suit if the giant U.S. Steel bought the Tennessee Coal and Iron Company. The economy recovered, and having declared he would not run in

1908, the 50-year-old Roosevelt prepared to give over his office to William Howard Taft, his handpicked successor.

## The Troubled Taft

On March 4, 1909, as snow swirled outside the White House, William Howard Taft readied himself for his inauguration. Over breakfast with Roosevelt, he basked in the glow of recent Republican victories. He had beaten Democrat William Jennings Bryan in the "Great Commoner's" third and last bid for the presidency. Republicans had retained control of Congress as well as a host of northern legislatures. Reform was at high tide, and Taft was eager to continue the Roosevelt program.

"Will," as Roosevelt liked to call him, was a distinguished jurist and public servant, the first American governor-general of the Philippines, and Roosevelt's secretary of war. Taft had great administrative skill and personal charm. But he disliked political maneuvering and preferred conciliation to confrontation. Even Roosevelt had doubts. "He's all right," TR had told a reporter on inauguration day. "But he's weak. They'll get around him. They'll"—and here Roosevelt pushed the reporter with his shoulder—"lean against him."

Trouble began early when progressives in the House moved to curb the near-dictatorial power of the conservative Speaker, Joseph Cannon. Taft waffled, first supporting them, then abandoning them to preserve the tariff reductions he was seeking. When progressives later broke Cannon's power without Taft's help, they scorned him. And Taft's compromise was wasted. Senate protectionists peppered the tariff bill with so many amendments that rates jumped nearly to their old levels.

Late in 1909, the rift between Taft and the progressives reached the breaking point in a dispute over conservation. Taft had appointed Richard Ballinger secretary of the interior over the objections of Roosevelt's old friend and mentor, Chief Forester Pinchot. When Ballinger opened a million acres of public lands for sale, Pinchot charged that shady dealings led Ballinger to transfer Alaskan public coal lands to a syndicate that included J. P. Morgan. Early in 1910, Taft fired Pinchot for insubordination. Angry progressives saw the Ballinger-Pinchot controversy as another betrayal by Taft. They began to look longingly across the Atlantic, where TR was stalking big game in Africa.

*Ballinger-Pinchot affair*

Despite his failures, Taft was no conservative pawn. For the next two years he pushed Congress to enact a progressive program regulating safety standards for mines and railroads, creating a federal children's bureau, and setting an eight-hour workday for federal employees. Taft's support of a graduated income tax—sometimes heated, sometimes tepid—was finally decisive. Early in 1913 it became the Sixteenth Amendment. Historians view it as one of the most important reforms of the century, for it eventually generated the revenue for many new social programs.

*Taft's accomplishments*

Yet no matter what Taft did, he managed to alienate conservatives and progressives alike. That spelled trouble for the Republicans as the presidential election of 1912 approached.

## Roosevelt Returns

In June 1910 Roosevelt came home, laden with hunting trophies and exuberant as ever. He found Taft unhappy and progressive Republicans threatening to defect. Party loyalty kept Roosevelt quiet through most of 1911, but in October, Taft pricked him personally on the sensitive matter of busting trusts. Like TR, Taft accepted trusts as natural, but he failed to make Roosevelt's distinction between "good" and "bad" ones. He demanded, more impartially, that all trusts be prevented from restraining trade. In four years as president, Taft had brought nearly twice the antitrust suits Roosevelt had in seven years.

In October 1911 the Justice Department charged U.S. Steel with having violated the Sherman Antitrust Act by acquiring the Tennessee Coal and Iron Company. Roosevelt regarded the action as a personal rebuke, since he himself had allowed U.S. Steel to proceed with the acquisition. Taft, complained TR, "was playing small, mean, and foolish politics."

Roosevelt decided to play big, high-minded, and presidential. Already, in a speech at Osawatomie, Kansas, in 1910, he had outlined a program of sweeping

*New Nationalism* | national reform. His "New Nationalism" recognized the value of consolidation in the economy—whether big business or big labor—but insisted on protecting the interests of individuals through big government. The New Nationalism went further, stressing planning and efficiency under a powerful executive, "a steward of the public welfare." It promised taxes on incomes and inheritances and greater regulation of industry. And it embraced social justice, specifically workers' compensation for accidents, minimum wages and maximum hours, child labor laws, and "equal suffrage"—a nod to women and loyal black Republicans. Roosevelt, a cautious reformer as president, grew daring as he campaigned for the White House.

## The Election of 1912

"My hat is in the ring!" Roosevelt announced in February 1912, to no one's surprise. Taft responded by claiming that the New Nationalism had won support only from "radicals," "emotionalists," and "neurotics." In fact, the enormously popular Roosevelt won most of the primaries; but by the time Republicans met in Chicago in June 1912, Taft had used presidential patronage and promises to secure the nomination.

A frustrated Roosevelt bolted and took progressive Republicans with

*Progressive party* | him. Two months later, amid choruses of "Onward Christian Soldiers," delegates to the newly formed Progressive party nominated Roosevelt for the presidency. "I'm feeling like a bull moose!" he bellowed. Progressives suddenly had a symbol for their new party.

The Democrats met in Baltimore, jubilant over the prospect of a divided Republican party. Delegates chose as their candidate Woodrow Wilson, the progressive governor of New Jersey. Wilson wisely concentrated his fire on Roosevelt. He countered the New Nationalism with his "New Freedom." It rejected the economic consolidation that Roosevelt embraced. Bigness was a sin, crowding out competition, promoting inefficiency, and reducing opportunity. Only by strictly limiting the size of businesses could the free market be preserved. And only by keeping government small could individual freedom be preserved. "Liberty," Wilson cautioned, "has never come from government," only from the "limitation of governmental power."

*New Freedom*

Increasingly voters found Taft beside the point. And in an age of reform, even the Socialists looked good. Better led, financed, and organized than ever, the Socialist party had increased its membership to nearly 135,000 by 1912. Socialist mayors ran 32 cities. The party also had an appealing candidate in Eugene V. Debs, a homegrown Indiana radical. He had won 400,000 votes for president in 1904. Now, in 1912, he summoned voters to make "the working class the ruling class."

On Election Day voters gave progressivism a resounding endorsement. Wilson won 6.3 million votes; Roosevelt, 4.1 million; Taft, just 3.6 million. Debs received almost a million votes. Together the two progressive candidates amassed a three-to-one margin. But the Republican split had broken the party's hold on national politics. For the first time since 1896, a Democrat would sit in the White House—and with his party in control of Congress.

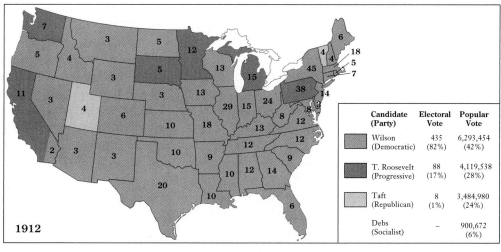

| Candidate (Party) | Electoral Vote | Popular Vote |
|---|---|---|
| Wilson (Democratic) | 435 (82%) | 6,293,454 (42%) |
| T. Roosevelt (Progressive) | 88 (17%) | 4,119,538 (28%) |
| Taft (Republican) | 8 (1%) | 3,484,980 (24%) |
| Debs (Socialist) | – | 900,672 (6%) |

THE ELECTION OF 1912

## WOODROW WILSON AND THE POLITICS OF MORALITY

Soon after the election Woodrow Wilson made a proud if startling confession to the chairman of the Democratic National Committee: "God ordained that I should be the next President of the United States." To the White House, Wilson brought a sense of destiny and a passion for reform. All his life, he believed he was meant to accomplish great things, and he did. Under him, progressivism peaked.

### Early Career

From the moment of his birth in 1856, Woodrow Wilson felt he could not escape destiny. It was all around him. In his family's Presbyterian faith, in the sermons of his minister father, in dinnertime talk ran the unbending belief in a world pre-determined by God and ruled by saved souls, an "elect." Wilson ached to be one of them and behaved as though he were.

To prepare to lead, Wilson studied the fiery debates of the British Parliament and wandered the woods reciting them from memory. Like most southerners, he loved the Democratic party, hated the tariff, and accepted racial separation. (Under his presidency, segregation returned to Washington for the first time since Reconstruction.)

An early career in law bored him, so he turned to history and political science and became a professor. His studies persuaded him that a modern president must act as a "prime minister," directing and uniting his party, molding legislation and public opinion, exerting continuous leadership. In 1910, after a stormy tenure as head of Princeton University, Wilson was helped by Democratic party bosses to win the governorship of New Jersey. In 1912 they helped him again, this time to the presidency of the country.

### The Reforms of the New Freedom

As governor, Wilson had led New Jersey on the path of progressive reform. As president, he was a model of progressive leadership. More than Theodore Roosevelt, he shaped policy and legislation. He went to Congress to let members know he intended to work personally with them. He kept party discipline tight and mobilized public opinion when Congress refused to act.

Lowering the high tariff was Wilson's first order of business. Progressives had long attacked the tariff as another example of the power of trusts. By protecting American manufacturers, Wilson argued, such barriers weakened the competition he cherished. When the Senate threatened to raise rates, the new president appealed directly to the public. "Industrious" and "insidious" lobbyists were blocking reform, he cried to reporters. A "brick couldn't be thrown without hitting one of them."

The Underwood-Simmons Tariff of 1913 marked the first downward revision in 19 years and the biggest since before the Civil War. To compensate for lost revenue, Congress enacted a graduated income tax under the newly adopted Sixteenth Amendment. It applied solely to corporations and the tiny fraction of Americans who earned more than $4000 a year. It nonetheless began a momentous shift in government revenue from its nineteenth-century base—public lands, alcohol taxes, and customs duties—to its twentieth-century base: personal and corporate incomes.

*Underwood-Simmons Tariff*

Wilson turned next to the perennial problems of money and banking. Early in 1913 a congressional committee under Arsène Pujo revealed that a few powerful banks controlled the nation's credit system. They could choke Wilson's free market by raising interest rates or tightening the supply of money. As a banking reform bill moved through Congress in 1913, opinion was divided among conservatives, who wanted centralized and private control, rural Democrats, who wanted regional banks under local bankers, and Populists and progressives—including Bryan and La Follette—who wanted government control.

Wilson split their differences in the Federal Reserve Act of 1913. The new Federal Reserve System contained 12 regional banks scattered across the country. But it also created a central Federal Reserve Board in Washington, appointed by the president, to supervise the system. The board could regulate credit and the money supply by setting the interest rate it charged member banks, by buying or selling government bonds, and by issuing paper currency called Federal Reserve notes. Thus the Federal Reserve System sought

*Federal Reserve Act*

In his 50s, Woodrow Wilson appeared robust when the picture on the left was taken during his governorship of New Jersey. Less than a decade later in 1920, two terms as president and a stroke in 1919 had taken their toll on his health, as the photograph on the right shows.

to stabilize the existing order by increasing federal control over credit and the money supply.

When Wilson finally took on the trusts, he inched toward the New Nationalism of Theodore Roosevelt. The Federal Trade Commission Act of

*Federal Trade Commission*

1914 created a bipartisan executive agency to oversee business activity. The end—to enforce orderly competition—was distinctly Wilsonian, but the means—an executive commission to regulate commerce— were pure Roosevelt.

Roosevelt would have stopped there, but Wilson made good on his campaign pledge to attack trusts. The Clayton Antitrust Act (1914) barred some of the worst

*Clayton Antitrust Act*

corporate practices: price discrimination, holding companies, and interlocking directorates (directors of one corporate board sitting on others). Yet despite Wilson's bias against size, the advantages of large-scale production and distribution were inescapable. In practice his administration chose to regulate rather than break up bigness. The Justice Department filed fewer antitrust suits than it had under the Taft administration.

## Labor and Social Reform

For all of Wilson's impressive accomplishments, voters seemed lukewarm toward the New Freedom. In the elections of 1914 Republicans cut Democratic majorities in the House and won important industrial and farm states. To strengthen his hand in the presidential election of 1916, Wilson began edging toward the social reforms of the New Nationalism he had once criticized as paternalistic and unconstitutional. He signaled the change early in 1916 when he nominated his close adviser Louis D. Brandeis to the Supreme Court. The progressive Brandeis had fought for the social reforms lacking from Wilson's agenda. His appointment also broke the tradition of anti-Semitism that had previously kept Jews off the Court.

In other ways, Wilson showed a new willingness to intervene more actively in the economy. He pressed for laws improving the working conditions of merchant seamen and setting an eight-hour day for workers on interstate railroads. He supported the Keating-Owen Child Labor Act (page 624). Farmers benefited from legislation providing them with low-interest loans. And just before the election Wilson intervened to avert a nationwide strike of rail workers.

## The Limits of Progressive Reform

Woodrow Wilson's administration capped a decade and a half of heady reform. Seeing chaos in the modern industrial city, progressive reformers had worked to reduce the damage of poverty and the hazards of industrial work, control rising immigration, and spread a middle-class ideal of morality. In city halls and state legislatures, they tried to break the power of corporate interests and entrenched political machines. In Washington, they enlarged government and broadened its mission from caretaker to promoter of public welfare.

Progressivism did not always succeed. Reformers sometimes betrayed their high ideals by denying equality to African Americans, Asians, and other minorities and by attempting to Americanize foreigners rather than accepting the contributions of their cultures. Too often government commissions meant to be "watchdog" agencies were captured by the interests they were supposed to oversee. Heavy regulation of industries like the railroads crippled them for decades. Although the direct primary, the popular election of senators, and other reforms weakened the power of political machines, boss rule survived.

For all its claims of sweeping change, progressivism left the system of market capitalism intact. Neither the New Nationalism of Theodore Roosevelt, with its emphasis on planning and regulation, nor Woodrow Wilson's New Freedom, which promoted competition through limits on corporate size, aimed to do more than improve the system. But the Gilded Age philosophy of laissez faire—of giving private enterprise a free hand—had clearly been rejected. Both state and federal governments established their right to regulate the actions of private corporations for the public good.

The reforms thus achieved, including the eight-hour day, woman suffrage, direct election of senators, graduated income taxes, and public ownership of utilities, began to address the problems of an urban industrial society. Under progressive leadership, the modern state—active and interventionist—was born.

American confidence soared as the new century unfolded. A golden age of peace, prosperity, and human advancement seemed within reach, at least to progressives. But in 1914, as progressivism crested in America, the guns of a hot August shattered the uneasy calm in Europe and plunged the world into war. Few people anywhere were prepared for the bloodbath that followed.

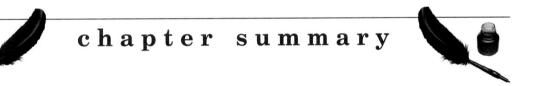

# chapter summary

Progressivism was a broad-based reform movement, the first truly national reform movement in American history, that attempted to address problems arising from industrialization, urbanization, and immigration.

- Progressive reform sprang from many impulses:
  - Desires to curb the advancing power of big business and to end political corruption.
  - Efforts to bring order and efficiency to economic and political life.

- Attempts by new interest groups to make business and government more responsive to the needs of ordinary citizens.
- Moralistic urges to rid society of industries such as the liquor trade that profited from human misery, to bridge the gap between immigrants and native-born Americans, and to soften the consequences of industrialization through social justice and social welfare.

- Led by members of the urban middle class, progressives were moderate modernizers, attempting to redeem such traditional American values as democracy, Judeo-Christian ethics, individualism, and the spirit of volunteerism and public service while employing the newest techniques of management and planning, coordinated systems, and specialized bureaucracies of experts.

- The twin drives for social justice and social welfare often relied on women, who extended their traditional sphere of home and family to become "social housekeepers" and crusaders for women's rights, especially the right to vote.

- Increasingly, progressivism animated politics, first at the local and state levels, then in the presidencies of Theodore Roosevelt and Woodrow Wilson.

- In the end, the weaknesses of progressivism—the fuzziness of its conception of the public interest, the exclusion of African Americans and other minorities, the ease with which its regulatory mechanisms were "captured" by those being regulated—were matched by its accomplishments in establishing the modern, activist state.

# interactive learning

The Primary Source Investigator CD-ROM offers the following materials related to this chapter:

- Interactive maps: **Election of 1912** (M7) and **Woman Suffrage, 1871–1919** (M16)

- Short documentary movies on the movement for woman suffrage (D15); and Edward Curtis and documenting Native American culture (D11)

- A collection of primary sources examining America during the progressive era: the promotional poster for the movie *The Jungle*, the Keating-Owen Child Labor Act, an article on conditions in Chicago's meatpacking plants, and the Meat Inspection Act of 1906. Other sources reveal the prominent role of environmentalism in the progressive era, including the congressional act establishing Yellowstone National Park.

 For quizzes and a variety of interactive resources, visit the book's Online Learning Center at www.mhhe.com/davidsonconcise4.

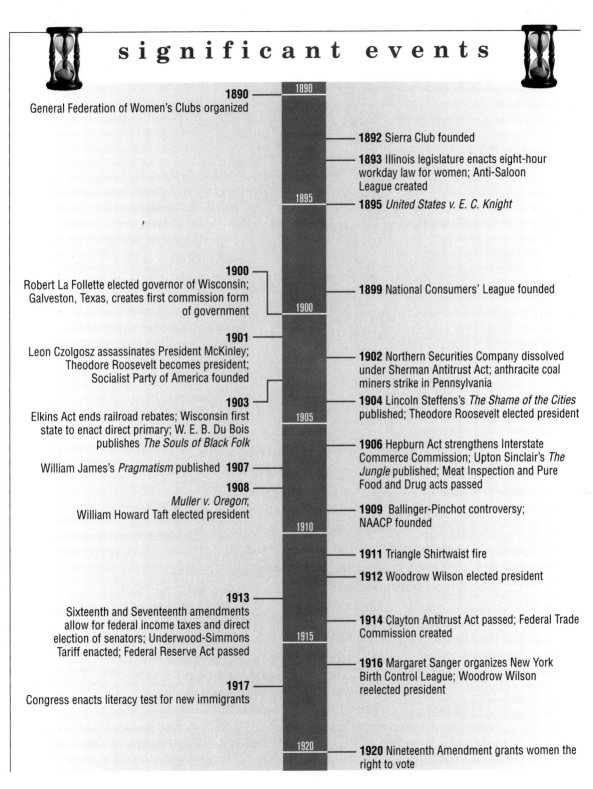

# significant events

**1890**
General Federation of Women's Clubs organized

**1892** Sierra Club founded

**1893** Illinois legislature enacts eight-hour workday law for women; Anti-Saloon League created

**1895** *United States v. E. C. Knight*

**1900**
Robert La Follette elected governor of Wisconsin; Galveston, Texas, creates first commission form of government

**1899** National Consumers' League founded

**1901**
Leon Czolgosz assassinates President McKinley; Theodore Roosevelt becomes president; Socialist Party of America founded

**1902** Northern Securities Company dissolved under Sherman Antitrust Act; anthracite coal miners strike in Pennsylvania

**1903**
Elkins Act ends railroad rebates; Wisconsin first state to enact direct primary; W. E. B. Du Bois publishes *The Souls of Black Folk*

**1904** Lincoln Steffens's *The Shame of the Cities* published; Theodore Roosevelt elected president

William James's *Pragmatism* published **1907**

**1906** Hepburn Act strengthens Interstate Commerce Commission; Upton Sinclair's *The Jungle* published; Meat Inspection and Pure Food and Drug acts passed

**1908**
*Muller v. Oregon*; William Howard Taft elected president

**1909** Ballinger-Pinchot controversy; NAACP founded

**1911** Triangle Shirtwaist fire

**1912** Woodrow Wilson elected president

**1913**
Sixteenth and Seventeenth amendments allow for federal income taxes and direct election of senators; Underwood-Simmons Tariff enacted; Federal Reserve Act passed

**1914** Clayton Antitrust Act passed; Federal Trade Commission created

**1916** Margaret Sanger organizes New York Birth Control League; Woodrow Wilson reelected president

**1917**
Congress enacts literacy test for new immigrants

**1920** Nineteenth Amendment grants women the right to vote

# CHAPTER 23

# The United States and the Old World Order

## 1901–1920

**Preview**  *With the outbreak of World War I, the old order of colonial imperialism and carefully balanced military alliances came crashing down. Wilson at first proclaimed Americans neutral, in hopes of brokering a peace settlement. But American economic and cultural ties to the Allies, along with German submarine warfare, brought Americans into the war. By its end, Woodrow Wilson's hopes for a progressive "peace without victory" and a new world order were dashed.*

In 1898, as tens of thousands of eager young men signed up to kill Spaniards in Cuba, the USS *Oregon* left San Francisco Bay on a roundabout route toward its battle station in the Caribbean. It first headed south through the Pacific, passing Central America and leaving it thousands of miles behind. Then in the narrow Strait of Magellan at South America's tip, the ship encountered a gale so ferocious that the shore could not be seen. All communication ceased, and Americans at home feared the worst. But the *Oregon* passed into the Atlantic and steamed north until finally, after 68 days and 13,000 miles at sea, it helped win the Battle of Santiago Bay.

The daring voyage electrified the nation but worried its leaders. Since the defeat of Mexico in 1848, the United States had stretched from the Atlantic to the Pacific without enough navy to go around. As an emerging power, the country needed a path between the seas, a canal across the narrow isthmus of Colombia's Panamanian province in Central America, to defend itself and to promote its growing trade.

"I took the isthmus," President Theodore Roosevelt later told a cheering crowd. In a way he did. In 1903 he reached an agreement with Colombia to lease the needed strip of land. Hoping for more money and greater control over the canal, the Colombian senate refused to ratify the agreement.

Privately, TR talked of seizing Panama. But when he learned of a budding independence movement there, he let it be known that he would welcome a revolt. On schedule and without bloodshed, the Panamanians rebelled late in 1903. The next day a U.S. cruiser dropped anchor offshore to prevent Colombia from landing troops. The United States quickly recognized the new Republic of Panama and concluded a treaty for a renewable lease on a canal zone 10 miles wide. Panama received $10 million plus an annual rent of $250,000, the same terms offered to Colombia. Critics called it "a rough-riding assault upon another republic." (In 1921, after oil had been discovered in Colombia, Congress voted $25 million to the country.)

In November 1906 Roosevelt pulled into port at Panama City aboard the *Louisiana*, newly launched and the biggest battleship in the fleet. He spent the next three days traveling the length of the canal in the pouring rain. Soaked from head to toe, his huge Panama hat and white suit sagging about his body, he splashed through labor camps, asking workers for their complaints. He toured the hospital at Ancon and met Dr. William Gorgas, conqueror of the yellow fever–bearing mosquito. He walked railroad ties at the cuts and made speeches in the mud. "This is one of the great works of the world," he told an assembly of black diggers.

The Panama Canal embodied Roosevelt's muscular policy of respect through strength. TR modernized the army and tripled its size, created a general staff for planning and mobilization, and established the Army War College. As a pivot point between the two hemispheres, his canal allowed the United States to flex its strength across the globe.

These expanding horizons came about largely as an outgrowth of American commercial and industrial expansion, just as the imperialist empires of Great Britain, France, Germany, Russia, and Japan reflected the spread of their own industrial and commercial might. The Americans, steeped in democratic ideals, frequently seemed uncomfortable with the naked ambitions of European empire-builders. Roosevelt's embrace of the canal, however, showed how far some Americans would go to shape the world.

Expansionist diplomats at home and abroad assured each other that global order could be maintained by balancing power through a set of carefully crafted alliances. But that system of alliances did not hold. In 1914, the year the Panama Canal opened, the old world order shattered in a terrible war.

## PROGRESSIVE DIPLOMACY

As the Panama Canal was being built, progressive diplomacy was taking shape. Like progressive politics, it stressed moralism and order as it stretched executive power to new limits, molding and remaking now the international environment. "Of all our race, [God] has marked the American people as His chosen nation to finally lead in the redemption of the world," said one senator in 1900. At the core of this missionary faith lay a belief in the superiority of Anglo-American institutions. Every Western leader assumed that northern Europeans were racially superior, too. The darker peoples of the tropical zones, observed a progressive educator, dwelled in "nature's asylum for

*Foundations of progressive diplomacy*

degenerates." In this global vision of Manifest Destiny, few progressives questioned the need to uplift them.

Economic expansion underlay the commitment to a "civilizing" mission. The depression of 1893 had encouraged American manufacturers and farmers to look overseas for markets, and that expansion continued after 1900. By 1918, at the end of World War I, the United States had become the largest creditor in the world. Every administration committed itself to opening doors of trade and keeping them open.

## *Big Stick in the Caribbean*

Theodore Roosevelt liked to invoke the old African proverb "Walk softly and carry a big stick." But in the Caribbean he moved both loudly and mightily. The Panama Canal gave the United States a commanding position in the Western Hemisphere. Its importance required the country to "police the surrounding premises," explained

*Platt Amendment*

Secretary of State Elihu Root. Before granting Cuba independence in 1902, the United States reorganized its finances and wrote into the Cuban constitution the Platt Amendment. It gave American authorities the right to intervene if Cuban independence or internal order were threatened. Claiming that power, U.S. troops occupied the island twice between 1906 and 1923.

In looking to enforce a favorable environment for trade in the Caribbean, Roosevelt also worried about European intentions. The Monroe Doctrine of 1823 had declared against further European colonization of the Western Hemisphere, but in the early twentieth century the rising debts of Latin Americans to Europeans invited intrusion. "If we intend to say hands off to the power of Europe, then sooner or later we must keep order ourselves," Roosevelt warned.

Going well beyond Monroe's concept of resisting foreign penetration, Roosevelt asserted American command of the Caribbean. In 1904, when the

*Roosevelt Corollary to the Monroe Doctrine*

Dominican Republic defaulted on its debts, he added the "Roosevelt Corollary" to the Monroe Doctrine by claiming the right to police the Americas. Under it, the United States assumed responsibility for several Caribbean states, including the Dominican Republic, Cuba, and Panama.

## *A "Diplomatist of the Highest Rank"*

In the Far East Roosevelt exercised ingenuity rather than force, since he considered Asia beyond the American sphere of influence. Like McKinley, TR committed himself only to maintaining an "open door" of equal access to trade in China and to protecting the Philippines, "our heel of Achilles."

The key lay in offsetting Russian and Japanese ambitions in the region. When Japan attacked Russian holdings in the Chinese province of Manchuria in 1904, Roosevelt offered to mediate. He worried that if unchecked, Japan might threaten

American interests in China and the Philippines. Both sides met at the U.S. Naval Base near Portsmouth, New Hampshire, and, under Roosevelt's guidance, produced the Treaty of Portsmouth in 1905. It recognized the Japanese victory (the first by an Asian power over a European country) and ceded to Japan Port Arthur, the southern half of Sakhalin Island, and in effect, control of Korea. Japan promised to leave Manchuria as part of China and keep trade open to all foreign nations. Both the balance of power in Asia and the open door in China had been preserved. Roosevelt's diplomacy earned him the Nobel Peace Prize in 1906.

*Treaty of Portsmouth*

Some Japanese nationalists resented the peace treaty for curbing Japan's ambitions in Asia. Their anger surfaced in a protest lodged, of all places, against the San Francisco school board. In 1906, rising Japanese immigration led San Francisco school authorities to place the city's 93 Asian students in a separate school. In Japan citizens talked of war over the insult. Roosevelt, fuming at the "infernal fools in California," summoned the mayor of San Francisco and seven school board members to the White House. In exchange for an end to the segregation order, Roosevelt offered to arrange a mutual restriction of immigration between Japan and the United States. In 1907 all sides accepted his "gentlemen's agreement."

*Gentlemen's agreement*

The San Francisco school crisis sparked wild rumors that Japan was bent on taking Hawaii, or the Philippines, or the Panama Canal. In case Japan or any other nation thought of upsetting the Pacific balance, Roosevelt sent 16 gleaming white battleships on a world tour. "By George, isn't it magnificent!" he crowed, as the "Great White Fleet" steamed out of Hampton Roads, Virginia, in 1907. The fleet made its most conspicuous stop in Japan. Some Europeans predicted disaster. Instead, cheering crowds turned out in Tokyo and Yokohama. The show of force heralded a new age of American naval might but had an unintended consequence that haunted Americans for decades: it spurred Japanese admirals to expand their own navy.

*Great White Fleet*

Watching Roosevelt in his second term, an amazed London *Morning Post* dubbed him a "diplomatist of the highest rank." Abroad as at home, his brand of progressivism was grounded in an enthusiastic nationalism that mixed force with finesse to achieve balance and order. Yet despite TR's efforts, imperial rivalries, an unchecked naval arms race, and unrest in Europe threatened to plunge the world into chaos.

## Dollar Diplomacy

Instead of force or finesse, William Howard Taft relied on private investment to promote economic stability, keep peace, and tie debt-ridden nations to the United States. "Dollar diplomacy" simply amounted to "substituting dollars for bullets," Taft explained. He and Philander Knox, his prickly secretary of state, treated the restless nations of Latin America like ailing corporations, injecting capital and reorganizing management. By the time Taft left office in 1913, half of all American investments abroad were in Latin America.

In Nicaragua dollar diplomacy was not enough. In 1909, when the Nicaraguan legislature balked at American demands to take over its customshouse and national bank, a U.S. warship dropped anchor off the coast. The lawmakers changed their minds, but in 1912 a revolution led Taft to dispatch 2000 marines to protect American lives and property. Sporadic American intrusions lasted more than a dozen years.

Failure dogged Taft overseas as it did at home. In the Caribbean his dollar diplomacy was linked so closely with unpopular regimes, corporations, and banks that Woodrow Wilson scrapped it as soon as he entered the White House. Taft's efforts to strengthen China with investments and trade only intensified rivalry with Japan and made China more suspicious of all foreigners, including Americans. In 1911 the southern Chinese provinces rebelled against foreign intrusion and overthrew the monarchy. Only persistent pressure from the White House kept dollar diplomacy in Asia alive at all.

## WOODROW WILSON AND MORAL DIPLOMACY

The Lightfoot Club had been meeting in Reverend Wilson's hayloft for months when the question of whether the pen was mightier than the sword came up. Young Tommy Wilson, who had organized the debating society, jumped at the chance to argue that written words were more powerful than armies. But when the boys drew lots, Tommy ended up on the other side. "I can't argue for something I don't believe in," he protested. Thomas Woodrow Wilson eventually dropped his first name, but he never gave up his boyhood conviction that morality, at least as he defined it, should guide conduct. To the diplomacy of order, force, and finance, Wilson added a missionary zeal for spreading capitalism, democracy, and the progressive values of harmony and cooperation.

### Missionary Diplomacy

As president, Woodrow Wilson revived and enlarged Jefferson's notion of the United States as a beacon of freedom. The country had a mission: "We are chosen, and prominently chosen, to show the way to the nations of the world how they shall walk in the paths of liberty." Such paternalism only thinly masked Wilson's assumption of Anglo-American superiority and his willingness to spread Western-style democracy, capitalism, and morality through force.

Wilson's missionary diplomacy had a practical side. In the twentieth century foreign markets would serve as America's new frontier. American industries "will burst their jackets if they cannot find free outlets in the markets of the world," he cautioned in 1912. Wilson's genius lay in reconciling this commercial

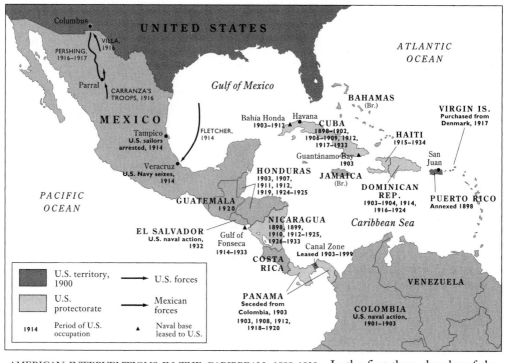

AMERICAN INTERVENTIONS IN THE CARIBBEAN, 1898–1930 In the first three decades of the twentieth century, armed and unarmed interventions by the United States virtually transformed the Caribbean into an American lake.

self-interest with a global idealism. In his eyes, exporting American democracy and capitalism would promote stability and progress throughout the world.

In Asia and the Pacific, Wilson moved to put "moral and public considerations" ahead of the "material interests of individuals." He pulled American bankers out of a six-nation railroad project in China backed by President Taft. The scheme encouraged foreign intervention and undermined Chinese sovereignty, Wilson said. The United States became the first major power to recognize the new democratic Republic of China in 1911 and in 1915 strongly opposed Japan's "Twenty-one Demands" for control of the country.

In the Caribbean and Latin America, Wilson discovered that interests closer to home could not be pursued through principles alone. In August 1914 he convinced Nicaragua, already occupied by American troops, to yield control of a naval base and grant the United States an alternative canal route. Upheavals in Haiti and the Dominican Republic brought in the U.S. Marines. By the end of his administration American troops were still stationed there and also in Cuba. All four nations were economically dependent on the United States and virtual protectorates. Missionary diplomacy, it turned out, could spread its gospel with steel as well as cash.

## Intervention in Mexico

A lingering crisis turned Wilson's "moral diplomacy" into a mockery in Mexico. A common border, 400 years of shared history, and millions of dollars in invest-

*Mexican Revolution* | ments made what happened in Mexico of urgent importance to the United States. In 1910 a revolution plunged Mexico into turmoil. Just as Wilson was entering the White House in 1913, the ruthless general Victoriano Huerta emerged as head of the government. Wealthy landowners and foreign investors endorsed Huerta, who was likely to protect their holdings. Soon a bloody civil war was raging.

Most European nations recognized the Huerta regime, but Wilson refused to accept the "government of butchers." (Huerta had murdered the popular leader Francisco Madero with the approval of the Taft administration.) When Huerta proclaimed himself dictator, Wilson banned arms shipments to Mexico. He threw his support to rebel leader Venustiano Carranza, on the condition that Carranza participate in American-sponsored elections. Carranza and his "constitutionalists" rejected such interference. With few options, Wilson armed the rebels anyway.

Wilson's distaste for Huerta was so great that he used a minor incident as a pretext for an invasion. In April 1914 the crew of the USS *Dolphin* landed without permission in the Mexican port city of Tampico. Local police arrested the sailors, only to release them with an apology. Unappeased, their squadron commander demanded a 21-gun salute to the American flag. Agreed, replied the Mexicans, but only if American guns returned the salute to Mexico. Learning of a German shipload of weapons about to land at Veracruz, Wilson broke the impasse by ordering American troops to take the city. Instead of the bloodless occupation they expected, U.S. marines encountered stiff resistance as they stormed ashore; 126 Mexicans and 19 Americans were killed before the city fell.

Only the combined diplomacy of Argentina, Brazil, and Chile staved off war between Mexico and the United States. When a bankrupt Huerta resigned in 1914,

*Pancho Villa* | Carranza formed a new constitutionalist government but refused to follow Wilson's guidelines. Wilson threw his support to Francisco "Pancho" Villa, a wily, peasant-born general who had broken from Carranza. Together with Emiliano Zapata, another peasant leader, Villa kept rebellion flickering.

A year later, when Wilson finally recognized the Carranza regime, Villa turned against the United States. In January 1916 he abducted 18 Americans from a train in Mexico and slaughtered them. In March, he galloped into Columbus, New Mexico, killed 19 people, and left the town in flames. Wilson ordered 6000 troops into Mexico to capture Villa. A reluctant Carranza agreed to yet another American invasion.

For nearly two years, General John "Black Jack" Pershing (nicknamed for the all-black unit he commanded in the Spanish-American War) chased Villa on horseback, in automobiles, and with airplanes. There were bloody skirmishes with government troops, but not a single one with Villa and his rebels. As the chase turned wilder and wilder, Carranza withdrew his consent for U.S. troops on Mexican soil. Early in 1917 Wilson pulled Pershing home. The "punitive expedition," as the president called it, poisoned Mexican-American relations for the next 30 years.

## THE ROAD TO WAR

In early 1917, around the time that Wilson recalled Pershing, the British liner *Laconia* was making its way home across the Atlantic. Passengers belowdecks talked almost casually of the war raging in Europe since 1914. "What do you think are our chances of being torpedoed?" asked Floyd Gibbons, an American reporter. Since Germany had stepped up its submarine attacks, the question was unavoidable. "I should put our chances at 250 to 1 that we don't meet a sub," replied a British diplomat.

"At that minute," recalled Gibbons, "the torpedo hit us." As warning whistles blasted, the passengers abandoned ship. From lifeboats they watched in horror as a second torpedo sent the *Laconia* to a watery grave. After a miserable night spent bobbing in the waves, Gibbons was rescued. But by 1917 other neutral Americans had already lost their lives at sea. Despite its best efforts, the United States found itself dragged into war.

### The Guns of August

For a century, profound strains had been pushing Europe toward war. Its population tripled, its middle and working classes swelled, and discontent with industrial society grew. Nationalism surged and with it, militarism and an aggressive imperialism. Led by Kaiser Wilhelm II and eager for empire, Germany aligned itself with Turkey and Austria-Hungary. The established imperial powers of England and France looked to contain Germany by supporting its foe, Russia. By the summer of 1914 Europe bristled with weapons, troops, and armor-plated navies. And these war machines were linked to one another through a web of diplomatic alliances—all of them committed to war, should someone or some nation set chaos in motion.

*Causes of World War I*

That moment came on June 28, 1914, in the streets of Sarajevo, the provincial capital of Bosnia in southwest Austria-Hungary. There, the heir to the Austro-Hungarian throne, Archduke Franz Ferdinand, was gunned down with his wife. The young assassin who carried out the deed belonged to the Black Hand, a terrorist group that had vowed to reunite Bosnia with Serbia in yet another Slavic nation on Austria-Hungary's border.

*Assassination of Archduke Ferdinand*

Austria-Hungary mobilized to punish all of Serbia. In response, rival Russia called up its 6-million-man army to help the Serbs. Germany joined with Austria-Hungary; France, with Russia. On July 28, after a month of insincere demands for apologies, Austria-Hungary attacked Serbia. Germany declared war on Russia on August 1 and, two days later, on France.

The guns of August heralded the first global war. Like so many dominoes, nations fell into line: Britain, Japan, Romania, and later Italy to the side of "Allies" France and Russia; Bulgaria and Turkey to the "Central Powers" of Germany and Austria-Hungary. Armies fought from the deserts of North Africa to the plains of Flanders. Fleets battled off the coasts of Chile and Sumatra. Soldiers came from as far away as Australia and India. Nearly 8 million never returned.

### Neutral but Not Impartial

The outbreak of war in Europe shocked most Americans. Few knew Serbia as anything but a tiny splotch on a world map. Fewer still were prepared to go to war in its defense. President Wilson issued an immediate declaration of neutrality and approved a plan for evacuating Americans stranded in Belgium. "The more

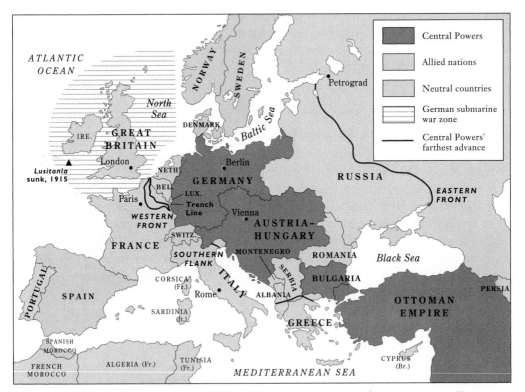

THE WAR IN EUROPE, 1914–1917  When World War I erupted, few countries in Europe remained neutral. The armies of the Central Powers penetrated as far west as France and as far east as Russia. By 1917, the war in Europe had settled into a hideous standoff along a deadly line of trenches on the western front.

I read about the conflict," Wilson wrote a friend, "the more open it seems to me to utter condemnation."

Wilson came to see the calamity as an opportunity. In his mind, a neutral America would lead warring nations to "a peace without victory" and a new world order. Selfish nationalism would give way to cooperative internationalism; power politics, to collective security in which nations joined together to ensure the safety of all and to isolate aggressors. Progressive faith in reason would triumph over irrational violence. Everything hinged on maintaining neutrality. Only if America stood above the fray could it lead the way to a higher peace. Americans must remain "impartial in thought as well as action," Wilson insisted in 1914.

But true impartiality was impossible. Americans of German and Austrian descent naturally sympathized with the Central Powers, as did Irish Americans, on the grounds of England's centuries-old domination of Ireland. But the bonds of language, culture, and history tied most Americans to Great Britain. And gratitude for French aid during the American Revolution still lived.

American economic ties to Britain and France created a financial investment in Allied victory. After faltering briefly in 1914, the American economy boomed with the flood of war orders. Between 1914 and 1916 trade with the Allies rocketed from $800 million to $3 billion. The Allies eventually borrowed more than $2 billion from American banks to finance their purchases. In contrast, a British blockade reduced American "contraband" commerce with the Central Powers to a trickle.

Germany aroused different sentiments. Although some progressives admired German social reforms, Americans generally saw Germany as an iron military power bent on conquest. Americans read British propaganda of spike-helmeted "Huns" raping Belgian women, bayoneting their children, pillaging their towns. Some of the stories were true, some embellished, some manufactured, but all worked against Germany in the United States.

## The Diplomacy of Neutrality

Wilson had admired Great Britain all his life and could not contain his sympathies. Although he insisted that all warring powers respect the right of neutrals to trade with any nation, he hesitated to retaliate against Great Britain's blockade. Britain's powerful navy was its key to victory over Germany, a land power. By the end of 1915 the United States had all but accepted the British blockade of Germany, while American supplies continued to flow to England. True neutrality was dead. America became the quartermaster of the Allies.

Early in 1915, Germany turned to a dreadful new weapon to even the odds at sea. It mounted a counterblockade of Great Britain with two dozen submarines, or *Unterseeboote*, called U-boats. Before submarines, sea raiders usually gave crews and passengers the chance to escape. But if thin-skinned U-boats surfaced to obey these conventions, they risked being rammed or blown from the water. So submarines attacked without warning and spared no lives.

*Submarine warfare*

Invoking international law and national honor, President Wilson threatened to hold Germany to "strict accountability" for any American losses. Germany promised not to sink any American ships, but soon a new issue grabbed the headlines: the safety of American passengers on vessels of nations at war.

On the morning of May 7, 1915, the British passenger liner *Lusitania* appeared out of a fog bank off the coast of Ireland on its way from New York to

**Lusitania**

Southampton. The commander of the German U-20 could hardly believe his eyes: the giant ship filled the viewfinder of his periscope. He fired a single torpedo. A tremendous roar followed as one of the *Lusitania*'s main boilers exploded. The ship listed so badly that lifeboats could barely be launched before the vessel sank. Nearly 1200 men, women, and children perished, including 128 Americans.

Wilson, though horrified at this "murder on the high seas," did little more than send notes of protest to Germany. Secretary of State Bryan, an advocate of what he called "real neutrality," wanted equal protests lodged against both German submarines and British blockaders. He suspected that the *Lusitania* carried munitions and was thus a legitimate target. (Much later, evidence proved him right.) Relying on passengers for protection against attack, Bryan argued, was "like putting women and children in front of an army." Rather than endorse Wilson's policy, Bryan resigned.

Battling on two fronts in Europe, Germany wanted to keep the United States out of the war. But in February 1916 a desperate Germany declared submarine warfare on all *armed* vessels, belligerent or neutral. A month later a U-boat commander mistook the French steamer *Sussex* for a mine layer and torpedoed the unarmed vessel as it ferried passengers and freight across the English Channel. Several Americans were injured.

In mid-April, Wilson issued an ultimatum. If Germany refused to stop sinking nonmilitary vessels, the United States would break off diplomatic relations.

**Sussex *pledge***

War would surely follow. Without enough U-boats to control the seas, Germany agreed to Wilson's terms, all but abandoning its counterblockade. This *Sussex* pledge gave Wilson a major victory but carried a grave risk. If German submarines resumed unrestricted attacks, the United States would have to go to war. "Any little German [U-boat] commander can put us into the war at any time," Wilson admitted to his cabinet.

### Peace, Preparedness, and the Election of 1916

While hundreds of young Yanks slipped across the border to enlist in the Canadian army, most Americans agreed that neutrality was the wisest course. Before the war a peace movement had taken seed in the United States. In 1914 social reformers Jane Addams, Charlotte Perkins Gilman, and Lillian Wald founded the Women's International League for Peace and Freedom and the American Union against Militarism. Calling on Wilson to convene a peace conference, they lobbied for open diplomacy, disarmament, an end to colonial empires, and an international organization to settle disputes. These would become the core of Wilson's peace plan.

Pacifists might condemn the war, but Republicans and corporate leaders argued that the nation was woefully unprepared to keep peace. The army numbered only 80,000 men in 1914; the navy, just 37 battleships and a handful of new "dreadnoughts," or supercruisers. Advocates of "preparedness" called for a navy larger than Great Britain's, an army of millions of reservists, and universal military training.

By the end of 1915, frustration with German submarines led Wilson to join the cause. He toured the country promoting preparedness and promising a "navy second to none." In Washington, he pressed Congress to double the army, increase the National Guard, and begin construction of the largest navy in the world. To foot the bill progressives pushed through new graduated taxes on higher incomes and on estates as well as additional levies on corporate profits.

Whoever paid for it, most Americans were thinking of preparedness for peace, not war. The Democrats discovered the political power of peace early in the presidential campaign of 1916. As their convention opened in St. Louis in June, the keynote speaker began what he expected to be a dull description of Wilson's recent diplomatic maneuvers—only to have the crowd roar back in each case, "What did we do? What did we do?" The speaker knew the answer and shouted it back: "We didn't go to war! We didn't go to war!" The next day Wilson was renominated by acclamation. "He Kept Us Out of War" became his campaign slogan.

*"He kept us out of war"*

The Republicans had already nominated Charles Evans Hughes, the former governor of New York. He endorsed "straight and honest" neutrality and peace. But despite his moderate stand, Democrats succeeded in painting him as a warmonger, partly because Theodore Roosevelt had rattled his own sabers so loudly. As the election approached, Democrats took out full-page advertisements in newspapers across the country: "If You Want WAR, Vote for HUGHES! If You Want Peace with Honor, VOTE FOR WILSON!"

By the time the polls closed, Wilson had squeaked out a victory. He carried the South and key states in the Midwest and West on a tide of prosperity, progressive reform, and, most of all, promises of peace.

## Wilson's Final Peace Offensive

Twice since 1915 Wilson had sent his trusted advisor Edward House to Europe to negotiate a peace among the warring powers, and twice House had failed. With the election over, Wilson opened his final peace offensive. But when he asked the belligerents to state their terms for a cease-fire, neither side responded. Frustrated, fearful, and genuinely agonized, Wilson called for "a peace among equals" in January 1917.

As Wilson spoke, a fleet of U-boats was cruising toward the British Isles. Weeks earlier German military leaders had persuaded the Kaiser to take one last gamble to starve the Allies into submission. On January 31, 1917, the German ambassador in Washington announced that unrestricted submarine warfare would resume the next day.

Wilson's dream of keeping the country from war collapsed. He asked Congress for authority to arm merchant ships and severed relations with Germany.

*Zimmermann telegram* | Then British authorities handed him a bombshell—an intercepted telegram from the German foreign secretary, Arthur Zimmermann, to the Kaiser's ambassador in Mexico. In the event of war, the ambassador was instructed to offer Mexico guns, money, and its "lost territory in Texas, New Mexico, and Arizona" to attack the United States. Already frustrated by Pancho Villa's raids across the U.S.-Mexico border, Wilson angrily released the Zimmermann telegram to the press. Soon after, he ordered gun crews aboard merchant ships and directed them to shoot U-boats on sight.

The momentum of events now propelled a reluctant Wilson toward war. On March 12, U-boats torpedoed the American merchant vessel *Algonquin*. On March 15, a revolution in Russia toppled Czar Nicholas II. A key ally was crumbling from within. By the end of the month U-boats had sunk nearly 600,000 tons of Allied and neutral shipping. For the first time reports came to Washington of cracking morale in the Allied ranks.

On April 2, accompanied by armed cavalry, Wilson rode down Pennsylvania Avenue. He trudged up the steps of the capitol and delivered to Congress a stirring war message, full of idealistic purpose. "We shall fight for the things we have always carried nearest our hearts—for democracy, for the right of those who submit to authority to have a voice in their own governments, for the rights and liberties of small nations."

Pacifists held up the war resolution until it finally passed on April 6. Six senators and 50 House members opposed it, including the first woman in Congress, Jeannette Rankin of Wyoming. Cultural, economic, and historical ties to the Allies, along with the German campaign of submarine warfare, had tipped the country toward war. Wilson had not wanted it, but now the battlefield seemed the only path to a higher peace.

## WAR AND SOCIETY

In 1915 the German zeppelin LZ-38, hovering at 8000 feet, dropped a load of bombs that killed seven Londoners. For the first time in history, civilians died in an air attack. Few aerial bombardments occurred during the First World War, but they signaled the growing importance of the home front in modern combat. Governments not only fielded armies but also mobilized industry, controlled labor, even rationed food. In the United States, traditions of cooperation and volunteerism helped to organize the home front and the battle front, often in ways that were peculiarly progressive.

## The Slaughter of Stalemate

While the United States debated entry into the Great War, the Allies were coming perilously close to losing it. Following the initial German assault in 1914, the war had settled into a grisly stalemate. A continuous, immovable front stretched south from Flanders to the border of Switzerland. Troops dug ditches, six to eight feet deep and four to five feet wide, to escape bullets, grenades, and artillery. Twenty-five thousand miles of these "trenches" slashed a muddy scar across Europe. Men lived in them for years, prey to disease, lice, and a plague of rats.

*Trench warfare*

War in the machine age gave the advantage to the defense. When soldiers bravely charged "over the top" of the trenches, they were shredded by machine guns that fired 600 rounds a minute. Poison gas choked them in their tracks. Giant howitzers lobbed shells on them from positions too distant to see. In the Battle of the Somme River in 1916 a million men were killed in just four months of fighting. Only late in the war did new armored "landships"—code-named "tanks"—return the advantage to the offense by surmounting the trench barriers with their caterpillar treads.

By then Vladimir Lenin was speeding home to Russia, where food riots, coal shortages, and protests against the government had led to revolution. Lenin had

Trench warfare, wrote one general, is "marked by uniform formations, the regulation of space and time by higher commands . . . fixed distances between units and individuals."
The reality of life in the trenches (as pictured here) was something else again.

been exiled to Switzerland during the early stages of the Russian Revolution but returned to lead the Bolshevik party to power in November 1917. Soon the Russians negotiated a separate peace with Germany, which then transferred a million soldiers to the western front for the coming spring offensive.

### "You're in the Army Now"

The Allies' plight drove the army into a crash program to send a million soldiers to Europe by the spring of 1918. The United States had barely 180,000 men in uniform. To raise the force, Congress passed the Selective Service Act in May 1917. Feelings about the draft ran high. "There is precious little difference between a conscript [draftee] and a convict," protested the House Speaker in 1917. Progressives were more inclined to see military service as an opportunity to unite America and promote democracy: "Universal [military] training will jumble the boys of America all together, . . . smashing all the petty class distinctions that now divide, and prompting a brand of real democracy."

*Selective Service Act*

At ten in the morning on July 20, 1917, Secretary of War Newton Baker tied a blindfold over his eyes, reached into a huge glass bowl, and drew the first number in the new draft lottery. Some 24 million men were registered. Almost 3 million were drafted; another 2 million volunteered. Most were white, and all were young, between the ages of 21 and 31. Several thousand women served as clerks, telephone operators, and nurses. In a nation of immigrants, nearly one draftee in five had been born in another country. Training often aimed at educating and Americanizing these ethnic recruits. In special "development battalions" drill sergeants barked out orders while volunteers from the YMCA taught American history and English.

Like Mexican Americans, African Americans volunteered in disproportionately high numbers. They quickly filled the four all-black army and eight National Guard units already in existence. Abroad, where 200,000 black troops served in France, only 42,000 were permitted in combat. Southern Democrats in Congress had opposed training African Americans to arms, fearful of putting "arrogant, strutting representatives of black soldiery in every community." But four regiments of the all-black Ninety-third Division, brigaded with the French army, were among the first Americans in the trenches and among the most decorated units in the U.S. Army.

Racial violence sometimes flared among the troops. The worst episode occurred in Houston in the summer of 1917. Harassed by white soldiers and by the city's Jim Crow laws, seasoned black regulars rioted and killed 17 white civilians. Their whole battalion was disarmed and sent under arrest to New Mexico. Thirteen troopers were condemned to death and hanged within days, too quickly for appeals even to be filed.

*Houston riot*

Black or white, recruits learned the ways of the army—rising before dawn, drilling in close order, marching for miles. But many of them also learned to wash regularly, use indoor toilets, and read. To fight sexually transmitted disease, the army produced thousands of pamphlets, films, and lectures. The drive constituted the first serious sex education young Americans ever received.

Progressive reformers did not miss the chance to put the social sciences to work in the army. Most recruits had fewer than seven years of education, yet they had to be classified and assigned quickly to units. Psychologists saw the chance to use new intelligence tests to help the army and prove their own theories about the value of "IQ" (intelligence quotient) in measuring the mind. In fact, these new "scientific" IQ tests often measured little more than class origins. Questions such as "Who wrote 'The Raven'?" exposed background rather than intelligence. More than half the Russian, Italian, and Polish draftees and almost 80 percent of the black draftees tested as "inferior." The army stopped the testing program in January 1919, but schools across the country adopted it after the war, reinforcing many ethnic and racial prejudices.

## Mobilizing the Economy

Armed against the enemy, clothed and drilled, the doughboys marched up the gangplanks of the "Atlantic Ferry"—the ships that conveyed them to Europe. (Infantrymen were called "doughboys," most likely because of the clay dough used by soldiers in the 1850s to clean belts.) To equip, feed, and transport an army of nearly 5 million required a national effort.

At the Treasury Department, Secretary William Gibbs McAdoo fretted over how to finance the war, which cost, finally, $32 billion. At the time the entire national debt ran to only $2 billion. New taxes paid about a third of the war costs. The rest came from loans financed through "Liberty" and "Victory" bonds and war savings certificates. By 1920 the national debt had climbed to $20 billion.

With sweeping grants of authority provided by Congress, President Wilson constructed a massive bureaucracy to mobilize the home front. What emerged was a managed economy similar to the New Nationalism envisioned by Theodore Roosevelt. A War Industries Board (WIB) coordinated | *War Industries Board* production through networks of industrial and trade associations. Although it had the authority to order firms to comply, the WIB relied instead on persuasion through publicity and "cost-plus" contracts that covered all production costs, plus a guaranteed profit. Antitrust suits, recalled one official, were simply put "to sleep until the war was over." Corporate profits tripled, and production soared.

The Food Administration encouraged farmers to grow more and citizens to eat less wastefully. Publicity campaigns promoted "wheatless" and "meatless" days and exhorted families to plant "victory" gardens. Spurred by rising prices, farmers brought more marginal lands into cultivation as their real income jumped 25 percent.

A Fuel Administration met the army's energy needs by increasing production and limiting domestic consumption. Transportation snarls required more drastic action. In December 1917 the U.S. Railroad Administration simply took over rail lines for the duration of the war. Government coordination, together with a new system of permits, got freight moving and kept workers happy. Rail workers saw their wages grow by $300 million. Railroad unions won recognition, an eight-hour day, and a grievance procedure. For the first time in decades labor unrest subsided, and the trains ran on schedule.

The modern bureaucratic state received a powerful boost during the 18 months of American participation in the war. Speeding trends already under way, some 5000 new federal agencies centralized authority and cooperated with business and labor. The number of federal employees more than doubled between 1916 and 1918, to over 850,000. The wartime bureaucracy was quickly dismantled at the end of the war, but it set an important precedent for the future.

*Bureaucratic state*

### *War Work*

The war benefited working men and women, though not as much as their employers. Government contracts guaranteed high wages, an eight-hour day, and equal pay for comparable work. To encourage people to stay on the job, federal contracting agencies set up special classes to teach employers the new science of personnel management in order to supervise workers more efficiently and humanely. American industry moved one step closer to the "welfare capitalism" of the 1920s, with its profit sharing, company unions, and personnel departments to forestall worker discontent.

Personnel management was not always enough to guarantee industrial peace. In 1917 American workers called over 4000 strikes, the most in American history. To keep factories running smoothly, President Wilson created the National War Labor Board (NWLB) early in 1918. The NWLB arbitrated more than 1000 labor disputes, helped to increase wages, and established overtime pay. In return for pledges not to strike, the board guaranteed the rights of unions to organize and bargain collectively. Membership in the American Federation of Labor jumped from 2.7 million in 1916 to nearly 4 million by 1919.

*National War Labor Board*

The wartime demand for workers brought about a million new women into the labor force. Most were young and single. Some took over jobs once held by men as railroad engineers, drill press operators, and electric lift truck drivers. The prewar trend toward higher-paying jobs intensified, though most women still earned less than the men they replaced. And some of the most spectacular gains in defense and government work evaporated after the war as male veterans returned and the country demobilized. Tens of thousands of army nurses, defense workers, and war administrators lost their jobs. Agencies such as the Women's Service Section of the Railroad Administration, which fought sexual harassment and discrimination, simply went out of business.

Women in war work nonetheless helped to energize several women's causes and organizations. Radical suffragist Alice Paul and others who had protested

Most posters of the day pictured women doing "women's" war work, such as nursing, but the demand for labor meant that women helped out in dirty and potentially dangerous jobs like those in this munitions factory, where women are working alongside men. Women doing this kind of work, previously handled by men alone, strengthened the case for extending voting rights to women on the basis of female equality.

against the war now argued for women's rights, including the right to vote, on the basis of it. As women worked beside men in wartime factories and offices, in nursing stations at home or on the front, and in patriotic and other volunteer organizations, they could argue more convincingly for both economic and political equality. One step in that direction came after the war with the ratification of the Nineteenth Amendment in 1919 granting women the right to vote.

## Great Migrations

War work sparked massive migrations of laborers. As the fighting abroad choked off immigration and the draft depleted the workforce, factory owners scoured the country for workers. Industrial cities, no matter how small, soon swelled with newcomers. Between 1917 and 1920, some 150,000 *Mexican migrations* Mexicans crossed the border into Texas, California, New Mexico, and Arizona. Some Mexican Americans left segregated barrios of western cities for war plants

## An African American Woman's
## View of the 1919 Race Riots

The Washington riot gave me the *thrill that comes once in a life time*. I . . . read between the lines of our morning paper that at last our men had stood like men, struck back, were no longer dumb driven cattle. When I could no longer read for my streaming tears, I stood up, alone in my room, held both hands high over my head and exclaimed aloud: "Oh I thank God, thank God." . . . Only colored women of the South know the extreme in suffering and humiliation.

We know how many insults we have borne silently, for we have hidden many of them from our men because we did not want them to die needlessly in our defense . . . , the deep humiliation of sitting in the Jim Crow part of a street car and hear the white men laugh and discuss us, point out the good and bad points of our bodies. . . .

And, too, a woman loves a strong man, she delights to feel that her man can protect her, fight for her if necessary, save her.

No woman loves a weakling, a coward be she white or black, and some of us have been near thinking our men cowards, but thank God for Washington colored men! All honor to them, for they first blazed the way and right swiftly did Chicago men follow [during the 1919 race riot]. They put new hope, a new vision into their almost despairing women.

God Grant that our men everywhere refrain from strife, provoke no quarrel, but they protect their women and homes at any cost.

*A Southern Colored Woman*

Source: *The Crisis*, Vol. 19 (November 1919), p. 339. Reprinted in William Loren Katy, ed., *Eyewitness: The Negro in American History* (New York: Pittman Publishing, 1976), p. 403.

in Chicago, Omaha, and other northern cities, pushed out by the cheaper labor from Mexico and seeking higher-paying jobs. But most worked on farms and ranches, freed from military service by the deferment granted to agricultural labor.

Northern labor agents fanned out across the rural South to recruit young African Americans, while black newspapers like the Chicago *Defender* summoned them up to the "Land of Hope." During the war more than 400,000 moved to the booming industries of the North. Largely unskilled and semiskilled, they worked in the steel mills of Pennsylvania, the war plants of Massachusetts, the brickyards of New Jersey. Southern towns were decimated by the drain. Finally, under pressure from southern politicians, the U.S. Employment Service suspended its program to assist blacks moving north.

*African Americans*

These migrations of African Americans—into the army as well as into the city—aggravated racial tensions. Lynching parties murdered 38 black southerners in 1917 and 58 in 1918. In 1919, after the war ended, more than 70 were hanged, some still in uniform. Housing shortages and job competition helped to ignite race riots across the North. In almost every city black citizens, stirred by war rhetoric of freedom and democracy, showed new militancy. During the bloody "red summer" of 1919 race wars broke out in Washington, D.C., Omaha, Nebraska, New York City, and Chicago, where thousands of African Americans were burned out of their homes and hundreds injured as they fought white mobs.

### Propaganda and Civil Liberties

"Once lead this people into war," President Wilson warned before American entry into the conflict, "and they'll forget there ever was such a thing as tolerance." Americans succumbed to a ruthless hysteria during World War I, but they had help. Wilson knew how reluctant Americans had been to enter the war, and in 1917 he created the Committee on Public Information (CPI) to cement American commitment to the war.

Under George Creel, a California journalist, the CPI launched a zealous publicity campaign that produced colorful war posters, 75 million pamphlets, and patriotic "war expositions" in two dozen cities across the country. An army of 75,000 fast-talking "Four-Minute Men" invaded theaters, schools, and churches to keep patriotism at "white heat" with four minutes of war tirades. The CPI organized "Loyalty Leagues" in ethnic communities and sponsored rallies, including a much-publicized immigrant "pilgrimage" to the birthplace of George Washington.

*Committee on Public Information*

As war fever mounted, voluntary patriotism blossomed into an orgy of "100 percent Americanism" that distrusted all aliens, radicals, pacifists, and dissenters. German Americans became special targets. In Iowa the governor made it a crime to speak German in public. When a mob outside of St. Louis lynched a naturalized German American who had tried to enlist in the navy, a jury found the leaders not guilty.

Congress gave hysteria more legal bite by passing the Espionage and the Sedition acts of 1917 and 1918. Both set harsh penalties for any actions that hindered the war effort or that could be viewed as even remotely unpatriotic. Following passage, 1500 citizens were arrested for offenses that included denouncing the draft, criticizing the Red Cross, and complaining about wartime taxes.

*Espionage and Sedition acts*

Radical groups received especially severe treatment. The Industrial Workers of the World (IWW), a militant union centered in western states, saw the war as a battle among capitalists and threatened to strike mining and lumber companies in protest. Federal agents raided IWW headquarters in Chicago and arrested 113 members. The crusade destroyed the union. Similarly, the Socialist party opposed the "capitalist" war. In response, the postmaster general banned a dozen Socialist publications from the mail, though the party was a legal organization that had elected mayors, municipal officials, and members of Congress. In June 1918 government agents arrested Eugene V. Debs, the Socialist candidate for president in 1912, for an antiwar speech. A jury found him guilty of sedition and sentenced him to 10 years in jail.

The Supreme Court endorsed such actions. In *Schenck v. United States* (1919), the Court unanimously affirmed the conviction of a Socialist party officer who

**Schenck v. United States** had mailed pamphlets urging resistance to the draft. The pamphlets, wrote Justice Oliver Wendell Holmes, created "a clear and present danger" to a nation at war.

## Over There

The first American doughboys landed in France in June 1917, but few saw battle. General John Pershing held back his raw troops until they could receive more training. He also separated them in a distinct American Expeditionary Force to preserve their identity and avoid Allied disagreements over strategy.

In the spring of 1918, as the Germans pushed toward Paris, Pershing rushed 70,000 American troops to the front. American units helped block the Germans both at the town of Château-Thierry and, a month later in June, at Belleau Wood. Two more German attacks, one at Amiens and the other just east of the Marne River, ended in costly German retreats. On September 12, 1918, half a million American soldiers and a smaller number of French troops overran the German stronghold at Saint-Mihiel in four days.

With their army in retreat and civilian morale low, Germany's leaders sought an armistice. They hoped to negotiate terms along the lines laid out by Woodrow

*Fourteen Points* Wilson in a speech to Congress in January 1918. Wilson's bright vision of peace had encompassed fourteen points. The key provisions called for open diplomacy, free seas and free trade, disarmament, democratic self-rule, and an "association of nations" to guarantee collective security. It was nothing less than a new world order to end selfish nationalism, imperialism, and war.

Allied leaders were not impressed. "President Wilson and his Fourteen Points bore me," French premier Georges Clemenceau said. "Even God Almighty has only ten!" But Wilson's idealistic platform was also designed to save the Allies deeper embarrassment. Almost as soon as it came to power in 1917, the new Bolshevik government in Moscow had begun publishing secret treaties from the czar's archives. They revealed that the Allies had gone to war for territory and colonies, not for high principles. Wilson's Fourteen Points had given their cause a nobler purpose.

Wilson's ideals also stirred German liberals. On October 6 Wilson received a telegram from Berlin requesting an immediate truce. Within a month Turkey and Austria-Hungary surrendered. Early in November the Kaiser was overthrown

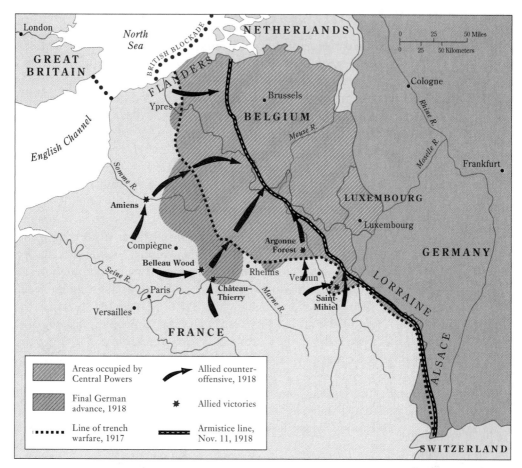

THE FINAL GERMAN OFFENSIVE AND ALLIED COUNTERATTACK, 1918   On the morning
of March 21, 1918, over 60 German divisions sliced through Allied lines. They then plunged
within 50 miles of Paris before being stopped at the Marne River in July. The Allied
counterattack was marked by notable American victories at Château-Thierry,
Belleau Wood, Saint-Mihiel, and Meuse-Argonne.

and fled to neutral Holland. On November 11, 1918, German officers filed into
Allied headquarters in a converted railroad car near Compiègne, France, and
signed the armistice.

Of the 2 million Americans who served in France, some 116,500 died. By comparison, the war claimed 2.2 million Germans, 1.7 million Russians, 1.4 million
French, 1.2 million Austro-Hungarians, and nearly a million Britons. The American contribution had nonetheless been crucial, providing vital convoys at sea and
fresh, confident troops on land. The United States emerged from the war stronger
than ever. Europe, on the other hand, looked forward—as one newspaper put it—
to "Disaster . . . Exhaustion . . . Revolution."

## The Influenza Pandemic of 1918–1919

In the months before the armistice, a scourge more lethal than war had begun to engulf the globe. It started innocently enough. At Fort Riley, Kansas, on the morning of March 11, 1918, company cook Albert Mitchell reported to the infirmary on sick call. His head and muscles ached, his throat was sore, and he had a low-grade fever.

It was the flu, dangerous for infants and the old but ordinarily no problem for a robust young man like Mitchell. By noon, however, 107 soldiers had reported similar symptoms. Within a week, the number had jumped to over 500. Cases of the flu were being reported in virtually every state in the Union, even on the isolated island of Alcatraz in San Francisco Bay. And robust young people were dying from it.

The first wave of flu produced few deaths in the United States. But as the virus mutated over the next year, its victims experienced more distressing symptoms: vomiting, dizziness, labored breathing, incessant sweating. Victims literally drowned in their own bodily fluids from the pneumonia that accompanied the infection.

Soldiers and others living in close quarters were especially vulnerable, and for reasons still unknown, so were young adults 20 to 34 years old, precisely the ages of most of those in the armed services. For every 50 people infected, one died. In the United States alone, the death toll rose to at least 675,000, more than the American battle deaths in World War I, World War II, the Korean War, and the war in Vietnam combined.

Ironically, the United States was the country least affected by this worldwide epidemic, called a "pandemic." American soldiers seem to have carried the disease

*Global spread of the pandemic*

to Europe, where it jumped from one country to another in the spring and summer of 1918. French troops and civilians soon were suffering from it, then British and German. General Eric von Ludendorff counted the flu as one of the causes of the failure of the final German offensive in July 1918, which almost won the war for Germany.

With steamships and railroads carrying people all over the globe, virtually no place was safe. By the summer of 1918, the virus had leapt from North America and Europe to Asia and Japan; by fall, to Africa and South America. As far north as the Russian city of Archangel, officials were reporting 30 influenza deaths a day by October 1918.

Sixteen months after Albert Mitchell first reported to sick call, the flu vanished as quickly and mysteriously as it had appeared. Conservative estimates placed the number of dead worldwide at 25 million, making the influenza pandemic of 1918–1919 the most lethal outbreak of disease on an annual basis in human history. Global war had helped spread the disease, but improvements in transportation and two centuries of global migrations had also spawned pandemics. As automobiles and airplanes continued to shrink the globe, similar pandemics, though less deadly, would be repeated in years to come. See Interactive Map 5 in the color insert for a depiction of the influenza pandemic.

Cartoon by D. C. Boonzaier in *De Burger*, 16/10/1918

In October 1918 artist D. C. Boonzaier drew this grim cartoon of the Spanish flu—
*Spaanse Griep*—when it came to South Africa. In his diary Boonzaier spoke of "the
presence of some universal calamity, from which there was no escape. Death stalked
by your side incessantly, you looked into its face wherever you turned."

## THE LOST PEACE

As the USS *George Washington* approached the coast of France in mid-December
1918, the mist suddenly lifted in an omen of good hope. Woodrow Wilson had
come to represent the United States at the Paris peace conference at Versailles,
once the glittering palace of Louis XIV. A world of problems awaited him and
the other Allied leaders. Europe had been shelled into ruin and scarred with the
debris of war. Fifty million people lay dead or maimed from the fighting.
Throughout the Balkans and the old Turkish empire, ethnic rivalries, social chaos,
and revolution loomed.

With the old world order in shambles, Wilson felt the need to take vigorous
action. Thus the president handpicked the Peace Commission of experts that
accompanied him. It included economists, historians, geographers, and political
scientists—but not a single member of the Republican-controlled Senate.
What promised to make peace negotiations easier created a crippling liability in
Washington, where Republicans were already casting hostile eyes on the mirrored
halls of Versailles.

## The Treaty of Versailles

Everywhere Wilson went, cheers greeted him. In Paris 2 million people showered him with flowers. In Italy they hailed him as the "peacemaker from America." And Wilson believed what he heard, unaware of how determined the victors were to punish the vanquished. David Lloyd George of England, Georges Clemenceau of France, Vittorio Orlando of Italy, and Wilson constituted the Big Four at the conference that included some 27 nations. War had united them; now peacemaking threatened to divide them.

Wilson's sweeping reforms had taken Allied leaders by surprise. Hungry for new colonies, eager to see Germany crushed and disarmed, they had already divided up the territories of the Central Powers in secret treaties. Germany had offered to surrender on the basis of Wilson's Fourteen Points, but the Allies refused to accept them. When Wilson threatened to negotiate peace on his own, Allied leaders finally agreed—but only for the moment.

Noticeably absent when the peace conference convened in January 1919 were the Russians. None of the Western democracies had recognized the Bolshevik regime in Moscow, out of fear that the communist revolution might spread. Instead, France and Britain were helping to finance a civil war to overthrow the Bolsheviks. Even Wilson had been persuaded to send several thousand American troops to join the Allied occupation of some northern Russian ports and to Siberia. The Soviets would neither forgive nor forget this intrusion.

Grueling negotiations forced Wilson to yield several of his fourteen points. Britain, with its powerful navy, refused even to discuss the issues of free trade and freedom of the seas. Wilson's "open diplomacy" was conducted behind closed doors by the Big Four. The only mention of disarmament involved Germany, which was permanently barred from rearming. Wilson's call for "peace without victory" gave way to a "guilt clause" that saddled Germany with responsibility for the war. Worse still, the victors imposed on the vanquished a burdensome debt of $33 billion in reparations.

Wilson did achieve some successes. His pleas for national self-determination led to the creation of a dozen new states in Europe, including Yugoslavia, Hungary, and Austria. (Poland and newly created Czechoslovakia, however, contained millions of ethnic Germans.) Former colonies gained new status as "mandates" of the victors, who were obligated to prepare them for independence. The old German and Turkish empires in the Middle East and Africa became the responsibility of France and England, while Japan took over German possessions in the Far East.

Wilson never lost sight of his main goal: a general association of nations. He had given so much ground precisely because he believed this new world organi-

*League of Nations* | zation would correct any mistakes in the peace settlement. Members promised to submit all war-provoking disagreements to arbitration and to isolate aggressors by cutting off commercial and military trade. Article X (Wilson called it "the heart of the covenant") bound members to respect one another's independence and territory and to join together against attack. "It is definitely a guarantee of peace," the president told the delegates in February 1919.

## The Battle for the Treaty

Wilson left immediately for home to address growing opposition in Congress. In the off-year elections of 1918, voters unhappy with wartime controls, new taxes, and attacks on civil liberties had given both houses to the opposition Republicans. A slim Republican majority in the Senate put Wilson's archrival, Henry Cabot Lodge of Massachusetts, in the chairman's seat of the all-important Foreign Relations Committee.

While most of the country favored the league, Lodge was against it. For decades he had fought to preserve American freedom of action in foreign affairs. Now he worried that the league would force Americans to subject themselves to "the will of other nations." And he certainly did not want Democrats to win votes by taking credit for the treaty. Securing the signatures of enough senators to block any treaty, Lodge rose in the Senate just before midnight on March 3, 1919, to read a "round robin" resolution against the league. "Woodrow Wilson's League of Nations died in the Senate tonight," concluded the New York *Sun*.

*Lodge opposes the league*

Wilson's only hope of winning the necessary two-thirds majority lay in compromise. Worn out by the concessions already wrung from him in Paris, afflicted by numbing headaches and a twitch in his left eye, he resisted all changes. Despite his doctor's warnings, Wilson took his case to the people in a month-long stump across the nation in 1919.

In Pueblo, Colorado, a crowd of 10,000 heard perhaps the greatest oration of his career. Wilson spoke of American soldiers killed in France and American boys whom the League one day would spare from death. Listeners wept openly. That evening, utterly exhausted, Wilson collapsed in a spasm of pain. On October 2, four days after being rushed to the White House, he fell to the bathroom floor, knocked unconscious by a stroke. He recovered slowly but never fully. More and more the battle for the treaty consumed his fading energies.

*Wilson's stroke*

Late in 1919 Lodge finally reported the treaty out of committee with 14 amendments to match Wilson's Fourteen Points. The most important asserted that the United States assumed no obligation under Article X to aid League members unless Congress consented. Wilson refused to accept any change. Whatever ill will Lodge bore Wilson, his objections did not destroy the treaty, but only weakened it by protecting the congressional power to declare war.

Wilson and Lodge refused to compromise. When the amended treaty finally came before the Senate in March 1920, enough Democrats broke from the president to produce a majority—but not the required two-thirds. The Treaty of

Versailles was dead in America. Not until July 1921 did Congress enact a joint resolution ending the war. The United States, which had fought separately from the Allies, made a separate peace as well.

### Red Scare

Peace abroad did not bring peace at home. On May Day 1919, six months after the war ended, mobs in a dozen cities broke up Socialist parades, injured hundreds, and killed three people. Later that month, when a spectator at a Victory Loan rally in Washington refused to stand for the national anthem, a sailor shot him in the back. The stadium crowd applauded.

The spontaneous violence and extremism occurred because Americans believed they were under attack by homegrown and foreign-sponsored radicals. *Radicals and labor unrest* When a rapid end to wartime controls brought skyrocketing prices and when unemployment grew in the wake of millions of returning veterans, a wave of labor unrest swept the country. Even the Boston police went on strike for higher pay. In Seattle a general strike paralyzed the city for five days in January 1919. Mayor Ole Hanson draped his car in an American flag and led troops through the streets in a show of force. Hanson blamed radicals, while Congress ascribed the national ills to Bolshevik agents, inspired by the revolution in Russia.

The menace of radicalism was entirely overblown. With Socialist Eugene Debs in prison, his dwindling party numbered only about 30,000. Radicals at first hoped that the success of the Russian Revolution would help reverse their fortunes in the United States. But most Americans found the prospect of "Bolshevik" agitators threatening, especially after March 1919, when the new Russian government formed the Comintern to spread revolution abroad. Furthermore, the Left itself splintered. In 1919 dissidents deserted the Socialists to form the more radical Communist Labor party. About the same time, a group of mostly Slavic radicals created a separate Communist party. The two organizations together counted no more than 40,000 members.

On April 28 Mayor Hanson received a small brown parcel at his office, evidently another present from an admirer of his tough patriotism. It was a homemade bomb. Within days, 20 such packages were discovered, including ones sent to John D. Rockefeller, Supreme Court justice Oliver Wendell Holmes, and the postmaster general. On June 2 bombs exploded simultaneously in eight different cities. One of them demolished the front porch of A. Mitchell Palmer, attorney general of the United States. The bomb thrower was blown to bits, but enough remained to identify him as an Italian anarchist from Philadelphia. Already edgy over Bolshevism and labor militancy, many Americans assumed that an organized conspiracy was being mounted to overthrow the government.

Palmer, a Quaker and a progressive, hardened in the wake of the bombings. In November 1919 and again in January 1920, he launched raids in over 30 cities across the United States. Government agents invaded private homes, meeting halls, and pool parlors, taking several thousand alleged communists into custody without warrants and beating those who resisted. Prisoners were marched through streets in chains, crammed into dilapidated jails, held without hearings. Over 200 aliens, most of whom had no criminal records, were deported to the Soviet Union.

*Palmer raids*

Such abuses of civil liberties provoked a backlash. After the New York legislature expelled five duly elected Socialists in 1919, responsible politicians—from former presidential candidate Charles Evans Hughes to Ohio senator Warren Harding—denounced the action. The "deportation delirium" ended early in 1920. Palmer finally overreached himself by predicting a revolutionary uprising for May 1, 1920. Buildings were put under guard and state militia called to readiness. Nothing happened. Four months later, when a wagonload of bombs exploded on Wall Street, Palmer blamed a Bolshevik conspiracy. Despite 35 deaths and more than 200 injuries, Americans saw it as the work of a few demented radicals (which it probably was) and went about business as usual.

On September 16, 1920, a wagonload of bombs exploded at the corner of Broad and Wall streets, killing 33 people and injuring more than 200. The nation was horrified but by and large saw no concerted communist plot behind the mysterious blast, as Attorney General A. Mitchell Palmer charged.

In early August 1914, the Panama Canal opened without fanfare. There had been plans for a tremendous celebration. The battleship *Oregon*, whose 1898 "race around the Horn" inspired the idea of an American-owned canal, would lead a flotilla of ships through the locks. But the plans had to be scrapped, for in that fateful month of August, the old world order of spheres of influence, balances of power, military alliances, and imperial colonies collapsed into world war.

When war came, it changed Americans. For the first time, they experienced a planned economy, a federal propaganda machine that united them in common purpose, and for some in uniform, a tour of duty in Europe. Progressivism furnished the bureaucratic tools to organize the fight, but the progressive push for social justice and toleration was quickly overshadowed by a patriotic frenzy. The abortive peace treaty left the nation disillusioned and self-absorbed. Americans turned from idealistic crusades to remake the world to the practical business of getting and spending.

Not for another 20 years would the United States assume a leading role in world affairs. At home the spirit of reform dimmed as a dynamic new era of prosperity dawned. Abroad an uneasy peace reigned in Europe and Asia. Yet in little more than a decade both prosperity and peace would vanish, victims of the failure to establish a new international order.

# chapter summary

The First World War marked the beginning of the end of the old world order of colonial imperialism, military alliances, and balances of power; it also marked a failed effort to establish a new world order based on the progressive ideals of international cooperation and collective security.

- Progressive diplomacy—whether through Theodore Roosevelt's big stick diplomacy, William Taft's dollar diplomacy, or Woodrow Wilson's missionary diplomacy—stressed moralism and order, championed "uplifting" nonwhites, and stretched presidential authority to its limits.

- With the outbreak of the First World War in 1914, Woodrow Wilson saw an opportunity for the United States to lead the world to a higher peace of international cooperation by remaining neutral and brokering the peace settlement.

- However, American sympathy for the Allies, heavy American investments in the Allies, and the German campaign of unrestricted submarine warfare finally drew the country into the war in 1917.

- Progressive faith in government, planning, efficiency, and publicity produced a greatly expanded bureaucratic state that managed the war effort on the home front.
  - The darker side of progressivism also flourished as the war transformed progressive impulses for assimilation and social control into campaigns for superpatriotism and conformity that helped to produce a postwar Red scare in 1919 and 1920.

# chapter summary

The New Era of the 1920s brought a booming economy and modern times to America, vastly accelerating the forces of change—bureaucracy, productivity, technology, advertising and consumerism, mass media, peer culture, and suburbanization. Urban-rural tensions peaked with shifts in population that gave cities new power, but as the decade wore on, weaknesses in the economy and a new ethos of getting and spending proved to be the New Era's undoing.

- Technology, advertising and consumer spending, and such boom industries as automobile manufacturing and construction fueled the largest peacetime economic growth in American history to that date.

- Key features of modern life—mass society, mass culture, and mass consumption—took hold, fed by mass media in the form of radio, movies, and mass-circulation newspapers and magazines.

- Modern life unsettled old ways and eroded social conventions that had limited life, especially for women and children, leading to the emergence of a New Woman and a youth culture.

- Great migrations of African Americans from the rural South to the urban North and of Latinos from Mexico to the United States reshaped the social landscape.

- Traditional culture, centered in rural America, hardened and defended itself against change through immigration restriction, Prohibition, Fundamentalism, and a reborn Ku Klux Klan.

- A galloping bull market in stocks reflected the commitment of government to big business and economic growth.

- When the stock market crashed in 1929, weaknesses in the economy—overexpansion, declining purchasing power, uneven distribution of wealth, weak banking and corporate structures, "sick" industries, and economic ignorance—finally brought the economy down, and with it the New Era came to a close.

# interactive learning

The Primary Source Investigator CD-ROM offers the following materials related to this chapter:

- Interactive maps: **Election of 1928** (M7); **Breakdown of Rural Isolation: Expansion of Travel Horizons in Oregon, IL** (M22); and **Areas of Population Growth, 1920–1930** (M25)

- Short documentary movie on the 1921 race riot in Tulsa (D19)

- A collection of primary sources revealing the rapid changes experienced by Americans in the 1920s: a photo of a Model T Ford and images of new women's fashions in the 1920s. Other documents recount the rise of racism and hate crimes in the United States: the constitution of the Ku Klux Klan, a political cartoon depicting Uncle Sam's resistance to illiterate voters, and a number of sources on the trial and execution of Sacco and Vanzetti.

For quizzes and a variety of interactive resources, visit the book's Online Learning Center at www.mhhe.com/davidsonconcise4.

# significant events

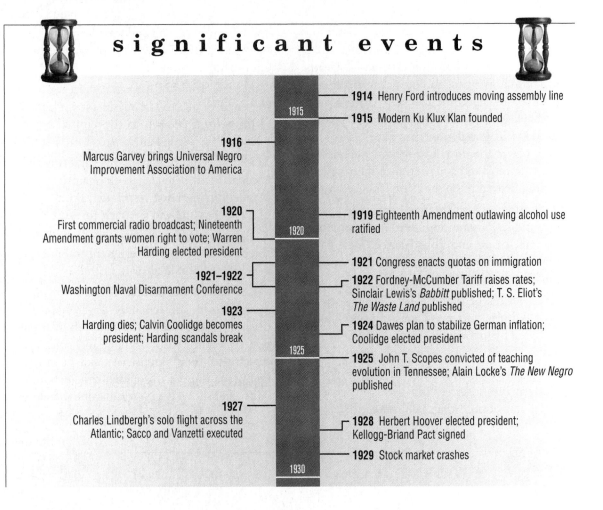

**1914** Henry Ford introduces moving assembly line

**1915** Modern Ku Klux Klan founded

**1916**
Marcus Garvey brings Universal Negro Improvement Association to America

**1919** Eighteenth Amendment outlawing alcohol use ratified

**1920**
First commercial radio broadcast; Nineteenth Amendment grants women right to vote; Warren Harding elected president

**1921** Congress enacts quotas on immigration

**1921–1922**
Washington Naval Disarmament Conference

**1922** Fordney-McCumber Tariff raises rates; Sinclair Lewis's *Babbitt* published; T. S. Eliot's *The Waste Land* published

**1923**
Harding dies; Calvin Coolidge becomes president; Harding scandals break

**1924** Dawes plan to stabilize German inflation; Coolidge elected president

**1925** John T. Scopes convicted of teaching evolution in Tennessee; Alain Locke's *The New Negro* published

**1927**
Charles Lindbergh's solo flight across the Atlantic; Sacco and Vanzetti executed

**1928** Herbert Hoover elected president; Kellogg-Briand Pact signed

**1929** Stock market crashes

# CHAPTER 25

# The Great Depression and the New Deal
## 1929–1939

Winner, South Dakota, November 10, 1933. "Dammit, I don't WANT to write to you again tonight. It's been a long, long day, and I'm tired." All the days had been long since Lorena Hickok began her cross-country trek. Four months earlier Harry Hopkins, the new federal relief administrator, had hired the journalist to report on the relief efforts of the New Deal. Forget about statistics or the "social worker angle," he told her. "Talk with the unemployed, those who are on relief and those who aren't, and when you talk to them," he added, "don't ever forget that but for the grace of God you, I, any of our friends might be in their shoes."

In 1933 and 1934, Hickok found that Roosevelt's relief program was falling short. Its half-billion-dollar subsidy to states, localities, and charities was still leaving out too many Americans, like the sharecropper Hickok discovered near Raleigh, North Carolina. He and his daughters had been living in a tobacco barn for two weeks on little more than weeds and table scraps. "Seems like we just keep goin' lower and lower," said the blue-eyed 16-year-old. To Hickok's surprise, hope still flickered in those determined eyes. Hickok couldn't explain it until she noticed a pin on the girl's chest. It was a campaign button from the 1932 election—"a profile of the President." Hope sprang from the man in the White House.

Before Franklin D. Roosevelt and the New Deal, the White House was far removed from ordinary citizens. The only federal agency with which they had any contact was the post office. And these days it usually delivered bad news. But as Hickok traveled across the country in 1933, she detected a change. People were

**Preview** *The Great Depression, the longest one in the history of the nation, left many Americans shaken. Rates of birth and marriage declined, and many women worked additional hours in and out of the home. Sufferings were most acute among agricultural migrants, African Americans, Latinos, and American Indians. Franklin Roosevelt's New Deal attacked the Depression along three broad fronts: recovery for the economy, relief for the needy, and reforms designed to ward off future depressions.*

In 1935, a news photographer captured this heartfelt exchange between the first lady and six-year-old Geraldine Walker in Detroit. The image fueled Eleanor Roosevelt's growing reputation as a champion of the downtrodden. But in a largely segregated society, the racial overtones of the snapshot shocked some observers. The *Georgia Woman's World* accompanied the photo with the indignant caption, "Believe it or not!" In 1998, in a different racial environment, the U.S. Post Office turned the once-controversial encounter into a commemorative stamp.

talking about government programs. Perhaps it was long-awaited contributions to relief or maybe reforms in securities and banking or the new recovery programs for industry and agriculture. Just as likely it was Franklin Roosevelt. Hickok seldom heard voters call themselves "Republicans" or "Democrats" anymore. Instead, she wrote, they were "for the president."

The message was clear: Franklin Roosevelt and the New Deal had begun to restore national confidence. Though it never brought full recovery, the New Deal did improve economic conditions and provided relief to millions of Americans. It reformed the economic system and committed the federal government to managing its ups and downs. In doing so it extended the progressive drive to soften industrialization and translated decades of growing concern for the disadvantaged into a federal aid program. For the first time, Americans believed Washington would help them through a terrible crisis. The liberal state came of age: active, interventionist, and committed to social welfare.

## THE HUMAN IMPACT OF THE GREAT DEPRESSION

Long breadlines snaked around corners. Vacant-eyed apple-sellers stood shivering in the wind. A man with his hat in his hand came to the back door asking for food in exchange for work. Fewer automobiles rode the streets; more hoboes rode the rails. Between 1929 and 1932 an average of 100,000 people lost their jobs every week until some 13 million Americans were jobless. At least one worker in four could find no work at all.

The Great Depression was a great leveler that reduced differences in the face of common want. The New York seamstress without enough piecework to pay her rent felt the same pinch of frustration and anger as the Berkeley student whose college education was cut short when the bank let her father go. Not everyone was devastated. Most husbands had some job. Most wives continued as home-makers. Most Americans got by as best they could, often cooperating with one another, practicing a ruthless underconsumption to make ends meet. "We lived lean," recalled one Depression victim. So did most of the American people—northern and southern, urban and rural, black, white, brown, yellow, and red.

## Hard Times

Hard times lasted for a decade. Even before the Great Crash many Americans were having trouble making a living. Economists calculated that for the barest necessities a family of four in the golden year of 1929 required $2000—more money than 60 percent of American families earned.

*Subsistence incomes*

As soup kitchens opened and breadlines formed in cities across the nation, survival often became the goal. Millions stayed alive by foraging like animals, and city hospitals began receiving new patients ill from starvation. Pellagra and other diseases associated with malnutrition increased.

Unable to pay mortgages or rent, many families lived off the generosity of forgiving landlords. Some traded down to smaller quarters or simply lost their homes. By 1932 between 1 million and 2 million Americans were homeless wanderers, among them an estimated 25,000 nomadic families. For the first time, emigration out of the United States exceeded immigration into it because Americans could find no work in their own country. Despite official claims that "no one has starved," the New York City Welfare Council reported 29 victims of starvation and 110 dead of malnutrition in 1932.

Marriages and births, symbols of faith in the future, decreased. For the first time in three centuries the curve of population growth began to level, as many young couples postponed having children. Experts worried about an impending "baby crop shortage." Strong families hung together and grew closer; weak ones languished or fell apart. Although divorce declined, desertion—the "poor man's divorce"—mushroomed. Under the strain, rates of mental illness and suicide rose as well.

*Marriage and family*

Many fathers, whose lives had been defined by work, suddenly had nothing to do. They grew listless and depressed. Most mothers stayed home and found their traditional roles as nurturer and household manager less disrupted than the bread-winning roles of their husbands. Between 1929 and 1933 living costs dropped 25 percent, but family incomes tumbled by 40 percent.

*Fathers and mothers*

Shantytowns (called "Hoovervilles" after the president) sprang up around most cities as the Depression deepened.

Homemakers watched household budgets with a closer eye than ever. They canned more food and substituted less expensive fish for meat. When they earned extra money they often did so within the confines of the "woman's sphere" by taking in boarders, laundry, and sewing, opening beauty parlors in their kitchens, and selling baked goods.

For those women who worked outside the home, prejudice still relegated them to so-called women's work. Over half the female labor force continued to work in domestic service or the garment trades, while others found traditional employment as schoolteachers, social workers, and secretaries. Only slowly did the female proportion of the workforce reach pre-Depression levels, until it rose finally to 25 percent by 1940, largely because women were willing to take almost any job.

*Psychological impact*

Whether in the renewed importance of homemaking or the reemergence of home industries, the Great Depression sent ordinary Americans scurrying for the reassuring shelter of past practices and left many of them badly shaken. Shame, self-doubt, and pessimism became epidemic as people blamed themselves for their circumstances and turned their anger inward. "Shame? You tellin' me?" recalled one man. "I would go stand on the relief line [and] bend my head low so nobody would recognize me." The lasting legacy of humiliation and fear—that you had caused your own downfall; that the bottom would drop out again; that life would be leveled once more; that the next depression might not end—was what one writer called an "invisible scar."

### The Golden Age of Radio and Film

By the end of the decade almost 9 out of 10 families owned radios. People depended on radios for nearly everything—news, sports, and weather; music and entertainment; advice on how to bake a cake or find God. Some pro- | *Programming* gramming helped change national habits. When *The Sporting News* conducted a baseball poll in 1932, editors were surprised to discover that a "new crop of fans has been created by radio . . . the women." Many women were at home during the day when most games were played, and broadcasters went out of their way to educate these new listeners. Night games soon outran day games in attendance, in part because husbands began taking wives and daughters, whose interest was sparked by radio.

Radio entered a golden age of commercialism. Advertisers hawked their products on variety programs like *Major Bowes' Amateur Hour* and comedy shows with entertainers such as George Burns and Gracie Allen. Daytime melodramas (called "soap operas" because they were sponsored by soap companies) aimed at women with stories of the personal struggles of ordinary folk.

Radio continued to bind the country together. A teenager in Splendora, Texas, could listen to the same wisecracks from Jack Benny, the same music from Guy Lombardo, as kids in New York and Los Angeles. In 1938 Orson Welles broadcast H. G. Wells's classic science fiction tale *The War of the Worlds*. Americans everywhere listened to breathless reports of an "invasion from Mars," and many believed it. In Newark, New Jersey, cars jammed roads as families rushed to evacuate the city. The nation, bombarded with reports of impending war in Europe and used to responding to radio advertising, was prepared to believe almost anything, even reports of invaders from Mars.

In Hollywood an efficient but autocratic studio system churned out a record number of feature films. Eight motion picture companies produced more than two-thirds of them. Color, first introduced to feature films in *Becky Sharp* (1935), soon complemented sound, which had debuted in the 1927 version of *The Jazz Singer*. Neither alone could keep movie theaters full. As attendance dropped early in the Depression, big studios such as Metro-Goldwyn-Mayer and Universal lured audiences back with films that shocked, titillated, and just plain entertained.

By the mid-1930s more than 60 percent of Americans were going to the movies at least once a week. They saw tamer films as the industry began regulating movie content in the face of growing criticism. In 1933 the Catholic Church created the Legion of Decency to monitor features. To avoid censorship and boycotts, studios stiffened their own regulations. Producers could not depict homosexuality, abortion, drug use, or sex. (Even the word *sex* was banned, as was all profanity.) If couples were shown in bed, they had to be clothed and one foot of each partner had to touch the floor. Middle-class morality reigned on the screen, and most Depression movies, like most of popular culture, preserved traditional values.

### "Dirty Thirties": An Ecological Disaster

Each year between 1932 and 1939 an average of nearly 50 dust storms, or "black blizzards," turned 1500 square miles between the Oklahoma panhandle and western

*Dust Bowl*

Kansas into a gigantic "Dust Bowl," whose baleful effects were felt as far north as the Dakotas and as far south as Texas. It was one of the worst ecological disasters in modern history. Nature played its part, scorching the earth and whipping the winds. But the "dirty thirties" were mostly human-made. The semiarid lands west of the 98th meridian were not suitable for agriculture or livestock. Sixty years of intensive farming and grazing had stripped the prairie of its natural vegetation and rendered it defenseless against the elements. When the dry winds came, one-third of the Great Plains just blew away.

The dust storms lasted anywhere from hours to days. Walking into one was like walking into "a wall of dirt." "This is the ultimate darkness," despaired a Kansan in the midst of one storm. "So must come the end of the world." Winds carried the dust aloft so high that yellow grit from Nebraska collected on the windowsills of the White House, and ships 300 miles off the East Coast found bits of Montana and Wyoming on their decks. Even the fish died—from lack of oxygen in dust-coated rivers.

Some 3.5 million plains people abandoned their farms. Landowners or corporations forced off about half of them as large-scale commercial farming

*Impact of commercial farming*

slowly spread into the heartland of America. Commercial farms were more common in California, where 10 percent of the farms grew more than 50 percent of the crops. As in industrial America, the strategy in agricultural America was to consolidate and mechanize. As farms grew in size, so did the number of tenants. In most Dust Bowl counties people owned less than half the land they farmed. American agriculture was turning from a way of life into an industry. And as the economy contracted, owners cut costs by cutting workers.

Relief offices around the country reported a change in migrant families. Rather than black or brown, more and more were white and native-born, typically a young married couple with one child. Most did not travel far, perhaps to the next county. Long-distance migrants from Oklahoma, Arizona, and Texas usually set their sights on California. Handbills and advertisements promised jobs picking fruit and harvesting vegetables. If they were like the Joad family in John Steinbeck's classic novel *The Grapes of Wrath* (1939), they drove west along Route 66 through Arizona and New Mexico, their belongings piled high atop rickety jalopies, heading for the West Coast.

More than 350,000 Oklahomans migrated to California—so many that "Okie" came to mean any Dust Bowler, even though most of Oklahoma lay outside the Dust Bowl. Only one in two or three migrants actually found work. The labor

"Black blizzards" dwarfed all human-made structures. The drought that helped bring them about lasted from 1932 to 1936. In a single day in 1934 dust storms dumped 12 million tons of western dirt on Chicago.

surplus allowed growers to set their own terms. A migrant family earned about $450 a year, less than a third the subsistence level. Families that did not work formed wretched enclaves called "little Oklahomas." The worst were located in the fertile Imperial Valley. There, at the end of the decade, relief officials discovered a family of 10 living in a 1921 Ford. When told to go, the mother responded vacantly, "I wonder where?"

### Mexican Americans and Repatriation

The Chavez family lost their farm in the North Gila River valley of Arizona in 1934. They had owned a small homestead near Yuma for two generations, but the Depression pushed them out. Cesar, barely six years old at the time, remembered only images of the departure: a "giant tractor" level- *Cesar Chavez* ing the corral; the loss of his room and bed; a beat-up Chevy hauling the family west; his father promising to buy another farm someday.

The elder Chavez could never keep his promise. Instead, he and his family lived on the road, "following the crops" in California. In eight years Cesar went to 37 schools. The family was forced to sell their labor to unscrupulous *engan-chistas*, or contractors, for less than $10 a week. The father joined strikers in the Imperial Valley in the mid-1930s, but they were crushed. "Some people put this out of their minds and forget it," said Cesar Chavez years later. "I don't." Thirty years later he founded the United Farm Workers of America, the first union of migratory workers in the country.

A deep ambivalence had always characterized American attitudes toward Mexicans, but the Great Depression turned most Anglo communities against them. Cities such as Los Angeles, fearing the burden of relief, found it cheaper to ship Mexicans home. Some migrants left voluntarily. Others were driven out *Repatriation* by frustrated officials or angry neighbors. Beginning in 1931 the federal government launched a series of deportations, or "repatriations," of Mexicans back to Mexico. These deportations often included the Mexicans' American-born children, who by law were citizens of the United States. During the decade the Latino population of the Southwest dropped by 500,000. In Chicago, the Mexican community shrank by almost half. Staying in the United States often turned out to be as difficult as leaving. The average income of Mexican American families in the Rio Grande valley of Texas was $506 a year. The sum represented the combined income of parents and children. Following the harvest made schooling particularly difficult: fewer than two Mexican American children in ten completed five years of school.

For Americans of Mexican descent, the Great Depression only deepened anxiety over identity. Were they Mexicans, as many Anglos regarded them, or were they Americans, as they regarded themselves? In the 1920s, such questions had produced several organizations founded to assert the American identity of native-born and naturalized Mexican Americans and to pursue their civil *LULAC and ethnic identity* rights. In 1929, on the eve of the Depression, many of these organizations were consolidated into the League of United Latin American Citizens (LULAC). By the early 1940s, "Flying Squadrons" of LULAC organizers had founded some 80 chapters nationwide, making it the largest Mexican American civil rights association in the country.

LULAC permitted only those Latinos who were American citizens to join, thus excluding hundreds of thousands of ethnic Mexicans who nonetheless regarded the United States as their home. It pointedly conducted meetings in English, relied heavily on the assimilated middle class for leadership, and stressed desegregation of public schools, voter registration, and an end to discrimination in public facilities and on juries.

Perhaps LULAC's clearest statement of intent in the 1930s came in its support for immigration restriction from Mexico as a means of both establishing the "Americanness" of its members and creating more jobs for Mexican Americans already here. Still, LULAC counted small farmers, ranchers, and wage laborers among its rank and file, many of whom identified strongly with Mexico. And despite LULAC's efforts to distance itself from Mexican immigrants, women members raised funds for milk, eyeglasses, Christmas toys, and clothes for the new arrivals.

## African Americans in the Depression

Hard times were nothing new to African Americans. "The Negro was born in depression," opined one black man. "It only became official when it hit the white man." Still, when the Depression struck, black unemployment surged. By 1932 it reached 50 percent, twice the national level. By 1933 several cities reported between 25 and 40 percent of their black residents with no support except relief payments. Even skilled black workers who retained their jobs saw their wages cut in half, according to one study of Harlem in 1935.

Migration out of the rural South, up 800,000 during the 1920s, dropped by 50 percent in the 1930s. As late as 1940 three of four African Americans still lived in rural areas; yet conditions there were just as bad as in cities. In 1934 one study estimated the average income for black cotton farmers at under $200 a year. Millions of African Americans made do by stretching meager incomes, as they had for years.

Like many African Americans, George Baker refused to be victimized by the Depression. Baker had moved from Georgia to Harlem in 1915. He changed his name to M. J. Divine and founded a religious cult that promised followers an afterlife of full equality. In the 1930s Father Divine preached economic cooperation and opened shelters, or "heavens," for regenerate "angels," black and white. In Detroit, Elijah Poole changed his name to Elijah Muhammad and in 1931 established the Black Muslims, a blend of Islamic faith and black nationalism. He exhorted African Americans to celebrate their African heritage, to live a life of self-discipline and self-help, and to strive for a separate all-black nation.

*Father Divine and Elijah Muhammad*

The Depression inflamed racial prejudice. Lynchings tripled between 1932 and 1933. In 1932 the Supreme Court ordered a retrial in the most celebrated racial case of the decade. A year earlier nine black teenagers had been accused of raping two white women on a train bound for Scottsboro, Alabama. Within weeks all-white juries had sentenced eight of them to death. The convictions rested on the testimony of the women, one of whom later admitted that the boys had been framed. Appeals kept the case alive for almost a decade. In the end charges against four of the "Scottsboro boys" were dropped. The other five received substantial prison sentences.

*Scottsboro boys*

## THE TRAGEDY OF HERBERT HOOVER

The presidency of Herbert Hoover began with great promise but soon became the worst ordeal of his life. "I have no fears for the future of our country," he had announced at his inauguration in March 1929. "It is bright with hope." Within seven months a "depression" had struck. (Hoover himself coined the term to minimize the crisis.) Try as he might, he could not beat it and the nation turned against him. "People were starving because of Herbert Hoover," sputtered an angry mother in 1932. "Men were killing themselves because of Herbert Hoover, and their fatherless children were being packed away to orphanages . . . because of Herbert Hoover." The charge was unfair, but it stuck. For all of Hoover's promise and innovative intelligence, his was to be a transitional presidency, important as a break from the do-nothing policies of past depression presidents and as a herald of the new, more active presidents to come.

## The Failure of Relief

By the winter of 1931–1932 the story was the same everywhere: relief organizations with too little money and too few resources to make much headway against

*Private charity*

the Depression. Once-mighty private charity had dwindled to 6 percent of all relief funds. Ethnic charities tried to stave off disaster for their own. Over the years Mexican Americans and Puerto Ricans had turned to *mutualistas,* traditional societies that provided members with social support, life insurance, and sickness benefits. In San Francisco, the Chinese Six Companies offered food and clothing to needy Chinese Americans. But as the head of the Federation of Jewish Charities warned, private efforts were failing. The government would be "compelled, by the cruel events ahead of us, to step into the situation and bring relief on a large scale."

An estimated 30 million needy people nationwide quickly depleted city treasuries, already pressed because nearly 30 percent of city taxpayers had fallen behind

*City services*

in paying the taxes they owed. In Philadelphia relief payments to a family of four totaled $5.50 a week, the highest in the country. Some cities gave nothing to unmarried people or childless couples, no matter how impoverished they were. By the end of 1931, Detroit, Boston, and scores of other cities were bankrupt.

Cities clamored for help from state capitals, but after a decade of extravagant spending and sloppy bookkeeping, many states were already running in the red.

*TERA*

As businesses and property values collapsed, tax bases shrank and with them state revenues. Michigan, one of the few states to provide any relief, reduced funds by more than half between 1931 and 1932. Until New York established its Temporary Emergency Relief Administration (TERA) in 1931, no state had any agency at all to handle the problem of unemployment.

## The Hoover Depression Program

From the fall of 1930 onward, President Herbert Hoover took responsibility for ending the crisis as humanely as possible. It was a mark of his character. Orphaned at nine, he became one of Stanford University's first graduates and, before the age of 40, the millionaire head of one of the most successful mine engineering firms in the world. As a good Quaker, he balanced private gain with public service, saving starving Belgian refugees in 1915 after war broke out in Europe. He worked 14 hours a day, paid his own salary, and convinced private organizations and businesses to donate food, clothing, and other necessities. In his honor, Finns coined a new word: to "hoover" meant to help.

As secretary of commerce under Harding and Coolidge, Hoover perfected his associational philosophy (see page 705). It rested on the notion that government should foster private solutions to public problems by promoting voluntary cooperation among businesses and between businesses and government. Even so, when the Depression struck, he was no do-nothing president. Past presidents had feared that any intervention at all by government would upset the natural workings of the economy and that their sole responsibility was to keep the budget balanced. But Hoover understood the vicious cycle in which rising unemployment drove down consumer demand, and he appreciated the need for stimulating investment. Thus he set in motion an unprecedented program of government activism.

Herbert Hoover

Despite the president's best efforts, his program failed. As a good associationalist, Hoover rallied business leaders, who pledged to maintain employment, wages, and prices—only to see those leaders back down as the economy sputtered. He pushed a tax cut through Congress in 1930 in order to increase the purchasing power of consumers. But when the cuts produced an unbalanced federal budget, Hoover reversed course. At bottom he firmly believed that capitalism would generate its own recovery and that a balanced federal budget was required in order to restore the confidence of business. Too much government action, he worried, might destory the very economic system he was seeking to save. So he agreed to tax increases in 1932, further undermining investment and consumption.

Equally disastrous, the president endorsed the Smoot-Hawley Tariff (1930) to protect the United States from cheap foreign goods. That bill brought a wave of retaliation from countries abroad, which choked world trade and reduced American sales overseas. Even the $1 billion that Hoover spent on public works—more than the total spent by all his predecessors combined—did not approach the $10 billion needed to employ only half the jobless. Spending such huge sums seemed unthinkable, for the entire federal budget at the time was only $3.2 billion.

Under pressure from Congress, Hoover took his boldest action to save the banks. Between 1930 and 1932 some 5100 failed as panicky depositors withdrew their funds. Hoover agreed to permit the creation of the Reconstruc- *Reconstruction* tion Finance Corporation (RFC) in 1932, an agency that could lend *Finance Corporation* money to banks and their chief corporate debtors—insurance companies and railroads. Modeled on a similar agency created during World War I, the RFC had a capital stock of $500 million and the power to borrow four times that amount. Within three months bank failures dropped from 70 a week to 1 every two weeks. The Glass-Steagall Banking Act (1932) made it easier for banks to loan money by adding $2 billion of new currency to the money supply, backed by Federal Reserve government bonds.

Yet in spite of this success, Hoover drew criticism for rescuing banks and not people. From the start he rejected the idea of federal relief for the unemployed. It was not that the president was insensitive—far from it. He never visited a bread-line or a relief shelter because he could not bear the sight of human suffering. He feared that a "dole," or giveaway program, would damage the initiative of recipients, perhaps even produce a permanent underclass. The bureaucracy that would be needed to police recipients would inevitably meddle in the private lives of citizens and bring a "train of corruption and waste." Hoover assumed that neighborliness and cooperation would be enough.

As unemployment continued to worsen, Hoover slowly softened his stand on federal relief. In 1932 he allowed Congress to pass the Emergency Relief and *Unemployment relief* Construction Act. It authorized the RFC to lend up to $1.5 billion for "reproductive" public works that paid for themselves—like toll bridges and slum clearance. Another $300 million went to states as loans for the direct relief of the unemployed. Yet in this Depression, $300 million was a pittance. When the governor of Pennsylvania requested loans to furnish the destitute with 13 cents a day for a year, the RFC sent only enough for 3 cents a day.

## Stirrings of Discontent

Unprecedented though they were, Hoover's efforts were too little, too late. "The word revolution is heard at every hand," one writer warned in 1932. Some won-dered if capitalism itself had gone bankrupt.

Here and there the desperate took matters into their own hands in 1932. In Wisconsin the Farm Holiday Association dumped thousands of gallons of milk *Farm Holiday* on highways in a vain attempt to raise prices. Ten thousand striking *Association* miners formed a 48-mile motorcar "Coal Caravan" that worked its way in protest across southern Illinois. In March a demonstration turned ugly when communist sympathizers led a hunger march on Henry Ford's Rouge Assembly Plant in Dearborn, Michigan. As 3000 protesters surged toward the gates, Ford police drenched them with hoses, then opened fire at point-blank range. Four marchers were killed and more than 20 wounded.

For all the stirrings of discontent, revolution was never a danger. In 1932 the Communist party of the United States had 20,000 members—up from 6500 only *Communist party* three years earlier but hardly large enough to constitute a political force. Deeply suspicious of Marxist doctrine, most Americans were unsympathetic to their cries for collectivism and an end to capitalism. Fewer than 1000 African Americans joined the party in the early 1930s. At first hostile to established politics, the Communists adopted a more cooperative strategy to con-tain Adolf Hitler when his Nazi party won control of Germany in 1933. The Soviet Union ordered Communist parties in Europe and the United States to join with liberal politicians in a "popular front" against Nazism. Thereafter party membership peaked in the mid-1930s at about 80,000.

## The Bonus Army

Hoover sympathized with the discontented but only to a point. In the summer of 1932, the "Bonus Army" learned the limits of his compassion. The army, a rag-tag collection of World War I veterans, was hungry and looking to cash in the bonus certificates they had received from Congress in 1924 as a reward for wartime service. By the time they reached Washington, D.C., in June 1932, their numbers had swelled to nearly 20,000, the largest protest in the city's history. Hoover dismissed them as a special-interest lobby and refused to see their leaders, but the House voted to pay them immediately. When the Senate blocked the bonus bill, most veterans left.

About 2000 stayed to dramatize their plight, camping with their families and parading peaceably. Despite the efforts of the Washington police to evict them, the protesters refused to leave. By the end of July, the president had had enough. He called in the U.S. Army under the command of Chief of Staff General Douglas MacArthur. MacArthur arrived with four troops of saber-brandishing cavalry, six tanks, and a column of infantry with bayonets ready for action. By the time the smoke cleared the next morning, the Bonus marchers had vanished except for 300 wounded veterans.

Though he had intended that the army only assist the police, Hoover accepted responsibility for the action. And the sight of unarmed and unemployed veterans under attack by American troops soured most Americans. In Albany, New York, Governor Franklin D. Roosevelt exploded at the president's failure: "There is nothing inside the man but jelly." Like the hero of a classical tragedy, Herbert Hoover, symbol of the New Era and the greatest humanitarian of his generation, came tumbling down.

## The Election of 1932

At their convention in Chicago, Republicans still stuck with Hoover and endorsed his Depression program to the last detail. Democrats countered with Franklin D. Roosevelt, the charismatic New York governor. As a sign of things to come, Roosevelt broke all precedent by flying to Chicago and addressing the delegates in person. "I pledge you, I pledge myself to a new deal for the American people," he told them.

Without a national following, Roosevelt zigged and zagged in an effort to appeal to the broadest possible bloc of voters. One minute he attacked Hoover as a "profligate spender" and vowed to balance the budget; the next he called for costly public works and aid to the unemployed. He promised to help business, then spoke vaguely of remembering the "forgotten man" and "distributing wealth and products more equitably." For his part, Hoover denounced Roosevelt's New Deal as a "dangerous departure" from time-honored traditions, one that would destroy American values and institutions and "build a bureaucracy such as we have never seen in our history." None of it mattered. The deepening Depression ensured that virtually any Democrat would defeat Hoover.

On Election Day, Roosevelt captured a thundering 58 percent of the popular vote and carried with him large Democratic majorities in the Congress. Just as telling as the margin of victory were its sources. Industrial workers in the North, poor farmers in the South and West, immigrants and big-city dwellers everywhere were being galvanized into a broad new coalition. These people had experienced firsthand the savage effects of the boom-and-bust business cycle and wanted change. But they were not radicals and found no appeal in the presidential campaigns of Socialist Norman Thomas or Communist William Z. Foster, both of whom had called for worker ownership of businesses. The Socialists polled less than a million votes, the Communists barely over 100,000. Instead, Depression-era voters turned to Roosevelt and the Democrats, who recognized that in a modern industrial state it was not enough to rally round business and hope that capitalism would right itself. Over 30 years of nearly unbroken Republican rule had come to an end.

## THE EARLY NEW DEAL (1933–1935)

On March 4, 1933, as the clocks struck noon, Eleanor Roosevelt wondered if it were possible to "do anything to save America now." She looked at her husband, who had just been sworn in as thirty-second president of the United States. Franklin faced the crowd of over 100,000. Heeding the nation's call for "action, and action now," he promised to exercise "broad Executive power to wage a war against the emergency." The crowd cheered. Eleanor was terrified: "One has the feeling of going it blindly because we're in a tremendous stream, and none of us know where we're going to land."

The early New Deal unfolded in the spring of 1933 with a chaotic 100-day burst of legislation. It stressed recovery through planning and cooperation with business but also tried to aid the unemployed and reform the economic system. Above all, the early New Deal broke the cycle of despair. With Roosevelt in the White House, most Americans believed that they were in good hands, wherever they landed.

### The Democratic Roosevelts

From the moment they entered it in 1933, Franklin and Eleanor—the Democratic Roosevelts—transformed the White House. No more footmen and no more buglers as Hoover had employed; above all, no more seven-course meals as Hoover had served. Instead, visitors got fare fit for a boardinghouse. Roosevelt's lunches of hash and a poached egg cost 19 cents. The gesture was symbolic, but it made the president's point of ending business as usual.

Such belt-tightening was new to Franklin Roosevelt. Born of an old Dutch family in New York, he grew up rich and pampered. He idolized his Republican cousin Theodore Roosevelt and mimicked his career, except as a Democrat. Like Theodore, Franklin graduated from Harvard University (in 1904), won a seat in the New York State legislature (in 1910), secured an appointment as assistant secretary of the navy (in 1913), and ran for the vice presidency (in 1920). Then disaster struck. On vacation in the summer of 1921, Roosevelt fell ill with poliomyelitis. The disease paralyzed him from the waist down. For the rest of his life, he walked only with the aid of crutches and heavy steel braces.

*Franklin Roosevelt*

Roosevelt emerged from the ordeal to win the governorship of New York in 1928. When the Depression struck, he created the first state relief agency in 1931, the Temporary Emergency Relief Administration. Aid to the jobless "must be extended by Government, not as a matter of charity, but as a matter of social duty," he explained. He considered himself a progressive but moved well beyond the cautious federal activism of most progressives. He adopted no single ideology. He cared little about economic principles. What he wanted were results. Experimentation became a hallmark of the New Deal.

Eleanor Roosevelt redefined what it meant to be first lady. Never had a president's wife been so visible, so much of a crusader, so cool under fire. She was the first first lady to hold weekly press conferences. Her column, "My Day," appeared in 135 newspapers, and her twice-weekly broadcasts made her a radio personality rivaling her husband. She became his eyes, ears, and legs, traveling 40,000 miles a year. Secret Service men code-named her "Rover."

*Eleanor Roosevelt*

Eleanor believed she was only a spur to presidential action. But she was active in her own right, as a teacher and social reformer before Franklin became president and afterward as a tireless advocate of the underdog. In the White House, she pressed him to hire more women and minorities but also supported antilynching and anti–poll tax measures, when he would not, and experimental towns for the homeless. By 1939 more Americans approved of her than of her husband.

## Saving the Banks

Before the election Roosevelt had gathered a group of economic advisers called the "Brains Trust." Out of their recommendations came the early, or "first," New Deal of government planning, intervention, and experimentation. Brains Trusters disagreed over the means of achieving their goals, but those goals they broadly shared: economic recovery, relief for the unemployed, and sweeping reform to ward off future depressions. All concurred that the first step was to save the banks. By the eve of the inauguration governors in 38 states had temporarily closed their banks to stem the withdrawal of deposits. Without a sound credit structure, there could be no recovery.

*The Brains Trust*

## "My Day":
## The First Lady Tours Tennessee

Johnson City, Tenn., May 31 [1939]—I looked out of the window of the train this morning while I was waiting for my breakfast, and it suddenly occurred to me that scenes from a train window might give a rather good picture of the variety in the conditions and occupations of our people in different parts of the country. I saw a little girl, slim and bent over, carrying two heavy pails of water across a field to an unpainted house. How far that water had to be carried, I do not know, but it is one thing to carry water on a camping trip for fun during a summer's holiday, and it is another thing to carry it day in and day out as part of the routine of living. On the outskirts of the town, I saw a wash line. On it hung two brown work shirts, a pair of rather frayed and faded blue dungarees, two child's sun suits and a woman's calico dress. Not much sign of wasteful living here.

Through its open door, I had a glimpse of the inside of a cabin in the hollow below us. It was divided into two rooms, one of them the bedroom with two beds in it. These two beds took up about all the available space in the room and it must have been necessary to leave the door open for air. There was a pad which looked rather like the cotton mattresses that have been made on WPA [Works Progress Administration], and a quilt neatly over each bed. I didn't notice any sheets or pillows.

There has been rain down here and the fields look in good condition. We passed a man plowing in a field with two women not far away hoeing. Beyond, in a grove of trees, there stood a stately house and under the trees was a baby carriage. I caught sight of someone in a flowered dress sitting on the porch. Then I again saw a yard of an unpainted house in the outskirts of a small town and a happy looking woman rocking a baby on the porch while a group of youngsters played in the yard. Happiness may exist under all conditions, given the right kind of people and sufficient economic security for adequate food and shelter.

Source: Excerpt from Rochelle Chadakoff, ed., *Eleanor Roosevelt's My Day: Her Acclaimed Columns, 1936–1945* (New York: Pharos Books), pp. 119–120. Copyright © 1989, UFS. Reprinted with permission.

On March 5, the day after his inauguration, Roosevelt ordered every bank in the country closed for four days. He shrewdly called it a "bank holiday." On March 9, the president introduced emergency banking legislation. The House passed the measure, sight unseen, and the Senate endorsed it later in the day. Roosevelt signed it that night.

Rather than nationalizing the banks as radicals wanted, the Emergency Banking Act followed the modest course of extending federal assistance to them.

*Emergency Banking Act*

Sound banks would reopen immediately with government support. Troubled banks would be handed over to federal "conservators," who would guide them to solvency. On Sunday, March 12, Roosevelt explained what was happening in the first of his many informal "fireside chat" radio broadcasts. When banks reopened the next day, deposits exceeded withdrawals.

To guard against another stock crash, financial reforms gave government greater authority to manage the currency and regulate stock transactions. In April 1933, Roosevelt dropped the gold standard and began experimenting with the value of the dollar to boost prices. Later that spring the Glass-Steagall Banking Act restricted speculation by banks and, more important, created fed- *Federal Deposit* eral insurance for bank deposits of up to $2500. Under the Federal *Insurance* Deposit Insurance Corporation, fewer banks failed for the rest of the decade than in the best year of the 1920s. The Securities Exchange Act (1934) established a new federal agency, the Securities and Exchange Commission, to oversee the stock market.

## Relief for the Unemployed

Saving the banks and financial markets meant little if human suffering could not be relieved. Mortgage relief for the millions who had lost their homes came eventually in 1934 in the Home Owners' Loan Act. But the need to alleviate starvation led Roosevelt to propose a bold new giveaway program. The Federal Emergency Relief Administration (FERA) opened its door in May 1933. Sitting amid unpacked boxes, gulping coffee and chain-smoking, former social worker Harry Hopkins spent $5 million of a $500 million appropriation in his first two hours as head of the new agency. In its two-year existence, FERA furnished more than $1 billion in grants to states, local areas, and private charities.

Hopkins persuaded Roosevelt to expand relief with an innovative shift from government giveaways to a work program to see workers through the winter of 1933–1934. Paying someone "to do something socially useful," *Work relief* Hopkins explained, "preserves a man's morale." The Civil Works Administration (CWA) employed 4 million Americans. Alarmed at the high cost of the program, Roosevelt disbanded the CWA in the spring of 1934. It nonetheless furnished a new weapon against unemployment and an important precedent for future relief programs.

Another work relief program established in 1933 proved even more creative. The Civilian Conservation Corps (CCC) was Roosevelt's pet project. It combined his concern for conservation with compassion for youth. The CCC took unmarried 18- to 25-year-olds from relief rolls and sent them into the woods and fields to plant trees, build parks, and fight soil erosion. During its 10 years, the CCC provided 2.5 million young men with jobs (which prompted some critics to chant, "Where's the she, she, she?").

New Dealers intended relief programs to last only through the crisis. But the Tennessee Valley Authority (TVA)—a massive public works project created

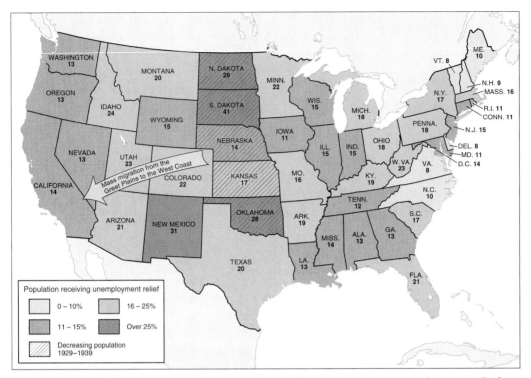

UNEMPLOYMENT RELIEF, 1934   The percentage of those receiving unemployment relief differed markedly throughout the nation. The farm belt of the plains was especially hard-hit, with 41 percent of South Dakota's citizens receiving federal benefits. In the East, the percentage dropped as low as 8 percent in some states.

in 1933—helped to relieve unemployment but also made a continuing contribution to regional planning. For a decade, planners had dreamed of transform-

*Tennessee Valley Authority*

ing the flood-ridden basin of the Tennessee River, one of the poorest areas of the country, with a program of regional development and social engineering. The TVA constructed a series of dams along the seven-state basin to control flooding, improve navigation, and generate cheap electric power. In cooperation with state and local officials, it also launched social programs to stamp out malaria, provide library bookmobiles, and create recreational lakes.

Like many New Deal programs, the TVA produced a mixed legacy. It saved 3 million acres from erosion, multiplied the average income in the valley tenfold, and repaid its original investment in federal taxes. Its cheap electricity helped to bring down the rates of private utility companies. But the experiment in regional planning also pushed thousands of families from their land, failed to end poverty, and created an agency that became one of the worst polluters in the country.

## Planning for Industrial Recovery

Planning, not just for regions but for the whole economy, seemed to many New Dealers the key to recovery. Some held that if businesses were allowed to plan and cooperate with one another, the ruthless competition that was driving down prices, wages, and employment could be controlled and the riddle of recovery solved. Business leaders had been urging such a course since 1931. In June 1933, under the National Industrial Recovery Act (NIRA), Roosevelt put planning to work for industry.

The legislation created two new agencies. The Public Works Administration (PWA) was designed to boost industrial activity and consumer spending with a $3.3 billion public works program. The companies put under contract and unemployed workers hired would help stimulate the economy through their purchases and leave a legacy of capital improvement. Harold Ickes, the prickly interior secretary who headed PWA, built the Triborough Bridge and Lincoln Tunnel in New York, the port city of Brownsville, Texas, and two aircraft carriers. But he was so fearful of waste and corruption that he never spent funds quickly enough to jumpstart the economy.

*Public Works Administration*

A second federal agency, the National Recovery Administration (NRA), aimed directly at controlling competition. Under NRA chief Hugh Johnson, representatives from government and business (and also from labor and consumer groups) drew up "codes of fair practices." Industry by industry, the codes established minimum prices, minimum wages, and maximum hours. No company could seek a competitive edge by cutting prices or wages below certain levels or by working a few employees mercilessly and firing the rest. It also required business to accept key demands of labor, including union rights to organize and bargain with management (thus ensuring that if prices jumped, so too might wages). And each code promised improved working conditions and outlawed such practices as child labor and sweatshops.

*National Recovery Administration*

No business was forced to comply, for New Dealers feared that such government coercion might be ruled unconstitutional. The NRA relied on voluntary participation. A publicity campaign of parades, posters, and public pledges exhorted businesses to join the NRA and consumers to buy only NRA-sanctioned products. More than two million employers eventually signed up. In store windows and on merchandise, shiny decals with blue-eagle crests alerted customers that "We Do Our Part."

## The NRA in Trouble

For all the hoopla, the NRA failed to bring recovery. Big businesses shaped the codes to their advantage. Often they limited production and raised prices, sometimes beyond what they normally had been. Not all businesses joined, and those that did often found the codes too complicated or costly to follow. The NRA tried to cover too many businesses, and its relatively few inspectors had trouble keeping up with all the complaints. Even NRA support for labor tottered, for it had no means of enforcing its guarantee of union rights. Business survived under the NRA, but without increasing production there was no incentive for expansion and new investment. Under such conditions hard times could last indefinitely. And in the short run, despite an enthusiastic start, the NRA was soon spawning little but evasion and criticism.

On May 27, 1935, the Supreme Court struck down the floundering NRA in *Schecter Poultry Corp. v. United States.* The justices unanimously ruled that the NRA had exceeded federal power over commerce among the states by regulating the Schecter brothers' poultry business in New York. Privately Roosevelt was relieved to be rid of the NRA. But he and other New Dealers were plainly shaken by the grounds of the decision. They were relying on a broad view of the commerce clause to fight the Depression. Their distress only grew when Justice Benjamin Cardozo added a chilling afterthought: the NRA's code making represented "an unconstitutional delegation of legislative power" to the executive branch. Without the ability to make rules and regulations, all the executive agencies of the New Deal might flounder.

## Planning for Agriculture

Like planning for industry, New Deal planning for agriculture relied on private interests—the farmers—to act as the principal planners. Under the Agricultural Adjustment Act of 1933, farmers limited their own production. The government, in turn, paid them for not producing, while a tax on millers, cotton ginners, and other processors financed the payments. In theory, production quotas would reduce surpluses, demand for farm commodities would rise (as would prices), and agriculture would recover.

In practice, the Agricultural Adjustment Administration (AAA) did help to increase prices. Unlike the code-ridden NRA, the AAA wisely confined coverage
*Agricultural Adjustment Administration* | to seven basic commodities. As a way to push prices even higher, the new Commodity Credit Corporation gave loans to farmers who stored their crops rather than sold them—a revival of the Populists' old subtreasury plan (see page 589). Farm income rose from $5.5 billion in 1932 to $8.7 billion in 1935.

Not all the gains in farm income were the result of government actions or free from problems. In the mid-1930s dust storms, droughts, and floods helped reduce harvests and push up prices. The AAA, moreover, failed to distribute its benefits equally. Large landowners controlled decisions over which plots would be left fallow. In the South these decisions frequently meant cutting the acreage of tenants and sharecroppers or forcing them out. Even when they reduced the acreage that they themselves plowed, big farmers could increase yields, since they had the money and equipment to cultivate more intensively.

In 1936 the Supreme Court voided the Agricultural Adjustment Act. In *Butler v. U.S.*, the six-justice majority concluded that the government had no right to regulate agriculture, either by limiting production or by taxing processors. A hastily drawn replacement, the Soil Conservation and Domestic Allotment Act (1936), addressed the complaints. Farmers were now subsidized for practicing "conservation"—taking soil-depleting crops off the land—and paid from general revenues instead of a special tax. A second Agricultural Adjustment Act in 1938 returned production quotas.

Other agencies tried to help impoverished farmers. The Farm Credit Administration refinanced about a fifth of all farm mortgages. In 1935 the Resettlement Administration gave marginal farmers a fresh start by moving them to better land. Beginning in 1937 the Farm Security Administration furnished low-interest loans to help tenants buy family farms. In neither case did the rural poor have enough political clout to obtain sufficient funds from Congress. Fewer than 5000 families of a projected 500,000 were resettled, and less than 2 percent of tenant farmers received loans.

In agriculture, as elsewhere, the net effect of such policies was mixed. New Deal programs helped to stabilize the farm economy and also provided an important precedent for future aid to farmers. At the same time, the favoritism shown large farmers squeezed out many small farmers and promoted large-scale agribusiness or corporate-run farming.

## A SECOND NEW DEAL (1935–1936)

"Boys—this is our hour," crowed the president's closest adviser, Harry Hopkins, in the spring of 1935. A year earlier voters had broken precedent by returning the party in power to Congress, giving the Democrats their largest majorities in decades. With the presidential election of 1936 only a year away, Hopkins figured that time was short: "We've got to get everything we want—a works program, social security, wages and hours, everything—now or never."

Hopkins calculated correctly. In 1935 politics, swept along by a torrent of protest, led to a "second hundred days" of lawmaking and a "Second New Deal." The emphasis shifted from planning and cooperation with business to greater regulation of business, broader relief, and bolder reform. A limited welfare state emerged in which the government was finally committed, at least symbolically, to guaranteeing the well-being of needy Americans.

### Voices of Protest

In 1934 a mob of 6000 stormed the Minneapolis city hall, demanding more relief and higher pay for government jobs. In San Francisco longshoremen walked off the job, setting off a citywide strike. By year's end, 1.5 million workers had joined

Louisiana governor and senator Huey Long promised to "make every man a king," but critics predicted that only Long would wear a crown. The "Kingfish" (a nickname taken from the *Amos 'n' Andy* radio show) made no secret of his presidential ambitions.

in 1800 strikes. Conditions were improving but not quickly enough, and across the country voices of protest gathered strength.

From the right came the charges of a few wealthy business executives and conservatives that Roosevelt was an enemy of private property and a dictator in the making. In August 1934 they founded the American Liberty League. Despite spending $1 million in anti–New Deal advertising, the league won little

*Liberty League* | support and only helped to convince the president that cooperation with business was failing.

In California discontented voters took over the Democratic party and turned sharply to the left by nominating novelist Upton Sinclair, a Socialist, for governor.

*End Poverty in California* | Running under the slogan "End Poverty in California" (EPIC), Sinclair proposed to confiscate idle factories and land and permit the unemployed to produce for their own use. Republicans mounted a no-holds-barred counterattack, including fake newsreels depicting Sinclair as a Bolshevik, atheist, and free-lover. Sinclair lost the election but won nearly 1 million votes.

Huey P. Long, the flamboyant senator from Louisiana, had ridden to power on a wave of rural discontent against banks, corporations, and political machines.

*Huey Long* | As governor of Louisiana, he pushed through reforms regulating utilities, building roads and schools, even distributing free schoolbooks. Opponents called him a "dictator"; most Louisianans simply called him the "Kingfish." Breaking with Roosevelt in 1933, Long pledged to bring about recovery by making "every man a king." "Share Our Wealth" was a drastic but simple plan: the government would limit the size of all fortunes and confiscate the rest. Every family would then be guaranteed an annual income of $2500 and an estate of $5000, enough to buy a house, an automobile, and a radio (over which Long had already built a national following).

By 1935, one year after its founding, Long's Share Our Wealth organization boasted 27,000 clubs with files containing nearly 8 million names. Democratic National Committee members shuddered at polls showing that Long might capture up to 4 million votes in 1936, enough to put a Republican in the White House. But late in 1935, in the corridors of the Louisiana capitol, Long was shot to death by a disgruntled constituent whose family had been wronged by the Long political machine.

Father Charles Coughlin was Long's urban counterpart. Where Long explained the Depression as the result of bloated fortunes, Coughlin blamed the banks. In weekly broadcasts from the Shrine of the Little Flower in suburban Detroit, the "Radio Priest" told his working-class, largely *Charles Coughlin* Catholic audience of the international bankers who had toppled the world economy by manipulating gold-backed currencies.

Coughlin promised to end the Depression with simple strokes: nationalizing banks, inflating the currency with silver, spreading work. (None would have worked because each would have dampened investment, the key to recovery.) Across the urban North, 30 to 40 million Americans—the largest audience in the world—huddled around their radios to listen. In 1934 Coughlin organized the National Union for Social Justice to pressure both parties. As the election of 1936 approached, the union loomed on the political horizon.

A less ominous challenge came from Dr. Francis Townsend. The 67-year-old physician had recently retired in California from the public health service. Moved by the plight of elderly Americans without pension plans or medical *Francis Townsend* insurance, Townsend set up Old Age Revolving Pensions, Limited, in 1934. He proposed to have the government pay $200 a month to those 60 years or older who quit their jobs and spent the money within 30 days. By 1936 Townsend clubs counted 3.5 million members, most of them small businesspeople and farmers at or beyond retirement age.

For all their differences, Sinclair, Long, Coughlin, Townsend, and other critics struck similar chords. Although the solutions they proposed were simplistic, the problems they addressed were serious: a maldistribution of goods and wealth, inadequacies in the money supply, the plight of the elderly. They attacked the growing control of corporations, banks, and government over individuals and communities. And they created mass political movements based on social as well as economic dissatisfaction. When Sinclair supporters pledged to produce for their own use and Long's followers swore to "share our wealth," when Coughlinites damned the "monied interests" and Townsendites thumped their Bibles at foul-ups in Washington, they were also trying to protect their freedom and their communities from the intrusion of big business and big government.

## The Second Hundred Days

By the spring of 1935, the forces of discontent were pushing Roosevelt to more action. And so was Congress. With Democrats accounting for more than two-thirds of both houses, they were prepared to outspend the president in extending the New Deal. The 100 days from April through mid-July, the "second hundred days," produced a legislative barrage that moved the New Deal toward Roosevelt's ultimate destination—"a little to the left of center," where government would seek to soften the impact of industrialism, protect the needy, and compensate for the boom-and-bust business cycle.

To help the many Americans who were still jobless Roosevelt proposed the Emergency Relief Appropriation Act of 1935, with a record $4.8 billion for relief and employment. Some of the money went to the new National Youth Administration (NYA) for more than 4.5 million jobs for young people. But the lion's share went to the new Works Progress Administration (WPA), where Harry Hopkins mounted the largest work relief program in history. Before its end in 1943, the WPA employed at least 8.5 million people and built or improved over 100,000 schools, post offices, and other public buildings. Constrained from competing with private industry and committed to spending 80 percent of his budget on wages, Hopkins showed remarkable ingenuity. WPA workers taught art classes in a Cincinnati mental hospital, drafted a Braille map for the blind in Massachusetts, and pulled a library by packhorse through the hills of Kentucky.

*Works Progress Administration*

The ambitious Social Security Act, passed in 1935, sought to help those who could not help themselves: the aged poor, the infirm, dependent children. In this commitment to the destitute—which the Roosevelt administration believed were actually few in number—it laid the groundwork for the modern welfare state. But Social Security also acted as an economic stabilizer by furnishing pensions for retirees and insurance for those suddenly laid off from their jobs. A payroll tax on both employer and employee underwrote pensions after age 65, while an employer-financed system of insurance made possible government payments to unemployed workers.

*Social Security*

Social Security marked a historic reversal in American political values. A new social contract between the government and the people replaced the gospel of self-help and the older policies of laissez faire. At last government acknowledged a broad responsibility to protect the social rights of citizens. The welfare state, foreshadowed in the aid given veterans and their families after the Civil War, was institutionalized, though its coverage was limited. To win the votes of southern congressmen hostile to African Americans, the legislation excluded farmworkers and domestic servants, doubtless among the neediest Americans but often black and disproportionately southern.

Roosevelt had hoped for social insurance that would cover Americans "from cradle to grave." Congress whittled down his plan, but its labor legislation pushed the president well beyond his goal of providing paternalistic aid for workers, such as establishing pension plans and unemployment insurance. New York senator Robert Wagner, the son of a janitor, wanted workers to fight their own battles. In 1933 he had included union recognition in the NRA. When the Supreme Court killed the NRA in 1935, Wagner introduced what became the National Labor Relations Act. (So important had labor support become to Roosevelt that he gave the bill his belated blessing.) The "Wagner Act" created a National Labor Relations Board (NLRB) to supervise the election of unions and ensure union rights to bargain. Most vital, the NLRB had the power to enforce these policies. By 1941, the number of unionized workers had doubled.

*National Labor Relations Act*

Roosevelt responded to the growing hostility of business by turning against the wealthy and powerful in 1935. The popularity of Long's tirades against the rich and Coughlin's against banks sharpened his points of attack. The Revenue Act of 1935 (called the "Wealth Tax Act") threatened to "soak the rich." By the time it worked its way through Congress, however, it levied only moderate taxes on high incomes and inheritances. The Banking Act of 1935 centralized authority over the money market in the Federal Reserve Board. By controlling interest rates and the money supply, government increased its ability to compensate for swings in the economy. The Public Utilities Holding Company Act (1935) limited the size of utility empires. Long the target of progressive reformers, the giant holding companies produced nothing but higher profits for speculators and higher prices for consumers. Diluted like the wealth tax, the utility law was still a political victory for New Dealers. "I am now on your bandwagon again," a Philadelphia voter told the president as the election of 1936 approached.

### The Election of 1936

In June 1936 Roosevelt traveled to Philadelphia, not to thank the loyal voter who had hopped aboard his bandwagon but to accept the Democratic nomination for a second term as president. "This generation of Americans has a rendezvous with destiny," he told a crowd of 100,000 packed into Franklin Field. Whatever destiny had in store for his generation, Roosevelt knew that the coming election would turn on a single issue: "It's myself, and people must be either for me or against me."

Roosevelt ignored his Republican opponent, Governor Alfred Landon of Kansas. Despite a bulging campaign chest of $14 million, Landon lacked luster as well as issues. He favored the regulation of business, a balanced budget, and much of the New Deal. For his part Roosevelt turned the election into a contest between haves and have-nots. The forces of "organized money are unanimous in their hate for me," he told a roaring crowd at New York's Madison Square Garden, "and I welcome their hatred."

The strategy deflated Republicans, discredited conservatives, and stole the thunder of the newly formed Union Party of Townsendites, Coughlinites, and old Long supporters. The election returns shocked even experienced observers. Roosevelt won the largest electoral victory ever—523 to 8—and a whopping 60.8 percent of the popular vote. The margin of victory came from those at the bottom of the economic ladder, grateful for help furnished by the New Deal.

A dramatic political realignment was now clearly in place, as important as the Republican rise to power in 1896. The Democrats reigned as the new majority party for the next 30 years. The "Roosevelt coalition" rested on three pillars: traditional Democratic support in the South; citizens of the big cities, particularly ethnics and African Americans; and labor, both organized and unorganized. The minority Republicans became the party of big business and small towns.

*Roosevelt coalition*

THE NEW DEAL AND THE AMERICAN PEOPLE

Before 1939, farmers in the Hill Country of Texas spent their evenings in the light of 25-watt kerosene lamps. Their wives washed eight loads of laundry a week, all by hand. Every day they hauled home 200 gallons—about 1500 pounds—of water from nearby wells. Farms had no milking machines, no washers, no automatic pumps or water heaters, no refrigerators, and no radios. "Living—just living—was a problem," recalled one woman.

Rural Electrification Administration

The reason for this limited life was simple: the Hill Country had no electricity. Thus no agency of the Roosevelt administration changed the way people lived more dramatically than the Rural Electrification Administration (REA), created in 1935. At the time less than 10 percent of American farms had electricity. Six years later 40 percent did, and by 1950, 90 percent. The New Deal did not always have such a marked impact. And its overall record was mixed. But time and again it changed the lives of ordinary people as government never had before.

## The New Deal and Western Water

In September 1936, President Roosevelt pushed a button in Washington, D.C., and sent electricity pulsing westward from the towering Boulder Dam in Colorado to cities as far away as Los Angeles. The waters thus diverted irrigated 2.5 million acres, while the dam's floodgates protected millions of people in southern California, Nevada, and Arizona. In its water management programs, the New Deal further extended federal power, literally across the country.

Boulder Dam was one of several multipurpose dams completed under the New Deal in the arid West. The aim was simple: to control whole river systems for regional use. Buchanan Dam on the lower Colorado River, the Bonneville and Grand Coulee dams on the Columbia, and many smaller versions curbed floods, generated cheap electricity, and developed river basins from Texas to Washington State. Beginning in 1938, the All-American Canal diverted the Colorado River to irrigate the Imperial Valley in California.

The environmental price of such rewards soon became evident, as it did with the New Deal's experiment in eastern water use, the Tennessee Valley Authority. The once mighty Columbia River, its surging waters checked by dams, flowed sedately from human-made lake to lake, but without the salmon whose spawning runs were also checked. Blocked by the All-American Canal from its path to the sea, the Colorado River slowly turned salty, until by 1950 its waters were unfit for drinking or irrigation.

## The Limited Reach of the New Deal

In the spring of 1939, the Daughters of the American Revolution refused to permit the black contralto Marian Anderson to sing at Constitution Hall in Washington,

D.C. Eleanor Roosevelt quit the DAR in protest, and Secretary of the Interior Harold Ickes began looking for another site. On a nippy Easter Sunday, in the shadow of the Lincoln Memorial, Anderson finally stepped to the microphone and sang to a crowd of 7500. Lincoln himself would not have missed the irony.

In 1932 most African Americans cast their ballots as they had since Reconstruction—for Republicans, the party of Abraham Lincoln and emancipation. But disenchantment with decades of broken promises was spreading, and by 1934 African Americans were voting for Democrats. "Let *African Americans* Jesus lead you and Roosevelt feed you," a black preacher told his congregation on the eve of the 1936 election. When the returns were counted, three of four black voters had cast their ballots for Roosevelt.

The New Deal accounted for this voting revolution. Sympathetic but never a champion, Roosevelt regarded African Americans as one of many groups whose interests he brokered. Even that was an improvement. Federal offices had been segregated since Woodrow Wilson's day, and in the 1920s black leaders called Hoover "the man in the lily-White House." Under Roosevelt racial integration slowly returned to government. Supporters of civil rights like Eleanor Roosevelt and Secretary of the Interior Ickes brought economist Robert C. Weaver and

California's multiethnic workforce is depicted in this detail from Paul Langley Howard's *California Industrial Scenes*. It was one of several murals painted on the walls of San Francisco's Coit Tower. The murals were begun in 1934 as a New Deal relief program for artists.

other black advisers into the administration. Mary McLeod Bethune, a sharecropper's daughter and founder of Bethune-Cookman College, ran a division of the National Youth Administration. Important as both symbols and activists, African American administrators created a "Black Cabinet" to help design federal policy.

Outside of government the Urban League continued to lobby for economic advancement, and the NAACP pressed to make lynching a federal crime. (Though publicly against lynching and privately in favor of an antilynching bill, Roosevelt refused to make it "must" legislation to avoid losing the white southern members of Congress he needed "to save America.") In New York's Harlem, Reverend John H. Johnson organized the Citizens' League for Fair Play in 1933 to persuade white merchants to hire black clerks. After picketers blocked storefronts, hundreds of African Americans got jobs with Harlem retailers and utility companies. Racial tension over employment and housing continued to run high, and in 1935 Harlem exploded in the only race riot of the decade.

Discrimination persisted under the New Deal. Black newspapers reported hundreds of cases of NRA codes resulting in jobs lost to white workers or wages lower than white rates of pay. Disgusted editors renamed the agency "Negroes Ruined Again." Federal efforts to promote grassroots democracy often gave control of New Deal programs to local governments, where discrimination went unchallenged. New Deal showplaces like the TVA's model town of Norris, Tennessee, and the homestead village of Arthurdale, West Virginia, were closed to African Americans.

African Americans reaped a few benefits from the New Deal. The WPA hired black workers for almost 20 percent of its jobs, even though African Americans made up less than 10 percent of the population. When it was discovered that the WPA was paying black workers less than whites, Roosevelt issued an executive order to halt the practice. Public Works administrator Ickes established the first quota system for hiring black Americans. By 1941 the percentage of African Americans working for the government exceeded their proportion of the population.

Civil rights never became a serious aspect of the New Deal, but for the nearly one million Mexican Americans in the United States, Latino culture sometimes
*Mexican Americans* frustrated meager federal efforts to help. Mexican folk traditions of self-help inhibited some from seeking aid; others remained unfamiliar with claim procedures. Still others failed to meet residency requirements. Meanwhile, low voter turnout hampered their political influence, and discrimination limited economic advancement.

In the Southwest and California, the Civilian Conservation Corps and the Works Progress Administration furnished some jobs, though fewer and for less pay than average. On Capitol Hill, Dennis Chavez of New Mexico, the only Mexican American in the Senate, channeled what funds he could into Spanish-speaking communities. But like African Americans, most Latinos remained mired in poverty. The many Mexican Americans who worked the fields as migratory laborers lay outside the reach of most New Deal programs.

## Tribal Rights

The New Deal renewed federal interest in Indians. Among the most disadvantaged Americans, Indian families on reservations rarely earned more than $100 a year. Their infant mortality rate was the highest in the country; their life expectancy, the shortest; their education level—usually no more than five years—the lowest. Their rate of unemployment was three times the national average.

In the 1930s, Indians had no stronger friend in Washington than John Collier. For years he had fought as a social worker among the Pueblos to restore tribal culture. As the new commissioner of Indian affairs, he reversed the decades-old policy of assimilation and promoted tribal life. Under the Indian Reorganization Act of 1934, elders were urged to celebrate festivals, artists to work in native styles, children to learn the old languages. A special Court of Indian Affairs removed Indians from state jurisdiction, and tribal governments ruled reservations. Perhaps most important, tribes regained control over Indian land. Since the Dawes Act of 1887, the land had been allotted to individual Indians, who were often forced by poverty to sell to whites. By the end of the 1930s, Indian landholding had increased.

*John Collier and Indians*

Indians split over Collier's policies. The Pueblos, with a strong communal spirit and already functioning communal societies, favored them. The tribes of Oklahoma and the Great Plains tended to oppose them. Individualism, the profit motive, and an unwillingness to share property with other tribe members fed resistance. So did age-old suspicion of all government programs. And some Indians genuinely desired assimilation. The Navajos, under the leadership of J. C. Morgan, rejected the Indian Reorganization Act in 1935. Morgan saw tribal government as a step backward.

## A New Deal for Women

As the tides of change washed across the country, a new deal for women was unfolding in Washington. The New Deal's welfare agencies offered unprecedented opportunity for social workers, teachers, and other women who had spent their lives helping the downtrodden. They were already experts on social welfare. Several were friends with professional ties, and together they formed a network of activists in the New Deal promoting women's interests and social reform. Led by Eleanor Roosevelt and Labor Secretary Frances Perkins, women served on the consumers' advisory board of the NRA, helped to administer the relief program, and won appointments to the Social Security Board.

In growing numbers women became part of the Democratic party machinery. Under the leadership of social worker Mary W. "Molly" Dewson, the Women's Division of the Democratic National Committee played a critical role in the election. Thousands of women mounted a "mouth-to-mouth" campaign, traveling from door to door to drum up support for Roosevelt and other

Democrats. When the ballots were tallied, women formed an important part of the new Roosevelt coalition.

Federal appointments and party politics broke new ground for women, but in general the New Deal abided by existing social standards. Gender equality, like

*Progress limited*

racial equality, was never high on its agenda. One-quarter of all NRA codes permitted women to be paid less than men, while WPA wages averaged $2 a day more for men. The New Deal gave relatively few jobs to women, and when it did, they were often in gender-segregated trades such as sewing. Government employment patterns for women fell below even those in the private sector. The WPA hired nearly half a million women in 1936, roughly 15 percent of all WPA workers, at a time when women constituted almost a quarter of the workforce.

Reflecting old conceptions of reform, New Dealers placed greater emphasis on aiding and protecting women than on employing them. The Federal Emergency Relief Administration built 17 camps for homeless women in 11 states. Social security furnished subsidies to mothers with dependent children, and the WPA established emergency nursery schools (which also became the government's first foray into early childhood education). But even federal protection fell short. Social security, for example, did not cover domestic servants, most of whom were women.

## The Rise of Organized Labor

Although women and minorities discovered that the New Deal had limits to the changes it promoted, a powerful union movement arose in the 1930s by taking full advantage of the new climate. It ended up pushing Roosevelt well beyond his limits. At the outset of the Depression barely 6 percent of the labor force belonged to unions. Though the New Deal left farmworkers officially outside its coverage, its promise of support encouraged these workers to act on their own. In California, where large agribusinesses employed migrant laborers to pick vegetables, fruit, and cotton, some 37 strikes involving over 50,000 workers swept the state after Roosevelt took office.

The most famous strike broke out in the cotton fields of the San Joaquin Valley under the auspices of the Cannery and Agricultural Workers Industrial Union

*CAWIU farm strike*

(CAWIU). Most of the strikers were Mexican, supported more by a complex network of families, friends, and coworkers than by the weak CAWIU. Before the strike was over, local farmers killed three people, and local officials threatened to cut off all relief aid to strikers and to send them back to Mexico. The government finally stepped in to arbitrate a wage settlement, which resulted in an end to the strike but at a fraction of the pay the workers sought.

Such government support was not enough to embolden the cautious American Federation of Labor, the nation's premier union. Historically bound to skilled labor and organized on the basis of craft, it ignored the unskilled workers who by the 1930s made up most of the industrial labor force, and it almost never organized women or black workers. Thus the AFL avoided major industries like rubber, automobiles, and steel.

John L. Lewis fought to unionize unskilled laborers. Tough, charismatic, and practical, Lewis headed the United Mine Workers (UMW), an affiliate of the AFL. When he met with Roosevelt in 1933, he received little more than consolation for his shrinking union. Yet the shrewd Lewis returned to the coalfields with a message the president had never given him: "The president wants you to join a union." Within a year the UMW had 400,000 members. Raising his sights, Lewis called for the creation of a Steel Workers' Organizing Committee (SWOC) and for the admission of the United Auto Workers (UAW) into the AFL.

At the annual AFL convention in Atlantic City in 1935, Lewis demanded a commitment to the "industrial organization of mass production workers." The delegates, mostly from craft unions, voted down the proposal. Near the end of the convention, as Lewis passed "Big Bill" Hutcheson of the carpenters union, angry words passed between the two. Lewis spun and with a single punch sent Hutcheson sprawling in a bloody heap.

The blow signaled the determination of industrial unions to break the AFL's domination of organized labor. A few weeks later, Lewis and the heads of seven other AFL unions announced the formation of the Committee for Industrial Organization (CIO). The AFL suspended the rogue unions in 1936. The CIO, later rechristened the Congress of Industrial Organizations, turned to the unskilled.

*Congress of Industrial Organizations*

## Campaigns of the CIO

CIO representatives concentrated on the mighty steel industry, which had clung to the "open," or nonunion, shop since 1919. In other industries, the rank and file did not wait. Emboldened by the recent passage of the Wagner Act, a group of rubber workers in Akron, Ohio, simply sat down on the job in early 1936. Since the strikers occupied the plants, managers could not replace them with strikebreakers. Nor could the rubber companies call in the military or police without risk to their property. The leaders of the United Rubber Workers Union opposed the "sit-downs," but when the Goodyear Tire & Rubber Company laid off 70 workers, 1400 rubber workers struck on their own. An 11-mile picket line sprang up outside. Eventually Goodyear settled by recognizing the union and accepting its demands on wages and hours.

*Sit-down strikes*

The biggest strikes erupted in the automobile industry. A series of spontaneous strikes at General Motors plants in Atlanta, Kansas City, and Cleveland spread to Fisher Body No. 2 in Flint, Michigan, late in December 1936. Singing the unionists' anthem, "Solidarity Forever," workers took over the plant while wives, friends, and fellow union members handed food and clothing through the windows. Local police tried to break up supply lines, only to be driven off by a hail of nuts, bolts, coffee mugs, and bottles.

Men looking through the broken windows of an automobile plant during the wave of sit-down strikes in 1937. The windows were smashed not by the men in this photograph but by women of the newly established "Emergency Brigade" when they heard that the workers inside were being gassed. Women played a vital role in supporting the strikes, collecting and distributing food to strikers and their families, setting up a first-aid station, and furnishing day care.

In the wake of this "Battle of Running Bulls" (a reference to the retreating police), Governor Frank Murphy finally called out the National Guard, not to arrest but to protect strikers. General Motors surrendered in February 1937. Less than a month later U.S. Steel capitulated without a strike. By the end of the year every automobile manufacturer except Henry Ford had negotiated with the UAW.

Bloody violence accompanied some drives. On Memorial Day 1937, 10 strikers lost their lives when Chicago police fired on them as they marched peacefully toward the Republic Steel plant. And sit-down strikes often alienated an otherwise sympathetic middle class. (In 1939 the Supreme Court outlawed the tactic.) Yet a momentous transfer of power had taken place. By 1940 nearly one worker in three belonged to a union. The unskilled had a powerful voice in the CIO. And the craft unions of the AFL outnumbered the organized unskilled by more than a million. Women's membership in unions tripled between

*Union gains*

1930 and 1940, and African Americans also made gains. Independent unions had become a significant part of industrial America.

Government played an important but secondary role in the industrial union movement by creating a hospitable environment for labor. Roosevelt courted workers, both organized and unorganized, but stood aside in the toughest labor battles. Yet doing nothing in favor of strikers was a vast improvement over the active hostility shown by earlier presidents. The Wagner Act afforded laborers an opportunity for organization and protection if they chose to request it, but nothing more. Leaders such as John L. Lewis, Walter Reuther of the United Auto Workers, and Philip Murray of the Steel Workers' Organizing Committee galvanized workers, who won their own victories.

### *"Art for the Millions"*

No agency of the New Deal touched more Americans than Federal One, the bureaucratic umbrella of the WPA's arts program. For the first time, thousands of unemployed writers, musicians, painters, actors, and photographers went on the federal payroll. Public projects—from massive murals to tiny guidebooks—would make "art for the millions."

A Federal Writers Project (FWP) produced about a thousand publications. Its 81 state, territorial, and city guides were so popular that commercial publishers happily printed them. A Depression-bred interest in American history prompted the FWP to collect folklore, study ethnic groups, and record the reminiscences of 200 former slaves. Meanwhile, the Federal Music Project (FMP) employed some 15,000 out-of-work musicians. For a token charge, Americans could hear the music of Bach and Beethoven. | *Federal arts programs*

In the Federal Art Project (FAP), watercolorists and drafters painstakingly prepared the Index of American Design, which offered elaborate illustrations of American material culture, from skillets to cigar-store Indians. At night artists taught sculpture, painting, clay modeling, and carving in country churches, settlement houses, and schools. Jackson Pollock, Willem de Kooning, and others destined to become important painters survived the Depression by painting for the government.

The most notable contribution of the FAP came in the form of murals. Under the influence of Mexican muralists Diego Rivera and José Clemente Orozco, American artists covered the walls of thousands of airports, post offices, and other government buildings with wall paintings glorifying local life | *Muralists* and work. (See, for example, the mural on page 741.) The rare treatment of class conflict later opened the FAP to charges of communist infiltration, but most of the murals stressed the enduring qualities of American life: family, work, community.

The Federal Theater Project (FTP) reached the greatest number of people— some 30 million—and aroused the most controversy. As its head, Hallie Flanagan made government-supported theater vital, daring, and relevant. Living Newspapers dramatized headlines of the day. Under the direction of Orson Welles and

John Houseman an all-black company (one of 16 "Negro Units") set Shake-speare's Macbeth in Haiti, with voodoo priestesses and African drummers. Occasionally frank depictions of class conflict riled congressional conservatives, and beginning in 1938, the House Un-American Activities Committee investigated the FTP as "a branch of the Communistic organization." A year later Congress slashed its budget and brought government-sponsored theater to an end.

**The New Deal government's pathbreaking documentary film *The River***

The documentary impulse to record life permeated the arts in the 1930s. Novels such as Erskine Caldwell's *Tobacco Road*, feature films like John Ford's *The Grapes of Wrath*, and such federally funded documentaries as Pare Lorentz's *The River* stirred the social conscience of the country. New Dealers had practical motives for promoting documentary realism. They wanted to blunt criticism of New Deal relief measures by documenting the distress. In 1937 Rexford Tugwell established an Information Division in his Resettlement Administration. He put

*Documentary realism* | Roy Stryker, his former Columbia University teaching assistant, in charge of its Historical Section. Stryker hired talented photographers to produce an unvarnished record of the Great Depression. Their raw and haunting photographs turned history into both propaganda and art.

## THE END OF THE NEW DEAL (1937–1940)

"I see one-third of a nation ill-housed, ill-clad, ill-nourished," the president lamented in his second inaugural address on January 20, 1937 (the first January inauguration under a new constitutional amendment). Industrial output had doubled since 1932; farm income had almost quadrupled. But full recovery remained elusive. Over seven million Americans were still out of work, and national income was only half again as large as it had been in 1933, when Roosevelt took office. At the height of his popularity, with bulging majorities in Congress, Roosevelt planned to expand the New Deal. Within a year, however, the New Deal was largely over, drowned in a sea of economic and political troubles—many of them Roosevelt's own doing.

### Packing the Courts

As Roosevelt's second term began, only the Supreme Court clouded the political horizon. In its first 76 years the Court had invalidated only two acts of Congress. Between 1920 and 1933 it struck down portions of 22 laws. This new judicial activism, spearheaded by a conservative majority, rested on a narrow view of the constitutional powers of Congress and the president. As the New Deal broadened those powers, the Supreme Court let loose a flood of nullifications.

In 1935 the Court wiped out the NRA on the grounds that manufacturing was not involved in interstate commerce and thus lay beyond federal regulation. In 1936 it canceled the AAA, reducing federal authority under the taxing power and the general welfare clause of the Constitution. In *Moorehead v. Tipaldo* (1936) the Court ruled that a New York minimum-wage law was invalid because it interfered with the right of workers to negotiate a contract. A frustrated Roosevelt complained that the Court had thereby created a "'no-man's land,' where no government—State or Federal" could act.

Roosevelt was the first president since James Monroe to serve four years without making a Supreme Court appointment. Among federal judges Republicans outnumbered Democrats by more than two to one in 1933. Roosevelt intended to redress the balance with legislation that added new judges *Roosevelt's plan* to the federal bench, including the Supreme Court. The federal courts were overburdened and too many judges "aged or infirm," he declared in February 1937. In the interests of efficiency, said Roosevelt, he proposed to "vitalize" the judiciary with new members. When a 70-year-old judge who had served at least 10 years failed to retire, the president could add another, up to 6 to the Supreme Court and 44 to the lower federal courts.

Roosevelt badly miscalculated. He unveiled his plan without warning, expecting widespread support. He regarded courts as political, not sacred, institutions and had ample precedent for altering even the Supreme Court. (As recently as 1869 Congress had increased its size to nine.) But most Americans clung to the courts as symbols of stability. Few accepted Roosevelt's efficiency argument, and no one on Capitol Hill (with its share of 70-year-olds) believed that seven decades of life necessarily made one incompetent. Worse still, the proposal ignited conservative-liberal antagonisms within the Democratic party. "Here's where I cash in my chips," declared the Democratic chairman of the House Judiciary Committee as he abandoned the president.

Suddenly the Court reversed itself. In April, *N.L.R.B. v. Jones and Laughlin Steel Corporation* upheld the Wagner Act by one vote. A month later the justices sustained the Social Security Act as a legitimate exercise of the commerce power. And when Justice Willis Van Devanter, the oldest and most conservative justice, retired later that year, Roosevelt at last made an appointment to the Supreme Court.

With Democrats deserting him, the president accepted a substitute measure that utterly ignored his proposal to appoint new judges. Roosevelt nonetheless claimed victory. After all, the Court shifted course (and eventually he appointed nine Supreme Court justices). But victory came at a high price. The momentum of the 1936 election was squandered, the unity of the Democratic party was destroyed, and opponents learned that Roosevelt could be beaten. A conservative coalition of Republicans and rural Democrats had come together around the first of several anti–New Deal causes.

## The New Deal at Bay

As early as 1936 Secretary of the Treasury Henry Morgenthau began to plead for fiscal restraint. With productivity rising and unemployment falling, it was time to reduce spending, balance the budget, and let business lead the recovery. "Strip off the bandages, throw away the crutches," and let the economy "stand on its own feet," he said.

Morgenthau was preaching to the converted. Although the president had been willing to run budget deficits in a time of crisis, he had never been comfortable

*John Maynard Keynes* | with them. To be sure, the British economist John Maynard Keynes had actually recommended the kind of deficit spending that Roosevelt had used. Keynes's startling theory called on government not to balance the budget but to spend its way out of depression. When prosperity returned, Keynes argued, government could pay off its debts through taxes. This deliberate policy of "countercyclical" action (spending in bad times, taxing in good) would compensate for swings in the economy.

Keynes's theory was precisely the path chosen by several industrial nations in which recovery came more quickly than it did to the United States. Germany in

*Recovery abroad* | particular built its rapid recuperation on spending. When Adolf Hitler and his National Socialist (Nazi) party came to power in 1933, they

went on a spending spree, constructing huge highways called autobahns, enormous government buildings, and other public works. Later they ran up deficits for rearmament as they prepared for war. Between 1933 and 1939 the German national debt almost quadrupled, while in the United States it rose by barely 50 percent. For Germans, the price in lost freedoms was incalculable, but by 1936, their depression was over.

Not all nations relied on military spending. And many of them, such as Great Britain and France, had not shared in the economic expansion of the 1920s, which meant their economies had a shorter distance to rise in order to reach pre-Depression levels. Yet spending of one kind or another helped solve the riddle of recovery in country after country. In Great Britain, for example, low interest rates plus government assistance to the needy ignited a housing boom, while government subsidies to the automobile industry and to companies willing to build factories in depressed areas slowed the slide. In the 1930s, Britons still endured what they called the "Great Slump," but their economy was the first to surpass its performance in 1929. By 1937 British unemployment had been cut nearly by half.

In the United States, Roosevelt ordered cuts in federal spending early in 1937. He slashed relief rolls by half and virtually halted spending on public works. Within six months, the economy collapsed. Industrial activity plummeted to 1935 levels. At the end of the year unemployment stood at 10.5 million as the "Roosevelt reces-

*Roosevelt recession* | sion" deepened. Finally spenders convinced him to propose a $3.75 billion omnibus measure in April 1938. Facing an election, Congress happily reversed relief cuts, quadrupled farm subsidies, and embarked on a new shipbuilding program. The economy revived but never recovered. Keynesian economics was vindicated, though it would take decades before becoming widely accepted.

With Roosevelt vulnerable, conservatives in Congress struck. They cut back on public housing programs and minimum wage guarantees in the South. The

FEDERAL BUDGET AND SURPLUS/DEFICIT, 1920–1940  During the 1920s, the federal government ran a modest surplus. Beginning in 1930, federal deficits mounted as spending for Depression programs climbed and revenues from taxes and tariffs sank.

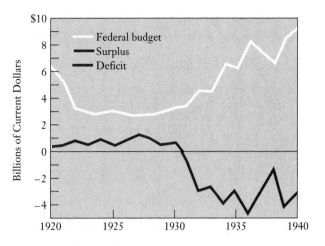

president's successes came where he could act alone, principally in a renewed attack on big business. At his urging, the Justice Department opened investigations of corporate concentration. Even Congress responded by creating the Temporary National Economic Committee to examine corporate abuses and recommend revisions in the antitrust laws. These were small consolations. The president, wrote Interior Secretary Harold Ickes in August 1938, "is punch drunk from the punishment."

Vainly Roosevelt fought back. In the off-year elections of 1938, he tried to purge Democrats who had deserted him. The five senators he targeted for defeat all won. Republicans posted gains in the House and Senate and won 13 governorships. Democrats still held majorities in both houses, but conservatives had the votes to block new programs. With the economy limping toward recovery, the New Deal passed into history, and the nation turned to a new crisis: a looming war abroad.

## The Legacy of the New Deal

The New Deal lasted only five years, from 1933 to 1938, and it never spent enough to end the Depression. Though it pledged itself to the "forgotten" Americans, it failed the neediest among them: sharecroppers, tenant farmers, migrant workers. In many ways, it was quite conservative. It left capitalism intact, even strengthened, and it overturned few cultural conventions. Even its reforms followed the old progressive formula of softening industrialism by strengthening the state.

Yet for all its conservatism and continuities, the New Deal left a legacy of change. Under it, government assumed a broader role in the economy than progressives had ever undertaken. To regulation was now added the complicated task of maintaining economic stability—compensating for swings in the business cycle. In its securities and banking regulations, unemployment insurance, and requirements for wages and hours, the New Deal created stabilizers to avoid future breakdowns. Bolstering the Federal Reserve system and enhancing control over credit strengthened government influence over the economy.

## The Chinese Intervene

MacArthur's success led Truman to a fateful decision. With the South liberated, he gave MacArthur permission to cross the 38th parallel, drive the Communists from the North, and reunite Korea under Syngman Rhee. Such a victory was just what Truman needed with Senator Joe McCarthy on the attack at home and the 1950 congressional elections nearing. By Thanksgiving American troops had roundly defeated northern forces and were advancing toward the frozen Yalu River, the boundary between Korea and China. MacArthur, made bold by success, promised that the boys would be home by Christmas.

Throughout the fall offensive, however, China's premier, Zhou Enlai, cautioned that his country would not tolerate an American presence on its border. Washington officials did not take the warning seriously. Mao Zedong, they assumed, was a Soviet puppet, and Stalin had declared the Korean conflict to be merely a "civil war" and off-limits. But on November 26, 400,000 Chinese troops poured across the Yalu, smashing through lightly defended UN lines. At Chosan they trapped 20,000 American and South Korean troops, inflicting one of the worst military defeats in American history. Within three weeks they had driven UN forces back behind the 38th parallel.

So total was the rout that Truman wondered publicly about using the atom bomb. That remark sent a frightened British prime minister Clement Attlee flying to Washington to dissuade Truman. The president readily agreed that the war must remain limited and withdrew his nuclear threat.

## Truman versus MacArthur

Military stalemate in Korea brought into the open a simmering feud between General MacArthur and Truman. The general had publicized his differences with Truman, arguing that UN forces should bomb Chinese and Russian supply bases across the Korean border, blockade China's coast, and unleash Chiang Kai-shek on mainland China. On March 23 he issued a personal ultimatum to Chinese military commanders demanding total surrender. To his Republican congressional supporters he sent a letter declaring, "We must win. There is no substitute for victory."

To Truman, MacArthur's strategy appeared to be an open invitation to another world war. Equally alarming, the general's insubordination threatened the tradition that the military remain under clear civilian control. When Truman made plans to discipline MacArthur, General Omar Bradley reported that MacArthur was threatening to resign before Truman could act. "The son of a bitch isn't going to resign on me," Truman retorted. "I want him fired!" Military leaders agreed that MacArthur had to go. On April 11 a stunned nation learned that the celebrated military commander had been relieved of his duties. When MacArthur returned to the States, cheering crowds welcomed him with a ticker-tape parade. Congress gave him the unprecedented opportunity to address a joint session before a national television audience.

## Harry Truman Disciplines
## His "Big General"

April 6, 1951

MacArthur shoots another political bomb through Joe Martin, leader of the Republican minority in the House.

This looks like the last straw.

Rank insubordination. Last summer he sent a long statement to the Vets of Foreign Wars—not through the high command back home, but directly! He sent copies to newspapers and magazines particularly hostile to me.

I was furnished a copy from the press room of the White House which had been *accidentally* sent there.

I ordered the release suppressed and then sent him a very carefully prepared directive dated Dec. 5, 1950, setting out Far Eastern policy after I'd flown 14,404 [miles] to Wake Island to see him and reach an understanding face to face.

He told me the war in Korea was over, that we could transfer a regular division to Germany Jan 1st. He was positive Red China would not come in. He expected to support our Far Eastern policy.

I call in Gen. Marshall, Dean Acheson, Mr. Harriman and Gen. Bradley before Cabinet to discuss situation. I've come to the conclusion that our Big General in the Far East must be recalled. I don't express any opinion or make known my decision.

Direct the four to meet again Friday afternoon and go over all phases of the situation.

April 9, 1951

. . . Meet with Acheson, Marshall, Bradley and Harriman. Go over recall orders to MacArthur and suggested public statement. Approve both and decide to send the orders to Frank Pace, Sec. of the Army, for delivery to MacArthur. . . . Gen. Bradley called about 9 P.M. Said there had been a leak. . . . I ordered messages sent at once and directly to MacArthur.

April 10, 1951

Quite an explosion. Was expected but I had to act.

Telegrams and letters of abuse by the dozens.

Source: Harry S. Truman, Diary. Reprinted in Robert H. Farrell, ed., *The Private Papers of Harry Truman* (Harper & Row: New York, 1980), pp. 210–211.

## The Global Implications of the Cold War

Behind the scenes Truman was winning this personal clash. At stake was not simply the issue of whether he or MacArthur would prevail. Rather, the outcome would determine the future direction of American foreign policy. The cold war crisis forced American leaders to think globally. Where in the world did the nation's interests lie? What region was most critical to the future? MacArthur believed that the Pacific basin would "determine the course of history in the next ten thousand years." The United States should make an all-out effort, not just to contain the Communist onslaught in Korea, but to play a major role throughout Asia. Many conservative Republicans and groups like the China Lobby shared MacArthur's view. As Senator Robert Taft put it, the United States should pursue "the same policy in the Far East as in Europe."

Truman and his advisers continued to see Western Europe as the center of the world's economic and military power. Political scientist Hans Morgenthau argued that "he who controls Europe is well on his way toward controlling the whole world." Secretary of State Acheson agreed with *Europe, not Asia, first* the Eurocentrists. Korea was to Acheson but a small link in a global "collective security system." The wider war in Asia that MacArthur favored would threaten American interests in Europe because American resources would be stretched too thinly. Or, as General Bradley told Congress, a war in Asia would lead to "the wrong war, at the wrong place, at the wrong time, and with the wrong enemy." In this debate the Eurocentric faction prevailed. Congressional leaders agreed with Truman that the war in Korea should remain limited and that American resources should go to rebuilding Europe's defenses.

Still, the continuing war in Korea took its toll on Truman's political fortunes. After July 1951, the war dragged on and so did the aimless peace talks. By March 1952 Truman's popularity had sunk so low that he lost the New *Korean stalemate* Hampshire presidential primary. With that defeat, he announced he would not run for reelection in 1952.

## K1C2: The Election of 1952

The Republican formula for victory in 1952 played on the Truman administration's weaknesses. Those did not include the economy, which remained remarkably healthy. Wage and price controls put in place by the administration prevented the sharp inflation that was expected to follow increased wartime spending. But the Republicans could capitalize on the stalemate over Korea. And several of Truman's advisers had been forced to resign for accepting gifts in return for political favors. The campaign strategy was summed up in the formula K1C2: Korea, corruption, and communism.

Republican party regulars and the conservative wing were committed to Robert Taft, who ran surprisingly well in the party primaries. But former military hero Dwight "Ike" Eisenhower was more popular with voters. His backers maneuvered their candidate to a first-ballot nomination. To heal the breach with the Taft delegates, the convention chose the staunch anti-Communist senator Richard Nixon as Eisenhower's running mate.

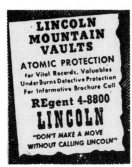

LINCOLN
MOUNTAIN
VAULTS
ATOMIC PROTECTION
for Vital Records, Valuables
Under Burns Detective Protection
For Informative Brochure Call
REgent 4-8800
LINCOLN
"DON'T MAKE A MOVE
WITHOUT CALLING LINCOLN"

Once the Soviet Union developed its own nuclear capability, Americans felt vulnerable to a surprise atomic attack. This advertisement from the *New York Times* in 1954 promised consumers that their valuables could be stored deep in a mountain vault.

The Democrats had no candidate as popular as Eisenhower. They drafted Illinois governor Adlai E. Stevenson, an unusually eloquent speaker. But, like Dewey before him, Stevenson lacked the common touch. The GOP's campaign against communism and corruption, led by Nixon, forced the Democrats on the defensive. Eisenhower, meanwhile, remained high above the mudslinging and promised voters that if elected, he would go to Korea to seek an end to the war.

The election outcome was never much in doubt. Ike's broad smile and confident manner won him over 55 percent of the vote. "The great problem of America today," he had said during the campaign, "is to take that straight road down the middle." Most Americans who voted for him were comforted to think that was just where they were headed.

*Eisenhower and Korea*

And Eisenhower kept his pledge "to go to Korea" and review the situation firsthand. Once in office, he renewed negotiations with North Korea but warned that unless the talks made speedy progress, the United States might retaliate "under circumstances of our choosing." The carrot-and-stick approach worked. On July 27, 1953, the Communists and the United Nations forces signed an armistice ending a "police action" in which nearly 34,000 Americans had died. Korea remained divided, almost as it had been in 1950. Communism had been "contained," but at a high price in human lives.

## The Fall of McCarthy

It was less clear whether anticommunism could be contained. When Eisenhower called himself a "modern" Republican, he distinguished himself from what he called the more "hidebound" members of the GOP. Their anti-Communist campaigns caused him increasing embarrassment. Senator McCarthy's reckless antics, at first directed at Democrats, began to hit Republican targets as well.

By the summer of 1953 the senator was on a rampage. He dispatched two young staff members, Roy Cohn and David Schine, to investigate the State Department's overseas information agency and the Voice of America radio stations. While there, they insisted on purging government libraries of "subversive" volumes. Some librarians, fearing for their careers, burned a number of books. That drove President Eisenhower to denounce "book burners," though soon after he reassured McCarthy's supporters that he did not advocate free speech for Communists.

The administration's own behavior contributed to the hysteria on which McCarthy thrived. The president launched a loyalty campaign, which he claimed resulted in 3000 firings and 5000 resignations of government employees. It was a godsend to McCarthyites: what further proof was needed that subversives were lurking in the federal bureaucracy? Furthermore, a well-publicized spy trial had led to the conviction of Ethel and Julius Rosenberg, a couple accused of passing atomic secrets to the Soviets. Although the evidence against Ethel was weak, the judge sentenced both Rosenbergs to the electric chair, an unusually harsh punishment even in cases of espionage. When asked to commute the death sentence to life imprisonment, Eisenhower refused, and the Rosenbergs were executed in June 1953.

*Rosenberg case*

In such a climate—where Democrats remained silent for fear of being called leftists and Eisenhower cautiously refused to "get in the gutter with *that* guy"— McCarthy lost all sense of proportion. When the army denied his staff aide David Schine an officer's commission, McCarthy decided to investigate communism in the army. The new American Broadcasting Company network, eager to fill its afternoon program slots, televised the hearings. The public had an opportunity to see McCarthy badger witnesses and make a mockery of Senate procedures. Soon after, his popularity began to slide and the anti-Communist hysteria ebbed as well. The Senate finally moved to censure him. He died three years later, destroyed by alcohol and the habit of throwing so many reckless punches.

*The army versus McCarthy*

With the Democrats out of the White House for the first time since the Depression and with McCarthyites in retreat, Eisenhower did indeed seem to be leading the nation on a course "right down the middle." Still, it is worth noting how much that sense of "middle" had changed.

Both the Great Depression and World War II made most Americans realize that the nation's economy was closely linked to the international order. The crash in 1929, with its worldwide effects, certainly made that clear. The New Deal demonstrated that Americans were willing to give the federal government power to influence American society in major new ways. And the war led the government to intervene in the economy even more directly.

Thus when peace came in 1945, it became clear that the "middle road" did not mean a return to the laissez-faire economics of the 1920s. Nor would most Americans support the isolationist policies of the 1930s. "Modern" Republicans accepted social welfare programs like Social Security and recognized that the federal government had the ability to lower unemployment, control inflation, and manage the economy in a variety of ways. Furthermore, the shift from war to peace demonstrated that it was no longer possible to make global war without making a global peace. Under the new balance of power in the postwar world, the United States and the Soviet Union stood alone as "superpowers," with the potential capability to annihilate each other and the rest of the world.

# chapter summary

The cold war between the Soviet Union and the United States affected every aspect of American domestic and foreign policy.

- Americans had long been suspicious of Soviet communism, but Stalin's aggressive posture toward Eastern Europe and the Persian Gulf region raised new fears among American policy makers.

- In response, the Truman administration applied a policy of containment through the Truman Doctrine, the Marshall Plan, and NSC-68.

- The domestic transition from war to peace was slowed because of inflation, labor unrest, and shortages of goods and housing, but the return of prosperity, fueled by consumer and government spending, eased the readjustment.

- Domestic fear of Communist subversion led the Truman administration to devise a government loyalty program and inspired the witch hunts of Senator Joseph McCarthy.

- The Soviet detonation of an atomic bomb and the fall of China to the Communists, followed by the Korean War, undermined the popularity of Harry Truman and the Democrats, opening the way for Dwight Eisenhower's victory in the 1952 presidential election.

# interactive learning

The Primary Source Investigator CD-ROM offers the following materials related to this chapter:

- Interactive map: **Election of 1948** (M7)

- A collection of primary sources exploring the onset of the cold war period, including the Marshall Plan, the treaty that created NATO, and the charter of the United Nations. Several documents illuminate fear and anxiety at the dawn of the nuclear age: a film clip of an early nuclear blast, students practicing "duck-and-cover" exercises, and images from the Korean War.

 For quizzes and a variety of interactive resources, visit the book's Online Learning Center at www.mhhe.com/davidsonconcise4.

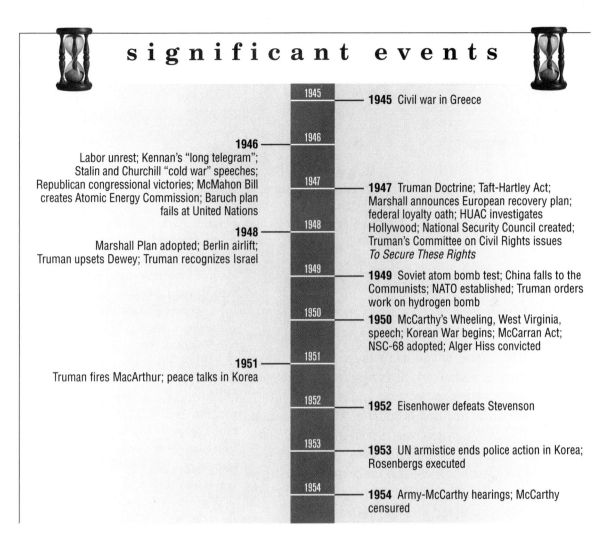

# significant events

**1945** Civil war in Greece

**1946**
Labor unrest; Kennan's "long telegram";
Stalin and Churchill "cold war" speeches;
Republican congressional victories; McMahon Bill
creates Atomic Energy Commission; Baruch plan
fails at United Nations

**1947** Truman Doctrine; Taft-Hartley Act;
Marshall announces European recovery plan;
federal loyalty oath; HUAC investigates
Hollywood; National Security Council created;
Truman's Committee on Civil Rights issues
*To Secure These Rights*

**1948**
Marshall Plan adopted; Berlin airlift;
Truman upsets Dewey; Truman recognizes Israel

**1949** Soviet atom bomb test; China falls to the
Communists; NATO established; Truman orders
work on hydrogen bomb

**1950** McCarthy's Wheeling, West Virginia,
speech; Korean War begins; McCarran Act;
NSC-68 adopted; Alger Hiss convicted

**1951**
Truman fires MacArthur; peace talks in Korea

**1952** Eisenhower defeats Stevenson

**1953** UN armistice ends police action in Korea;
Rosenbergs executed

**1954** Army-McCarthy hearings; McCarthy
censured

# CHAPTER 28

The company that epitomized the corporate culture of the 1950s was General Motors. GM executives sought to blend in rather than to stand out. They chose their suits in drab colors—dark blue, dark gray, or light gray—to increase their anonymity. Not head car designer Harley Earl. Earl brought a touch of Hollywood into the world of corporate bureaucrats. He had a closet filled with colorful suits. His staff would marvel as he headed off to a board meeting dressed in white linen with a dark blue shirt and *blue suede shoes*—the same shoes that Elvis Presley sang so protectively about.

# The Suburban Era

## 1945–1963

**Preview** *The culture of the automobile in many ways defined America at midcentury. Superhighways encouraged newly prosperous Americans to move into suburban homes boasting green lawns and new televisions. The middle-class "consensus" of an American dream revolved around single-family homes, religious observance of some sort, and women who cared for the family at home. And the continuing cold war cast a long shadow culminating in a confrontation over Cuba in 1962 that skirted the edge of all-out nuclear war.*

Mr. Earl—no one who worked for him ever called him Harley—could afford to be a maverick. He created the cars that brought customers into GM showrooms across the country. Before he came to Detroit, engineering sold cars. Advertising stressed mechanical virtues—the steady ride, reliable brakes, or, perhaps, power steering. Earl made style the distinctive feature. Unlike the boxy look other designs favored, an Earl car was low and sleek, suggesting motion even when the car stood still. No feature stood out more distinctively than the fins he first put on the 1948 Cadillac. By the mid-1950s jet planes inspired Earl to design ever-more-outrageous fins, complemented by huge, shiny chrome grills and ornaments. These features served no mechanical purpose. Some critics dismissed Earl's designs as jukeboxes on wheels.

To Earl and GM that did not matter. Design sold cars. "It gave [customers] an extra receipt for their money in the form of visible prestige marking for an expensive car," Earl said. The "Big Three" auto manufacturers—General Motors, Ford, and Chrysler—raced one another to redesign their annual models, the more outrageous the better. Earl once joked, "I'd put smokestacks right in the middle of the sons of bitches if I thought I could sell more cars." The goal was not a

Like a freak of evolution run riot, automotive tailfins during the 1950s were elongated until they reached the monstrous proportions of the 1959 Cadillac, which also sported bomblike taillights.

better car but what Earl called "dynamic obsolescence," or simply change for change's sake. "The 1957 Ford was great," its designer remarked, "but right away we had to bury it and start another." Even though the mechanics of cars changed little from year to year, dynamic obsolescence persuaded Americans in the 1950s to buy new cars in record numbers.

Fins, roadside motels, "gaseterias," drive-in burger huts, interstate highways, shopping centers, and, of course, suburbs—all these were part of a culture of mobility in the 1950s. Americans continued their exodus from rural areas to cities and from cities to the suburbs. African Americans left the South, heading for industrial centers in the Northeast, in the Midwest, and on the West Coast. Mexican Americans concentrated in southwestern cities, while Puerto Ricans came largely to New York. And for Americans in the Snowbelt, the climate of the West and South (at least when civilized by air conditioning) made the Sunbelt attractive.

The mobility was social, too. As the economy continued to expand, the size of the American middle class grew. In an era of prosperity and peace, some commentators began to speak of a "consensus"—a general agreement in American culture, based on values of the broad middle class. In a positive light consensus reflected the agreement among most Americans about fundamental democratic values. Most citizens embraced the material benefits of prosperity as evidence of the virtue of "the American way." And they opposed the spread of communism abroad.

*The 1950s as an era of consensus*

But consensus had its dark side. Critics worried that too strong a consensus bred a mindless conformity. Were Americans becoming too homogenized? Was there a depressing sameness in the material goods they owned, in the places they lived, and in the values they held? The baby boomers born into this era seldom agonized over such issues. In the White House President Eisenhower radiated a comforting sense that the affairs of the nation and the world were in capable hands. That left teenagers free to worry about what really mattered: a first date, a first kiss, a first job, a first choice for college, and whether or not to "go all the way" in the back seat of one of Harley Earl's fin-swept Buicks.

## THE RISE OF THE SUBURBS

Suburban growth accelerated sharply at the end of World War II. During the 1950s suburbs grew 40 times faster than cities, so that by 1960 half of the American people lived in them. The return of prosperity brought a baby boom and a need for new housing. Automobiles made the suburbs accessible. But the spurt in suburban growth took its toll on the cities, which suffered as the middle class fled urban areas.

### A Boom in Babies and in Housing

The Great Depression caused many couples to delay beginning a family. In the 1930s birthrates had reached their low point in American history, about 18 to 19 per thousand. As prosperity returned during the war, birthrates began to rise. By 1952 they had passed 25 per thousand to reach one of the highest fertility rates in the world. New brides were also younger, which translated into unusual fertility. Americans chose to have larger families, as the number with three children tripled and those with four or more quadrupled. "Just imagine how much these extra people, these new markets, will absorb—in food, in clothing, in gadgets, in housing, in services," one journalist predicted.

Historians and demographers have been hard-pressed to explain this extraordinary population bulge. It was not limited to the United States. In several other

*The boom worldwide*

industrialized nations fertility rates also soared, Australia, New Zealand, Britain, and West Germany prime among them. France and Czechoslovakia saw similar, shorter rises in the first few years after the war, but these increases seemed merely to have been a kind of catching up after the war's disruptions. Yet as the chart on page 829 indicates, the long-term trend in American fertility rates was downward, as it was in other industrialized nations. Fertility rates peaked in Australia and New Zealand in 1961, and three years later, in Great Britain and West Germany. Hence the baby boom stands as an anomaly, one that remains hard to explain.

Perhaps Americans were "making up for lost time" after the war. Rising income allowed more people to afford marriage and children. But Americans should have caught up by the early 1950s, whereas the baby boom continued. Furthermore, rising standards of living tend to reduce, not increase, birthrates. In 1950 the most industrialized and urban nations had a birthrate of 21.8 per thousand, while in less developed and less densely settled sub-Saharan Africa the

S ix-year-old Ruby knew the lessons. She was to look straight ahead—not to one side or the other—and especially not at them. She was to keep walking. Above all, she was not to look back once she'd passed, because that would encourage them. Ruby knew these things, but it was hard to keep her eyes straight. The first day of school, her parents came, along with federal marshals to keep order. And all around hundreds of angry white people were yelling things like, "You little nigger, we'll get you and kill you." Then she was within the building's quiet halls and alone with her teacher. She was the only person in class: none of the white students had come. As the days went by during that autumn of 1960, the marshals stopped walking with her but the hecklers still waited. And once in a while Ruby couldn't help looking back, trying to see if she recognized the face of one woman in particular.

Ruby's parents were not social activists. They signed their daughter up for the white school in this New Orleans neighborhood because "we thought it was for all the colored to do, and we never thought Ruby would be alone." Her father's white employer fired him; letters and phone calls threatened the family. Through it all Ruby seemed to take things in stride, though her parents worried that she was not eating well. Often she left her school lunch untouched or refused anything other than packaged food such as potato chips. It was only after a time that the problem was traced to the hecklers. "They tells me I'm going to die, and that it'll be soon. And that one lady tells me every morning I'm getting poisoned soon, when she can fix it." Ruby was convinced that the woman owned the variety store nearby and would carry out her threat by poisoning the family's food.

# Civil Rights and the Crisis of Liberalism
## 1947–1969

**Preview** *Largely walled out from the prosperity of the 1950s, African Americans and Latinos campaigned to gain the freedoms denied them through widespread racism and, in the South, a system of segregation. As the civil rights movement blossomed, young, relatively affluent baby boomers spread the revolution to other areas of American life. Their radical goals sometimes clashed with President Lyndon Johnson's liberal strategy of using federal programs to alleviate inequality and create a "Great Society."*

*Desegregation in New Orleans, 1960*

Over the course of a year, white students gradually returned to class and life settled into a new routine. By the time Ruby was 10, she had developed a remarkably clear perception of herself. "Maybe because of all the trouble going to school in the beginning I learned more about my people," she told Robert Coles, a psychologist studying children and the effects of segregation. "Maybe I would have anyway; because when you get older you see yourself and the white kids; and you find out the difference. You try to forget it, and say there is none; and if there is you won't say what it be. Then you say it's my own people, and so I can be proud of them instead of ashamed."

The new ways were not easy for white southerners either—even those who saw the need for change. One woman, a teacher from Atlanta, recalled for Robert Coles the summer 10 years earlier, when she went to New York City to take courses in education. There were black students in her dormitory, an integrated situation she was not used to. One day as she stepped from her shower, so did a black student from the nearby stall. "When I saw her I didn't know what to do," the woman recalled. "I felt sick all over, and frightened. What I remember—I'll

Overton Park Zoo in Memphis, Tennessee, was segregated like thousands of other public facilities throughout the South in the late 1950s. In the case of the zoo, Tuesdays were "colored" days, the only time when blacks could attend—except if the Fourth of July fell on a Tuesday. Then "colored" day was moved to Thursday.

never forget it—is that horrible feeling of being caught in a terrible trap, and not knowing what to do about it. . . . My sense of propriety was with me, though— miraculously—and I didn't want to hurt the woman. It wasn't her that was upsetting me. I knew that, even in that moment of sickness and panic." So she ducked back into the shower until the other woman left.

It took most of the summer before she felt comfortable eating with black students. Back in Atlanta, she told no one about her experiences. "At that time people would have thought one of two things: I was crazy (for being so upset and ashamed) or a fool who in a summer had become a dangerous 'race mixer.'" She continued to love the South and to defend its traditions of dignity, neighborliness, and honor, but she saw the need for change. And so in 1961 she volunteered to teach one of the first integrated high school classes in Atlanta. "I've never felt so useful," she concluded after two years; ". . . not just to the children but to our whole society. American as well as Southern. Those children, all of them, have given me more than I've given them."

For Americans in all walks of life, the changes that swept the United States in the 1960s were wrenching. From the schoolrooms and lunch counters of the South to the college campuses of the North, from eastern slums to western migrant labor camps, American society was in ferment.

On the face of it, such agitation seemed to be a dramatic reversal of the placid 1950s. Turbulence and change had overturned stability and consensus. Yet the events of the 1960s grew naturally out of the social conditions that preceded them. The civil rights movement was brought about not by a group of farsighted leaders in government but by ordinary folk who sought change, often despite the reluctance or even fierce opposition of people in power. After World War II, grassroots organizations like the NAACP for blacks and the American GI Forum for Latinos acted with a new determination. Both peoples sought to achieve the equality of opportunity promised by the American creed.

## THE CIVIL RIGHTS MOVEMENT

The struggle of African Americans for equality during the postwar era is filled with ironies. By the time barriers to legal segregation in the South began to fall, millions of black families were leaving for regions where discrimination was less easily challenged in court. The South they left behind was in the early stages of an economic boom. The cities to which many migrated had entered a period of decline. Yet, as if to close a circle, the rise of large black voting blocs in major cities created political pressures that forced the nation to dismantle the worst legal and institutional barriers to racial equality.

### The Changing South and African Americans

Before World War II, 80 percent of African Americans lived in the South. Most raised cotton as sharecroppers and tenant farmers. But the war created a labor shortage at home, as millions went off to fight and others to armament factories. This shortage gave cotton growers an incentive to mechanize cotton picking. In

*Mechanized cotton farming*

1950 only 5 percent of the crop was picked mechanically; by 1960 at least half was. Tenant farmers, sharecroppers, and hired labor of both races left the countryside for the city.

The national level of wages also profoundly affected southern labor. When federal minimum wage laws forced lumber or textile mills to raise their pay scales, the mills no longer expanded. In addition, steel and other industries with strong national unions and manufacturers with plants around the country set wages by national standards. That brought southern wages close to the national average by the 1960s. As the southern economy grew, what had for many years been a distinct regional economy became more diversified and more integrated into the national economy.

As wages rose and unskilled work disappeared, job opportunities for black southerners declined. Outside of cotton farming, the lumber industry provided the largest number of jobs for young black men. There, the number of black teenagers hired by lumber mills dropped 74 percent between 1950 and 1960. New high-wage jobs were reserved for white southerners, since outside industries arriving in the South made no effort to change local patterns of discrimination. So the ultimate irony appeared. As per capita income rose and industrialization brought in new jobs, black laborers poured out of the region in search of work. They arrived in cities that showed scant tolerance for racial differences and little willingness or ability to hire unskilled black labor.

## The NAACP and Civil Rights

In the postwar era the National Association for the Advancement of Colored People (NAACP) led the legal fight against racial segregation. Their hard-hitting campaign reflected the increased national political influence of African Americans as they migrated out of the South. No longer could northern politicians readily ignore the demands that black leaders made for greater equality. At first, however, the NAACP focused its campaign on the courts.

Thurgood Marshall was the association's leading attorney. Marshall had attended law school in the 1930s at Howard University in Washington. There,

*Thurgood Marshall*

the law school's dean, Charles Houston, was in the midst of revamping the school and turning out sharp, dedicated lawyers. Not only was Marshall sharp; he had the common touch as well. "Before he came along," one observer noted,

> the principal black leaders—men like Du Bois and James Weldon Johnson and Charles Houston—
> didn't talk the language of the people. They were upper-class and upper-middle-class Negroes.
> Thurgood Marshall was of the people. . . . Out in Texas or Oklahoma or down the street here in
> Washington at the Baptist church, he would make these rousing speeches that would have 'em all
> jumping out of their seats.

During the late 1930s and early 1940s Marshall toured the South (in "a little old beat-up '29 Ford"), typing out legal briefs in the backseat, trying to get teachers to sue for equal pay, and defending blacks accused of murder in a Klan-infested county in Florida. He was friendly with whites and not shy. Black citizens who had never even considered the possibility that a member of their race might win a legal battle "would come for miles, some of them on mule-back or horseback, to see 'the nigger lawyer' who stood up in white men's court-rooms."

For years NAACP lawyers supported members of the community willing to risk their jobs, property, and lives to challenge segregation. But the NAACP chose not to attack head-on the Supreme Court decision (*Plessy v. Ferguson*, 1896) that permitted "separate but equal" segregated facilities. They simply demonstrated that a black college or school might be separate, but it was hardly equal if it lacked a law school or even indoor plumbing.

## *The* Brown *Decision*

In 1950 the NAACP changed tactics: it would now try to convince the Supreme Court to overturn the separate but equal doctrine itself. Oliver Brown of Topeka, Kansas, was one of the people who provided a way. Brown was dissatisfied that his daughter Linda had to walk past an all-white school on her way to catch the bus to her segregated black school. A three-judge federal panel rejected Brown's suit because the schools in Topeka, while segregated, did meet the legal standards for equality. The NAACP appealed the case to the Supreme Court and, in 1954, won a striking decision. *Brown v. Board of Education of Topeka* overturned the lower court ruling and overthrew the doctrine of "separate but equal."

Marshall and his colleagues succeeded in part because of a change in the Court itself. The year before, President Eisenhower had appointed Earl Warren, a liberal Republican from California, as chief justice. Warren, a force- *Overturning* Plessy
ful advocate, managed to persuade even his reluctant judicial col-
leagues that segregation as defined in *Plessy* rested on an insupportable theory of racial supremacy. The Court ruled unanimously that separate facilities were inherently unequal. To keep black children segregated solely on the basis of race, it ruled, "generates a feeling of inferiority as to their status in the community that may affect their hearts and minds in a way unlikely ever to be undone."

At the time of the *Brown* decision, 21 states and the District of Columbia operated segregated school systems. All had to decide, in some way, how to comply with the new ruling. The Court allowed some leeway, handing down a second ruling in 1955 that required states to carry out desegregation "with all deliberate speed." Some border states reluctantly decided to comply, but in the Deep South, many pledged die-hard defiance. In 1956, a "Southern Manifesto" was issued by 19 U.S. senators and 81 representatives: they intended to use "all lawful means" to reestablish legalized segregation.

## Latino Civil Rights

Mexican Americans also considered school desegregation a key to their civil rights campaign. After World War II, only 1 percent of children of Mexican descent graduated from Texas high schools. Two Latino organizations, the American GI Forum and the League of United Latin American Citizens (LULAC, see page 722), supported legal challenges to the Texas system of school segregation.

In 1947 the superintendent in the town of Bastrop, Texas, had refused a request to enroll first-grader Minerva Delgado in a nearby all-white school. Civil

*Delgado and segregated schools*

rights activist Gus Garcia, a legal adviser to both LULAC and the GI Forum, helped bring a case on Minerva's behalf against the school district. But before *Delgado et al. v. Bastrop et al.* could even be tried, a Texas judge ordered an end to segregated schools beyond the first grade (the exception was based on the assumption that the youngest Mexican American children needed special classes to learn English). *Delgado* served notice that Mexicans would no longer accept second-class citizenship. It also served as a precedent in *Brown v. Board of Education* in 1954.

Two weeks before the Supreme Court made that landmark civil rights ruling, it also decided a case of great importance to Latinos. Unlike African Americans, Latinos did not face a Jim Crow system of laws imposing segregation. Throughout the Southwest the states recognized just two races: black and white. That left Mexican Americans in legal limbo. Though legally grouped with whites, by long-standing social custom they were barred from many public places, could not serve on juries, and faced widespread job discrimination. To remedy the situation, Mexican Americans had to establish themselves in the courts as a distinct class of people. Only then could they seek legal remedies.

An opportunity to make that point arose in the case of Pete Hernández, who had been convicted of murder by an all-white jury in Jackson County, Texas. As Gus Garcia and other Mexican American attorneys realized, no Mexican American had served on a Jackson jury in the previous 25 years. Taking a leaf from the tactics of Thurgood Marshall, they appealed the Hernández case before the Supreme Court, hoping to extend to Mexicans the benefits of the Fourteenth Amendment's equal protection clause.

The key to the Hernández case was ingenious but direct. Lawyers for Texas argued that because Mexicans were white, a jury without Mexicans was still a jury

*Hernández and desegregation*

of peers. Yet the courthouse in which Hernández was convicted had two men's rooms. One said simply "MEN." The other had a crude, hand-lettered sign that read "COLORED MEN" and below that in Spanish, "HOMBRES AQUÍ" [MEN HERE]. As one of Garcia's colleagues recalled, "In the jury pool, Mexicans may have been white, but when it came to nature's functions they were not." Such examples of discrimination persuaded the Supreme Court, in *Hernández v. Texas*, to throw out the state's argument. Latinos in south Texas, like African Americans across the South, were held to be a discrete group whose

Attorney Gus Garcia (left) was one of the key leaders of the American GI Forum, founded by Mexican American veterans to pursue their civil rights. He and his colleagues successfully appealed the conviction of Pete Hernández (center) before the Supreme Court in 1954.

members deserved equal protection under the law. "The Fourteenth Amendment is not directed solely against discrimination due to a 'two-class theory,' that is, based upon differences between 'white' and Negro," ruled Chief Justice Earl Warren. Warren's reasoning made it possible for Latinos to seek redress as a group rather than as individuals. After *Hernández*, the Mexican American community had both the legal basis and the leadership to broaden its attack against discrimination.

## A New Civil Rights Strategy

Neither the *Brown* nor the *Hernández* decision ended segregation, but they combined with political and economic forces to usher in a new era of southern race relations. In December 1955 Rosa Parks, a 43-year-old black civil rights activist, was riding the bus home in Montgomery, Alabama. When the driver ordered her to give up her seat for a white man, as Alabama Jim Crow laws required, she refused. Police took her to jail and eventually fined her $14.

*Rosa Parks*

Determined to overturn the law, a number of women from the NAACP, led by Jo Ann Robinson, met secretly at midnight to draft a letter of protest:

Another Negro woman has been arrested and thrown into jail because she refused to get up out of her seat on the bus and give it to a white person. . . . Until we do something to stop these arrests, they will continue. The next time it may be you, or you or you. This woman's case will come up Monday. We are, therefore, asking every Negro to stay off the buses on Monday in protest of the arrest and trial.

Thousands of copies of the letter were distributed, and the Monday boycott was such a success it was extended indefinitely. Many in the white community, in an effort to halt the unprecedented black challenge, resorted to various forms of legal and physical intimidation. No local insurance agent would insure cars used to carpool black workers. A bomb exploded in the house of the Reverend Martin Luther King Jr., the key boycott leader. Still the boycotters held out until November 23, 1956, when the Supreme Court ruled that bus segregation was illegal.

The triumph was especially sweet for Martin Luther King Jr., whose leadership in Montgomery brought him national fame. Before becoming a minister at the Dexter Street Baptist Church, King had had little personal contact with the

*Martin Luther King Jr.*  worst forms of white racism. He had grown up in the relatively affluent middle-class black community of Atlanta, Georgia, the son of one of the city's most prominent black ministers. He attended Morehouse College, an academically respected black school in Atlanta, and Crozer Theological Seminary in Philadelphia before entering the doctoral program in theology at Boston University. As a graduate student, King embraced the pacifism and nonviolence of the Indian leader Mohandas Gandhi and the activism of Christian reformers of the progressive era.

As boycott leader, it was King's responsibility to rally support without triggering violence. Since local officials were all too eager for any excuse to use force, King's nonviolent approach proved an effective strategy. "In our protest there will be no cross burnings. No white person will be taken from his home by a hooded Negro mob and brutally murdered." And he evoked the Christian and republican ideals that would become the themes of his civil rights crusade. "If we protest courageously, and yet with dignity and Christian love," he said, "when the future history books are written, somebody will have to say, 'There lived a race of people, of black people, of people who had the moral courage to stand up for their rights. And thereby they injected a new meaning into the history of civilization.'"

Indeed, the African Americans of Montgomery did set an example of moral courage that attracted national attention and rewrote the pages of American race relations. King and his colleagues were developing the tactics needed to launch a more aggressive phase of the civil rights movement.

### Little Rock and the White Backlash

The civil rights spotlight moved the following year to Little Rock, Arkansas. There, reluctant white officials had adopted a plan to integrate the schools with a most deliberate lack of speed. Nine black students were scheduled to enroll in September 1957 at the all-white Central High School. Instead, the school board urged them to stay home. Governor Orval Faubus, generally a moderate on race relations, called out the Arkansas National Guard on the excuse of maintaining order. President Eisenhower, who had refused to endorse the *Brown* decision, tacitly supported Faubus in his defiance of court-ordered integration by remarking that "you cannot change people's hearts merely by laws."

Still, the Justice Department could not let Faubus defy the federal courts. It won an injunction against the governor, but when the nine blacks returned on September 23, a mob of 1000 abusive protesters greeted them. So great was national attention to the crisis that President Eisenhower felt compelled to send in a thousand federal troops and take control of the National Guard. For one year the Guard preserved order until Faubus, in a last-ditch maneuver, closed all the schools. Only in 1959, under the pressure of another federal court ruling, did the Little Rock schools reopen and resume the plan for gradual integration.

In the face of such attitudes, King and other civil rights leaders recognized that the skirmishes of Montgomery and Little Rock were a beginning, not the end. Cultural attitudes and customs were not about to give way overnight. Black leaders were unable to achieve momentum on a national scale until 1960. Then, a series of spontaneous demonstrations by young people changed everything.

## A MOVEMENT BECOMES A CRUSADE

On January 31, 1960, Joseph McNeill got off the bus in Greensboro, North Carolina, a freshman on the way back to college. When he looked for something to eat at the lunch counter, the waitress gave the familiar reply. "We don't serve Negroes here."

It was a refrain repeated countless times and in countless places. Yet for some reason this rebuke particularly offended McNeill. He and his roommates had read a pamphlet describing the 1955 bus boycott in Montgomery, Alabama. They decided it was time to make their own protest against segregation. Proceeding the next day to the "whites only" lunch counter at a local store, they sat politely waiting for service. Rather than serve them, the manager closed the counter. Word of the action spread. A day later—Tuesday— the four students were joined by 27 more. Wednesday, the number jumped

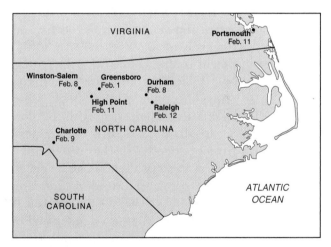

THE SPONTANEOUS SPREAD OF SIT-INS, FEBRUARY 1960
Sit-ins began in Greensboro the week of February 1. After a weekend rally, they spread to Durham and Winston-Salem on Monday, February 8. Tuesday, the demonstrations jumped to Charlotte; Thursday, High Point and Portsmouth, Virginia. A radio news broadcast in Raleigh assured white residents that black students there would not follow Greensboro's example. In response, angry black students demonstrated in Raleigh.

to 63, Thursday, to over 300. Come the weekend, 1600 students rallied to plan further action. Within two weeks, the courage of the Greensboro students had inspired 15 sit-ins across the South. By year's end, 70,000 people had demonstrated; thousands had gone to jail.

*Greensboro sit-ins*

The campaign for black civil rights gained momentum not so much by the power of national movements as through a host of individual decisions by local groups and citizens. When New Orleans schools were desegregated in 1960, young Ruby's parents had not intended to make a social statement. But once involved, they refused to back down. The students at Greensboro had not been approached by the NAACP, but acted on their own initiative.

## Riding to Freedom

Of course, organizations channeled these discontents and aspirations. But the new generation of younger activists also shaped and altered the organizations. Beginning in the 1960s, the push for desegregation moved from court actions launched by the NAACP and the Urban League to newer groups determined to take direct action. Martin Luther King's Southern Christian Leadership Conference (SCLC) hinted at newer, more direct challenges to the social order. Since organizing the Montgomery boycott, King had continued to advocate nonviolent protest: "To resist without bitterness; to be cursed and not reply; to be beaten and not hit back." A second organization, the Congress of Racial Equality (CORE), was even more prepared to force nonviolent confrontations with the segregationist system. A new group, the Student Non-Violent Coordinating Committee (SNCC, pronounced "Snick"), grew out of the Greensboro sit-in. SNCC represented the militant, younger generation of black activists, impatient with the slow pace of reform.

*The SCLC, CORE, and SNCC*

In May 1961 CORE director James Farmer led a group of black and white "freedom riders" on a bus trip from Washington to New Orleans. They intended to focus national attention on the inequality of segregated facilities. Violent southern mobs gave the freedom riders the kind of attention they feared. In South Carolina, thugs beat divinity student John Lewis as he tried to enter an all-white waiting room. Mobs in Anniston and Birmingham, Alabama, assaulted the freedom riders as police ignored the violence. One of the buses was burned.

Sensitive to the power of conservative southern Democrats, President Kennedy tried to avoid sending federal forces to protect the demonstrators. But his hopes were dashed. From a phone booth outside the bus terminal, John Doar, a Justice Department official in Montgomery, relayed the horror to Attorney General Robert Kennedy:

> Now the passengers are coming off. They're standing on a corner of the platform. Oh, there are fists; punching! A bunch of men led by a guy with a bleeding face are beating them. There are no cops. It's terrible! It's terrible! There's not a cop in sight. People are yelling. "There those niggers are! Get 'em; get 'em!" It's awful.

Vietnam's difficult terrain of mountains, jungles, and rice paddies made helicopters especially useful to move troops quickly.

it, and move on—only to be ordered back days or weeks later because the enemy had moved in again. Since success could not be measured in territory gained, the measure became the "body count": the number of Vietcong killed. *Body counts* Unable to tell who was friendly and who was hostile, GIs regularly took out their frustrations on innocent civilians. Officers counted those victims to inflate the numbers that suggested the Americans were winning.

Most Americans assumed that superior military technology could guarantee success. But technology alone could not tell friend from foe. Since the Vietcong routinely mixed with the civilian population, the chances for deadly *Technology and* error increased. Bombs of napalm (jellied gasoline) and white *its limits* phosphorus rained liquid fire from the skies, coating everything from village huts to the flesh of fleeing humans. To clear jungle canopies and expose Vietcong camps and roads, American planes spread more than 100 million pounds of defoliants. The forests destroyed totaled more than one-third of South Vietnam's timberlands—an area approximately the size of the state of Rhode Island. The long-term health and ecological effects were severe.

The miracles of modern technology also made the war more demanding. Helicopters could whisk GIs from one firefight to another or from the front lines of a steaming jungle back to Saigon. There they could catch overnight flights to

Hawaii or the mainland. The sudden shift from the hell of war to civilian peace could be wrenching. "I fell asleep [on the plane to New York] and woke up yelling, probably a nightmare," recalled John Kerry, a candidate for president in 2004. "The other passengers moved away from me—a reaction I noticed more and more in the months ahead. . . . The feeling toward [Vietnam vets] was, 'Stay away—don't contaminate us with whatever you've brought back from Vietnam.'"

By 1967 the war was costing more than $2 billion a month. The United States dropped more bombs on Vietnam than it had during all of World War II. After one air attack on a Communist-held provincial capital, American troops walked into the smoldering ruins. "We had to destroy the town in order to save it," an officer explained. As the human and material costs of the war increased, that statement stuck in the minds of many observers. What sense was there in a war that saved people by burning their homes?

## The War at Home

As the war dragged on, such questions provoked anguished debate among Americans, especially on college campuses. Faculty members held "teach-ins" to explain the
*Teach-ins* | issues to concerned students. Scholars familiar with Southeast Asia questioned every major assumption the president used to justify escalation. The United States and South Vietnam had brought on the war, they charged, by violating the Geneva Accords of 1954. Moreover, the Vietcong were an indigenous rebel force with legitimate grievances against Saigon's corrupt government. The war was a civil war among the Vietnamese, not an effort by Soviet or Chinese Communists to conquer Southeast Asia, as Eisenhower, Kennedy, and Johnson had claimed.

By 1966 national leaders had similarly divided into opposing camps of "hawks" and "doves." The hawks argued that America must win in Vietnam to save Southeast Asia from communism, to preserve the nation's prestige, and to protect the lives of
*Hawks and doves* | American soldiers fighting the war. Most Americans supported those views. The doves were nonetheless a prominent minority. African Americans as a group were far less likely than white Americans to support the war. Some resented the diversion of resources from the cities to the war effort. Many black Americans' heightened sense of racial consciousness led them to identify with the Vietnamese people. Martin Luther King, SNCC, and CORE all opposed the war. Heavyweight boxing champion Muhammad Ali, a black Muslim, refused on religious grounds to serve in the army, even though the decision cost him his title.

By 1967 college students and faculty turned out in crowds to express their outrage: "Hey, hey, LBJ, how many kids have you killed today?" Over 300,000
*Antiwar demonstrations* | people demonstrated in April 1967 in New York City. Some college protesters even burned their draft cards in defiance of federal law. In the fall more violent protests erupted as antiwar radicals stormed a draft induction center in Oakland, California. The next day 55,000 protesters ringed the Pentagon in Washington. Again, mass arrests followed.

As protests flared, key moderates became increasingly convinced the United States could not win the war. Senator William Fulbright of Arkansas was among them. Having helped President Johnson push the Tonkin Gulf Resolution through the Senate, Fulbright now held hearings sharply critical of American policy.

Defense Secretary Robert McNamara became the most dramatic defector. For years the statistically minded secretary struggled to quantify the success of the war effort. By 1967 McNamara had become skeptical. If Americans were killing 300,000 Vietnamese, enemy forces should be shrinking. *McNamara loses faith* Instead, intelligence estimates indicated that North Vietnamese infiltration had risen from 35,000 a year in 1965 to 150,000 in 1967. McNamara came to have deep moral qualms about continuing the war indefinitely. "The picture of the world's greatest superpower killing or seriously injuring 1,000 non-combatants a week, while trying to pound a tiny, backward nation into submission on an issue whose merits are hotly disputed, is not a pretty one," he advised. When Johnson, who did not want to be remembered as the first American leader who lost a war, continued to side with the hawks, McNamara resigned.

As the war's cost soared to more than $50 billion a year, it fueled a rising inflation. Medicare, education, housing, and other Great Society programs raised the domestic budget sharply too. Through it all Johnson refused to raise taxes, even though wages and prices rose rapidly. From 1965 to 1970 inflation jumped from about 2 percent to around 4 percent. The economy was headed for trouble.

## THE UNRAVELING

Almost all the forces dividing America seemed to converge in 1968. Until January of that year, most Americans had reason to believe General Westmoreland's estimate of the war. There was, he suggested, "light at the end of the tunnel." Johnson and his advisers, whatever their private doubts, in public painted an optimistic picture. With such optimism radiating from Washington, few Americans were prepared for the events of the night of January 30, 1968.

### Tet Offensive

As the South Vietnamese began their celebration of Tet, the Vietnamese lunar New Year, Vietcong guerrillas launched a series of concerted attacks. Assault targets included Saigon's major airport, the South Vietnamese presidential palace, and Hue, the ancient Vietnamese imperial capital. Most unnerving to Americans, 19 Vietcong commandos blasted a hole in the American embassy compound in Saigon and stormed in. They fought in the courtyard until all 19 lay dead. One reporter, stunned by the carnage, compared the courtyard to a butcher shop.

Tet must rank as one of the great American intelligence failures, on a par with the failure to anticipate Japan's attack on Pearl Harbor or China's intervention in the Korean War. For nearly half a year the North Vietnamese had lured American troops away from Vietnam's cities into pitched battles at remote outposts. As American forces dispersed, the Vietcong infiltrated major population areas of Saigon and the Mekong Delta region. A few audacious VC, disguised as South Vietnamese soldiers, even hitched rides on American jeeps and trucks. Though surprised by the Tet offensive, American and South Vietnamese troops repulsed most of the assaults. General Westmoreland announced that the Vietcong's "well-laid plans went afoul."

In a narrow military sense, Westmoreland was right. The enemy had been driven back, sustaining perhaps 40,000 deaths. Only 1100 American and

*Stalemate* | 2300 South Vietnamese soldiers had been killed. But Americans at home received quite another message. Tet created a "credibility gap" between the administration's optimistic reports and the war's harsh reality. The president had repeatedly claimed that the Vietcong were on their last legs. Yet as Ho Chi Minh had coolly informed the French after World War II, "You can kill ten of my men for every one I kill of yours . . . even at those odds, you will lose and I will win." Respected CBS news anchor Walter Cronkite drew a gloomy lesson of Tet for his national audience: "To say that we are mired in stalemate seems the only realistic, yet unsatisfactory, conclusion."

The Tet offensive sobered Lyndon Johnson as well as his new secretary of defense, Clark Clifford. Clifford was a Johnson loyalist and a stalwart believer in

*Clark Clifford* | the war. But as he reviewed the American position in Vietnam, he could get no satisfactory answers from the Joint Chiefs of Staff, who had requested an additional 206,000 troops. "How long would it take to succeed in Vietnam?" Clifford recalled asking them:

> They didn't know. How many more troops would it take? They couldn't say. Were two hundred thousand the answer? They weren't sure. Might they need more? Yes, they might need more. Could the enemy build up [their own troop strength] in exchange? Probably. So what was the plan to win the war? Well, the only plan was that attrition would wear out the Communists, and they would have had enough. Was there any indication that we've reached that point? No, there wasn't.

Clifford decided to build a case for deescalation. To review policy, he formed a panel of "wise men," respected pillars of the cold war establishment. The war could not be won, they concluded, and Johnson should seek a negotiated settlement.

Meanwhile, the antiwar forces had found a political champion in Senator Eugene McCarthy from Wisconsin. McCarthy was something of a maverick

*"Clean for Gene"* | who wrote poetry in his spare time. He announced that no matter how long the odds, he intended to challenge Lyndon Johnson in the 1968 Democratic primaries. Idealistic college students got haircuts and shaves in order to look "clean for Gene" as they campaigned for McCarthy in New Hampshire. Johnson won the primary, but his margin was so slim (300 votes) that it amounted to a stunning defeat. To the anger of McCarthy supporters, Robert Kennedy, John Kennedy's younger brother, quickly announced his own antiwar candidacy.

"I've got to get me a peace proposal," the president told Clifford. White House speechwriters finally put together an announcement that bombing raids against North Vietnam would be halted, at least partially, in hopes that peace talks could begin. They were still trying to write an ending when *LBJ withdraws* Johnson told them, "Don't worry; I may have a little ending of my own." On March 31 he supplied it, announcing: "I have concluded that I should not permit the presidency to become involved in the partisan divisions that are developing in this political year. . . . Accordingly I shall not seek, and I will not accept, the nomination of my party for another term as your president."

The announcement shocked nearly everyone. The Vietnam War had pulled down one of the savviest, most effective politicians of the era. North Vietnam responded to the speech by sending delegates to a peace conference in Paris, where negotiations quickly bogged down. And American attention soon focused on the chaotic situation at home, where all the turbulence, discontent, and violence of the 1960s seemed to be coming together.

## The Shocks of 1968

On April 4 Martin Luther King Jr. traveled to Memphis to support striking sanitation workers. He was relaxing on the balcony of his motel when James Earl Ray, an escaped convict, fatally shot him with a sniper's rifle. King's campaign of nonviolence was overshadowed by the violent reaction to his *King and Kennedy* murder. Riots broke out in ghetto areas of the nation's capital; by the *killed* end of the week, disturbances rocked 125 more neighborhoods across the country. Then on the evening of June 5, a disgruntled Arab nationalist, Sirhan Sirhan, assassinated Robert Kennedy. Running in opposition to the war, Kennedy had just won a crucial primary victory in California.

The deaths of King and Kennedy pained Americans deeply. In their own ways, both men exemplified the liberal tradition, which reached its high-water mark in the 1960s. King had retained his faith in a Christian theology of nonviolence. He sought reform for the poor of all races without resorting to the language of the fist and the gun. Robert Kennedy had come to reject the war his brother had supported, and he seemed genuinely to sympathize with the poor and minorities. At the same time, he was popular among traditional white ethnics and blue-collar workers. Would the liberal political tradition have flourished longer if these two charismatic figures had survived the turbulence of the 1960s?

Once violence silenced the clearest liberal voices, it became clear that Democrats would choose Hubert Humphrey to replace Lyndon Johnson. Humphrey had begun his career as a progressive and a strong supporter of civil rights. But as Johnson's loyal vice president, he was intimately associated with the war and the old-style liberal reforms that could never satisfy radicals. The Republicans had chosen Richard Nixon, a traditional anti-Communist (now reborn as the "new," more moderate Nixon). As much as radicals disliked Johnson, they truly abhorred Nixon, "new" or old.

Chicago, where the Democrats met for their convention, was the fiefdom of Mayor Richard Daley, long a symbol of machine politics and backroom deals.

*A tumultuous Democratic convention*

Daley was determined that the dissatisfied radicals who poured into Chicago would not disrupt "his" Democratic convention. The radicals were equally determined that they would. For a week the police skirmished with demonstrators: police clubs, riot gear, and tear gas versus the demonstrators' eggs, rocks, and balloons filled with paint and urine. When Daley refused to allow a peaceful march past the convention site, the radicals marched anyway, and then the police, with the mayor's blessing, turned on the crowd in what a federal commission later labeled a police riot. In one pitched battle, many officers took off their badges and waded into the crowd, nightsticks swinging, chanting "Kill, kill, kill." Reporters, medics, and other innocent bystanders were injured; at 3 A.M. police invaded candidate Eugene McCarthy's hotel headquarters and pulled some of his assistants from their beds.

With feelings running so high, President Johnson did not dare appear at his own party's convention. Theodore White, a veteran journalist covering the assemblage, scribbled his verdict in a notebook as police chased hippies down Michigan Avenue. "The Democrats are finished," he wrote.

## Revolutionary Clashes Worldwide

The clashes in Chicago seemed homegrown, but they took place against the backdrop of a global surge in radical, often violent, student upheavals. In 1966 Chinese students were in the vanguard of Mao Zedong's Red Guards, formed to enforce a Cultural Revolution that sought to purge China of all bourgeois cultural influences. Although that revolution persecuted millions among the educated classes and left the country in economic shambles, Mao became a hero to radicals outside China. Radicals also lionized other revolutionaries who took up arms: Fidel Castro and Che Guevara in Cuba and Ho Chi Minh in Vietnam.

Radical targets varied. In Italy students denounced the official Marxism of the Soviet Union and Italian Communist party. French students at the Sorbonne in Paris rebelled against the university's efforts to discipline political activists. Students in Czechoslovakia launched a full-scale rebellion, known as Prague Spring, against the Soviet domination of their nation until Soviet tanks crushed the uprising. Though their agenda varied from country to country, student revolutionaries reached near unanimity on one point: they condemned the American war in Vietnam.

## Whose Silent Majority?

Radicals were not the only Americans alienated from the political system in 1968. Governor George Wallace of Alabama sensed the frustration among the "average man on the street, this man in the textile mill, this man in the steel mill, this barber, this beautician, the policeman on the beat." In running for president, Wallace sought the support of blue-collar workers and the lower middle classes.

Wallace had first come to national attention in 1963, when he barred integration of the University of Alabama. Briefly, he pursued the Democratic presidential nomination in 1964. For the race in 1968 he formed his own American Independent party with the hawkish General Curtis | *George Wallace*
LeMay as his running mate. (LeMay spoke belligerently of bombing North Vietnam "back to the stone age.") Wallace's enemies were the "liberals, intellectuals, and long hairs [who] have run this country for too long."

Wallace did not simply appeal to law and order, militarism, and white backlash; he was too sharp for that. With roots in southern Populism, he called for federal job-training programs, stronger unemployment benefits, national health insurance, a higher minimum wage, and a further extension of union rights. Polls in September revealed that many Robert Kennedy voters had shifted to Wallace. A quarter of all union members backed him.

In fact, Wallace had tapped true discontent among the working class. Many blue-collar workers despised hippies and peace marchers yet wanted the United States out of Vietnam. And they were suspicious, as Wallace was, of the upper-class "establishment" that held power. "We can't understand how all those rich kids—the kids with beards from the suburbs—how they got off when my son had to go over there and maybe get his head shot off," one blue-collar parent complained.

Richard Nixon too sought the votes of these traditionally Democratic voters, especially disaffected southern Democrats. The Republicans, of course, had been reviled by the Populists of old as representatives of the money power, | *Nixon and the silent*
monopoly, and the old-line establishment. But Nixon himself had | *majority*
modest roots. His parents owned a general store in Whittier, California, where he had worked to help the family out. At Duke Law School he was so pinched for funds he lived in an abandoned toolshed. His dogged hard work earned him the somewhat dubious nickname of "iron pants." If ever there had been a candidate who could claim to be self-made, it was Nixon. And he well understood the disdain ordinary laborers felt for "kids with beards from the suburbs" who seemed always to be insisting, protesting, *demanding*. Nixon believed himself a representative of the "silent majority," as he later described it, not a vocal minority.

He thus set two fundamental requirements for his campaign: to distance himself from President Johnson on Vietnam and to turn Wallace's "average Americans" into a Republican majority. The Vietnam issue was delicate, because Nixon had generally supported the president's efforts to end the war. He told his aide Richard Whalen, "I've come to the conclusion that there's no way to win the war. But we can't say that, of course. In fact, we have to seem to say the opposite." For most of his campaign he hinted that he had a secret plan to end the war but steadfastly refused to disclose it. He pledged only to find an honorable solution. As for Wallace's followers, Nixon promised to promote "law and order" while cracking down on "pot," pornography, protest, and permissiveness.

Hubert Humphrey had the more daunting task of surmounting the ruins of the Chicago convention. All through September antiwar protesters dogged his campaign *The 1968 election* with "Dump the Hump" posters. Although Humphrey picked up steam late in the campaign (partly by cautiously criticizing Johnson's war policies), the last-minute surge was not enough. Nixon captured 43.4 percent of the popular vote to 42.7 percent for Humphrey and 13.5 percent for Wallace. Some voters had punished the Democrats not just for the war but also for supporting civil rights. The majority of the American electorate had turned its back on liberal reform.

## THE NIXON ERA

In Richard Nixon, Americans had elected two men to the presidency. On the public side, he appeared as the traditional small-town conservative who cherished individual initiative, chamber-of-commerce capitalism, Fourth of July patriotism, and middle-class Victorian values. The private Nixon was a troubled man. His language among intimates was caustic and profane. He waxed bitter toward those he saw as enemies. Never a natural public speaker, he was physically rather awkward—a White House aide once found toothmarks on a "child-proof" aspirin cap the president had been unable to pry open. But Nixon seemed to search out challenges— "crises" to face and conquer.

### Vietnamization—and Cambodia

A settlement of the Vietnam "crisis" thus became one of Nixon's first priorities. He found a congenial ally in National Security Advisor Henry Kissinger. *Henry Kissinger* Kissinger, an intensely ambitious Harvard academic, shared with the new president a global vision of foreign affairs. Like Nixon, Kissinger had a tendency to pursue his ends secretly, circumventing the traditional channels of government such as the Department of State.

Nixon and Kissinger wanted to bring the war to an end but insisted on "peace with honor." That meant leaving a pro-American South Vietnamese government behind. The strategy Nixon adopted was "Vietnamization," which involved a carrot and a stick. On its own initiative, the United States began gradually withdrawing troops as a way to advance the peace talks in Paris. The burden of fighting would shift to the South Vietnamese army. Critics likened this strategy to little more than "changing the color of the corpses." All the same, as the media shifted their focus to the peace talks, the public had the impression the war was winding down.

Using the stick, President Nixon hoped to drive the North Vietnamese into negotiating peace on American terms. Quite consciously, he traded on his reputation as a cold warrior who would stop at nothing. As he explained to his chief of staff, Robert Haldeman,

> I call it the Madman Theory, Bob. I want the North Vietnamese to believe that I've reached the point where I might do anything to stop the war. We'll just slip the word to them that, "for God's sake, you know Nixon is obsessed about Communists. We can't restrain him when he's angry—and he has his hand on the nuclear button"—and Ho Chi Minh himself will be in Paris in two days begging for peace.

To underline his point, in the spring of 1969 Nixon launched a series of bombing attacks against North Vietnamese supply depots inside neighboring Cambodia. Johnson had refused to widen the war in this manner, fearing domestic reaction. Nixon simply kept the raids secret.

The North Vietnamese refused to cave in to the bombing. Ho Chi Minh's death in 1969 changed nothing. His successors continued to reject any offer that did not end with complete American withdrawal and an abandonment of the *Cambodian invasion* South Vietnamese military government. Once again Nixon turned up the heat. Over the opposition of his secretaries of defense and state, he ordered American troops into Cambodia to wipe out North Vietnamese bases there. On April 30, 1970, he announced the "incursion" of American troops, proclaiming that he would not allow "the world's most powerful nation" to act "like a pitiful helpless giant."

The wave of protests that followed included the fatal clashes between authorities and students at Kent State and Jackson State as well as another march on Washington by 100,000 protesters. Even Congress was upset enough to repeal the Tonkin Gulf Resolution, a symbolic rejection of Nixon's invasion. After two months American troops left Cambodia, having achieved little.

## Fighting a No-Win War

For a time, Vietnamization seemed to be working. As more American troops went home, the South Vietnamese forces improved modestly. But for American GIs still in the country, morale became a serious problem. Obviously the United States was gradually pulling out its forces. After Tet, it was clear there would be no victory. So why were the "grunts" in the field still being asked to put their lives on the line? The anger surfaced increasingly in incidents known as "fragging," in which GIs threw fragmentation grenades at officers who pursued the war too aggressively.

Nor could the army isolate itself from the trends dividing American society. Just as young Americans "turned on" to marijuana and hallucinogens, so soldiers in Vietnam used drugs. Black GIs brought with them the black power issues from home. One white medic noticed that Muhammad Ali's refusal to be drafted *GIs and black power* caused the blacks in his unit "to question why they were fighting the Honky's war against other Third World people. I saw very interesting relationships happening between your quick-talking, sharp-witted Northern blacks and your kind of easygoing, laid-back Southern blacks. . . . Many Southern blacks changed their entire point of view by the end of their tour and went home extremely angry."

The problem with morale only underlined the dilemma facing President Nixon. As the troops became restive, domestic opposition to the war grew and the North Vietnamese refused to yield.

## The Move toward Détente

Despite Nixon's insistence on "peace with honor," Vietnam was not a war he had chosen to fight. And both Kissinger and Nixon recognized that by 1968 the United States no longer had the resources to exercise unchallenged dominance around the globe. The Soviet Union remained their prime concern. Ever since Khrushchev had backed down at the Cuban missile crisis in 1962, the Soviets had steadily expanded their nuclear arsenal. Furthermore, the growing economies of Japan and Western Europe challenged American leadership in world trade. Continued instability in Southeast Asia, the Middle East, and other Third World areas threatened the strength of the non-Communist bloc. Thus Vietnam diverted valuable military and economic resources from more critical areas.

In what the White House labeled the "Nixon Doctrine," the United States would shift some of the military burden for containment to other allies: Japan in the Pacific, the shah of Iran in the Middle East, Zaire in central Africa, and the apartheid government in South Africa. Over the next six years American foreign military sales jumped from $1.8 billion to $15.2 billion. At the same time, Nixon and Kissinger looked for new ways to contain Soviet power not simply by the traditional threat of arms but through negotiations to ease tensions. This policy was named, from the French, détente.

*Nixon Doctrine*

Kissinger and Nixon looked to create "linkages" among many cold war issues. For example, the arms race burdened the Soviet economy. To ease that pressure, they would make concessions to the Soviets on nuclear arms. The Soviets in return would have to limit their arms buildup and, in a linked concession, pressure North Vietnam to negotiate an end to the war. To add leverage, Nixon and Kissinger developed a "China card." The United States would stop treating Communist Mao Zedong as an archenemy and, instead, open diplomatic relations with the Chinese. Fearful of a more powerful China, the Soviets would be more conciliatory toward the United States.

*The China card*

It took a shrewd diplomatist to sense an opportunity to shift traditional cold war policy. Conservative Republicans denounced the idea of recognizing Mao's government, even after 20 years. They believed that the Soviets responded only to force and that they were united with China in a monolithic Communist conspiracy. Now Richard Nixon, the man who had built a career fighting communism, made overtures to the Communist powers. Kissinger slipped off to China on a secret mission (he was nursing a stomachache, his aides assured the press) and then reappeared having arranged a trip to China for the president. During that visit in early 1972, Nixon pledged to normalize relations, a move the public enthusiastically welcomed.

Richard Nixon's trip to China included this visit to the Great Wall. Perhaps precisely because he had been so staunch an anti-Communist, Nixon appreciated the enormous departure his trip marked in Sino-American relations.

A new overture to the Soviet Union followed the China trip. Eager to acquire American grain and technology, Soviet premier Leonid Brezhnev invited Nixon to Moscow in May 1972. Nixon saw in the Soviet market a chance to ease American trade deficits by selling surplus wheat to the Russians. But *SALT I* the meeting's most important result was the signing of the first Strategic Arms Limitation Treaty (SALT I). In the agreement, both sides pledged not to develop a new system of antiballistic missiles (ABMs), which would have accelerated the costly arms race. And they agreed to limit the number of intercontinental ballistic missiles (ICBMs) each side would deploy.

Americans were pleased at the prospect of lower cold war tensions. But it was not clear that the linkages achieved in Moscow and Beijing would help extricate the United States from Vietnam.

## THE NEW IDENTITY POLITICS

During the 1968 campaign Richard Nixon noticed a placard carried by a hopeful voter: "Bring Us Together." That phrase became his campaign theme. Yet given the deep divisions of the 1960s, unity was elusive. George Wallace had attracted voters fed up with protest and social unrest. If Nixon could add those discontented southerners and blue-collar workers to his traditional Republican base, his enlarged "silent majority" would guarantee his return to the White House in 1972.

To the silent majority, it seemed that the consensus of the 1950s was being ripped apart. In their campaign for civil rights, many African Americans had insisted that because they were not treated equally, they belonged to a separate, oppressed group. In the 1960s this sense of separate identity blossomed as African Americans took pride in proclaiming black power or even embracing, like the Nation of Islam, a doctrine of separation. Latinos, American Indians, Asian Americans, feminists, and gay Americans all applied a similar critique to their own social situations. Out of an increased pride in distinctive values and group identities came a new political and social assertiveness. Where earlier activists had sought assimilation into American society, these movements looked to establish their identities in opposition to the prevailing culture.

## Latino Activism

Part of the increased visibility of minorities resulted from a new wave of immigration from Mexico and Puerto Rico after World War II. Many Cubans also arrived after the 1959 revolution that brought Castro to power. Historical, cultural, and ethnic differences among the three major Latino groups made it difficult to develop a common political agenda. Still, some activists did seek a greater unity.

After World War II a weak island economy and the lure of prosperity on the mainland brought more than a million Puerto Ricans into New York City. As citizens of the United States, they could move freely to the mainland and back home again. That dual consciousness discouraged many from establishing deep roots stateside. Equally important, the newcomers were startled to discover that, whatever their status at home, on the mainland they were subject to racial discrimination and often segregated into urban slums. In 1964 about half of all recent immigrants lived below the poverty level. Light-skinned migrants escaped those conditions by blending into the middle class as "Latin Americans." The Puerto Rican community thereby lost some of the leadership it needed to assert its political rights.

*Puerto Rican migration*

Still, during the 1960s, the urban barrios gained greater political consciousness as groups like Aspira adopted the strategies of civil rights activists and organizations like the Black and Puerto Rican Caucus created links with other minority groups. The Cubans who arrived in the United States after 1959—some 350,000 over the course of the decade—forged fewer ties with other Latinos. Most settled around Miami. An unusually large number came from Cuba's professional, business, and government class and were racially white and politically conservative.

Mexican Americans, on the other hand, constituted the largest segment of the Latino population. Until the 1940s most were farmers and farm laborers in Texas, New Mexico, and California. But during the 1950s, the process of mechanization had affected them, just as it had black southerners. By 1969 about 85 percent of

Living conditions were harshest for Mexican Americans among agricultural workers. Cesar Chavez mobilized migrant workers into the United Farm Workers Union. His demands for recognition of the union by California growers led to a bitter strike (in Spanish, *huelga*) in 1966.

Mexican Americans had settled in cities. With urbanization came a slow improvement of the range and quality of jobs they held. A body of skilled workers, middle-class professionals, and entrepreneurs emerged.

Yet Mexican agricultural workers continued to face harsh working conditions and meager wages. Attempts to unionize faltered partly because workers migrated from job to job and strikebreakers were easily imported. In 1963 a soft-spoken but determined farmworker, Cesar Chavez, recruited fellow organizers Gil Padilla and Dolores Huerta to make another attempt. Their efforts over the next several years led to the formation of the United Farm Workers labor union.

*Cesar Chavez and the UFW*

Chavez, like Martin Luther King, proclaimed an ethic of nonviolence. Also like King, he was guided by a deep religious faith (Roman Catholicism in the case of Chavez and most Mexican American farmworkers). During a strike of Mexican and Filipino grape workers in the summer of 1966, Chavez led a 250-mile march on Sacramento ("Dr. King had been very successful" with such marches, he noted). Seeking additional leverage, the union looked to use consumers as an economic weapon by organizing a boycott of grapes in supermarkets across the nation. Combined with a 24-day hunger strike by Chavez—a technique borrowed from Gandhi—the boycott forced growers to negotiate contracts with the UFW beginning in 1970.

Just as Martin Luther King found his nonviolent approach challenged by more radical activists, Chavez saw a new generation of Mexican Americans take

*Chicano activists*

up a more aggressive brand of identity politics. Many began calling themselves Chicanos. Like blacks, Chicanos saw themselves as a people whose culture had been taken from them. Their heritage had been rejected, their labor exploited, and their opportunity for advancement denied. In Denver, Rodolfo "Corky" Gonzales laid out a blueprint for a separatist Chicano society, with public housing set aside for Chicanos and the development of economically independent barrios where a new cultural pride could flourish. "We are Bronze People with a Bronze Culture," declared Gonzales. "We are a Nation. We are a union of free pueblos. We are Aztlán."

The new activism came from both college and high school students. Like others of the baby-boom generation, Mexican Americans attended college in increasing numbers. In addition, Lyndon Johnson's Educational Opportunity Programs, part of the War on Poverty, brought thousands more Latinos onto college campuses, especially in California. By 1968 some 50 student Mexican American organizations had sprung up on college campuses. In Los Angeles that year thousands of Chicano high school students walked out to protest substandard educational conditions. Two years later the new ethnic militancy led to the formation of La Raza Unida (The Race United). This third-party movement sought to gain power in communities in which Chicanos were a majority and to extract concessions from the Democrats and Republicans. The more militant "Brown Berets" adopted the paramilitary tactics and radical rhetoric of the Black Panthers.

## The Choices of American Indians

Like African Americans and Latinos, Indians began to protest; yet the unique situation of Native Americans (as many had begun to call themselves) set them apart

*Termination and urbanization*

from other minorities. A largely hostile white culture had in past centuries sought to either exterminate or assimilate American Indians. Ironically, the growing strength of the civil rights movement created another threat to Indian tribal identities. Liberals came to see the reservations not as oases of Indian culture but as rural ghettos. During the 1950s they joined conservatives eager to repeal the New Deal and western state politicians eyeing tribal resources to adopt a policy of "termination." The Bureau of Indian Affairs would reduce federal services, gradually sell off tribal lands, and push Indians into the "mainstream" of American life. Although most full-blooded Indians objected to the policy, some people of mixed blood and Indians already assimilated into white society supported the move. The resulting relocation of approximately 35,000 Indians accelerated a shift from rural areas to cities. The urban Indian population, which had been barely 30,000 in 1940, reached more than 300,000 by the 1970s.

The social activism of the 1960s inspired Indian leaders to shape a new political agenda. In 1968 urban activists in Minneapolis created AIM, the American Indian Movement. A year later like-minded Indians living around San Francisco

Bay formed Indians of All Tribes. Because the Bureau of Indian Affairs refused to address the problems of urban Indians, more militant members of the organization dramatized their dissatisfaction by seizing the abandoned federal prison on Alcatraz Island in San Francisco Bay. The Alcatraz action inspired calls for a national Pan-Indian rights movement. *American Indian Movement*

Then in 1973, AIM organizers Russell Means and Dennis Banks led a dramatic takeover of a trading post at Wounded Knee, on a Sioux reservation in South Dakota. Ever since white cavalry gunned down over a hundred Sioux in 1890 (page 505), Wounded Knee had symbolized for Indians the betrayal of white promises and the bankruptcy of reservation policy. *Occupation of Wounded Knee* Even more, Wounded Knee now demonstrated the problems that Indian activists faced. When federal officers surrounded the trading post, militants discovered that other Indians did not support their tactics and were forced to leave. A Pan-Indian movement was difficult to achieve when so many tribes were determined to go their own ways, as distinct, self-regulating communities. During the 1970s more than 100 different organizations were formed to unite various tribes pursuing political and legal agendas at the local, state, and federal levels.

### Asian Americans

The 1965 Immigration Reform Act had set out to end quotas that discriminated against non-European immigration. In doing so it led to a rapid increase in the numbers of immigrants from Asia. Asians who in 1960 constituted less than one percent of the American population (about a million people) were by 1985 two percent (about five million). This new wave included many middle-class professionals, a lower percentage of Japanese, and far more newcomers from Southeast and South Asia. Earlier civil rights reforms had swept away the legal barriers to full citizenship that had once stigmatized Asians.

Many Americans saw these new immigrants as "model minorities." They possessed skills in high demand, worked hard, were often Christian, and seldom protested. The 1970 census showed Japanese and Chinese Americans with incomes well above the median for white Americans. Such statistics hid fault lines within communities. Although many professionals assimilated into the American mainstream, agricultural laborers and sweatshop workers remained trapped in poverty. And no matter how much Anglos praised their industry, Asian Americans still wore what one sociologist defined as a "racial uniform." They were nonwhites in a white society. *The myth of the model minority*

Few Americans were aware of Asian involvement in identity politics. That was in part because the large majority of Asian Americans lived in just three states—Hawaii, California, and New York. Further, Asian Americans were less likely to join the era's vocal protests. Nonetheless, Asian students did join with African Americans, Chicanos, and Native Americans to advocate a "third world revolution" against the white establishment. Asian students, too, wanted a curriculum that recognized their histories and cultures.

voluntary restraints on prices and wages while seeking to restore the strength of the dollar in international trade. But even before the president's economic remedies could be tried, OPEC raised the price of oil again. Interest rates shot up to almost 20 percent. Such high rates struck hard at American consumers addicted to buying on credit. Mortgage money disappeared. With the Federal Reserve raising interest rates to dampen inflation, the recession grew worse. As the economy slumped, so did Carter's political future. At the same time he found himself bedeviled by crises abroad.

### Leadership through Idealism

Carter approached foreign policy with a set of ambitious yet reasonable goals. Like Nixon and Kissinger, he accepted the fact that in a postcolonial world, American influence could not be heavy-handed. Unlike Nixon and Kissinger, Carter believed that a knee-jerk fear of Soviet ambition had led Americans to support too many right-wing dictators simply because they claimed to be anti-Communist. Carter reasserted the nation's moral purpose by giving a higher priority to preserving human rights.

*Human rights*

Though foreign policy "realists" often jeered at this idealistic policy, it did make a difference. At least one Argentinian Nobel Peace Prize winner, Adolfo Pérez Esquivel, claimed he owed his life to it. So did hundreds of others in countries like the Philippines, South Korea, Argentina, and Chile, where dissidents were routinely tortured and murdered. The Carter administration exerted economic pressures to promote more humane policies.

Debate over American influence in the Third World soon focused on the Panama Canal, long a symbol of American intervention in Latin America. Most Americans were under the impression that the United States owned the canal—or if it didn't, at least deserved to. Senator S. I. Hayakawa of California spoke for defenders of the American imperial tradition when he joked, "It's ours. We stole it fair and square." In reality the United States held sovereignty over a 10-mile-wide strip called the Canal Zone and administered the canal under a perpetual lease. Since the 1960s Panamanians had resented, and sometimes rioted against, the American presence. Secretary of State Vance believed conciliation would reduce anti-American sentiment in the region. He convinced Carter in 1977 to sign treaties that would return the canal to Panama by 1999. The United States did reserve the right to defend and use the waterway.

*Panama Canal*

From 1979 on, however, it was not Vance but National Security Advisor Zbigniew Brzezinski who dominated foreign policy. Brzezinski preferred a hard-line anti-Communist approach, even in Latin America. Unrest troubled the region's struggling nations, especially Nicaragua. Its dictator, Anastasio Somoza, proved so corrupt that he alienated even the normally conservative propertied classes. The United States, at Brzezinski's urging,

*Brzezinski in charge*

continued to support Somoza, but with cooperation from Nicaragua's business leaders, the Marxist Sandinistas toppled him. They then rejected American aid in favor of a nonaligned status and closer ties to Cuba. Hard-line American anti-Communists grew especially alarmed when the Sandinistas began supplying leftist rebels in neighboring El Salvador. To contain the threat, Carter agreed to assist the brutal right-wing dictatorship in El Salvador while encouraging the overthrow of the leftist government in Nicaragua.

### Saving Détente

The United States was not the only superpower with a flagging economy and problems in the Third World. The Soviet Union struggled with an aging leadership and an economy that produced few consumer goods. Even though the Russians led the world in oil production, income from rising oil prices was drained off by an inefficient economy. Support for impoverished allies in Eastern Europe, Cuba, and Vietnam and attempts to extend Soviet influence elsewhere proved costly.

Economic weakness made the Soviets receptive to greater cooperation with the United States. But in the matter of détente, Carter again found himself pulled in two directions. Brzezinski was eager to revive Henry Kissinger's *A revived China card* "China card" strategy, the hope of playing off the two Communist superpowers against each other. A visit to Beijing by Brzezinski smoothed the way for the United States to extend formal recognition to China in 1979. Meanwhile, Carter met Russian premier Brezhnev at a summit meeting in Vienna the same *SALT II* year. The talks produced an arms control treaty building on the one negotiated by Ford and Kissinger—SALT II—to limit nuclear launchers and missiles with multiple warheads. Still, neither the Americans nor the Soviets would agree to scrap key weapons systems, and conservatives in the Senate blocked ratification of the treaty.

Such hostility to détente encouraged Carter to adopt Brzezinski's harder line. Confrontation and a military buildup replaced the Vance policy of negotiation and accommodation. The president expanded the defense budget, built American bases in the Persian Gulf region, and sent aid to anti-Communist dictators whatever their record on human rights. The Soviet Union responded with similar hostility.

### The Middle East: Hope and Hostages

What the unstable Balkans were to Europe before World War I, the Middle East promised to be for the superpowers in the 1970s and 1980s. Oil and the Soviets' nearby southern border gave the area its geopolitical importance. The United States had strong ties to oil-rich Saudi Arabia, a commitment to the survival of Israel, and a determination to prevent the Soviet Union from extending its influence into the area. That commitment was tested each time war broke out between Israel and its Arab neighbors, in 1948, 1956, 1967, and 1973.

Preservation of the peace was one key to American policy. As a result, Americans were greatly encouraged when President Anwar Sadat of Egypt made an unprecedented trip to Israel to meet with Prime Minister Menachem Begin. To encourage the peace process, Carter invited Begin and Sadat to Camp David in September 1978. After 13 difficult days of heated debate, Carter brought the two archrivals to an agreement. Israel agreed to withdraw from the Sinai peninsula, which it had occupied since defeating Egypt in 1967; Carter compensated Israel by offering $3 billion in military aid. Begin and Sadat shared a Nobel Peace Prize that might just as fairly have gone to Carter.

*Camp David Accords*

The shah of Iran, with his American-equipped military forces, was another key to American hopes for stability in the Middle East. A strong Iran, after all, blocked Soviet access to the Persian Gulf and its oil. But in the autumn of 1978, the shah's regime was challenged by Iranian Islamic fundamentalists. They objected to the Western influences flooding their country, especially the tens of thousands of American advisers. Brzezinski urged Carter to support the shah with troops if necessary; Vance recommended meetings with the revolutionary leaders, distance from the shah, and military restraint.

*The Iranian Revolution*

Carter waffled between the two approaches. He encouraged the shah to use force but refused any American participation. When the shah's regime collapsed

Jimmy Carter brought together Israeli prime minister Menachem Begin (right) and Egypt's Anwar Sadat (left). Together at Camp David they hammered out a "Framework for Peace in the Middle East."

in February 1979, fundamentalists established an Islamic republic, led by a religious leader, the Ayatollah Ruhollah Khomeini. The new government was particularly outraged when Carter admitted the ailing shah to the United States for cancer treatment. In November student revolutionaries stormed the American embassy in Teheran, occupying it and taking 53 hostages. In the face of this insult the United States seemed helpless to act. Would Muslim Shiite fundamentalists spread their revolution to neighboring Arab states? Worse yet, would the Soviets prey upon a weakened Iran?

In fact, the Soviets were equally worried that religious zeal might spread to their own restless minorities, especially to Muslims within their borders.

*U.S.S.R. invasion of Afghanistan*

In December 1979 Leonid Brezhnev ordered Soviet troops to subdue anti-Communist Muslim guerrillas in neighboring Afghanistan. President Carter condemned the invasion, but the actions he took to protest were largely symbolic, especially the decision to withdraw the American team from the 1980 Olympic games in Moscow. And he announced a Carter Doctrine: the United States would intervene unilaterally if the Soviet Union threatened American interests in the Persian Gulf.

## A President Held Hostage

Even more than the 53 Americans in Teheran, the president himself seemed to have been taken hostage by events. His ratings in national polls sank to record lows (77 percent negative). Carter responded by reviving the cold war rhetoric of the 1950s and accelerating the development of nuclear weapons. But where the CIA in 1953 had successfully overthrown an Iranian government, an airborne rescue mission launched in 1980 ended in disaster. Eight marines died when two helicopters and a plane collided in Iran's central desert. Cyrus Vance, a lonely voice of moderation, finally resigned.

By 1980 the United States was mired in what Carter himself described as "a crisis of confidence." Turmoil in Vietnam, Central America, and the Middle East

*Crisis of confidence*

produced a nightmare of waning American power. Economic dislocations at home revived fears of a depression. None of these problems had begun with Jimmy Carter. The inflationary cycle and declining American productivity had their roots in the Vietnam era. And ironically, America's declining influence abroad reflected long-term success in bringing economic growth to Europe and the Pacific Rim.

In that sense, Carter's failure was largely symbolic. But the uneasiness of the late 1970s reflected a widespread disillusionment with liberal social programs, and even with pragmatic "engineers" like Carter. Had the government become a drag on the American dream? Tom Wolfe's "Me Generation" seemed to be rejecting Carter's appeals to sacrifice. It turned instead to promoters of self-help therapy, fundamentalist defenders of the faith, and staunch conservatives who promised both spiritual and material renewal for the 1980s.

# chapter summary

In the aftermath of Vietnam, Watergate, an economic recession, and the energy crisis, the United States found itself mired in what President Jimmy Carter described as a "crisis of confidence."

- Despite the fragmentation of the left in the 1970s, consumer advocates and environmentalists kept alive the spirit of reform.

- Unpopular domestic political strategies like impoundment and the secret activities of the plumbers made Richard Nixon vulnerable to political attacks that followed revelations of White House involvement in the Watergate break-in and subsequent cover-up.

- Following a Senate investigation and the discovery of White House tapes containing the smoking gun linking the president to the cover-up, Richard Nixon resigned rather than face inevitable impeachment.

- As the nation's first unelected president, Gerald Ford inherited an office weakened by scandal, by the determination of Congress to rein in an "imperial presidency," and by Ford's own decision to pardon Richard Nixon for his role in Watergate.

- Under President Ford, Henry Kissinger became the real power in Washington as he pursued peace between Israel and its Arab neighbors, détente with the Soviet Union, and an easing of oil prices that burdened the American economy with high inflation.

- Jimmy Carter, unable to end the recession at home, pursued success abroad with a human rights policy and the negotiation of the Camp David Accords between Israel and Egypt—only to have the Soviet invasion of Afghanistan and the Iranian hostage crisis undermine his foreign policy.

# interactive learning

The Primary Source Investigator CD-ROM offers the following materials related to this chapter:

- Interactive map: **The Middle East** (M28)

- A collection of primary sources exploring the age of limits that emerged in the wake of the Watergate scandal and the Vietnam War.

Sources include Nixon's letter of resignation, a cartoon about the scandal, and an excerpt from Ford's speech after being sworn in. Other sources explore a new awareness of environmental problems, including the founding legislation of the Environmental Protection Agency.

For quizzes and a variety of interactive resources, visit the book's Online Learning Center at www.mhhe.com/davidsonconcise4.

# significant events

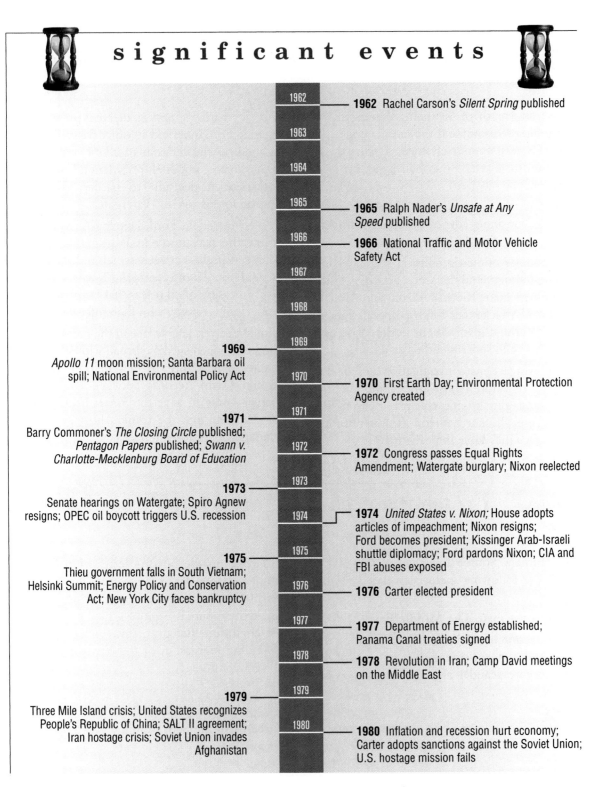

**1962** Rachel Carson's *Silent Spring* published

1962
1963
1964
1965
1966
1967
1968
1969

**1965** Ralph Nader's *Unsafe at Any Speed* published

**1966** National Traffic and Motor Vehicle Safety Act

**1969**
*Apollo 11* moon mission; Santa Barbara oil spill; National Environmental Policy Act

1970

**1970** First Earth Day; Environmental Protection Agency created

**1971**
Barry Commoner's *The Closing Circle* published; *Pentagon Papers* published; *Swann v. Charlotte-Mecklenburg Board of Education*

1971
1972

**1972** Congress passes Equal Rights Amendment; Watergate burglary; Nixon reelected

**1973**
Senate hearings on Watergate; Spiro Agnew resigns; OPEC oil boycott triggers U.S. recession

1973
1974

**1974** *United States v. Nixon;* House adopts articles of impeachment; Nixon resigns; Ford becomes president; Kissinger Arab-Israeli shuttle diplomacy; Ford pardons Nixon; CIA and FBI abuses exposed

**1975**
Thieu government falls in South Vietnam; Helsinki Summit; Energy Policy and Conservation Act; New York City faces bankruptcy

1975
1976

**1976** Carter elected president

1977

**1977** Department of Energy established; Panama Canal treaties signed

1978

**1978** Revolution in Iran; Camp David meetings on the Middle East

**1979**
Three Mile Island crisis; United States recognizes People's Republic of China; SALT II agreement; Iran hostage crisis; Soviet Union invades Afghanistan

1979
1980

**1980** Inflation and recession hurt economy; Carter adopts sanctions against the Soviet Union; U.S. hostage mission fails

I n the early 1970s San Diego city officials looked out at a downtown that was growing seedier each year, as stores and shoppers fled to more than a dozen suburban malls ringing the city. Nor was San Diego's experience unusual. Across the nation many downtown retail centers were disintegrating, becoming virtual ghost towns at the close of the business day. But San Diego found a way to bounce back. The city launched a $3 billion redevelopment plan, calling for a convention center, a marina, hotels, and apartment complexes.

# The Conservative Challenge
## 1980–1992

At the core of the plan was Horton Plaza, a mall designed to look like a quaint Italian hill town. When it opened in 1985, stucco facades and Renaissance arches lured customers to upscale stores like Banana Republic, jewelers, and sporting goods shops. Jugglers wandered the mall's thoroughfares, while guitarists serenaded passersby. Horton Plaza soon ranked just behind the zoo and Sea World as one of San Diego's prime tourist attractions.

**Preview** *As frustration mounted over an era of limits, conservatives pressed to restore traditional religious and social values. Ronald Reagan led the charge with a program to reduce government regulations, raise military spending, and lower taxes. A newly conservative Supreme Court set limits on government intervention in the areas of civil rights, abortion, and the separation of church and state. But as the national debt rose sharply and a recession deepened, voters reined in the conservative movement.*

For all its extravagance, Horton Plaza was hardly an innovation. The first enclosed mall, Southdale Center, had been completed nearly 20 years earlier in Edina, Minnesota, near Minneapolis. With chilling winters and 100 days a year of rain, shopping conditions in Edina were hardly ideal. Southdale provided an alternative: a climate-controlled marketplace where shoppers could browse or get a bite to eat without dodging cars. At first, retailers had worried that customers who couldn't drive by or park in front of their stores wouldn't stop and shop. But the success of the new malls quickly dispelled such fears. By 1985, when Horton Plaza opened, there were more shopping centers nationwide (25,000) than either school districts or hospitals.

With their soaring atriums and splashing fountains, malls became for consumers the cathedrals of American material culture. Shopping on Sunday rivaled churchgoing as the weekly family ritual. Where American youth culture centered on high schools in the 1950s and on college campuses in the 1960s, in the 1970s and 1980s it had gravitated toward mall fast-food stores and video amusement arcades. Older people in search of moderate exercise discovered that the controlled climate was ideal for "mall walking." Malls even had their counterculture: "mall rats" who "hung out" and survived by shoplifting.

*Malls as the symbol of an age*

Malls as cathedrals of consumption reflected a society turning away from social protest to more private paths of personal expression. Some people expressed themselves through material consumption. Others adopted a spiritual direction. Evangelical religions offered them redemption in the prospect of being "born again." Still others preached a return to traditional family values. Personal responsibility, private charity, and volunteerism, they believed, should replace the intrusive modern welfare state. Along less orthodox paths, the "human potential movement" offered yoga, transcendental meditation, Rolfing, and a host of other techniques for discovering inner fulfillment.

So it was not surprising, perhaps, that in 1980 Ronald Reagan chose to evoke Puritan John Winthrop's seventeenth-century vision of an American "city on a hill"—that city Winthrop hoped would inspire the rest of the world. The image carried strong religious overtones: of a Puritan Christian commonwealth that was both well ordered and moral. Reagan's vision, of course, had been updated. It embraced nineteenth-century ideals of "manifest destiny." (America should "stand tall," he insisted, as the world's number one military power.) And Reagan affirmed the laissez-faire ideals of the late nineteenth century, encouraging citizens to promote the public good through the pursuit of private wealth. "Government is not the solution to our problem," he asserted. "Government is the problem."

Critics contended that Reagan was no more likely than the Puritans to succeed with his revolution. History, they argued, had shown that private enterprise was unable to prevent or regulate the environmental damage caused by acid rain, oil spills, or toxic waste dumps. Furthermore, a severely limited federal government would prove unable to cope with declining schools, urban violence, or the AIDS epidemic. To many liberals the Reagan agenda amounted to a flight from public responsibility into a fantasy world no more authentic than the Italian hill town nestled in downtown San Diego. John Winthrop's austere vision risked being transformed into a city on a hill with climate control, where the proprietors of Muzak-filled walkways banished all problems beyond the gates of the parking lots.

Throughout the 1980s Americans gravitated between the born-again vision of the conservative revolution and more secular, centrist politics. Ronald Reagan and his successor, George Bush, both championed the causes of social conservatives, such as the right to life, the call to allow prayer in public schools, and an end to affirmative action. But in an increasingly secular society, those social causes received less attention than Reagan's economic and military agenda: to cut taxes and increase military spending.

## THE CONSERVATIVE REBELLION

In 1964 billboards for conservative candidate Barry Goldwater had proclaimed across America: "In Your Heart You Know He's Right." Beneath one of the billboards an unknown Democratic wag unfurled his own banner: "Yes—Extreme Right." Most citizens voted with the wag, perceiving Goldwater's platform as too conservative, too extreme, too dangerous for the times.

By 1980 rising prices, energy shortages, and similar economic uncertainties fed a growing opposition to a liberal agenda. Hard-pressed workers resented increased competition from minorities, especially those supported by affirmative action quotas. Citizens resisted the demands for higher taxes to support social welfare spending. The family, too, seemed *Issues of the 1970s and 1980s* under siege, as divorce rates and births to single mothers soared. Sexually explicit media, an outspoken gay rights movement, and the availability of legal abortions struck many conservatives as part of a wholesale assault on decency. Increasingly the political agenda was determined by those who wanted to restore a strong family, traditional religious values, patriotism, and limited government.

The United States was not the only nation to experience a resurgence of political conservatism, nationalism, and religious revival. The year before Ronald Reagan became president, Great Britain chose Margaret Thatcher as its first woman prime minister. Under her conservative leadership, *The conservative tide worldwide* "Thatcherism" became a synonym for cutting social programs, downsizing government, and privatizing state-controlled industries. Even within the Soviet bloc rumblings could be felt as more citizens turned to religion after becoming disillusioned with the communist system. In China, the successors to revolutionary leader Mao Zedong begin to introduce market capitalism into the economy during the 1980s.

In some regions the conservative revival reflected a questioning of the liberal values that emerged from Europe's eighteenth-century Enlightenment. That era's faith in the rational spirit of science and technology had dominated Western thought for 200 years. Increasingly, fundamentalists were demanding that traditional religion become the center of public life. The student radicals in Iran who seized the American embassy feared that Western ideas would destroy their Islamic faith. In Israel, religious conservatives became a political force as they, too, resisted secular trends in their society. And as we shall see, leadership of the Roman Catholic Church fell to Pope John Paul II, who rejected calls to liberalize doctrine on such issues as birth control, abortion, and the acceptance of female priests.

## Born Again

At one center of the conservative rebellion was the call for a revival of religion. It came most insistently from white Protestant evangelicals. Fundamentalist Protestants had since the 1920s increasingly separated themselves from the older, more liberal denominations. In the decades after World War II their membership grew dramatically—anywhere from 400 to 700 percent, compared with less than 90 percent for mainline denominations. By the 1980s they had become a significant third force in Christian America, after Roman Catholics and traditional Protestants. The election of Jimmy Carter, himself a born-again Christian, reflected their newfound visibility.

*Evangelicals*

Like fundamentalists of the 1920s who battled evolution at the Scopes trial (pages 702–703), evangelicals of the 1980s resisted the trend toward more secular ideas, especially in education. Some pressed states and the federal government to adopt a "school prayer" amendment allowing officially sanctioned prayer in classrooms. Others urged the teaching of "creationism" as an alternative to Darwinian evolution. Frustrated with public schools, some parents created private Christian academies to insulate their children from the influence of "secular humanism." Fundamentalists applied this term to the modernist notions of a materially determined world in which all truths are relative and in which circumstances rather than moral precepts determine ethical behavior.

Although evangelicals condemned the secularism of the modern media, they used broadcast technology to sell their message. Cable and satellite broadcasting brought televangelists to national audiences. The Reverend Pat Robertson introduced his 700 Club over the Christian Broadcast Network from Virginia Beach, Virginia. Another 700 Club regular, Jim Bakker, launched a spinoff program called the Praise the Lord Club—PTL for short. Within a few years PTL had the largest audience of any daily show in the world.

*The Moral Majority*

But it was the Reverend Jerry Falwell, spiritual leader of the Thomas Road Baptist Church in Lynchburg, Virginia, who first made the step from religious to political activism. In 1979 Falwell formed the Moral Majority, Inc., an organization to attract campaign contributions and examine candidates around the country on issues important to Christians. In the 1980 election the Moral Majority sent out more than a billion pieces of mail in an attempt to unseat liberals in Congress.

## The Catholic Conscience

American Catholics faced their own decisions about the lines between religion and politics. In the 1960s Catholic social activism had been inspired by the Vatican II church council (see page 880). The reforms of Vatican II invited greater participation by ordinary church members and encouraged closer ties to other Christians and to Jews. Disturbed by these currents, Catholic conservatives

*Catholic conservatism*

Many conservative Christians adopted the militant style of 1960s radicals to protest issues like abortion. Here they clash with pro-choice demonstrators outside Faneuil Hall in Boston.

found support for their views when the magnetic John Paul II became pope in 1979. Pope John Paul reined in the modern trends inspired by Vatican II. The pope resisted a wider role for women and stiffened church policy against birth control. That put him at odds on such issues with a majority of American Catholics.

Though conservative Catholics and Protestant evangelicals were sometimes wary of one another, they shared certain views. Both groups lobbied the government to provide federal aid to parochial schools and fundamentalist academies. And on the issue of abortion, Pope John Paul reaffirmed the church's teaching that all life begins at conception, so that any abortion amounts to the murder of the unborn. Evangelicals, long suspicious of the power of secular technology and science, attacked abortion as another instance in which science had upset the natural moral order of life.

## The Media as Battleground

Both evangelicals and political conservatives viewed the mass media as an establishment that was politically liberal and morally permissive. Certainly by the 1980s

American popular culture had come to portray sex and violence more explicitly, as well as to treat openly such sensitive social issues as racial and ethnic prejudice. Because television played such a prominent role in American life, it became a battleground where conservatives and liberals clashed.

The conflict could be seen in producer Norman Lear's situation comedy *All in the Family*, introduced in 1971. Its main character, Archie Bunker, was a blue-collar father seething with fears and prejudices. Americans were supposed to laugh at Archie's outrageous references to "Hebes," "Spics," and "Commie crapola," but many in the audience were not laughing. Some minority leaders charged that by making Archie lovable, the show legitimized the very prejudices it seemed to attack.

*Topical sitcoms*

*M\*A\*S\*H*, a popular sitcom launched in 1972, was more clearly liberal in tone. Although set in a medical unit during the Korean War, its real inspiration was the growing disillusionment with the Vietnam War. *M\*A\*S\*H* twitted bureaucracy, authority, bigotry, and snobbery. For conservatives, the antiauthoritarian bent of such shows seemed to spill over into newspaper and television reporting. On the other hand, feminists and minority groups complained that television portrayed them through stereotypes, if it portrayed them at all.

Perhaps inevitably, the wars for the soul of prime time spilled into the political arena. Norman Lear, Archie Bunker's creator, went on to form People for the American Way, a lobbying group that campaigned for more diversity in American life and attempted to counteract pressure groups like the Moral Majority. Conservatives, looking to make a stronger political impact, in 1980 embraced an amiable former movie actor who had long preached their gospel.

## The Election of 1980

Jimmy Carter might be born again, but Ronald Reagan spoke the language of true conservatism. "I think there is a hunger in this land for a spiritual revival, a return to a belief in moral absolutes," he told his followers. Such a commitment to fundamentalist articles of faith was more important than the fact that Reagan actually had no church affiliation and seldom attended services.

The defection of many evangelical Protestants meant that the Democrats had lost the majority of white southern voters. The Republican Party became the home of most conservatives. When undecided voters saw Reagan as the candidate with the power to lead, the race turned into a landslide. Equally impressive, Republicans won their first majority in the Senate since 1954. They cited the margin of victory as a popular mandate for a conservative agenda. "It's a fed-up vote," countered Carter's political analyst Patrick Caddell. Still, the New Deal Democratic coalition had been splintered. Although Reagan's majority was greatest among white voters over 45 who earned more than $50,000 a year, he made striking gains among union workers, southern white Protestants, Catholics, and Jews.

*Reagan supporters*

## PRIME TIME WITH RONALD REAGAN

Ronald Reagan brought the bright lights of Hollywood to Washington. His managers staged one of the most extravagant inaugurations in the nation's history, and Nancy Reagan became the most fashion-conscious first lady since Jackie Kennedy. Yet poverty rates rose, too, as the gulf between rich and poor widened.

### The Great Communicator

Ronald Reagan brought a simple message to Washington. "It is time to reawaken the industrial giant, to get government back within its means, and to lighten our punitive tax burden," he announced on inauguration day. Commentators began referring to the president as "the great communicator," because of his mastery of television and radio.

Reagan used his skill as an actor to obscure contradictions between his rhetoric and reality. With his jaunty wave and jutting jaw, he projected physical vitality and the charismatic good looks of John Kennedy. Yet at age 69, he was the oldest president to take office, and none since Calvin Coolidge had slept so soundly or so much. Reagan had begun his political life as a New Deal Democrat, but by the 1950s he had become an ardent anti-Communist Republican. In 1966 he began two terms as governor of California with a promise to pare down government programs and balance budgets. In fact, spending jumped sharply during his term in office.

*The Reagan style*

Similar inconsistencies marked Reagan's leadership as president. Outsiders applauded his "hands-off" management: Reagan set the tone and direction, letting his advisers take care of the details. On the other hand, many within the administration, like Secretary of the Treasury Donald Regan, were shocked to find the new president remarkably ignorant about and uninterested in important matters of policy. "The Presidential mind was not cluttered with facts," Regan lamented. Yet Reagan's cheerful ability to deflect responsibility for mistakes earned him a reputation as the "Teflon president," since no criticism seemed to stick.

In addition, Reagan was blessed by remarkably good luck. The deaths of three aging Soviet leaders, from 1982 through 1985, compounded that country's economic weakness and reduced Russian influence abroad.

As president, Ronald Reagan often evoked the image of a cowboy hero. Yet the Reagan revolution in practice led to sharply increased federal spending and federal deficits.

Members of the OPEC oil cartel quarreled among themselves, exceeded production quotas, and thus forced oil prices lower. That removed a major inflationary pressure on the American economy. And when a would-be assassin shot the president in the chest on March 30, 1981, the wound was not life threatening. His courage in the face of danger impressed even his critics.

*Reagan's fortune*

## The Reagan Agenda

Reagan's primary goal as president was to weaken big government. His budget would become an instrument to reduce bureaucracy and to undermine activist federal agencies in the areas of civil rights, environmental and consumer protection, poverty programs, the arts, and education. In essence, the new president wanted to return government to the size and responsibility it possessed in the 1950s before the reforms of Kennedy and Johnson.

At the heart of the Reagan revolution was a commitment to "supply-side" economics, a program that in many ways resembled the trickle-down economic theories of the Harding-Coolidge era. Supply-side theorists argued that high taxes and government regulation stifled enterprising businesses and economic expansion. The key to revival lay in a large tax cut, a politically popular though economically controversial proposal. Such a cut threatened to reduce revenues and increase an already large deficit. Not so, argued economist Arthur Laffer. The economy would be so stimulated that tax revenues would actually rise, even though the tax rate was cut.

*Supply-side economics*

The president's second target for action was inflation, the "silent thief" that had burdened the economy during the Ford-Carter years. Reagan resisted certain traditional cures for inflation: tight money, high interest rates, and wage and price controls. He preferred two approaches unpopular with Democrats: higher unemployment and weakened unions to reduce labor costs.

Lower public spending, a favorite Republican remedy, might have seemed one likely method of reducing inflation. But the third element of Reagan's agenda was a sharp rise in military outlays: a total of $1.5 trillion to be spent over five years. The president wanted to create an American military presence with the strength to act unilaterally anywhere in the world. This was a remarkably expansive goal: Presidents Nixon, Ford, and Carter had all looked to scale back American commitments, either through détente or by shifting burdens to allies in Western Europe. Reagan recognized no such limits. And rather than emphasize either nuclear defense or conventional weapons, Defense Secretary Caspar Weinberger successfully lobbied Congress for both.

*Military buildup*

## The Reagan Revolution in Practice

The administration soon found an opportunity to "hang tough" when air traffic controllers went on strike, claiming that understaffing and long working hours threatened air safety. Because the controllers were civil service employees, the strike

## The President's Budget Director Discusses the Reagan Revolution

Like all revolutionaries, we wanted to get our program out of the fringe cell group where it had been hatched and into the mainstream. . . . So we pitched it in tones that were music to every politician's ears. We highlighted the easy part—the giant tax cut. The side of the doctrine that had to do with giving to the electorate, not taking from it.

My blueprint for sweeping, wrenching change in national economic governance would have hurt millions of people in the short run. . . . It meant complete elimination of subsidies to farmers and businesses. It required an immediate end to welfare for the able-bodied poor. It meant no right to draw more from the Social Security fund than retirees had actually contributed, which was a lot less than most were currently getting.

These principles everywhere clashed with the political reality. Over the decades, the politicians had lured tens of millions of citizens into milking . . . cows, food stamps, Social Security, the Veterans Hospitals, and much more. . . . For the Reagan Revolution to add up, they had to be cut off. The blueprint was thus riddled with the hardship and unfairness of unexpected change. Only an iron chancellor would have tried to make it stick. Ronald Reagan wasn't that by a long shot.

Even [after I criticized the administration publicly] my private exoneration at lunch in the Oval Office by a fatherly Ronald Reagan showed why a Reagan Revolution couldn't happen. He should have been roaring mad like the others—about either the bad publicity or my admission of a flawed economic plan.

But Ronald Reagan proved to be too gentle and sentimental for that. He always went for the hard luck stories. He sees the plight of real people before anything else. Despite his right-wing image, his ideology and philosophy always takes a back seat when he learns that some individual human being might be hurt.

That's also why he couldn't lead a real revolution in American economic policy.

Source: Selected excerpts from David Stockman, *The Triumph of Politics: Why the Reagan Revolution Failed* (New York, Harper-Collins, 1986), pp. 9–12. Copyright © 1986 by David A. Stockman. Reprinted by permission of HarperCollins Publishers, Inc.

was technically illegal. Without addressing the merits of the controllers' complaints, Reagan simply fired them for violating their contract. The defeat of the air controllers signaled a broader attack on unions. When a recession enveloped the nation, major corporations wrung substantial concessions on wages and work rules. Organized labor witnessed a steady decline in membership and political power.

The president's war against government regulation took special aim at environmental rules. Conservatives, especially in the West, complained that preservation of wild lands restricted mining, cattle grazing, farming, and real estate development—all powerful western industries. Reagan appointed westerner James Watt, an outspoken champion of this "sagebrush rebellion," to head the

*Environmental controversy*

Interior Department. Watt, in turn, devoted himself to opening federal lands for private development, including lumbering and offshore oil drilling. After offending Indians, African Americans, Jews, and the handicapped as well as many Republicans, Watt was forced to resign in 1983, but administration policies remained unchanged.

Most important to conservatives, Reagan pushed his supply-side legislation through Congress during his first year in office. The Economic Recovery Tax Act

*Tax cuts*

provided a 25 percent across-the-board reduction for all taxpayers. The president hailed it, along with recently passed budget cuts, as an antidote to "big government's" addiction to spending and a stimulus to the economy.

### The Impact of Reaganomics

The impact of Reagan's supply-side economics (nicknamed "Reaganomics" by the press) was mixed. By 1982 a recession had pushed unemployment above 10 percent. But the following year marked the beginning of an economic expansion that lasted through Reagan's presidency, thanks in part to increased federal spending and lowered interest rates. Then, too, falling energy costs and improved industrial productivity contributed to renewed prosperity.

Even so, the Reagan tax cut was one of a series of policy changes that brought about a substantial transfer of wealth from poor and lower-middle-class workers to the upper middle classes and the rich. For the wealthiest Americans, the 1980s were the best of times. The top 1 percent commanded a greater share of the nation's wealth (37 percent) than at any time since 1929. Their earnings averaged about $560,000 per year, as opposed to $20,000 or less for the bottom 40 percent. What counterculture hippies were to the 1960s, high-salaried "yuppies" (young, upwardly mobile professionals) were to the 1980s.

On the surface, the buoyant job market seemed to signal a more general prosperity as well. By the end of Reagan's second term, more than 14.5 million jobs

*Factors encouraging the transfer of wealth*

had been created for Americans. Yet these jobs were spread unevenly by region, class, and gender. More than 2 million were in finance, insurance, real estate, and law, all services used more by the wealthy than the poor. In highly paid Wall Street jobs—those involving financial services—more than 70 percent went to white males, only 2 percent to African Americans. New employment for women was concentrated in the areas of health, education, social services, and government, where approximately 3 million jobs opened, most dependent on government support. New jobs for the poor (more than 3 million) were largely restricted to minimum-wage, part-time, dead-end jobs in hotels, fast-food restaurants, and retail stores.

Because Reaganomics preached the virtues of free markets and free trade, the administration did little to discourage high-wage blue-collar jobs from flowing to cheap labor markets in Mexico and Asia. Furthermore, Reagan aimed the sharpest

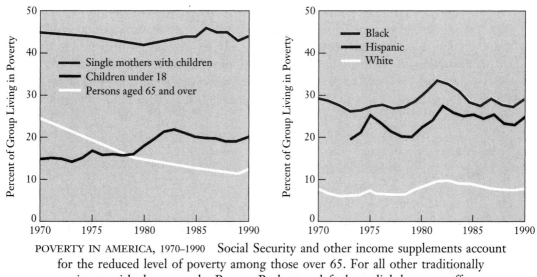

POVERTY IN AMERICA, 1970–1990   Social Security and other income supplements account for the reduced level of poverty among those over 65. For all other traditionally impoverished groups, the Reagan-Bush years left them slightly worse off.

edge of his budget axe at programs for the poor: food stamps, Aid to Families with Dependent Children, Medicaid, school lunches, and housing assistance. The programs trimmed back least were middle-class entitlements like Social Security and Medicare. Those programs affected Americans over 65 who, as social activist Michael Harrington observed, as a general class "are not now, and for a long time have not been, poor."

As more income flowed toward the wealthy and as jobs were lost to overseas competitors, the percentage of Americans below the poverty level rose from 11.7 percent in 1980 to 15 percent by 1982. There the level remained through the Bush administration. Reagan's successful war on inflation, which dropped to less than 2 percent by 1986, contributed to a rise in unemployment. Even during the recovery, the figure dropped below 6 percent of the workforce only in the months before the 1988 election. (In contrast, the highest rate under Jimmy Carter was 5.9 percent.) Thus the Reagan boom was an uneven one, despite continued economic expansion.

## The Military Buildup

Reagan described the Soviet Union as an "evil empire." To defeat communism he supported a sharp rise in military spending. Outlays rose from less than $200 billion under Presidents Ford and Carter to almost $300 billion in 1985. The largest increases were for expensive strategic nuclear weapons systems.

Huge costs were not the only source of criticism. When Reagan's tough-talking defense planners spoke about "winning" a nuclear exchange, they revived the antinuclear peace movement across Europe and America.

*Star Wars*

The bishops of the American Catholic Church announced their opposition to nuclear war. Scientists warned that the debris in the atmosphere from an atomic exchange might create a "nuclear winter" fatal to all life on Earth. Other critics singled out runaway Pentagon costs. One of the president's favorite programs was the Strategic Defense Initiative, or SDI. Nicknamed "Star Wars" after a popular science fiction film, it spent billions of dollars trying to establish a space-based missile defense system. Most scientists contended that the project was as fantastic as the movie.

The combination of massive defense spending and substantial tax cuts left the federal government awash in red ink. Annual deficits climbed to more than $200 billion. Furthermore, with interest rates so high, the value of the dol-

*Growing deficits*

lar soared on world markets, pushing up the cost of American exports. As American exports declined, imports from abroad (such as Japanese autos) competed more successfully in America. The United States, a creditor nation since World War I, had by 1986 become the world's largest debtor.

The high cost of the Reagan agenda would come to haunt his conservative successors. For the time being, however, Ronald Reagan's popularity was unassailable. In 1984 he easily won a second term, gaining 59 percent of the vote in his run against Democrat Walter Mondale of Minnesota. (Mondale's running mate, Geraldine Ferraro of New York, was the first female candidate for the vice presidency.) Reagan remained his sunny, unflappable self. "The 75-year-old man is hitting home runs," rhapsodized *Time* magazine at the beginning of his second term. In reality, Reagan would soon be tested by a series of crises arising out of his aggressive foreign policy.

## STANDING TALL IN A CHAOTIC WORLD

Reagan brought to the conduct of foreign policy the same moral ardor that shaped his approach to domestic affairs. Reagan wanted the United States to stand tall: to adopt a policy that drew bold, clear lines as a means of restoring American prestige and defeating communism. But turmoil abroad demonstrated that bold policies were not always easy to carry out. And because the president remained indifferent to most day-to-day details, he was at the mercy of those officials who put into effect his aggressive anti-Communist foreign policy.

### Terrorism in the Middle East

In the Middle East, the passions of religious factions suggested how difficult it was to impose order, even for a superpower like the United States. In 1982 President Reagan sent American marines into Lebanon as part of a European-American peacekeeping force. His hope was to bring a measure of stability to a region torn by civil war. But in trying to mediate between Lebanon's religious and political sects, the American "peacekeepers" found themselves dragged into the fighting.

Terrorists retaliated by blowing up a U.S. Marine barracks in October 1983, killing 241. The president then ordered American troops withdrawn.

Just as hostage taking in Iran had frustrated the Carter administration, terrorist attacks by Islamic fundamentalists bedeviled Reagan. In 1985 terrorists took new hostages in Lebanon; others hijacked American airline flights, killed an American hostage on a Mediterranean cruise ship, and bombed a nightclub where American soldiers met in West Germany. Reagan's public response was always uncompromising: "Let terrorists beware: . . . our policy will be one of swift and effective retribution."

But against whom should the United States seek revenge? American intelligence agencies found it extremely difficult to collect reliable information on the many political and terrorist factions. In 1986 the president sent bombers to attack targets in Libya, whose anti-American leader, Colonel Muammar Qaddafi, had links to terrorists. But so did the more powerful states of Syria and Iran.

## Mounting Frustrations in Central America

At first, a policy of standing tall seemed easier closer to home. In 1983, the administration launched an invasion of Grenada, a small Caribbean island whose government was challenged by pro-Castro revolutionaries. U.S. forces crushed the rebels, but the invasion was largely a symbolic gesture. *Grenada invasion*

More frustrating to the president, Nicaragua's left-wing Sandinista government had established increasingly close ties with Cuba. In 1981 Reagan extended aid to the antigovernment Contra forces. When critics warned that Nicaragua could become another Vietnam, the president countered that the Contras were freedom fighters, battling in the spirit of America's Founding Fathers. Although the Contras did include some moderate democrats and disillusioned Sandinistas, most of their leaders had served the brutal Somoza dictatorship that the Sandinistas had toppled in 1979.

Reagan might have sought a negotiated settlement between the Contras and the Sandinistas; instead he allowed the CIA to help the Contras mine Nicaraguan harbors in hopes of overthrowing the Sandinistas outright. When some of the mines exploded, damaging foreign ships in violation of international law, even some conservative senators were dismayed. Congress adopted an amendment sponsored by Representative Edward Boland of Massachusetts that explicitly forbade the CIA or "any other agency or entity involved in intelligence activities" to spend money to support the Contras "directly or indirectly." The president signed the Boland Amendment, though only grudgingly. *Boland Amendment*

## The Iran-Contra Connection

Thus by mid-1985 Reagan policy makers felt two major frustrations. First, Congress had forbidden support of the Nicaraguan Contras. Second, Iranian-backed terrorists continued to hold American hostages in Lebanon. In the summer of 1985 a course of events was set in motion that linked these two issues.

The president let his advisers know that he wanted to find a way to free the remaining hostages. National Security Advisor Robert McFarlane suggested opening a channel to "moderate factions" in the Iranian government. If the United States sold Iran a few weapons, the grateful moderates might use their influence in Lebanon to free the hostages. But an agreement to exchange arms for hostages would violate the president's often-repeated vow never to pay ransom to terrorists. Still, Reagan apparently approved the initiative. Over the following year, four secret arms shipments were made to Iran. One hostage was set free.

Reagan's secretaries of state and defense both had strongly opposed the trading of arms for hostages. "This is almost too absurd to comment on," *Arms for hostage deals* | Defense Secretary Weinberger protested. Thus, both men were kept largely uninformed of the arms shipments, precisely because their opposition was well known. McFarlane's successor, Admiral John Poindexter, had the president sign a secret intelligence "finding" that allowed him and his associates to pursue their mission without informing Congress or even the secretaries of defense and state. Since the president ignored the details of foreign policy, McFarlane, Poindexter, and their aides had assumed the power to act on their own.

The man most often pulling the strings seemed to be Lieutenant Colonel Oliver "Ollie" North, a junior officer under McFarlane and later Poindexter. *Oliver North* | A Vietnam veteran with a flair for the dramatic, North was impatient with bureaucratic rules and procedures. He and McFarlane had already discovered a way to evade the Boland Amendment in order to secretly aid the Nicaraguan Contras. McFarlane told Saudi Arabia and several other American allies that the Contras desperately needed funds. As a favor, the Saudis deposited at least $30 million in Swiss bank accounts used to launder the money. North then arranged to spend the money to buy the weapons that were delivered to Central America.

The two secret strands came together in January 1986. North hit upon the idea that the profits made selling arms to Iran could be siphoned off to buy weapons for the Contras. The Iranian arms dealer who brokered the deal thought it a great idea. "I think this is now, Ollie, the best chance, because . . . we never get such good money out of this," he laughed, as he was recorded on a tape North himself made. "We do everything. We do hostages free of charge; we do all terrorists free of charge; Central America free of charge."

### Cover Blown

Through much of 1986 secrecy surrounded both operations. Then a Lebanese newspaper broke the story of the Iranian arms deal. Astonished reporters besieged

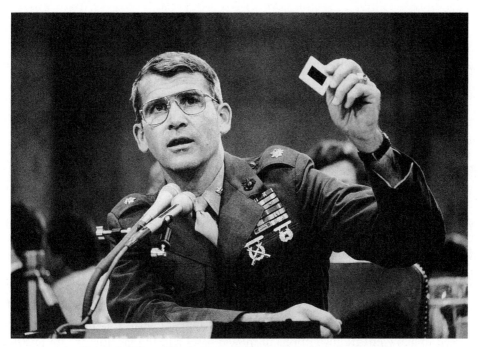

As Colonel Oliver North himself admitted during the Iran-Contra
hearings, he purposely misled Congress about the Reagan
administration's secret aid to the Contras.

the administration. How did secret arms sales to a terrorist regime benefit the
president's antiterrorist campaign, they asked. Further inquiry revealed the link
between the arms sales and the Contras. Attorney General Edwin Meese moved
so slowly to investigate that North and his secretary had time to shred crucial
documents. Still, enough evidence remained to make the dimensions of the illegal operations clear.

The press immediately began referring to the scandal as "Irangate," compar-
ing it to Richard Nixon's Watergate scandal. But Irangate raised more troubling
issues. Watergate sprang from political tricks that ran amok. The pres- *Irangate*
ident had led the cover-up to save his own political skin. The Irangate hearings, held during the summer of 1987, left the role of the president unex-
plained. Admiral Poindexter testified that he had kept Reagan in ignorance, "so
that I could insulate him from the decision and provide some future deniability
for the president if it ever leaked out." In that way, Iran-Contra revealed a presidency out of control. An unelected segment within the government had taken
upon itself the power to pursue its own policies beyond legal channels. In doing
so, Reagan, North, Poindexter, and McFarlane subverted the constitutional system
of checks and balances.

## From Cold War to Glasnost

Since few in Congress wanted to impeach a popular president, the Iran-Contra hearings came to a sputtering end. Reagan's popularity returned, in part because of substantial improvement in Soviet-American relations.

In 1985 a fresh spirit entered the Kremlin. Unlike the aged leaders who preceded him, Mikhail Gorbachev was young, saw the need for reform within the Soviet

*Mikhail Gorbachev*

Union, and rivaled Reagan as a shaper of world opinion. Gorbachev's fundamental restructuring, or perestroika, set about improving relations with the United States, reducing military commitments, and adopting a policy of openness (glasnost) about problems in the Soviet Union. In October, the two leaders held a summit meeting in Reykjavík, Iceland. Gorbachev dangled the possibility of abolishing all nuclear weapons. Reagan seemed receptive, apparently unaware that if both sides eliminated all nuclear weapons, Soviet conventional forces would far outnumber NATO troops in Europe. In the end, the president refused to sacrifice his Star Wars system for so radical a proposal.

Despite the immediate impasse, negotiations continued. In December 1987 Reagan traveled to Moscow to sign the Intermediate Nuclear Force treaty, which eliminated an entire class of intermediate-range nuclear missiles. Both sides agreed to allow on-site inspections of missile bases and the facilities where missiles would be destroyed. That agreement greatly eased cold war tensions.

## The Election of 1988

As the election of 1988 approached, the president could claim credit for improved relations with the Soviet Union. Loyalty to Reagan made Vice President George Bush the Republican heir. The Democratic challenger, Governor Michael Dukakis of Massachusetts, tried to call attention to weaknesses in the American economy. An alarming number of savings and loan institutions had failed, and Dukakis recognized that poor and even many middle-class Americans had lost ground during the 1980s. But with the economy reasonably robust, Bush won by a comfortable margin, taking 54 percent of the popular vote. The Reagan agenda remained on track.

### AN END TO THE COLD WAR

President George Herbert Walker Bush was born to both privilege and politics. The son of a powerful Connecticut senator, he attended an exclusive boarding school and Yale University. That background made him part of the eastern establishment often condemned by more populist Republicans. Yet once the oil business lured Bush to Texas, he moved to the right, becoming a Goldwater Republican when he ran unsuccessfully for the Senate in 1964. Although he once supported Planned Parenthood and a woman's right to abortion, Bush eventually adopted the conservative right-to-life position. In truth, however, foreign policy interested him far more than domestic politics.

### A Post–Cold War Foreign Policy

To the astonishment of most Western observers, Mikhail Gorbachev's reform policies led not only to the collapse of the Soviet empire but also to the breakup of the Soviet Union itself. In December 1988, Gorbachev spoke in the United Nations of a "new world order." To that end he began liquidating the Soviet cold war legacy, as the last Russian troops began leaving Afghanistan and then Eastern Europe.

Throughout 1989 Eastern Europeans began to test their newfound freedom. In Poland, Hungary, Bulgaria, Czechoslovakia, and most violently Romania, Communist dictators fell from power. Nothing inspired the world more than the stream of celebrating East Germans pouring through the Berlin Wall in November 1989. Within a year the wall, a symbol *The fall of communism* of Communist oppression, had been torn down and Germany reunified. Although Gorbachev struggled to keep together the 15 republics that made up the U.S.S.R., the forces of nationalism and reform pulled the Soviet Union apart. The Baltic republics—Lithuania, Latvia, and Estonia—declared their independence in 1991. Then in December, the Slavic republics of Ukraine, Belarus, and Russia formed a new Commonwealth of Independent States. By the end of December eight more of the former Soviet republics had joined the loose

President George Bush met with Soviet president Mikhail Gorbachev at a Moscow summit meeting in 1991. Clearly the policy of glasnost extended to American beverages: the Kremlin's conference table is stocked with Coke.

federation. Boris Yeltsin, the charismatic president of Russia, became the Commonwealth's dominant figure. With no Soviet Union left to preside over, Gorbachev resigned as president.

President Bush responded cautiously to these momentous changes. Although the president increasingly supported Gorbachev's reforms, he distrusted the more popular yet unpredictable maverick Yeltsin. Even if Bush had wished to launch a campaign to aid Eastern Europe and the new Commonwealth states, soaring deficits and a stagnant American economy limited his options. The administration seemed to support the status quo in Communist China, too. When in June 1989 China's aging leadership crushed students rallying for democratic reform in Beijing's Tiananmen Square, Bush muted American protests.

The fall of the Soviet Union signaled the end of a cold war that, more than once, had threatened a nuclear end to human history. At a series of summits with

**START Treaty** | Russian leaders, the United States and its former rivals agreed to sharp reductions in their stockpiles of nuclear weapons. The Strategic Arms Reduction Treaty (or START), concluded in July 1991, far surpassed the limits negotiated in earlier SALT talks. By June 1992 Bush and Yeltsin had agreed to even sharper cuts.

## The Persian Gulf War

With two superpowers no longer facing off against each other, what would the "new world order" look like? If anything, regional crises loomed larger. Civil wars in Eastern Europe and Africa demonstrated that a world order beyond the shadow of the cold war might be more chaotic and unpredictable than ever.

Yet it was instability in the Middle East that brought Bush's greatest foreign policy challenge. From 1980 to 1988 Iran and Iraq had battered each other in a

**Saddam Hussein** | debilitating war. During those years the Reagan administration assisted Iraq with weapons and intelligence, until at last it won a narrow victory over Iran's fundamentalists. But Iraq's ruthless dictator, Saddam Hussein, had run up enormous debts. To ease his financial crisis, Saddam cast a covetous eye on his neighbor, the small oil-rich sheikdom of Kuwait. In August 1990, 120,000 Iraqi troops invaded and occupied Kuwait, catching the Bush administration off guard. Would Saddam stop there?

"We committed a boner with regard to Iraq and our close friendship with Iraq," admitted Ronald Reagan. Embarrassed by having supported the pro-Iraqi policy, Bush was determined to thwart Saddam's invasion of Kuwait. He worried also that Iraq might threaten American supplies of oil not only from Kuwait but also from Kuwait's oil-rich neighbor, Saudi Arabia. The president successfully coordinated a United Nations–backed economic boycott. Increasing the pressure further, he deployed half a million American troops in Saudi Arabia and the Persian Gulf. By November Bush had won a resolution from the Security Council permitting the use of military force if Saddam did not withdraw.

On January 17, 1991, planes from France, Italy, Britain, Saudi Arabia, and the United States began bombing Baghdad and Iraqi bases. Operation Desert Storm had begun. After weeks of merciless pounding from the air, ground operations shattered Saddam's vaunted Republican Guards in less than 100 hours. By the end of February Kuwait was liberated and nothing stood between Allied forces and Baghdad. Bush was unwilling to go that far—and most other nations in the coalition agreed. If Hussein were toppled, it was not clear who in Iraq would fill the vacuum of power. But long after the war ended, the United States still worried about Saddam and his potential possession of biological and atomic weapons.

*Operation Desert Storm*

## Domestic Doldrums

Victory in the Gulf War so boosted the president's popularity that aides brushed aside the need for any bold domestic program. "Frankly, this president doesn't need another single piece of legislation, unless it's absolutely right," asserted John Sununu, his cocky chief of staff. That attitude suggested a lack of direction that proved fatal to Bush's reelection hopes.

At first, Bush envisioned a domestic program that would soften the harsher edges of the Reagan revolution. He promised to create a "kinder, gentler" nation. Yet pressures from conservative Republicans kept the new president from straying too far in the direction of reform. Although Bush appointed a well-respected conservationist, William Reilly, to head the Environmental Protection Agency, Reilly often found his programs opposed by others in the administration. When delegates from 178 nations met at an Earth Summit in Rio de Janeiro in 1992, the president opposed efforts to draft stricter rules to lessen the threat of global warming. Bush did sign into law the sweeping Clean Air Act passed by Congress in 1990. But soon after, Vice President Dan Quayle established a Council on Competitiveness to rewrite environmental regulations that corporations found burdensome.

*Environmental issues*

## The Conservative Court

Although Presidents Reagan and Bush both spoke out against abortion, affirmative action, the banning of prayer in public schools, and other liberal social positions, neither made action a legislative priority. Even so, both presidents shaped social policy through their appointments to the Supreme Court. Reagan placed three members on the bench, including in 1981 Sandra Day O'Connor, the first woman to sit on the high court. Bush nominated two justices. As more liberal members of the Court retired (including William Brennan and Thurgood Marshall), the decisions handed down became distinctly more conservative.

On two occasions, the Senate challenged this trend. In 1987, it rejected Robert Bork, a nominee whose opposition to long-established Court policies on privacy and civil rights led even some Republicans to oppose him. But this fight proved so exhausting that the Senate quickly approved President Reagan's alternate choice, Antonin Scalia. Scalia proved to be the Court's most conservative member.

In 1991 the Senate also hotly debated President Bush's nomination of Clarence Thomas, an outspoken black conservative and former member of the Reagan administration. The confirmation hearings became even more

*The Clarence Thomas hearings*

heated when Anita Hill, a woman who had worked for Thomas, testified that he had sexually harassed her. Because Hill was a professor of law and herself a Reagan conservative, her often graphic testimony riveted millions of television viewers. Suddenly the hearings raised new issues. Women's groups blasted the all-male Judiciary Committee for keeping Hill's allegations private until reporters uncovered the story. Thomas and his defenders accused his opponents of using a disgruntled woman to help conduct a latter-day lynching. In the end the Senate narrowly voted to confirm, and Thomas joined Scalia as a conservative member of the Court.

Law professor Anita Hill polarized Senate hearings on the nomination of Clarence Thomas to the Supreme Court when she accused her former boss of sexual harassment. Women's groups were disturbed that the all-male Judiciary Committee had at first kept her allegations private.

Evidence of the Court's changing stance came most clearly in its attitude toward affirmative action, those laws that gave preferred treatment to minority groups in order to remedy past racial discrimination. State and federal courts and legislatures had used techniques like busing and the setting of quotas as ways to overturn past injustices. As early as 1978, however, even before Reagan's appointments, the Court began to set limits on affirmative action. In *Bakke v. Regents of the University of California* (1978), the majority ruled that college admissions staffs could not set fixed quotas, although they could still use race as a guiding factor in trying to create a more diverse student body. Increasingly, the Court made it easier for white citizens to challenge affirmative action programs. At the same time, it set higher standards for those who wished to put forward a claim of discrimination. "An amorphous claim that there has been past discrimination in a particular industry cannot justify the use of an unyielding racial quota," wrote Justice O'Connor in 1989.

Court decisions on abortion and religion in public schools demonstrated a similar desire to set limits on earlier precedents. *Planned Parenthood v. Casey* (1992) upheld a woman's constitutional right to an abortion, but it also allowed states to place new restrictions on the procedure. And while the Court affirmed that religious teachings or prayer could have no official status in public schools, it allowed students to engage in voluntary prayer as well as to form religious clubs meeting after school.

### Disillusionment and Anger

Ronald Reagan had given a sunny face to conservatism. He assured voters that if taxes were cut, the economy would revive and deficits fall. Yet after a decade of conservative leadership, the deficit had ballooned and state and local governments were larger than ever. A growing number of Americans felt that the institutions of government had come seriously off track.

A series of longer-term crises contributed to this disillusionment. One of the most threatening centered on the nation's savings and loan institutions. By the end of the 1980s these "thrifts" were failing at the highest rate since *S&L crisis* the Great Depression. To help banks, the Reagan administration and Congress had cut back federal regulations, allowing savings banks to invest their funds more speculatively. Reagan's advisers ignored the warnings that fraud and mismanagement were increasing sharply. Only during the Bush administration did it become clearer that the cost of restoring solvency would run into hundreds of billions of taxpayers' dollars.

The late 1980s also brought a public health crisis. Americans were spending a higher percentage of their resources on medical care than citizens in other nations, yet they were no healthier. As medical costs soared, more than *Health crises* 30 million Americans had no health insurance. The crisis was worsened by a fatal disorder that physicians began diagnosing in the early 1980s: acquired immune deficiency syndrome, or AIDS. With no cure available, the disease threatened to take on epidemic proportions, not only in the United States but around the globe. Yet because the illness was at first most common in the male homosexual community and intravenous drug abusers, many groups in American society resisted addressing the problem.

Bank failures, skyrocketing health costs, an increase in unemployment and poverty—by themselves none of these problems could derail the conservative tide that had swept Ronald Reagan into office. Still, the crises demonstrated how pivotal government had become in providing social services and limiting the abuses of powerful private interests in a highly industrialized society. Neither the Reagan nor the Bush administration had developed a clear way to address such problems

Recess of the Legislature of any State, the Executive thereof may make temporary Appointments until the next Meeting of the Legislature, which shall then fill such Vacancies.

No Person shall be a Senator who shall not have attained to the Age of thirty Years, and been nine Years a Citizen of the United States, and who shall not, when elected, be an Inhabitant of that State for which he shall be chosen.

The Vice President of the United States shall be President of the Senate, but shall have no vote, unless they be equally divided.

The Senate shall chuse their other Officers and also a President pro tempore, in the absence of the Vice President, or when he shall exercise the Office of President of the United States.

The Senate shall have the sole Power to try all Impeachments. When sitting for that purpose they shall be on Oath or Affirmation. When the President of the United States is tried, the Chief Justice shall preside: And no person shall be convicted without the Concurrence of two thirds of the Members present.

Judgment in Cases of Impeachment shall not extend further than to removal from Office, and disqualification to hold and enjoy any Office of honor, Trust, or Profit under the United States: but the Party convicted shall nevertheless be liable and subject to Indictment, Trial, Judgment, and Punishment, according to Law:

**Section 4.** The Times, Places and Manner of holding Elections for Senators and Representatives, shall be prescribed in each State by the Legislature thereof; but the Congress may at any time by Law make or alter such Regulations, except as to the Places of Chusing Senators.

The Congress shall assemble at least once in every Year, and such Meeting shall be on the first Monday in December, unless they shall by Law appoint a different Day.

**Section 5.** Each House shall be the Judge of the Elections, Returns and Qualifications of its own Members, and a Majority of each shall constitute a Quorum to do Business; but a smaller number may adjourn from day to day, and may be authorized to compel the Attendance of absent Members, in such Manner, and under such Penalties, as each House may provide.

Each House may determine the Rules of its Proceedings, punish its Members for disorderly Behaviour, and, with the Concurrence of two thirds, expel a Member.

Each House shall keep a Journal of its Proceedings, and from time to time publish the same, excepting such Parts as may in their Judgment require Secrecy; and the Yeas and Nays of the Members of either House on any question shall, at the Desire of one fifth of those Present, be entered on the Journal.

Neither House, during the Session of Congress, shall, without the Consent of the other, adjourn for more than three days, nor to any other Place than that in which the two Houses shall be sitting.

**Section 6.** The Senators and Representatives shall receive a Compensation for their Services, to be ascertained by Law, and paid out of the Treasury of the United States. They shall in all Cases, except Treason, Felony, and Breach of the Peace, be privileged from Arrest during their Attendance at the Session of their respective Houses, and in going to and returning from the same; and for any Speech or Debate in either House, they shall not be questioned in any other Place.

No Senator or Representative shall, during the Time for which he was elected, be appointed to any civil Office under the Authority of the United States, which shall have been created, or the Emoluments whereof shall have been increased, during such time; and no Person holding any Office under the United States shall be a Member of either House during his continuance in Office.

**Section 7.** All Bills for raising Revenue shall originate in the House of Representatives; but the Senate may propose or concur with Amendments as on other bills.

Every Bill which shall have passed the House of Representatives and the Senate, shall, before it become a Law, be presented to the President of the United States; If he approve he shall sign it, but if not he shall return it, with his Objections, to that House in which it shall have originated, who shall enter the Objections at large on their Journal, and proceed to reconsider it. If after such Reconsideration two thirds of that House shall agree to pass the bill, it shall be sent, together with the objections, to the other House, by which it shall likewise be reconsidered, and if approved by two thirds of that House, it shall become a Law. But in all such Cases the Votes of both Houses shall be determined by Yeas and Nays, and the Names of the Persons voting for and against the Bill shall be entered on the Journal of each House respectively. If any Bill shall not be returned by the President within ten Days (Sundays excepted) after it shall have been presented to him, the Same shall be a Law, in like Manner as if he had signed it, unless the Congress by their Adjournment prevent its Return, in which Case it shall not be a Law.

Every Order, Resolution, or Vote to which the Concurrence of the Senate and House of Representatives may be necessary (except on a question of Adjournment) shall be presented to the President of the United States; and before the Same shall take Effect, shall be approved by him, or being disapproved by him, shall be repassed by two thirds of the Senate and House of Representatives, according to the Rules and Limitations prescribed in the Case of a Bill.

**Section 8.** The Congress shall have Power To lay and collect Taxes, Duties, Imposts and Excises, to pay the Debts and provide for the common Defence and general Welfare of the United States; but all Duties, Imposts and Excises shall be uniform throughout the United States;

To borrow money on the credit of the United States;

To regulate Commerce with foreign Nations, and among the several States, and with the Indian Tribes;

To establish an uniform rule of Naturalization, and uniform Laws on the subject of Bankruptcies throughout the United States;

To coin Money, regulate the Value thereof, and of foreign Coin, and fix the Standard of Weights and Measures;

To provide for the Punishment of counterfeiting the Securities and current Coin of the United States;

To establish Post Offices and post Roads;

To promote the Progress of Science and useful Arts, by securing for limited Times to Authors and Inventors the exclusive Right to their respective Writings and Discoveries;

To constitute Tribunals inferior to the Supreme Court;

To define and punish Piracies and Felonies committed on the high Seas, and Offenses against the Law of Nations;

To declare War, grant Letters of Marque and Reprisal, and make Rules concerning Captures on Land and Water;

To raise and support Armies, but no Appropriation of Money to that Use shall be for a longer Term than two Years;

To provide and maintain a Navy;

To make Rules for the Government and Regulation of the land and naval forces;

To provide for calling forth the Militia to execute the Laws of the Union, suppress Insurrections and repel Invasions;

To provide for organizing, arming, and disciplining the Militia, and for governing such Part of them as may be employed in the Service of the United States, reserving to the States respectively, the Appointment of the Officers, and the Authority of training the Militia according to the discipline prescribed by Congress;

To exercise exclusive Legislation in all Cases whatsoever, over such District (not exceeding ten Miles square) as may, by Cession of particular States, and the acceptance of Congress, become the Seat of the Government of the United States, and to exercise like Authority over all Places purchased by the Consent of the Legislature of the State in which the Same shall be, for the Erection of Forts, Magazines, Arsenals, Dock-yards, and other needful Buildings;—And

To make all Laws which shall be necessary and proper for carrying into Execution the foregoing Powers, and all other Powers vested by this Constitution in the Government of the United States, or in any Department or Officer thereof.

**Section 9.** The Migration or Importation of such Persons as any of the States now existing shall think proper to admit, shall not be prohibited by the Congress prior to the Year one thousand eight hundred and eight, but a tax or duty may be imposed on such Importation, not exceeding ten dollars for each Person.

The privilege of the Writ of Habeas Corpus shall not be suspended, unless when in Cases of Rebellion or Invasion the public Safety may require it.

No bill of Attainder or ex post facto Law shall be passed.

No capitation, or other direct, Tax shall be laid unless in Proportion to the Census or Enumeration herein before directed to be taken.

No Tax or Duty shall be laid on Articles exported from any State.

No Preference shall be given by any Regulation of Commerce or Revenue to the Ports of one State over those of another: nor shall Vessels bound to, or from, one State, be obliged to enter, clear, or pay Duties in another.

No Money shall be drawn from the Treasury, but in Consequence of Appropriations made by Law; and a regular Statement and Account of the Receipts and Expenditures of all public Money shall be published from time to time.

No Title of Nobility shall be granted by the United States: And no Person holding any Office of Profit or Trust under them, shall, without the Consent of the Congress, accept of any present, Emolument, Office, or Title, of any kind whatever, from any King, Prince, or foreign State.

**Section 10.** No State shall enter into any Treaty, Alliance, or Confederation; grant Letters of Marque and Reprisal; coin Money; emit Bills of Credit; make any Thing but gold and silver Coin a Tender in Payment of Debts; pass any Bill of Attainder, ex post facto Law, or Law impairing the Obligation of Contracts, or grant any Title of Nobility.

No State shall, without the Consent of the Congress, lay any Imposts or Duties on Imports or Exports, except what may be absolutely necessary for executing its inspection Laws; and the net Produce of all Duties and Imposts, laid by any State on Imports or Exports, shall be for the use of the Treasury of the United States; and all such Laws shall be subject to the Revision and Control of the Congress.

No state shall, without the Consent of Congress, lay any duty of Tonnage, keep Troops, or Ships of War in time of Peace, enter into any Agreement or Compact with another State, or with a foreign Power, or engage in War, unless actually invaded, or in such imminent Danger as will not admit of delay.

## ARTICLE II

**Section 1.** The executive Power shall be vested in a President of the United States of America. He shall hold his Office during the Term of four years, and, together with the Vice President, chosen for the same Term, be elected, as follows:

Each State shall appoint, in such Manner as the Legislature thereof may direct, a Number of Electors, equal to the whole Number of Senators and Representatives to which the State may be entitled in the Congress: but no Senator or Representative, or Person holding an Office of Trust or Profit under the United States, shall be appointed an Elector.

[The Electors shall meet in their respective States, and vote by Ballot for two persons, of whom one at least shall not be an Inhabitant of the same State with themselves. And they shall make a List of all the Persons voted for, and of the Number of Votes for each; which List they shall sign and certify, and transmit sealed to the Seat of the Government of the United States, directed to the President of the Senate. The President of the Senate shall, in the Presence of the Senate and House of Representatives, open all the Certificates, and the Votes shall then be counted. The Person having the greatest Number of Votes shall be the President, if such Number be a Majority of the whole Number of Electors appointed; and if there be more than one who have such Majority, and have an equal Number of Votes, then the House of Representatives shall immediately chuse by Ballot one of them for President; and if no Person have a Majority, then from the five highest on the List the said House shall in like Manner chuse the President. But in chusing the President, the Votes shall be taken by States, the Representation from each State having one Vote; a quorum for this Purpose shall consist of a Member or Members from two-thirds of the States, and a Majority of all the States shall be necessary to a Choice. In every Case, after the Choice of the President, the Person having the greatest Number of Votes of the Electors shall be the Vice President. But if there should remain two or more who have equal votes, the Senate shall chuse from them by Ballot the Vice President.][4]

The Congress may determine the Time of chusing the Electors, and the Day on which they shall give their Votes; which Day shall be the same throughout the United States.

No person except a natural-born Citizen, or a Citizen of the United States, at the time of the Adoption of this Constitution, shall be eligible to the Office of President; neither shall any Person be eligible to that Office who shall not have attained to the Age of thirty-five years, and been fourteen Years a Resident within the United States.

In Case of the Removal of the President from Office, or of his Death, Resignation, or Inability to discharge the Powers and Duties of the said Office, the same shall devolve on the Vice President, and the Congress may by Law provide for the Case of Removal, Death, Resignation, or Inability, both of the President and Vice President, declaring what Officer shall then act as President, and such Officer shall act accordingly, until the disability be removed, or a President shall be elected.

The President shall, at stated Times, receive for his Services a Compensation, which shall neither be increased nor diminished during the Period for which he shall have been elected, and he shall not receive within that Period any other Emolument from the United States, or any of them.

Before he enter on the execution of his Office, he shall take the following Oath or Affirmation:—"I do solemnly swear (or affirm) that I will faithfully execute the Office of President of the United States, and will, to the best of my Ability, preserve, protect, and defend the Constitution of the United States."

**Section 2.**  The President shall be Commander in Chief of the Army and Navy of the United States, and of the Militia of the several States, when called into the actual Service of the United States; he may require the Opinion, in writing, of the principal Officer in each of the executive Departments, upon any subject relating to the Duties of their respective Offices, and he shall have Power to Grant Reprieves and Pardons for Offenses against the United States, except in Cases of Impeachment.

---

[4]Revised by the Twelfth Amendment.

He shall have Power, by and with the Advice and Consent of the Senate, to make Treaties, provided two-thirds of the Senators present concur; and he shall nominate, and by and with the Advice and Consent of the Senate, shall appoint Ambassadors, other public Ministers and Consuls, Judges of the Supreme Court, and all other Officers of the United States, whose Appointments are not herein otherwise provided for, and which shall be established by Law: but the Congress may by Law vest the Appointment of such inferior Officers, as they think proper, in the President alone, in the Courts of Law, or in the Heads of Departments.

The President shall have Power to fill up all Vacancies that may happen during the Recess of the Senate, by granting Commissions which shall expire at the End of their next Session.

**Section 3.**  He shall from time to time give to the Congress Information of the State of the Union, and recommend to their Consideration such Measures as he shall judge necessary and expedient; he may, on extraordinary occasions, convene both Houses, or either of them, and in Case of Disagreement between them, with respect to the Time of Adjournment, he may adjourn them to such Time as he shall think proper; he shall receive Ambassadors and other public Ministers; he shall take care that the Laws be faithfully executed, and shall Commission all the Officers of the United States.

**Section 4.**  The President, Vice President and all civil Officers of the United States, shall be removed from Office on Impeachment for, and Conviction of, Treason, Bribery, or other high Crimes and Misdemeanors.

## ARTICLE III

**Section 1.**  The judicial Power of the United States, shall be vested in one supreme Court, and in such inferior Courts as the Congress may from time to time ordain and establish. The Judges, both of the supreme and inferior Courts, shall hold their Offices during good Behaviour, and shall, at stated Times, receive for their Services, a Compensation, which shall not be diminished during their Continuance in Office.

**Section 2.**  The judicial Power shall extend to all Cases, in Law and Equity, arising under this Constitution, the Laws of the United States, and Treaties made, or which shall be made, under their Authority;—to all Cases affecting ambassadors, other public ministers and consuls;—to all cases of admiralty and maritime Jurisdiction;—to Controversies to which the United States shall be a Party;—to Controversies between two or more States;—between a State and Citizens of another State;[5]—between Citizens of different States—between Citizens of the same State claiming Lands under Grants of different States, and between a State, or the Citizens thereof, and foreign States, Citizens, or Subjects.

In all Cases affecting Ambassadors, other public Ministers and Consuls, and those in which a State shall be Party, the supreme Court shall have original Jurisdiction. In all the other Cases before mentioned, the supreme Court shall have appellate Jurisdiction, both as to Law and Fact, with such Exceptions, and under such Regulations as the Congress shall make.

The trial of all Crimes, except in Cases of Impeachment, shall be by Jury; and such Trial shall be held in the State where the said Crimes shall have been committed; but when not committed within any State, the Trial shall be at such Place or Places as the Congress may by Law have directed.

---

[5]Qualified by the Eleventh Amendment.

**Section 3.** Treason against the United States, shall consist only in levying War against them, or in adhering to their Enemies, giving them Aid and Comfort. No Person shall be convicted of Treason unless on the Testimony of two Witnesses to the same overt Act, or on Confession in open Court.

The Congress shall have power to declare the Punishment of Treason, but no Attainder of Treason shall work Corruption of Blood, or Forfeiture except during the Life of the Person attainted.

## ARTICLE IV

**Section 1.** Full Faith and Credit shall be given in each State to the public Acts, Records, and judicial Proceedings of every other State. And the Congress may by general Laws prescribe the Manner in which such Acts, Records and Proceedings shall be proved, and the Effect thereof.

**Section 2.** The Citizens of each State shall be entitled to all Privileges and Immunities of Citizens in the several States.

A Person charged in any State with Treason, Felony, or other Crime, who shall flee from Justice, and be found in another State, shall on demand of the executive Authority of the State from which he fled, be delivered up, to be removed to the State having Jurisdiction of the crime.

No Person held to Service or Labour in one State, under the Laws thereof, escaping into another, shall, in Consequence of any Law or Regulation therein, be discharged from such Service or Labour, but shall be delivered up on Claim of the Party to whom such Service or Labour may be due.

**Section 3.** New States may be admitted by the Congress into this Union; but no new State shall be formed or erected within the Jurisdiction of any other State; nor any State be formed by the Junction of two or more States, or parts of States, without the Consent of the Legislatures of the States concerned as well as of the Congress.

The Congress shall have Power to dispose of and make all needful Rules and Regulations respecting the Territory or other Property belonging to the United States; and nothing in this Constitution shall be so construed as to Prejudice any Claims of the United States, or of any particular State.

**Section 4.** The United States shall guarantee to every State in this Union a Republican Form of Government, and shall protect each of them against Invasion; and on Application of the Legislature, or of the Executive (when the Legislature cannot be convened) against domestic Violence.

## ARTICLE V

The Congress, whenever two-thirds of both Houses shall deem it necessary, shall propose Amendments to this Constitution, or, on the Application of the Legislatures of two-thirds of the several States, shall call a Convention for proposing Amendments, which, in either Case, shall be valid to all Intents and Purposes, as part of this Constitution, when ratified by the Legislatures of three-fourths of the several States, or by Conventions in three-fourths thereof, as the one or the other Mode of Ratification may be proposed by the Congress; Provided that no Amendment which may be made prior to the Year One thousand eight hundred and eight shall in any Manner affect the first and fourth Clauses in the Ninth Section of the first Article; and that no State, without its Consent, shall be deprived of its equal Suffrage in the Senate.

## ARTICLE VI

All Debts contracted and Engagements entered into, before the Adoption of this Constitution, shall be as valid against the United States under this Constitution, as under the Confederation.

This Constitution, and the Laws of the United States which shall be made in Pursuance thereof; and all Treaties made, or which shall be made, under the Authority of the United States, shall be the supreme Law of the Land; and the Judges in every State shall be bound thereby, any Thing in the Constitution or Laws of any State to the Contrary notwithstanding.

The Senators and Representatives before mentioned, and the Members of the several State Legislatures, and all executive and judicial Officers, both of the United States and of the several States, shall be bound by Oath or Affirmation to support this Constitution; but no religious Tests shall ever be required as a qualification to any Office or public Trust under the United States.

## ARTICLE VII

The Ratification of the Conventions of nine States shall be sufficient for the Establishment of this Constitution between the States so ratifying the same.

Done in Convention by the Unanimous Consent of the States present the Seventeenth Day of September in the Year of our Lord one thousand seven hundred and Eighty seven, and of the Independence of the United States of America the Twelfth. In Witness whereof We have hereunto subscribed our Names.[6]

## GEORGE WASHINGTON

PRESIDENT AND DEPUTY FROM VIRGINIA

**New Hampshire**
John Langdon
Nicholas Gilman

**Massachusetts**
Nathaniel Gorham
Rufus King

**Connecticut**
William Samuel
  Johnson
Roger Sherman

**New York**
Alexander Hamilton

**New Jersey**
William Livingston
David Brearley
William Paterson
Jonathan Dayton

**Pennsylvania**
Benjamin Franklin
Thomas Mifflin
Robert Morris
George Clymer
Thomas FitzSimons
Jared Ingersoll
James Wilson
Gouverneur Morris

**Delaware**
George Read
Gunning Bedford, Jr.
John Dickinson
Richard Bassett
Jacob Broom

**Maryland**
James McHenry
Daniel of
  St. Thomas Jenifer
Daniel Carroll

**Virginia**
John Blair
James Madison, Jr.

**North Carolina**
William Blount
Richard Dobbs
  Spaight
Hugh Williamson

**South Carolina**
John Rutledge
Charles Cotesworth
  Pinckney
Charles Pinckney
Pierce Butler

**Georgia**
William Few
Abraham Baldwin

---

[6]These are the full names of the signers, which in some cases are not the signatures on the document.

*Articles in Addition to, and Amendment of, the Constitution of the United States of America, Proposed by Congress, and Ratified by the Legislatures of the Several States, Pursuant to the Fifth Article of the Original Constitution*[7]

## [AMENDMENT I]

Congress shall make no law respecting an establishment of religion, or prohibiting the free exercise thereof; or abridging the freedom of speech, or of the press; or the right of the people peaceably to assemble, and to petition the Government for a redress of grievances.

## [AMENDMENT II]

A well regulated Militia, being necessary to the security of a free State, the right of the people to keep and bear Arms shall not be infringed.

## [AMENDMENT III]

No Soldier shall, in time of peace, be quartered in any house, without the consent of the Owner, nor in time of war, but in a manner to be prescribed by law.

## [AMENDMENT IV]

The right of the people to be secure in their persons, houses, papers, and effects, against unreasonable searches and seizures, shall not be violated, and no Warrants shall issue, but upon probable cause, supported by Oath or affirmation, and particularly describing the place to be searched, and the persons or things to be seized.

## [AMENDMENT V]

No person shall be held to answer for a capital or otherwise infamous crime, unless on a presentment or indictment of a Grand Jury, except in cases arising in the land or naval forces, or in the Militia, when in actual service in time of War or public danger; nor shall any person be subject for the same offence to be twice put in jeopardy of life or limb; nor shall be compelled in any criminal case to be a witness against himself, nor be deprived of life, liberty, or property, without due process of law; nor shall private property be taken for public use, without just compensation.

## [AMENDMENT VI]

In all criminal prosecutions, the accused shall enjoy the right to a speedy and public trial, by an impartial jury of the State and district wherein the crime shall have been committed, which

---

[7]This heading appears only in the joint resolution submitting the first ten amendments, known as the Bill of Rights.

district shall have been previously ascertained by law, and to be informed of the nature and cause of the accusation; to be confronted with the witnesses against him; to have compulsory process for obtaining witnesses in his favour, and to have the Assistance of Counsel for his defence.

## [AMENDMENT VII]

In suits at common law, where the value in controversy shall exceed twenty dollars, the right of trial by jury shall be preserved, and no fact tried by a jury, shall be otherwise reexamined in any Court of the United States, than according to the rules of the common law.

## [AMENDMENT VIII]

Excessive bail shall not be required, nor excessive fines imposed, nor cruel and unusual punishments inflicted.

## [AMENDMENT IX]

The enumeration of the Constitution, of certain rights, shall not be construed to deny or disparage others retained by the people.

## [AMENDMENT X]

The powers not delegated to the United States by the Constitution, nor prohibited by it to the States, are reserved to the States respectively, or to the people.
[Amendments I–X, in force 1791.]

## [AMENDMENT XI][8]

The Judicial power of the United States shall not be construed to extend to any suit in law or equity, commenced or prosecuted against one of the United States by Citizens of another State, or by Citizens or Subjects of any Foreign State.

## [AMENDMENT XII][9]

The Electors shall meet in their respective States and vote by ballot for President and Vice-President, one of whom, at least, shall not be an inhabitant of the same State with themselves; they shall name in their ballots the person voted for as President, and in distinct ballots the person voted for as Vice-President, and they shall make distinct lists of all persons voted for

---

[8]Adopted in 1798.
[9]Adopted in 1804.

as President, and of all persons voted for as Vice-President, and of the number of votes for each, which lists they shall sign and certify, and transmit sealed to the seat of the government of the United States, directed to the President of the Senate;—The President of the Senate shall, in the presence of the Senate and House of Representatives, open all the certificates and the votes shall then be counted;—The person having the greatest number of votes for President, shall be the President, if such number be a majority of the whole number of Electors appointed; and if no person have such majority, then from the persons having the highest numbers not exceeding three on the list of those voted for as President, the House of Representatives shall choose immediately, by ballot, the President. But in choosing the President, the votes shall be taken by states, the representation from each state having one vote; a quorum for this purpose shall consist of a member or members from two-thirds of the states, and a majority of all the states shall be necessary to a choice. And if the House of Representatives shall not choose a President whenever the right of choice shall devolve upon them, before the fourth day of March next following, then the Vice-President shall act as President, as in the case of the death or other constitutional disability of the President.—The person having the greatest number of votes as Vice-President, shall be the Vice-President, if such number be a majority of the whole number of Electors appointed, and if no person have a majority, then from the two highest numbers on the list, the Senate shall choose the Vice-President; a quorum for the purpose shall consist of two-thirds of the whole number of Senators, and a majority of the whole number shall be necessary to a choice. But no person constitutionally ineligible to the office of President shall be eligible to that of Vice-President of the United States.

## [AMENDMENT XIII][10]

**Section 1.**   Neither slavery nor involuntary servitude, except as a punishment for crime whereof the party shall have been duly convicted, shall exist within the United States, or any place subject to their jurisdiction.

**Section 2.**   Congress shall have power to enforce this article by appropriate legislation.

## [AMENDMENT XIV][11]

**Section 1.**   All persons born or naturalized in the United States, and subject to the jurisdiction thereof, are citizens of the United States and of the State wherein they reside. No State shall abridge the privileges or immunities of citizens of the United States; nor shall any State deprive any person of life, liberty, or property, without due process of law; nor deny to any person within its jurisdiction the equal protection of the laws.

**Section 2.**   Representatives shall be apportioned among the several States according to their respective numbers, counting the whole number of persons in each State, excluding Indians not taxed. But when the right to vote at any election for the choice of electors for President and Vice-President of the United States, Representatives in Congress, the Executive and Judicial officers of a State, or the members of the Legislature thereof, is denied to any of the male inhabitants of such State, being twenty-one years of age, and citizens of the United States, or in any

[10]Adopted in 1865.
[11]Adopted in 1868.

way abridged, except for participation in rebellion, or other crime, the basis of representation therein shall be reduced in the proportion which the number of such male citizens shall bear to the whole number of male citizens twenty-one years of age in such State.

**Section 3.**   No person shall be a Senator or Representative in Congress, or elector of President and Vice-President, or hold any office, civil or military, under the United States, or under any State, who, having previously taken an oath, as a member of Congress, or as an officer of the United States, or as a member of any State legislature, or as an executive or judicial officer of any State, to support the Constitution of the United States, shall have engaged in insurrection or rebellion against the same, or given aid or comfort to the enemies thereof. But Congress may by a vote of two-thirds of each House, remove such disability.

**Section 4.**   The validity of the public debt of the United States, authorized by law, including debts incurred for payment of pensions and bounties for services in suppressing insurrection or rebellion, shall not be questioned. But neither the United States nor any State shall assume or pay any debts or obligation incurred in aid of insurrection or rebellion against the United States, or any claim for the loss or emancipation of any slave; but all such debts, obligations, and claims shall be held illegal and void.

**Section 5.**   The Congress shall have the power to enforce, by appropriate legislation, the provisions of this article.

# [AMENDMENT XV][12]

**Section 1.**   The right of citizens of the United States to vote shall not be denied or abridged by the United States or by any State on account of race, color, or previous condition of servitude—

**Section 2.**   The Congress shall have power to enforce this article by appropriate legislation.

# [AMENDMENT XVI][13]

The Congress shall have power to lay and collect taxes on incomes, from whatever source derived, without apportionment among the several States, and without regard to any census or enumeration.

# [AMENDMENT XVII][14]

The Senate of the United States shall be composed of two Senators from each State, elected by the people thereof, for six years; and each Senator shall have one vote. The electors in each State shall have the qualifications requisite for electors of the most numerous branch of the State legislatures.

---

[12]Adopted in 1870.
[13]Adopted in 1913.
[14]Adopted in 1913.

When vacancies happen in the representation of any State in the Senate, the executive authority of such State shall issue writs of election to fill such vacancies: *Provided*, That the legislature of any State may empower the executive thereof to make temporary appointments until the people fill the vacancies by election as the legislature may direct.

This amendment shall not be so construed as to affect the election or term of any Senator chosen before it becomes valid as part of the Constitution.

## [AMENDMENT XVIII][15]

**Section 1.**　After one year from the ratification of this article the manufacture, sale, or transportation of intoxicating liquors within, the importation thereof into, or the exportation thereof from the United States and all territory subject to the jurisdiction thereof for beverage purposes is hereby prohibited.

**Section 2.**　The Congress and the several States shall have concurrent power to enforce this article by appropriate legislation.

**Section 3.**　This article shall be inoperative unless it shall have been ratified as an amendment to the Constitution by the legislatures of the several States, as provided in the Constitution, within seven years from the date of the submission hereof to the States by the Congress.

## [AMENDMENT XIX][16]

The right of citizens of the United States to vote shall not be denied or abridged by the United States or by any State on account of sex.

Congress shall have power to enforce this article by appropriate legislation.

## [AMENDMENT XX][17]

**Section 1.**　The terms of the President and Vice-President shall end at noon on the 20th day of January, and the terms of Senators and Representatives at noon on the 3d day of January, of the years in which such terms would have ended if this article had not been ratified; and the terms of their successors shall then begin.

**Section 2.**　The Congress shall assemble at least once in every year, and such meeting shall begin at noon on the 3d day of January, unless they shall by law appoint a different day.

**Section 3.**　If, at the time fixed for the beginning of the term of the President, the President elect shall have died, the Vice-President elect shall become President. If a President shall not have been chosen before the time fixed for the beginning of his term or if the President elect shall have failed to qualify, then the Vice-President elect shall act as President until a President

---

[15]Adopted in 1918.
[16]Adopted in 1920.
[17]Adopted in 1933.

*Cairo, and Tehran Conferences* (1985); Gaddis Smith, *American Diplomacy during the Second World War, 1941–1945* (1985); Michael B. Stoff, *Oil, War, and American Security: The Search for a National Policy on Foreign Oil, 1941–1947* (1980) and, as ed., *The Manhattan Project: A Documentary Introduction* (1991); J. Samuel Walker, *Prompt and Utter Destruction: Truman and the Use of the Atomic Bomb against Japan* (1997); Randall B. Woods, *A Changing of the Guard: Anglo-American Relations, 1941–1946* (1990).

## CHAPTER 27: COLD WAR AMERICA (1945–1954)

### The Postwar Era
Paul Boyer, *By the Bomb's Early Light* (1986); H. W. Brands, *The Devil We Knew: America and the Cold War* (1993); Robert Ferrell, *Harry S Truman: A Life* (1994); Eric Goldman, *The Crucial Decade and After* (1960); Margot Henriksen, *Dr. Strangelove's America: Society and Culture in the Atomic Age* (1997); Landon Jones, *Great Expectations: America and the Babyboom Generation* (1980); George Lipsitz, *Class and Culture in Postwar America* (1981); James O'Connor, ed., *American History/American Television* (1983); William O'Neill, *American High* (1986); Richard Pells, *The Liberal Mind in a Conservative Age* (1985); Dana Polan, *Power and Paranoia: History, Narrative, and the American Cinema, 1940–1950* (1986); Leila Rupp and Verta Taylor, *Survival in the Doldrums: The American Women's Rights Movement, 1945 to the 1960s* (1987); Mark Silk, *Spiritual Politics: Religion and America since World War II* (1988); Athan Theoharis, *Chasing Spies: How the FBI Failed in Counterintelligence but Promoted the Politics of McCarthyism in the Cold War Years* (2002); Jules Tygiel, *Baseball's Great Experiment: Jackie Robinson and His Legacy* (1983); Martin Walker, *The Cold War: A History* (1994).

### The Cold War in the West
Dean Acheson, *Present at the Creation* (1969); Stephen Ambrose, *The Rise to Globalism* (1983); Douglas Brinkley, ed., *Dean Acheson and the Making of American Foreign Policy* (1993); Herbert Druks, *The Uncertain Friendship: The U.S. and Israel from Roosevelt to Kennedy* (2001); Richard Wightman Fox, *Reinhold Niebuhr: A Biography* (1985); Richard Freeland, *The Truman Doctrine and the Origins of McCarthyism* (1970); John L. Gaddis, *The Long Peace: Inquiries into the History of the Cold War* (1987), *Strategies of Containment* (1982), and *We Now Know* (1997); Lloyd Gardner, *Architects of Illusion* (1970); Gregg Herken, *The Winning Weapon* (1980); Michael

Hogan, *The Marshall Plan: America, Britain, and the Reconstruction of Western Europe, 1947–1952* (1987); Walter Isaacson and Evan Thomas, *The Wise Men* (1986); Fred Kaplan, *The Wizards of Armageddon* (1983); Laurence Kaplan, *The United States and NATO* (1984); George Kennan, *Memoirs*, 2 vols. (1967, 1972); Bruce Kuniholm, *The Origins of the Cold War in the Near East* (1980); Mark H. Lytle, *The Origins of the Iranian-American Alliance, 1941–1953* (1987); James Miller, *The United States and Italy, 1940–1950* (1986); Ronald Pruessen, *John Foster Dulles* (1982); Cheryl Rubenberg, *Israel and the American National Interest* (1986); Gaddis Smith, *The Last Years of the Monroe Doctrine, 1945–1993* (1994); Lawrence Wittner, *American Intervention in Greece, 1943–1949* (1982); Randall B. Woods and Howard Jones, *Dawning of the Cold War* (1991).

### The Cold War in Asia
Robert Blum, *Drawing the Line: The Origin of the American Containment Policy in East Asia* (1982); Bruce Cumings, *The Origins of the Korean War*, vol. 1 (1981) and vol. 2 (1990) and, as ed., *Child of Conflict: The Korean-American Relationship, 1943–1953* (1983); William Head, *America's China Sojourn* (1983); Gary Hess, *The United States' Emergence as a Southeast Asian Power, 1940–1950* (1987); Akira Iriye, *The Cold War in Asia* (1974); Burton Kaufman, *The Korean War* (1986); Michael Schaller, *The United States and China in the Twentieth Century* (1979) and *The American Occupation of Japan: The Coming of the Cold War to Asia* (1985); John W. Spanier, *The Truman-MacArthur Controversy and the Korean War* (1959); William Stueck Jr., *The Road to Confrontation* (1981), *The Korean War: An International History* (1995), and *Rethinking the Korean War: A New Diplomatic and Stratgic History* (2002); Nancy Tucker, *Patterns in the Dust: Chinese-American Relations and the Recognition Controversy, 1949–1950* (1983).

### The Domestic Cold War
Michael Belknap, *Cold War Political Justice: The Smith Act, the Communist Party, and American Civil Liberties* (1977); David Caute, *The Great Fear* (1978); Bernard F. Dick, *Radical Innocence: A Critical Study of the Hollywood Ten* (1988); Stanley I. Kutler, *The American Inquisition: Justice and Injustice in the Cold War* (1982); Robert Lamphere and Tom Shachtman, *The FBI-KGB War* (1986); Victor Navasky, *Naming Names* (1980); Robert Newman, *Owen Lattimore and the "Loss" of China* (1992); William O'Neill, *A Better World: Stalinism and the American Intellectuals* (1983); Michael Oshinsky, *A Conspiracy So Immense: The World of Joe McCarthy*

(1983); Ronald Radosh and Joyce Radosh, *The Rosenberg File* (1983); Thomas Reeves, *The Life and Times of Joe McCarthy* (1982); Richard Rovere, *Senator Joe McCarthy* (1959); Ellen Shrecker, *Many Are the Crimes: McCarthyism in America* (1998) and *No Ivory Tower: McCarthyism and the Universities* (1984); Athan Theoharis, *Seeds of Repression: Harry S Truman and the Origins of McCarthyism* (1971); Allen Weinstein, *Perjury: The Hiss-Chambers Case* (1978); Robert Williams, *Klaus Fuchs: Atom Spy* (1987).

**The Truman Administration**
Jack Ballard, *The Shock of Peace: Military and Economic Demobilization after World War II* (1983); James Chace, *Acheson* (1998); Clark Clifford with Richard Holbrooke, *Counsel to the President, A Memoir* (1991); Richard Dalfiume, *Desegregation of the U.S. Armed Forces* (1969); Robert Ferrell, *Harry S Truman and the Modern American Presidency* (1983); Donald Fixico, *Termination and Relocation: Federal Indian Policy, 1945–1960* (1986); Kari Frederickson, *The Dixiecrat Revolt and the End of the Solid South* (2001); David Goldfield, *Black, White, and Southern: Race Relations and Southern Culture* (1990); Allen Matusow, *Farm Politics and Policies in the Truman Years* (1967); Donald McCoy, *The Presidency of Harry S Truman* (1984); Donald McCoy and Richard Ruetten, *Quest and Response: Minority Rights and the Truman Administration* (1973); Merle Miller, *Plain Speaking* (1973); Richard Miller, *Truman: The Rise to Power* (1986); Arnold Offner, *Another Such Victory: President Truman and the Cold War, 1945–1953* (2002); Allen Yarnell, *Democrats and Progressives: The 1948 Presidential Election as a Test of Postwar Liberalism* (1974).

**CHAPTER 28: THE SUBURBAN ERA (1945–1963)**

**General Histories**
Alan Brinkley, *Liberalism and Its Discontents* (1998); Paul Carter, *Another Part of the Fifties* (1983); John Diggins, *The Proud Decades: America in War and Peace, 1941–1960* (1988); James Gilbert, *A Cycle of Outrage* (1986); Godfrey Hodgson, *America in Our Time* (1976); Martin Jezer, *The Dark Ages: Life in the United States, 1945–1960* (1982); William Leuchtenberg, *A Troubled Feast* (1979); Douglas Miller and Marion Nowak, *The Fifties: The Way We Really Were* (1977); Ronald Oakley, *God's Country: America in the 1950s* (1986); Jon R. Stone, *On the Boundaries of American Evangelicalism* (1997); Steven Watts, *The Magic Kingdom: Walt Disney*

*and the American Way of Life* (1997); Stephen Whitfield, *The Culture of the Cold War* (1991).

**American Life and Culture**
Erik Barnouw, *Tube of Plenty: The Evolution of American Television* (1975); James L. Baughman, *The Republic of Mass Culture: Journalism, Filmmaking, and Broadcasting in America since 1941* (1992); Daniel Bell, *The End of Ideology* (1960); Carl Belz, *The Story of Rock* (1972); Michael Bertrand, *Race, Rock, and Elvis* (2000); Wini Breines, *Young, White, and Miserable: Growing Up Female in the Fifties* (1992); Victoria Byerly, *Hard Times Cotton Mill Girls* (1986); Stephanie Coontz, *The Way We Never Were: American Families and the Nostalgia Trap* (1992); John D'Emilio and Estelle Freedman, *Intimate Matters: A History of Sexuality in America* (1988); Colin Escott, *Good Rockin' Tonight: Sun Records and the Birth of Rock and Roll* (1991); Betty Friedan, *The Feminine Mystique* (1963); Neil Gabler, *Winchell: Gossip, Power, and the Culture of Celebrity* (1994); John Kenneth Galbraith, *The Affluent Society* (1958); Herbert Gans, *The Levittowners* (1967); Carol George, *God's Salesman: Norman Vincent Peale and the Power of Positive Thinking* (1994); Serge Gilbaut, *How New York Stole the Idea of Modern Art* (1983); Charlie Gillett, *The Sound of the City: The Rise of Rock and Roll* (1970); William Graebner, *Coming of Age in Buffalo: Youth and Authority in the Postwar Era* (1990); Will Herberg, *Protestant-Catholic-Jew* (1956); Thomas Hine, *Populux* (1986); Kenneth Jackson, *Crabgrass Frontier: The Suburbanization of the United States* (1985); James H. Jones, *Alfred Kinsey: A Public/Private Life* (1997); Wendy Kozol, *Life's America: Family and Nation in Postwar Photojournalism* (1994); William Martin, *A Prophet with Honor: The Billy Graham Story* (1991); C. Wright Mills, *The Power Elite* (1956) and *White Collar* (1951); George Nash, *The Conservative Intellectual Movement in America* (1976); David Potter, *People of Plenty* (1956); David Riesman, *The Lonely Crowd* (1950); Adam Rome, *The Bulldozer and the Countryside: Suburban Sprawl and the Rise of American Environmentalism* (2001); Lynn Spiegel, *Make Room for TV: Television and the Family Ideal in Postwar America* (1992); Gaye Tuchman et al., eds., *Hearth and Home: Images of Women in the Mass Media* (1978); Brian Ward, *Just My Soul Responding: Rhythm and Blues, Black Consciousness, and Race Relations* (1998); Ed Ward et al., *Rock of Ages: The Rolling Stone History of Rock and Roll* (1986); Carol Warren, *Madwives: Schizophrenic Women in the 1950s* (1987); William Whyte, *The Organization Man* (1956); Bradford Wright, *Comic Book Nation: The Transformation of Youth Culture in America* (2001).

**Foreign Policy in the Eisenhower-Kennedy Era**
Graham Allison, *Essence of Decision: Explaining the Cuban Missile Crisis* (1971); Stephen Ambrose, *Ike's Spies: Eisenhower and the Espionage Establishment* (1981); Michael Beschloss, *The Crisis Years, Kennedy and Khrushchev, 1960–1963* (1991); Thomas Borstelmann, *The Cold War and the Color Line: American Race Relations in a Global Arena* (2001); Blanche Wiesen Cook, *The Declassified Eisenhower* (1981); Campbell Craig, *Destroying the Village: Eisenhower and Thermonuclear War* (1998); Robert Divine, *Blowin' in the Wind: The Nuclear Test Ban Debate, 1954–1960* (1978) and *Eisenhower and the Cold War* (1981); Aleksandr Fursenko and Timothy Naftali, *"One Hell of a Gamble": Khrushchev, Castro, and Kennedy, 1958–1964* (1997); Trumbell Higgins, *Perfect Failure: Kennedy, Eisenhower, and the Bay of Pigs* (1987); Elizabeth Hoffman, *All You Need Is Love: The Peace Corps and the Spirit of the 1960s* (1998); Townsend Hoopes, *The Devil and John Foster Dulles* (1973); Richard Immerman, *The CIA in Guatemala* (1982); Madeline Kalb, *The Congo Cables: The Cold War in Africa from Eisenhower to Kennedy* (1982); Stephen Kinzer, *All the Shah's Men: An American Coup and the Roots of Terror in the Middle East* (2003); Frederick Marks III, *Power and Peace: The Diplomacy of John Foster Dulles* (1993); Ernest May and Philip Zelikow, *The Kennedy Tapes: Inside the White House during the Cuban Missile Crisis* (1997); Richard Melanson and David Mayers, eds., *Reevaluating Eisenhower: American Foreign Policy in the 1950s* (1987); Thomas Paterson, *Contesting Castro: The United States and the Triumph of the Cuban Revolution* (1994); Brenda Gayle Plummer, *Rising Wind: Black Americans and U.S. Foreign Policy, 1935–1960* (1996); Richard Rhodes, *Dark Sun: The Making of the Hydrogen Bomb* (1995); Gerald Rice, *The Bold Experiment: JFK's Peace Corps* (1985); R. B. Smith, *An International History of the Vietnam War: The Kennedy Strategy* (1985); Philip Taubman, *Secret Empire: Eisenhower, the CIA and the Hidden Story of America's Space Espionage* (2003); Evan Thomas, *The Very Best Men—Four Who Dared: The Early Years of the CIA* (1995); Richard Welch Jr., *Response to Revolution: The United States and the Cuban Revolution, 1954–1961* (1985).

**Domestic Politics**
Stephen Ambrose, *Eisenhower the President* (1984); Piers Brendon, *Ike* (1986); Jeff Broadwater, *Eisenhower and the Anti-Communist Crusade* (1992); David Burner and Thomas West, *The Torch Is Passed: The Kennedy Brothers and American Liberalism* (1984); Larry Burt, *Tribalism in Crisis: Federal Indian Policy, 1953–1961* (1982); Robert Caro, *Master of the Senate: The Years of Lyndon Johnson* (2002); Barbara Clowse, *Brainpower for the Cold War: The Sputnik Crisis and the National Defense Education Act of 1958* (1981); Robert Dallek, *An Unfinished Life: John F. Kennedy, 1917–1963* (2003); Donald Fixico, *Termination and Relocation: Federal Indian Policy, 1945–1960* (1986); John Giglio, *The Presidency of John F. Kennedy* (1991); Fred Greenstein, *The Hidden Hand Presidency: Eisenhower as Leader* (1982); Seymour Hersh, *The Dark Side of Camelot* (1997); Chester Pach, *The Presidency of Dwight D. Eisenhower* (1991); Thomas Reeves, *A Question of Character: A Life of John F. Kennedy* (1992); Mark Rose, *Interstate Express Highway Politics, 1939–1989* (1991); Arthur Schlesinger Jr., *Robert Kennedy and His Times* (1978) and *The Thousand Days* (1965); Mary Ann Watson, *The Expanding Vista, American Television in the Kennedy Years* (1990); Theodore White, *The Making of the President, 1960* (1961); Gary Wills, *Nixon Agonistes* (1970).

## CHAPTER 29: CIVIL RIGHTS AND THE CRISIS OF LIBERALISM (1947–1969)

**General Histories**
John M. Blum, *Years of Discord: American Politics and Society, 1961–1974* (1991); David Faber, *The Age of Great Dreams: America in the 1960s* (1994) and, as ed., *The Sixties: From Memory to History* (1994); Richard Goodwin, *Remembering America: A Voice from the Sixties* (1988); Godfrey Hodgson, *America in Our Time* (1976); Maurice Isserman and Michael Kazin, *America Divided: The Civil War of the 1960s* (1999); Lisa McGerr, *Suburban Warriors: The Origins of the New American Right* (2001); Edward P. Morgan, *The 60s Experience: Hard Lessons about Modern America* (1991); David Steigenwald, *The Sixties and the End of the Modern Era* (1995); Lawrence Wright, *The New World: Growing Up in America, 1960–1984* (1988).

**The Civil Rights Revolution**
Michael Belknap, *Federal Law and Southern Order: Racial Violence and Constitutional Conflict in the Post-Brown South* (1987); Derrick Bell, *And We Are Not Saved: The Elusive Quest for Racial Justice* (1987); Jack Bloom, *Class, Race, and the Civil Rights Movement* (1987); Taylor Branch, *Parting the Waters: America in the King Years, 1954–1963* (1988) and *Pillar of Fire: America in the King Years, 1963–65* (1998); Eric Burner, *And Gently He Shall Lead Them: Robert Parris Moses and Civil Rights in Mississippi* (1994); Stokely Carmichael and Charles Hamilton, *Black Power* (1967); Clayborne

Carson, *In Struggle: SNCC and the Black Awakening of the 1960s* (1981); Dan T. Carter, *The Politics of Rage: George Wallace and the New Conservatism* (1995); William Chafe, *Civilities and Civil Rights* (1980); Claude Clegg III, *An Original Man: The Life and Times of Elijah Muhammad* (1997); Edward E. Curtis IV, *Islam in Black America: Identity, Liberation, and Difference in African-American Islamic Thought* (2002); John Dittmar, *Local People: The Struggle for Civil Rights in Mississippi* (1994); James Duram, *Moderate among Extremists: Dwight D. Eisenhower and the School Desegregation Crisis* (1981); Michael Eric Dyson, *Making Malcolm: The Myth and Meaning of Malcolm X* (1995); Seth Forman, *Blacks in the Jewish Mind* (1998); Ignacio Garcia, *Viva Kennedy: Mexican Americans in Search of Camelot* (2000); David Garrow, *Bearing the Cross* (1986) and *The FBI and Martin Luther King* (1981); Henry Louis Gates Jr., *Colored People: A Memoir* (1994); Hugh Davis Graham, *Civil Rights and the Presidency: Race and Gender in American Politics, 1960–1972* (1992); David Halberstam, *The Children* (1988); James C. Hall, *Mercy, Mercy Me: African-American Culture and the American Sixties* (2001); Vincent Harding, *There Is a River: The Black Struggle for Freedom in America* (1981); Elizabeth Huckaby, *The Crisis at Central High: Little Rock, 1957–1958* (1980); Otto Kerner et al., *The Report of the National Advisory Commission on Civil Disorders* (1968); Richard Kluger, *Simple Justice: The History of Brown v. Board of Education and Black America's Struggle for Equality* (1975); Anthony Lewis et al., *Portrait of a Decade* (1964); Doug McAdam, *Freedom Summer* (1988); Malcolm X (with Alex Haley), *The Autobiography of Malcolm X* (1966); August Meier and Elliott Rudwick, *CORE: A Study in the Civil Rights Movement, 1942–1968* (1975); Adam Nossiter, *Of Long Memory: Mississippi and the Murder of Medgar Evers* (1994); Stephen Oates, *Let the Trumpet Sound: The Life and Times of Martin Luther King, Jr.* (1982); James T. Patterson, *Brown v. Board of Education: A Civil Rights Milestone and Its Troubled Legacy* (2001); Bruce Perry, *Malcolm* (1992); Bernard Schwartz, *Inside the Warren Court* (1983); Harvard Sitkoff, *The Struggle for Black Equality, 1954–1992* (1993); Mark Stern, *Calculating Visions: Kennedy, Johnson, and Civil Rights* (1992); Harris Wofford, *Of Kennedy and Kings* (1980); Juan Williams, *Eyes on the Prize: America's Civil Rights Years, 1954–1965* (1987); Eugene Wolfenstein, *The Victims of Democracy: Malcolm X and the Black Revolutionaries* (1981); Miles Wolff, *Lunch at the 5 & 10* (1990); C. Vann Woodward, *The Strange Career of Jim Crow* (1974).

### The Counterculture and New Left

John Andrew III, *The Other Side of the Sixties: Young Americans for Freedom and the Rise of Conservative Politics* (1997); Peter Braunstein and Michael William Doyle, eds., *Imagine Nation: The American Counterculture of the 1960s and 1970s* (2002); Howard Brick, *Age of Contradiction: American Thought and Culture in the 1960s* (1998); Serge Denisoff, *Great Day Coming: Folk Music and the American Left* (1971); Morris Dickstein, *The Gates of Eden* (1976); Robert S. Ellwood, *The Sixties Spiritual Awakening* (1994); James Farrell, *The Spirit of the Sixties: The Making of Postwar Radicalism* (1997); Thomas Frank, *The Conquest of the Cool: Business Culture, Counterculture, and the Rise of Hip Consumerism* (1997); Todd Gitlin, *The Whole World Is Watching: The Mass Media in the Making and Unmaking of the New Left* (1981); Richard Goldstein, *Reporting the Counterculture* (1989); Paul Goodman, *Growing Up Absurd* (1960); Emmett Grogan, *Ringolevio* (1972); Maurice Isserman, *If I Had a Hammer . . . : The Death of the Old Left and the Birth of the New Left* (1987); Judy Kaplan and Linn Shapiro, *Red Diaper Babies: Children on the Left* (1985); Martin Lee and Bruce Shlain, *Acid Dreams: The CIA, LSD, and the Sixties Rebellion* (1985); Christine Mamiya, *Pop Art and the Consumer Culture: American Super Market* (1992); Kirse Granat May, *Golden State, Golden Youth: The California Image in Popular Culture, 1955–66* (2002), Timothy Miller, *The Hippies and American Values* (1991); W. J. Rorabaugh, *Berkeley at War: The 1960s* (1989); Doug Rossinow, *The Politics of Authenticity: Liberalism, Christianity, and the New Left in America* (1998); Theodore Roszak, *The Making of a Counter Culture* (1969); Kirkpatrick Sale, *SDS* (1973); Mark Spitz, *Dylan: A Biography* (1989); Students for a Democratic Society, *The Port Huron Statement* (1962); Hunter Thompson, *Hell's Angels* (1967) and *Fear and Loathing in Las Vegas* (1971); Ed Ward et al., *Rock of Ages: The Rolling Stone History of Rock and Roll* (1986); Tom Wolfe, *Electric Kool-Aid Acid Test* (1968); Eric Zolov, *Refried Elvis: The Rise of the Mexican Counterculture* (1999).

### Politics and Foreign Policy in the Great Society

James Anderson and Jared Hazelton, *Managing Macroeconomic Policy: The Johnson Presidency* (1986); Michael Beschloss, ed., *Taking Charge: The Johnson White House Tapes, 1963–1964* (1997); H. W. Brands, *The Wages of Globalism: Lyndon Johnson and the Limits of American Power* (1994); Warren Cohen, *Dean Rusk* (1980); Robert Dallek, *Flawed Giant* (1998); Hugh Graham Davis, *Uncertain Trumpet* (1984); Herbert Druks, *The*

*Uncertain Alliance: The U.S. and Israel from Kennedy to the Peace Process* (2001); Greg Duncan, *Years of Poverty, Years of Plenty* (1984); Morton Horowitz, *The Warren Court and the Pursuit of Justice* (1998); Diane Kunz, ed., *The Diplomacy of the Crucial Decade: American Foreign Policy in the 1960s* (1995); Richard Mahoney, *JFK: Ordeal in Africa* (1983); Alan Matusow, *The Unraveling of America: A History of Liberalism in the 1960s* (1984); Walter McDougall, *The Heavens and the Earth: A Political History of the Space Age* (1985); Charles Murray, *Losing Ground: American Social Policy, 1950–1980* (1984); Thomas Noer, *Cold War and Black Liberation: The United States and White Rule in Africa, 1948–1968* (1985); Rick Perlstein, *Barry Goldwater and the Unmaking of the American Consensus* (2001); Earl Warren et al., *The Report of the Warren Commission* (1964); Bryce Wood, *The Dismantling of the Good Neighbor Policy* (1985).

## CHAPTER 30: THE VIETNAM ERA (1963–1975)

### The United States and the Vietnam War

Christian Appy, *Working Class War: American Combat Soldiers and Vietnam* (1993); Loren Baritz, *Backfire: A History of How American Culture Led Us into Vietnam and Made Us Fight the Way We Did* (1985); Larry Berman, *Planning a Tragedy* (1982); Larry Cable, *Conflict of Myths: The Development of American Counterinsurgency Doctrine and the Vietnam War* (1986); Mark Clodfelter, *The Limits of Airpower* (1989); Francis Fitzgerald, *Fire in the Lake* (1972); Lloyd Gardner, *Pay Any Price: Lyndon Johnson and the War for Vietnam* (1995); Leslie Gelb and Richard Betts, *The Irony of Vietnam: The System Worked* (1979); Mike Gravel et al., *The Pentagon Papers* (1975); David Halberstam, *The Best and the Brightest* (1972) and *The Making of Quagmire* (1987); Le Ly Hayslip, *When Heaven and Earth Changed Places* (1989); Le Ly Hayslip and James Hayslip, *Child of War, Woman of Peace* (1993); George Herring, *LBJ and Vietnam* (1994); George Kahin, *Intervention* (1986); Stanley Karnow, *Vietnam* (1983); Gabriel Kolko, *Anatomy of a War* (1985); Andrew Krepinevich Jr., *The Army and Vietnam* (1986); A. J. Langguth, *Our Vietnam: The War, 1954–1975* (2000); David Levy, *The Debate over Vietnam* (1991); Robert Mann, *A Grand Delusion: America's Descent into Vietnam* (2001); Kathryn Marshall, *In the Combat Zone: An Oral History of Women in the Vietnam War, 1966–1975* (1987); H. R. McMaster, *Dereliction of Duty: Lyndon Johnson, Robert McNamara, the Joint Chiefs of Staff, and the Lies That Led to Vietnam* (1997); Harold G. Moore and Joseph Galloway, *We Were Soldiers Once . . . and Young* (1992); Tim Page, *Nam* (1983); Bruce Palmer Jr., *The 25-Year War* (1984); Archimedes Patti, *Why Viet Nam?* (1983); Norman Podhoretz, *Why We Were in Vietnam* (1982); Al Santoli, *Everything We Had: An Oral History of the Vietnam War by Thirty-Three American Soldiers Who Fought It* (1981); Neil Sheehan, *A Bright Shining Lie: John Paul Vann and America in Vietnam* (1988); Ronald Spector, *After Tet: The Bloodiest Year in Vietnam* (1993) and *The United States Army in Vietnam* (1983); Harry Summers Jr., *On Strategy: A Critical Analysis of the Vietnam War* (1981); Wallace Terry, *Bloods: An Oral History of the Vietnam War by Black Veterans* (1984); William Turley, *The Second Indochina War: A Short Political and Military History* (1986); James Westheider, *Fighting on Two Fronts: African Amerians and the Vietnam War* (1997); Jim Wilson, *The Sons of Bardstown* (1994).

### Dissent against the War

William Berman, *William Fulbright and the Vietnam War* (1988); David Caute, *The Year of the Barricades, 1968* (1988); Charles DeBenedetti and Charles Chatfield, *An American Ordeal: The Antiwar Movement and the Vietnam Era* (1990); David Farber, *Chicago '68* (1988); Myra MacPherson, *Long Time Passing: Vietnam and the Haunted Generation* (1984); Norman Mailer, *Armies of the Night* (1968) and *Miami and the Siege of Chicago* (1969); Kim McQuaid, *The Anxious Years* (1989); James Miller, *Democracy Is in the Streets* (1987); Melvin Small, *Covering Dissent: The Media and the Anti–Vietnam War Movement* (1994); William Strauss, *Chance and Circumstance* (1978); Amy Swerdlow, *The Women's Strike for Peace: Traditional Motherhood and Radical Politics in the 1960s* (1993); Lawrence Wittner, *Rebels against War: The American Peace Movement, 1933–1983* (1984); Nancy Zaroulis and Gerald Sullivan, *Who Spoke Up? American Protest against the War in Vietnam* (1984).

### Identity Politics

Rodolfo Acuña, *Occupied America* (1981); Barry D. Adam, *The Rise of a Gay and Lesbian Movement* (1987); Rae Andre, *Homemakers: The Forgotten Workers* (1981); Mario Barerra, *Race and Class in the Southwest* (1979); Peter Berger and Brigitte Berger, *The War over the Family: Capturing the Middle Ground* (1983); Mary Frances Berry, *The Politics of Parenthood: Childcare, Women's Rights, and Feminism* (1993) and *Why ERA Failed:*

*Politics, Women's Rights, and the Amending Process of the Constitution* (1986); Susan Brownmiller, *Against Our Will: Men, Women, and Rape* (1975); John Burma, ed., *Mexican-Americans in the United States* (1970); Albert Camarillo, *Hispanics in a Changing Society* (1979); Tony Castro, *Chicano Power* (1974); Robert Coles and Geoffrey Stokes, *Sex and the American Teenager* (1985); Angela Davis, *Women, Race, and Class* (1981); Vine Deloria, *Behind the Veil of Broken Treaties* (1974); John D'Emilio, *Sexual Politics, Sexual Communities: The Making of a Homosexual Minority in the United States, 1940–1970* (1983); Susan Douglas, *Where the Girls Are: Growing Up Female with the Mass Media* (1994); Martin Duberman, *Stonewall* (1993); Andrea Dworkin, *Right-Wing Women* (1983); Barbara Ehrenreich, *The Hearts of Men: American Dreams and the Flight from Commitment* (1983); Amy Erdman, *Yours in Sisterhood: Ms. Magazine and the Promise of Popular Feminism* (1998); Susan Esterbrook, *If All We Did Was to Weep at Home: A History of White Working-Class Women in America* (1979); Shulamith Firestone, *The Dialectic of Sex: The Case for the Feminist Revolution* (1970); Donald Fixico, *The Urban Indian Experience in America* (2000); Jo Freeman, *The Politics of Women's Liberation* (1975); Patrick Gallagher, *The Cuban Exile* (1980); David Garrow, *Liberty and Sexuality: The Right and Privacy in the Making of Roe v. Wade* (1994); Carol Gilligan, *In Another Voice: Psychological Theory and Women's Development* (1982); Germaine Greer, *The Female Eunuch* (1972); Alice Kessler Harris, *Out to Work* (1982); Hazel W. Hertzberg, *The Search for an American Indian Identity: Modern Pan-Indian Movements* (1971); Gloria Hull et al., *But Some of Us Are Brave: Black Women's Studies* (1982); Peter Iverson, *The Navajo Nation* (1981); Christopher Lasch, *Haven in a Hostile World* (1979); Kristen Luker, *Abortion and the Politics of Motherhood* (1984); Norma McCorvey, *I Am Roe: My Life, Roe v. Wade, and Freedom of Choice* (1994); Darcy McNickle, *Native American Tribalism* (1973); Guadalupe San Miguel Jr., *Not White: School Integration and the Chicano Movement in Houston* (2001); Kate Millett, *Sexual Politics* (1970); Steven Mintz and Susan Kellogg, *Domestic Revolutions: A Social History of American Family Life* (1988); Joan Moore and Harry Pachon, *The Hispanics in the United States* (1985); Joan Moore et al., *Homeboys* (1978); Robin Morgan, ed., *Sisterhood Is Powerful: An Anthology* (1970); Maureen Muldoon, *Abortion Debate in the United States and Canada: A Source Book* (1991); Christopher Nealon, *Foundlings: Lesbian and Gay Historical Emotions before Stonewall* (2001); Roger Nichols, *The American Indian: Past and Present* (1986); James Olsen and Raymond Wilson, *Native Americans in the Twentieth Century* (1984); Hugh Pearson, *The Shadow of the Panther: Huey Newton and the Price of Black Power in America* (1994); A. Petit, *Images of the Mexican-American in Fiction and Film* (1980); Craig Rimmerman, *From Identity to Politics: The Lesbian and Gay Movements in the United States* (2002); La Frances Rodgers-Rose, ed., *The Black Woman* (1980); John William Sayer, *Ghost Dancing the Law: The Wounded Knee Trials* (1997); Gloria Steinem, *Outrageous Acts and Everyday Rebellions* (1983); Roger Streitmatter, *Unspeakable: The Rise of the Gay and Lesbian Press in America* (1995); Ronald Taylor, *Chavez and the Farm Workers* (1975); Arnulfo Trejo, ed., *The Chicanos: As We See Ourselves* (1979); Karl Wagenheim, *Puerto Rico: A Profile* (1975).

## CHAPTER 31: THE AGE OF LIMITS (1965–1980)

### Environmentalism

Edward Abbey, *The Monkey Wrench Gang* (1975); Rachel Carson, *Silent Spring* (1962); Barry Caspar and Paul Wellstone, *Powerline* (1981); Barry Commoner, *The Closing Circle* (1971); Albert Cowdry, *This Land, This South: An Environmental History* (1983); Irene Diamond and Gloria Feman Orenstein, *Reweaving the World: The Emergence of Ecofeminism* (1990); Thomas Dunlap, *DDT: Scientists, Citizens, and Public Policy* (1981); J. Brooks Flippen, *Nixon and the Environment* (2000); Robert Booth Fowler, *The Greening of Protestant Thought* (1995); Robert Gottlieb, *Forcing the Spring: The Transformation of the American Environmental Movement* (1993); Linda Lear, *Rachel Carson: Witness for Nature* (1997); Daniel Martin, *Three Mile Island* (1980); Robert N. Mayer, *The Consumer Movement* (1989); Ian McHarg, *Design with Nature* (1969); Lester Milbrath, *Environmentalists: Vanguard for a New Society* (1984); Roderick Nash, *The Rights of Nature* (1989); Shannon Petersen, *Acting for Endangered Species: The Statutory Ark* (2002); Marc Reisner, *Cadillac Desert: The American West and Its Disappearing Water* (1986); Charles Rubin, *The Green Crusade: Rethinking the Roots of Environmentalism* (1994); Kirkpatrick Sale, *The Green Revolution: The American Environmental Movement, 1962–1993* (1993); Philip Shabecoff, *A Fierce Green Fire: The American Environmental Movement* (1993); Andrew Szasz, *EcoPopulism: Toxic Waste and the Movement for Environmental Justice* (1994); James Trefethen, *An American Crusade for Wildlife* (1975); Donald Worster, *Rivers of Empire: Water, Aridity, and the Growth of the American West* (1985).

## American Society and the Economy in the 1970s

Barry Bluestone and Bennett Harrison, *The Deindustrialization of America* (1982); Paul Boyer, *When Time Shall Be No More: Prophecy Belief in Modern American Culture* (1992); Peter Calleo, *The Imperious Economy* (1982); Barry Commoner, *The Politics of Energy* (1979); Jay P. Dolan, *In Search of an American Catholicism* (2002); Ronald Formisano, *Boston against Busing: Race, Class, and Ethnicity in the 1960s and 1970s* (1991); Dean Kotlowski, *Nixon's Civil Rights: Politics, Principle, and Policy* (2001); Christopher Lasch, *The Culture of Narcissism* (1978); Michael Lienesch, *Redeeming America: Piety and Politics in the New Christian Right* (1993); J. Anthony Lukas, *Common Ground: A Turbulent Decade in the Lives of Three American Families* (1986); George Marsden, *Fundamentalism and Evangelicalism* (1991); Martin Melosi, *Coping with Abundance: Energy and Environment in Industrial America* (1985); Timothy O'Neill, *Bakke and the Politics of Equality* (1985); Daniel Yergin, *The Prize* (1991).

## Richard Nixon and Watergate

Stephen Ambrose, *Nixon: Ruin and Recovery, 1973–1990* (1991) and *Nixon, The Triumph of a Politician, 1962–1972* (1989); John Dean, *Blind Ambition* (1976); John Erlichmann, *Witness to Power* (1982); H. R. Haldeman, *The Haldeman Diaries: Inside the Nixon White House* (1994); Seymour Hersh, *The Price of Power: Kissinger in the Nixon White House* (1983); Stanley Kutler, *Abuse of Power* (1997) and *The Wars of Watergate* (1990); J. Anthony Lukas, *Nightmare: The Underside of the Nixon Years* (1988); Richard Nixon, *RN* (1978); John Sirica, *To Set the Record Straight* (1979); Theodore White, *Breach of Faith* (1975); Tom Wicker, *One of Us: Richard Nixon and the American Dream* (1991); Bob Woodward and Carl Bernstein, *All the President's Men* (1974) and *The Final Days* (1976).

## Politics and Diplomacy in the Age of Limits

James Bill, *The Eagle and the Lion: The Tragedy of American-Iranian Relations* (1987); Zbigniew Brzezinski, *Power and Principle* (1983); William Bundy, *A Tangled Web: The Making of Foreign Policy in the Nixon Presidency* (1998); James Cannon, *Time and Chance: Gerald Ford's Appointment with History* (1993); Peter Carroll, *It Seemed Like Nothing Happened* (1982); Jimmy Carter, *Keeping the Faith* (1982); Rosalynn Carter, *First Lady from Plains* (1984); John Dumbull, *The Carter Presidency: A Reevaluation* (1993); Gary Fink and Hugh Graham Davis, eds., *The Carter Presidency* (1998); Gerald Ford, *A Time to Heal* (1979); Raymond Garthoff, *Détente and Confrontation: American-Soviet Relations from Nixon to Reagan* (1985); Millicent Gates and Bruce Geelhoed, *The Dragon and the Snake: An American Account of the Turmoil in China, 1976–1977* (1986); Michael Hogan, *The Panama Canal in American Politics* (1986); Walter Isaacson, *Kissinger* (1992); Henry Jackson, *From the Congo to Soweto: U.S. Foreign Policy toward Africa since 1960* (1982); Burton Kaufman, *The Presidency of James Earl Carter Jr.* (1993); Henry Kissinger, *The White House Years* (1979) and *Years of Upheaval* (1982); Walter LaFeber, *The Panama Canal*, rev. ed. (1989); Robert Litwack, *Détente and the Nixon Doctrine* (1984); Alan Matusow, *Nixon's Economy: Booms, Busts, Dollars, and Votes* (1998); Morris Morley, *The United States and Chile* (1975); Richard Pipes, *U.S.-Soviet Relations in the Era of Détente* (1981); William Quandt, *Camp David* (1986); A. James Reichley, *Conservatives in an Age of Change: The Nixon and Ford Administrations* (1981); Robert Schulzinger, *Henry Kissinger: Doctor of Diplomacy* (1989); William Shawcross, *Sideshow: Nixon, Kissinger, and the Destruction of Cambodia* (1978); Gary Sick, *All Fall Down* (1985); Gaddis Smith, *Morality, Reason, and Power* (1986); Robert Sutter, *The China Quandary* (1983); Seth Tillman, *The U.S. in the Middle East* (1982); Cyrus Vance, *Hard Choices* (1983); Theodore White, *The Making of the President, 1968* (1969).

## CHAPTER 32: THE CONSERVATIVE CHALLENGE (1980–1992)

### American Society

Bruce Bawer, *A Place at the Table: The Gay Individual and American Society* (1994); Robert Bellah et al., *The Good Society* (1991) and *Habits of the Heart: Individualism and Commitment in American Life* (1985); Dallas Blanchard, *The Anti-Abortion Movement* (1994); Stephen Carter, *The Culture of Disbelief: How American Law and Politics Trivialize Religious Devotion* (1993); William Dietrich, *In the Shadow of the Rising Sun: The Political Roots of American Economic Decline* (1991); Thomas Byrne Edsall, *The New Politics of Inequality* (1984); Barbara Ehrenreich, *Fear of Falling: The Inner Life of the Middle Class* (1989) and *The Worst Years of Our Lives* (1990); Susan Faludi, *Backlash: The Undeclared War against American Women* (1991); Elizabeth Fee and Daniel Fox, eds., *AIDS: The Burdens of History* (1992); Henry Louis Gates Jr., *Loose Canons: Notes on the Culture Wars* (1993); Michael Goldfield, *The Decline of Organized Labor in the United States* (1987); Otis Graham Jr., *Losing Time: The Industrial*

Policy Debate (1992); Michael Harrington, The New American Poverty (1984); Richard Herrnstein and Charles Murray, The Bell Curve: Intelligence and Class Structure in American Life (1994); Godfrey Hodgson, The World Turned Right Side Up: A History of the Conservative Ascendancy in America (1996); Robert Hughes, Culture of Complaint: The Fraying of America (1993); Paul Krugman, Peddling Prosperity: Economic Sense and Nonsense in the Age of Diminished Expectations (1994); Frank Levy, Dollars and Dreams: The Changing American Income Distribution (1987); Steve Levy, Insanely Great: The Life and Times of Macintosh, the Computer That Changed Everything (1994); Jane Maysbridge, Why We Lost the ERA (1986); Ruth Milkman, Farewell to the Factory: Autoworkers in Late Twentieth Century America (1997); Joseph Nocera, A Piece of the Action: How the Middle Class Joined the Money Class (1994); Juliet Schor, The Overworked American: The Unexpected Decline of Leisure (1991); Studs Terkel, The Great Divide (1988); Thomas Toch, In the Name of Excellence: The Struggle to Reform the Nation's Schools (1991).

**Conservative Politics**
Ken Auletta, The Underclass (1982); Earl Black and Merle Black, The Vital South: How Presidents Are Elected (1992); Sidney Blumenthal, The Rise of the Counter-Establishment from Conservative Ideology to Political Power (1988); Sidney Blumenthal and Thomas Byrne Edsall, eds., The Reagan Legacy (1988); Paul Boyer, ed., Reagan as President: Contemporary Views of the Man, His Politics, and His Policies (1990); William Brennan, America's Right Turn from Nixon to Bush (1994); Barbara Bush, Barbara Bush: A Memoir (1994); Michael Deaver, Behind the Scenes (1987); Theodore Draper, A Very Thin Line: The Iran-Contra Affairs (1991); Ken Gross, Ross Perot: The Man behind the Myth (1992); David Hoeveler Jr., Watch on the Right: Conservative Intellectuals in the Reagan Era (1991); Peter Irons, Brennan vs. Rehnquist: The Battle for the Constitution (1994); Jonathan Kwitny, The Crimes of Patriots: A True Tale of Dope, Dirty Money, and the CIA (1987); Jonathan Lash, A Season of Spoils: The Story of the Reagan Administration's Attack on the Environment (1984); Theodore Lowi, The End of the Republican Era (1995); Kevin Phillips, Boiling Point: Republicans, Democrats, and the Decline of Middle Class Prosperity (1993) and The Politics of Rich and Poor: Wealth and the American Electorate in the Reagan Aftermath (1990); John Podhoretz, Hell of a Ride: Backstage at the White House Follies, 1989–1993 (1993); Dan Quayle, Standing Firm: A Vice-Presidential Memoir (1994); Donald Regan, For the Record (1988); Tom Rosenstiel, Strange Bedfellows:

How Television and the Presidential Candidates Changed American Politics, 1992 (1993); Randy Shilts, And the Band Played On: Politics, People, and the AIDS Epidemic (1987); David Stockman, The Triumph of Politics: The Inside Story of the Reagan Revolution (1986); Stephen Vaugh, Ronald Reagan in Hollywood: Movies and Politics (1994); Gary Wills, Reagan's America (1987); Daniel Wirls, The Politics of Defense in the Reagan Era (1992).

**Foreign Policy into the 1990s**
Michael Beschloss and Strobe Talbott, At the Highest Levels: The Inside Story of the End of the Cold War (1993); Raymond Bonner, Weakness and Deceit: U.S. Policy and El Salvador (1984); William Broad, Teller's War: The Top Secret Story behind the Star Wars Deception (1992); Bradford Burns, At War with Nicaragua (1987); Leslie Cockburn, Out of Control (1987); Christopher Coker, The United States and South Africa, 1968–1985 (1986); Thomas Friedman, From Beirut to Jerusalem (1989); John Lewis Gaddis, The United States and the End of the Cold War (1992); Roy Gutman, Banana Diplomacy (1988); Alexander Haig Jr., Caveat: Realism, Reagan, and Foreign Policy (1984); Delip Hiro, Desert Shield to Desert Storm (1992); Bruce Jentleson, Pipeline Politics: The Complex Political Economy of East-West Trade (1986); Robert Kaplan, Balkan Ghosts (1993); Walter LaFeber, Inevitable Revolutions (1993); William LeoGrande, Our Own Backyard: The United States in Central America, 1977–1992 (1998); John Mueller, Policy and Opinion in the Gulf War (1994); Robert Pastor, Condemned to Repetition: The United States and Nicaragua (1987); Jonathan Schell, The Fate of the Earth (1982); David Schoenbaum, The United States and the State of Israel (1993); Strobe Talbott, Deadly Gambits: The Reagan Administration and the Stalemate in Nuclear Arms Control (1984); Sanford Ungar, Africa (1985); William Vogele, Stepping Back: Nuclear Arms Control and the End of the Cold War (1994); Thomas Walker, ed., Reagan versus the Sandinistas (1987); Bob Woodward, Veil: The Secret Wars of the CIA (1987).

**Minorities and American Culture**
Roger Daniels et al., eds., Japanese-Americans: From Relocation to Redress (1986); Reynolds Farley and Walter Allen, The Color Line and the Quality of Life in America (1987); Lawrence Fuchs, The American Kaleidoscope: Race, Ethnicity, and the Civic Culture (1990); Douglas Glasgow, The Black Underclass (1980); Andrew Hacker, Two Nations: Black and White, Separate, Hostile, Unequal (1992); Denis Heyck, ed., Barrios and Borderlands:

*Cultures of Latinos and Latinas in the United States* (1993); Bill Ong Hing, *Making and Remaking Asian America through Immigration Policy, 1850–1990* (1993); Christopher Jencks, *The Homeless* (1994); Jonathan Kozol, *Savage Inequalities: Children in America's Schools* (1991); Joan Moore and Harry Pachon, *Hispanics in the United States* (1985); Adolph Reed, *The Jesse Jackson Phenomenon: The Crisis of Purpose in Afro-American Politics* (1986); Sam Roberts, *Who Are We? A Portrait of America Based on the Latest U.S. Census* (1994); Arthur Schlesinger Jr., *The Disuniting of America* (1991); Peter Skerry, *Mexican-Americans: The Ambivalent Minority* (1993); Robert C. Smith, *Racism in the Post–Civil Rights Era: Now You See It, Now You Don't* (1995); The Staff of the Chicago Tribune, *The American Millstone: An Examination of the Nation's Permanent Underclass* (1986); Shih-Shan Henry Tsai, *The Chinese Experience in America* (1986); William Wei, *The Asian American Movement* (1993).

## CHAPTER 33: NATION OF NATIONS IN A GLOBAL COMMUNITY (1980–2004)

### Domestic Politics in the Clinton Era

Charles Allen, *The Comeback Kid: The Life and Times of Bill Clinton* (1992); Stuart Banner, *The Death Penalty: An American History* (2002); Elizabeth Drew, *The Corruption of American Politics: What Went Wrong and Why* (1999) and *Whatever It Takes: The Struggle for Political Power in America* (1997); Theodore Lowi, *The End of the Republican Era* (1995); David Maraness, *The Clinton Enigma* (1998) and *First in His Class: The Biography of Bill Clinton* (1996); Mary Matlin and James Carville, *All's Fair in Love and Running for President* (1994); Joyce Milton, *The First Partner: Hillary Rodham Clinton* (1999); Roger Morris, *Partners in Power: The Clintons and their America* (1999); *The New Yorker Special Politics Issue* (October 21 and 28, 1996); Mark Rosell, ed., *The Clinton Scandel and the Future of American Government* (2000); James Stewart, *Bloodsport: The President and His Adversaries* (1997); James Trabor and Eugene Gallagher, *Why Waco? Cults in the Battle for Religious Freedom* (1995); Bob Woodward, *The Agenda: Inside the Clinton White House* (1994) and *Shadow: Five Presidents and the Legacy of Watergate* (1999).

### Foreign Policy in the 1990s

Madeleine Albright, *Madam Secretary* (2003); G. Pope Atkins and Lamar Wilson, *The Dominican Republic and the United States* (1998); Richard Barnet and John Cavanaugh, *Global Dreams: Imperial Corporations and the New World Disorder* (1996); Wayne Bert, *The Reluctant Superpower: The United States Policy in Bosnia* (1997); Steven Burg and Paul Shoup, *The War in Bosnia-Herzegovina* (1999); Michael Cox, *U.S. Foreign Policy after the Cold War* (1995); James Cronin, *The World the Cold War Made* (1996); Michael Dobbs, *Madeline Albright* (1999); H. Richard Frimen, *NarcoDiplomacy* (1996); David Fromkin, *Kosovo Crossing: American Ideals Meet Reality in the Balkan Battlefield* (1999); George W. Grayson, *The North American Free Trade Agreement* (1995); William Greider, *Fortress America* (1998); Avigdor Haselkorn, *The Continuing Storm: Iraq, Poisonous Weapons, and Deterrence* (1999); John Hirsch and Robert Oakley, *Somalia and Operation Restore Hope* (1995); Stanley Hoffman, *World Disorders* (1999); Robert Kaplan, *The Ends of the Earth: A Journey to the Frontiers of Anarchy* (1996); Walter LaFeber, *The Clash: U.S.-Japan Relations throughout History* (1997); Noel Malcolm, *Bosnia* (1994); John Martz, *United States Policy in Latin America* (1995); Julie Mertus, *Kosovo: How Myths and Truths Started a War* (1999); Ilan Pape, *The Israel/Palestine Question* (1999); Randall Ripley and James Lindsey, eds., *U.S. Foreign Policy after the Cold War* (1997); Stephen Schwartz, ed., *Atomic Audit* (1998); Ronald Steele, *Temptations of a Superpower* (1995); Lawrence Susskind, *Environmental Diplomacy* (1994); Robert Thomas, *The Politics of Serbia* (1999); Susan Woodward, *Balkan Tragedy* (1995).

### The Global Economy and Environment in the 1990s

Janet Abbate, *Inventing the Internet* (1999); Paul Andrews, *How the Web Was Won* (1999); Sharon Beder, *Global Spin: The Corporate Assault on the Environment* (1998); Tim Berners-Lee, *Weaving the Web: The Original Design and Ultimate Destiny of the World Wide Web by the Inventor* (1999); Mark Bowie, *Losing Ground: American Environmentalism at the Close of the Twentieth Century* (1996); Charles Ferguson, *High Stakes and No Prisoners: A Winner's Tale of Greed and Glory in the Internet Wars* (1999); David Helvarg, *The War against the Greens: The "Wise-Use" Movement, the New Right, and Anti-Environmental Violence* (1997); Charles Johnson, *The Evolution of Wired Life: From the Alphabet to the Soul-Catcher Chip* (1999); Jason Olim et al., *The CDnow Story: Rags to Riches on the Internet* (1999); Robert Reid, *Architects of the Web: 1,000 Days That Built the Future of Business* (1997); Robert Solomon, *Money on the Move: The Revolution in International Finance since*

*1980* (1999); Kara Swisher, *aol.com: How Steve Case Beat Bill Gates, Nailed the Netheads, and Made Millions in the War for the Web* (1998); Brian Tokar, *Earth for Sale: Reclaiming Ecology in the Age of Corporate Greenwash* (1997); Art Wolinsky, *The History of the Internet and the World Wide Web* (1999).

## Multicultural America

Lawrence Auster, *The Path to National Suicide: An Essay on Immigration and Multiculturalism* (1990); Frank Bean et al., *At the Crossroads: Mexico and U.S. Immigration Policy* (1998); Roy Beck, *The Case against Immigration* (1996); Richard Bernstein, *Multiculturalism and the Battle for America's Future* (1994); Peter Brimelow, *Alien Nation: Common Sense about America's Immigration Disaster* (1995); Ellis Cose, *A Nation of Strangers: Prejudice, Politics, and the Populating of America* (1992) and *The Rage of a Privileged Class: Why Are Middle-Class Blacks Angry?* (1994); Greg Critser, *Fat Land: How Americans Became the Fattest People in the World* (2003); Jose Cruz, *Identity and Power: Puerto Rican Politics and the Challenge of Ethnicity* (1998); Jay P. Dolan, *In Search of an American Catholicism* (2002); Timothy Dunn, *The Militarization of the U.S.-Mexico Border* (1996); Susan Faludi, *Stiffed: The Betrayal of the American Man* (1999); Joshua Gamson, *Fresh Talk Back: Tabloid Talk Shows and Sexual Nonconformity* (1998); Garrett Hardin, *The Immigration Dilemma: Avoiding the Tragedy of the Commons* (1995); Richard Herrnstein and Charles Murray, *The Bell Curve: Intelligence and Class Structure in American Life* (1994); David Hollinger, *Postethnic America: Beyond Multiculturalism* (1995); Laura Hyun Yi Kung, *Compositional Subjects: Enfiguring Asian/American Women* (2002); Robert Lee, *Orientals: Asian Americans in Popular Culture* (1999); Maxine Margolis, *An Invisible Minority: Brazilians in New York City* (1998); Oscar Martinez, *Border People: Life and Society in the U.S.-Mexico Borderlands* (1994); Joel Millman, *The Other Americans: How Immigrants Renew Our Country, Our Economy, and Our Values* (1997); Juan Perea, eds., *Immigrants Out: The New Nativism and Anti-Immigration Impulse in the United States* (1997); Peter Slains, *Assimilation American Style* (1997); Alex Stepick, *Pride against Prejudice: Haitians in the United States* (1998); Michael S. Teitelbaum and Myron Wiener, eds., *Threatened Peoples, Threatened Borders* (1995); Sanford Ungar, *Fresh Blood: The New American Immigrants* (1995); Bernard Wong, *Ethnicity and Entrepreneurship: The New Chinese Immigrants in the San Francisco Bay Area* (1998); Jun Xing, *Asian Americans through the Lens* (1998).

## Post 9/11

Richard Clarke, *Against All Enemies: Inside America's War on Terror* (2004); David Frum, *The Right Man: The Surprise Presidency of George W. Bush* (2003); Jacob S. Hacker, *The Divided Welfare State: The Battle over Public and Private Benefits in the United States* (2003); Walter LaFeber, *America, Russia, and the Cold War, 1945–2003*, 10th ed. (2003); James Moore, *Bush's Brain: How Karl Rove Made George W. Bush Presidential* (2003); Williamson Murray and Robert H. Scales Jr., *The Iraq War: A Military History* (2003); National Commission on Terrorist Attacks, *The 9/11 Commission Report: Final Report of the National Commission on Terrorist Attacks Upon the United States* (2004); Todd S. Purdum, *A Time of Our Choosing: America's War in Iraq* (2003); Joel Slemrod and Jon Bakija, *Taxing Ourselves to Death: A Citizens' Guide to the Great Debate over Tax Reform* (2003); Bob Woodward, *Bush at War* (2003).

# Credits

*Chapter 9* **Page 228** *Thomas Jefferson* by Rembrandt Peale, 1805. Oil on canvas, 28 × 23 in. Collection of The New-York Historical Society, accession no. 1867.306; **236** Illustration by A. Rider, Library of Congress; **238** The Granger Collection, New York.

*Chapter 10* **Page 257** American Clock & Watch Museum, Bristol, CT; **265** Beinecke Rare Book and Manuscript Library, Yale University; **268** Missouri Historical Society (Neg. #CT SS831); **275** *Pawtucket Falls, Rhode Island* by Jacques Gerard Milbert, 1828–1829. Lithograph on India paper. The New York Public Library. The New York Public Library/Art Resource, NY.

*Chapter 11* **Page 286** *The Butcher* by Nicolino Calyo, c. 1840–1844. Museum of the City of New York, Gift of Mars. Francis P. Garvan in memory of Francis P. Garvan; **291** *The County Election* by George Caleb Bingham, 1852. Oil on canvas, 38 × 52 in. (96.5 × 132.1 cm). Gift of Bank America. The Saint Louis Art Museum; **294** *Andrew Jackson* by Asher B. Durand, 1835. Oil on canvas, 30 × 25 in. Collection of The New-York Historical Society, accession no. 1858.11; **299** *Portrait of a black man wearing a bow tie*, Unknown maker, American (Daguerreotypist). The J. Paul Getty Museum, Los Angeles, 84.XT.441.3. © The J. Paul Getty Museum; **307** Museum of the City of New York, The J. Clarence Davies Collection.

*Chapter 12* **Page 314** Harriet Beecher Stowe Center, Hartford, CT; **321** Stock Montage, Inc.; **325** Print Collection Miriam & Ira D. Wallach Division of Art, Prints and Photographs. The New York Public Library. Astor, Lenox and Tilden Foundations. The New York Public Library/Art Resource NY; **328** Bettmann/CORBIS; **332** Madison County Historical Society, Oneida, NY; **334** Coline Jenkins, Elizabeth Cady Stanton Trust.

*Chapter 13* **Page 341** The Historic New Orleans Collection, accession no. 1960.46; **351** The Historic New Orleans Collection, accession no. 1975.93.5; **352** *The Squatters* by George Caleb Bingham, 1850. Oil on canvas, 23 1/8 × 28 1/4 in. (58.74 × 71.75 cm). Museum of Fine Arts, Boston, Bequest of Henry Lee Shattuck, in memory of the late Ralph W. Gray, 1971.154. Photograph © 2005 Museum of Fine Arts, Boston; **359** *After the Sale: Slaves Being Sent South from Richmond, Va.* by Eyre Crowe, 1853. Chicago Historical Society, 1957.0027; **360** *Virginia Slaves Dancing* by Lewis Miller, 1853. Print Collection Miriam & Ira D. Wallach Division of Art, Prints and Photographs. The

New York Public Library. Astor, Lenox and Tilden Foundations. The New York Public Library/Art Resource NY; **363** *Heading Herring* by David Hunter Strother, 1856. West Virginia and Regional History Collection, West Virginia University Libraries.

*Chapter 14* **Page 374** Seaver Center for Western History Research, Los Angeles County Museum of Natural History; **387** *San Francisco*, general view, by S. Frank Marryat. Engraving published by M. & N. Hanhart, 1850–1852. Collection of The New-York Historical Society, negative no. 26280; **390** Library of Congress.

*Chapter 15* **Page 415 (left)** Bettmann/CORBIS; **415 (right)** Illinois State Historical Society; **422** *An Eminent Southern Clergyman*, pictorial envelope, 3 × 5 1/2 in. Collection of The New-York Historical Society, negative no. aj45013.

*Chapter 16* **Page 428** Chicago Historical Society, ICHi-09975; **437** Chicago Historical Society, ICHi-07774; **439** The Museum of the Confederacy, Richmond, Virginia; **443** Department of the U.S. Army, U.S. Army Military History Institute, Carlisle Barracks, PA; **453 (left)** Library of Congress; **453 (right)** Cook Collection, Valentine Richmond History Center.

*Chapter 17* **Page 462** Culver Pictures, Inc.; **463** Library of Congress; **469** Courtesy of the Abraham Lincoln Presidential Library; **478** Stock Montage, Inc.

*Chapter 18* **Page 492** National Archives; **496** Library of Congress; **510** Huntington Library/SuperStock; **515** Image courtesy of Circus World Museum, Baraboo, Wisconsin.

*Chapter 19* **Page 523** Bettmann/CORBIS; **536** *Colliers National Weekly*, April 8, 1905, pg. 7; **541** Courtesy MetLife Archive; **547** Culver Pictures, Inc.

*Chapter 20* **Page 552** *Cliff Dwellers* by George Bellows, 1913. Oil on canvas, 40 3/16 × 42 1/16 in. (102.07 × 106.83 cm). Los Angeles County Museum of Art, Los Angeles County Fund (16.4). Photograph © 2005 Museum Associates/LACMA; **561** Albert H. Wiggins Collection, by Courtesy of the Trustees of the Boston Public Library; **563** Photo reproduced courtesy Thomas W. Chinn. From *Bridging the Pacific: SF Chinatown and Its People* by Thomas W. Chinn. © 1989 Chinese Historical Society of America, San Francisco; **566** Trade Catalog of Reed & Barton, Taunton, Massachusetts, 1885. Courtesy, Winterthur Library: Joseph Downs Collection of Manuscripts and Printed Ephemera.

# Index

Note: Page numbers in *italics* indicate illustrations, page numbers followed by "m" indicate maps; and page numbers followed by "n" indicate footnotes.

# Primary Source Investigator CD-ROM

History comes alive through narrative; but the building blocks of that narrative are primary sources. McGraw-Hill's Primary Source Investigator (PSI) CD-ROM provides instant access to hundreds of the most important and interesting documents, images, artifacts, audio recordings, and videos from our past. You can browse the collection across time, source types, subjects, historical questions, textbook chapters, or your own custom search terms. Clicking on a source opens it in our Source Window, packed with annotations, investigative tools, transcripts, and interactive questions for deeper analysis.

As close companions to the primary sources, three kinds of original secondary sources are also included on the PSI: 5- to 8-minute documentaries and interactive maps complete with underlying statistical data. Together these features weave a rich historical narrative or argument on topics that are difficult to fully grasp from primary sources alone. Each secondary source also provides links back to related primary sources, enabling you to test a secondary source's argument against the historical record.

While examining any of these sources you can use our notebook feature to take notes, bookmark key sources, and save or print copies of all the sources for use outside of the archive. After researching a particular theme or time period, you can use our argument-outlining tool to walk you through the steps of composing a historical essay or presentation.

Through its browsing and inspection tools, Primary Source Investigator helps you practice the art of historical detection using a real archive of historical sources. This process of historical investigation follows three basic steps:

- *Ask* Use our browsing panels to search and filter the sources
- *Research* Use the Source Window to examine sources in detail and the Notebook to record your insights
- *Argue* Practice outlining historical arguments based on archival sources.